Managing British Colonial and Post-Colonial Development

Managing British Colonial and Post-Colonial Development

The Crown Agents, 1914–74

David Sunderland

THE BOYDELL PRESS

First published 2007
The Boydell Press, Woodbridge

ISBN 978-1-84383-301-7

The Boydell Press is an imprint of Boydell & Brewer Ltd
PO Box 9, Woodbridge, Suffolk IP12 3DF, UK
and of Boydell & Brewer Inc.
668 Mt Hope Avenue, Rochester, NY 14620, USA
website: www.boydellandbrewer.com

A catalogue record for this book is available
from the British Library

This publication is printed on acid-free paper

Printed in Great Britain by
Biddles Ltd, King's Lynn

Contents

List of figures and tables vi

Acknowledgements ix

Abbreviations xi

Introduction 1

1 The public issue of loans 9

2 Other sources of finance 42

3 The management of colonial investment Funds 69

4 The management of the Joint Colonial Fund and the Joint Miscellaneous Fund 97

5 The cost of supplies 115

6 Procurement from the early 1960s and delivery delays 143

7 Miscellaneous roles 160

8 The move into secondary banking 179

9 The collapse of the secondary banking venture 221

Conclusion 241

Appendices

1. The Crown Agents, 1920–74 254
2. Market finance, 1914–68 256
3. Non-market finance, 1920–65 260
4. 1954 Investment Funds, Wartime gifts and loans, 1936 procurement and 1954 colonial appointments 265
5. Crown Agents' own account activities 269
6. FMI investment in associated companies, 1969–74 270

Bibliography 279

Index 287

List of Figures and Tables

Figures

1.1. Publicly issued loans and JCF/JMF advances, 1914–74 10
1.2. Annual average yields, 1920–69 14
1.3. Total value of stock domiciled with the CAs and amount held by the CAs on behalf of colonial funds, 1947–62 31
1.4. Conversions, loans sold to the market/placed, and Inter-Colonial loans, 1922–68 34
2.1. Nominal share and loan capital of UK companies that operated in British Africa, Ceylon, Malaya and the British West Indies, 1938–57 and CDC expenditure 1949–65 48
2.2. UK government aid, 1919/20 to 1964/5 60
3.1. Value of Colonial Investment Funds and JCF/JMF at year ends, 1920–74 70
3.2. Distribution of Colonial Investment Fund and JCF/JMF investments, 1930–62 72
4.1. JCF monies at banks, in securities and lent to colonies, 1929–69 99
4.2. JCF dividend rates relative to comparable investments, 1929–71 101
5.1. Supplies purchased, inspected and insured, 1920–74 116
7.1. Appointments, passages and pension and salary payments, 1920–67 161
8.1. Finvest account, 1970–74 180
8.2. Finvest lending, 1971–74 183

Tables

1.1. Characteristics of a sample of final purchasers of the Barbados 6pc, 1971/73 Loan 37
2.1. Finance of development, 1920–65 64
3.1. Distribution of Fund investments, 1935 and 1958 74
5.1. Stores purchased and shipped by territory, 1936 and 1964 117
5.2. Geographical location of contractors, 1937 128

For my sister, Mrs Ann Metcalfe

Acknowledgements

This book owes its existence to the Economic and Social Research Council, which financed the three year project on which it is based (grant no. RES–000–23–0152), and to the Crown Agents, who gave me full access to their files.

Many institutions have assisted me in my research. I would therefore like to thank the staff of the Bank of England archive; of the National Archives, Kew; and of the archive of the National Westminster Bank, London, and the Librarians at the British Library, London; at the Central Reference Library, Manchester; at the Guildhall Library, London; at the John Rylands Library, Manchester; at the London School of Economics Library; and at Manchester Metropolitan University All Saints and Aytoun Libraries.

Individuals from the Crown Agents who have helped me include John Shuter, the Deputy Head of Finance from 1967 to 1972 and later the Head of Investment, and David Johns, the International Fund Investment Manager from 1967 to 1970 and later Assistant to the Director of Finance, who generously gave up their time to answer my often impertinent questions, and read and commented on the draft chapters of the book; Philip Knights, Company Secretary during the late 1960s and the early 1970s and later Archivist, who gave me a greater understanding of the culture of the Agency; Mrs Vivienne Challis, the widow of Allan Challis; and four people who prefer to remain anonymous. I would also like to thank Lynn Hale, the Crown Agents' present Company Secretary, for all his help over the past few years; Jim McMahon who patiently ferried me back and forth to and from the Agents' Liverpool file store; and the late A. W. Abbott, a former CA Company Secretary and Archivist, for his work on the history of the Agency. Thanks are also due to Peter Sowden, the History Editor of Boydell & Brewer for his great efficiency and interest in my work.

Academic help came from Professor David Jeremy, who helped me devise the ESRC application and read and commented on draft chapters; Dr Geoff Tweedale, who patiently listened to my often boring accounts of the progress of my research and directed me to relevant books and articles; Professor Andrew Pendleton for his advice on ESRC applications; and, as ever, Professor Avner Offer, my doctorial supervisor at Oxford University, who taught me so much.

Abbreviations

ADM	Bank of England files, Bank of England Archive (see Bibliography)
B of E	Bank of England
BT	Board of Trade files, National Archives (see Bibliography)
B of T	Board of Trade
C	Bank of England files, Bank of England Archive (see Bibliography)
CA	Crown Agent
CA (m)	Crown Agent files, Crown Agent Archive, Sutton (see Bibliography)
CAB	Cabinet Office files, National Archives
CAOG	Crown Agent files, National Archives (see Bibliography)
CDC	Colonial (later Commonwealth) Development Corporation
CO	Colonial Office files, National Archives (see Bibliography)
DTC	Department of Technical Co-operation
EARH	East Africa Railway and Harbour Board
ECGD	Export Credits Guarantee Department
FCO	Foreign and Commonwealth Office files, National Archives (see Bibliography)
Finvest	Finance Department Investment Account
FMI	Four Millbank Investments Ltd
FNFC	First National Finance Corporation Ltd
G	Bank of England files, Bank of England Archive (see Bibliography)
HO	Home Office files, National Archives (see Bibliography)
IC loan	Inter-colonial loan
IR	Inland Revenue files, National Archives (see Bibliography)
JCF	Joint Colonial Fund
JMF	Joint Miscellaneous Fund
L	Crown Agent files, Crown Agent Archive, Liverpool (see Bibliography)
LA	Crown Agent Archive, Liverpool
LCC	London Chamber of Commerce
MTS	Millbank Technical Services
OD	Ministry of Overseas Development files, National Archives (see Bibliography)
ODA	Overseas Development Administration
ODM	Ministry of Overseas Development
OV	Bank of England files, Bank of England Archive (see Bibliography)
NA	The National Archives, Kew, London
PP	Parliamentary Papers
Prem	Prime Minister's Office, National Archives (see Bibliography)
RC	Crown Agent files, Crown Agent Archive, Sutton (see Bibliography)

S	Crown Agent files, Crown Agent Archive, Sutton (see Bibliography)
SA	Crown Agent Archive, Sutton
SF	Sinking Fund
SIS	Sterling Industrial Securities Ltd
T	Treasury files, National Archives (see Bibliography)
WN	Crown Agent files, Crown Agent Archive, Liverpool (see Bibliography)

Introduction

The literature on the British Empire during the twentieth century is now immense. It includes general studies of the operation of the Empire, regional surveys that examine the effects of policy decisions on the periphery, books on the provision of aid and the development of colonies, and countless monographs on decolonisation.[1] In addition, the impact of colonial development on Britain has been discussed at length in books and articles on the growth of the British economy during the period, and there have been a number of works on the financial relationship between colonial administrations and London, largely concentrating on the Empire's role in the maintenance of the sterling area.[2] There has been little investigation, however, of the 'nuts and bolts' of development. Hardly any research has been undertaken on how colonial administrations and their independent successors raised non-aid finance in the UK, how they purchased construction materials and other goods not available locally, how their investments in the London money market were managed, or how they acquired a range of other services that could not be obtained within their own countries.

The reason for this gap in the literature is that, until now, there has been no in-depth study of the twentieth century work of the Office of the Crown Agents for the colonies, which performed these tasks.[3] The Crown Agent office was established in 1833, and, until independence, acted for the administrations of Crown colonies and protectorates, and for public authorities, such as municipalities and utilities boards, that operated in these territories. Thereafter, it worked for the governments of independent countries within and outside the Commonwealth, public corporations, and a number of international aid organizations, such as the World Bank and the United Nations.

1 For example, P. J. Cain and A. G. Hopkins, *British Imperialism: Crisis and Deconstruction, 1914–1990*, London 1993; J. D. B. Miller, *Survey of Commonwealth Affairs: Problems of Expansion and Attrition 1953–1969*, London 1974; Yusuf Bangura, *Britain and Commonwealth Africa: The Politics of Economic Relations 1951–75*, Manchester 1983; D. J. Morgan, *The Official History of Colonial Development, Volumes 1–5*, London 1979–80; John Darwin, 'British decolonisation since 1945: A pattern or a puzzle?', *Journal of Imperial and Commonwealth History*, 12 (2) (1984), pp. 187–209; Max Beloff, *Imperial Sunset: Britain's Liberal Empire, 1897–1921*, London 1989; Ronald Hyam, *Britain's Imperial Century, 1815–1914: A St udy of Empire and Expansion*, New York 1976.

2 For example, Andrew Shonfield, *British Economic Policy Since the War*, Harmondsworth 1958; Alec Cairncross, *The British Economy Since 1945: Economic Policy and Performance, 1945–1990*, Oxford 1992; Catherine R. Schenk, *Britain and the Sterling Area. From Devaluation to Convertability in the 1950s*, London 1994; Gerold Krozewski, *Money and the End of Empire. British International Economic Policy and the Colonies 1947–58*, London 2001.

3 The work of the nineteenth century Crown Agents is described in David Sunderland, *Managing the British Empire. The Crown Agents 1833–1914*, London 2004. In 1954, the Office was renamed the Crown Agents for Oversea Governments and Administrations.

Until the late 1970s, it was a quasi-independent body. Although under the supervision of the Colonial Office and the successor departments, which appointed the Agents and monitored their activities, it was administratively and financially independent of the government. It had a wide latitude as to how it conducted its affairs and covered its own salaries and expenses through a system of commissions for work done. Clients were charged fees, generally some percentage of the cost of the work performed, which were fixed at levels sufficient only to cover administration costs and to maintain a Reserve Fund that met pension costs and financed deficits and was pegged at £167,500 in 1929 and £350,000 in 1948. After 1930, any excess revenue was redistributed to customers, each of whom received a sum proportionate to the amount of business it did with the Agents.

From 1920 to 1974, there were 22 Crown Agents, who, on average, served for ten years and decided policy, represented the office in meetings with clients and government officials, and supposedly managed its day-to-day activities, though this task was largely undertaken by departmental heads (Appendix 1). Most were brought up in upper middle class Anglican families in the South East of England and had been educated at public school and University, almost half at the Universities of Oxford and Cambridge. They therefore had assimilated the gentlemanly ethos of fair play and honesty and could easily form close relationships with Governors and Colonial Office officials, who had similar backgrounds and who they met socially.[4] The majority were recruited from the Colonial Office and the colonies – half had worked at the Colonial Office, three as Under- Secretaries, and nine had been employed in some capacity by the colonial service – and the remainder were senior CA staff members who were promoted to the position. They thus had knowledge of the Agency's operations and the problems and needs of its clients, and strong relationships with governors and Colonial Office officials. The Secretary of State was also well aware of their capabilities and could use former colleagues to monitor the activities of the Agency and to ensure that it followed his rulings.

Unfortunately, many of those who came from the Colonial Office and the colonial service lacked financial and engineering skills, and a number could contribute little to the Agency. The position of Crown Agent was seen as a reward for long years of service and as a dumping ground for individuals who were incompetent or could no longer adequately perform their duties because of ill health, lack of drive or 'uncongenial personalities'.[5] Sir Harold Downie (CA 1942–53), for example, came to the Agency 'a worn out man, having been closely involved in protracted and frustrating negotiations about the termination of the mandate for Palestine', and Sir Claude Hayes (1968–74) was 'unloaded' on the CAs because of his 'abrasiveness' and aggression towards his colleagues.[6] Others were moved to the Agency as a result of internal Colonial Office machinations. Sir Henry Lambert (1921–32), for instance, possessed strong views on

4 Many belonged to the same clubs. See SA, CA (m) 64, Past CAs, no date; NA, CAOG 17/20, Fleming to Beckett, 25 Feb. 1935.

5 CA (m) 64, Past CAs, no date.

6 *Ibid.*; CA (m) 67, vol. 1, Abbott, 12 Aug. 1980; NA, OD 18/240, Cohen, 5 April 1968. See also Abbott's comments on Sir William Bottomley (1938–43), Sir Hugh Thornton (1920–43), and Sir J. Flood (1938–40) (CA (m) 64, Past CAs, no date).

South Africa, which were not shared by the Secretary of State, and Sir Hugh Thornton (1920–43) had allied himself far too closely with Lord Milner, with the result that when Milner relinquished his post as Colonial Secretary he found himself 'marooned at the Colonial Office, who seized an early opportunity of extruding this "foreign body"'.[7] Many of the CAs thus performed their duties poorly, though a very select few were judged to be highly effective. Sir George Beresford-Stooke (1953–54), for example, 'entered with zest into the procedures and technique of the work and was equally assiduous in the fostering of personal contact both at home and overseas', and Sir George Seel's period of office (1953–54) 'was marked by sustained activity ... infinite common sense and insistence upon ... achieving the highest standard of efficiency'.[8]

To help them complete their work, the Agents employed 276 people in 1914, 790 in 1945, 1,428 in 1955 and 1,637 in 1967, all of whom worked in specialised task orientated departments.[9] Theoretically, their clerical staff was recruited through the Civil Service Commission and had permanent contracts. In reality, because the Commission was unable to meet all of their needs, a large number of their employees, 56 per cent in 1945 and 29 per cent in 1955, were employed on a temporary basis, recruited through press adverts. Prior to and occasionally after 1920, a number of permanent clerks were also appointed as a result of personal recommendation and tended to be friends or relatives of existing employees.[10] Such recruitment was normal practice in the private sector, reduced the cost and difficulty of finding suitable workers, and minimized the likelihood that candidates would lie about their abilities. The Agents had personal knowledge of the capabilities and honesty of their friends and relatives and could be confident that their staff would recommend only competent candidates, as each clerk was aware that a poor recommendation would reflect badly on themselves.

Like the Crown Agents, many of the staff employed performed their work poorly. Those recruited through the Civil Service Commission tended to be young and lacked commercial experience and were often the less impressive candidates, as those who did well in the compulsory exam generally preferred to take up posts in the Home Civil Service.[11] Many of those who opted for the Agency also often stayed a relatively short period of time before moving on to jobs in the private sector. The CAs were required to adopt Civil Service salary scales, which were relatively low, there were few valuable fringe benefits, such as cheap mortgages, and the routine work undertaken was often boring and unsatis-

7 CA (m) 64, Past CAs, no date.

8 *Ibid.*

9 A. W. Abbott, *A Short History of the Crown Agents and their Office*, London 1959 (privately published), pp. 33, 57; CAOG 16/349.

10 For example, Edward Antrobus, the Chief Accountant and Clerk from 1902–20 was the brother of the Colonial Office official and later CA Sir Reginald Antrobus (1909–18); Henry Purcell, Chief Clerk from 1933–47, was the son of Sir John Purcell, who worked in the Stamps department of the Inland Revenue and recommended him to the CA Sir Percy Ezechiel; Henry Purcell, in turn, recommended the employment of K. W. Barley, Director of Finance from 1966–68, a son of one of his close friends; and, in July 1950, Walter Curtis, a Head of the Purchasing Department, obtained a temporary clerkship for his son, who later became an Executive Officer (Sunderland, *Managing*, p. 26; SA, Pen Portraits, Morris to Knights, Jan. 1991).

11 LA, L 18/9, p. 11.

fying.[12] As regards the temporary clerks, these lacked motivation, often had poor or no skills, and tended to be relatively old and unproductive, 58 per cent in 1950 being over the age of forty.[13] Like their permanent colleagues, they again tended to work at the Agency for only a short time, though turnovers fell in the 1950s when they were allowed to apply to become permanent members of staff after a given number of years service.[14]

Other reasons for the general staff inefficiency was the pre-1920 recruitment of friends and relatives of existing employees, some of whom completed their work poorly, but received preferential treatment, leading to much resentment, and the Agency's promotion and staff movement policies. Until around 1930, promotion was by seniority and many of those given advancement lacked the skills necessary to complete their new jobs.[15] Thereafter, although promotion was primarily on merit, seniority continued to play an important part in decisions, largely because of pressure placed on the Agents by the relevant trade unions.[16] The CAs also had a policy of moving Executive Officers every few years to a new department, which ensured 'a freshening of ideas and wide experience at the top', but meant that in the first few months of occupying a new post an Executive Officer was relatively unproductive.[17] From the mid-1960s, moreover, the more capable and efficient Executive Officers tended to be 'creamed off' by the Finance Department and Millbank Technical Services Ltd, a private firm created by the Agency to complete some of its engineering business.[18]

Although relatively inefficient, the CAs' clerical staff, nevertheless, strongly identified with their employer and with the interests of its clients. They worked closely and formed deep relationships with colonial administrators and were well aware that the growth and survival of the Agency depended on the fulfilment of their clients' needs. There also existed a very strong office culture. The clerks employed shared similar characteristics – most were male and lower middle class, Anglican, had a conservative political outlook and had been born and brought up in London or the South East of England. Those in executive positions had generally worked for the Agency since leaving school and therefore had fully imbibed its values and goals, formed deep friendships with their colleagues, and were conscious that they had little chance of gaining similar employment elsewhere. Identification with the Agency was further encouraged through the provision of gifts and the development of strong staff bonds. Although they earned relatively low wages, clerks could look forward to good pensions, could purchase household and horticultural goods at cost prices from the CA Horticultural Society and cheap lunches and teas from the CA Refreshment Club, obtained free morning and afternoon tea or coffee, and could make use of a men's and ladies' rest room, a rifle range, a sports ground and a cinema, where lunch time

12 L 35, meeting, 29 Aug. 1973.
13 CAOG 16/162, Morris, 1 July 1966; L 18/9, report of sub-committee on CA costs, 23 March 1960, p. 11.
14 Five years service in 1951 and two years in 1955 (CAOG 16/22, weeding note).
15 CA (m) 64, Past CAs, no date.
16 SA, File no. 54, Abbot, 1966; CAOG 16/240, memo, 26 Feb. 1963.
17 CA (m) 102, note on the Salmon report, 14 July 1949.
18 L 3, G. Dept. report, Aug. 1967.

concerts were occasionally held.[19] Employee bonds, meanwhile, were generated through the family relationships that existed between some members of staff, the policy of moving Executive Officers between departments, the accommodation of the whole Agency in one office complex at Millbank, London, and the existence of a myriad of clubs, societies and social events. Most staff belonged to a Civil Service trade union, and could attend dances and annual flower and vegetable shows, and join a bridge, a chess, a darts, a language, a rifle and a Sunday football club.[20]

Approach and structure of the book

Turning to the approach and the structure of the study, the book seeks to describe how the Agency performed its various roles and to determine whether its existence was beneficial to its clients or to the UK. Like many of the companies that provided it with supplies or services, it often acted in its own interests rather than in those of its customers. Moreover, it was occasionally prevented from doing the best for its clients by Bank of England, Colonial Office and Treasury officials, who forced it to act in ways that would benefit the British economy or their own organizations.

To aid understanding, the book is roughly divided into four parts. The first two chapters investigate how the Agency raised non-aid funds for its clients. Chapter one concentrates on the sale to UK investors of colonial loan stock. It seeks to explain how the Agents sought to maximize the demand for these securities and ensure that they were sold at a relatively high price, and how their efforts to achieve these goals were obstructed by the Bank of England, the Treasury and a variety of City institutions. The following chapter then looks at the other ways the Agents raised funds and how their attempts to act in the interests of their clients were again hindered by the Bank of England and the Treasury. It also summarises the various other sources of development money available and assesses the impact the outflow of all these funds had on the UK economy.

The second part examines the Agents' other financial role – the management of the sums their clients invested in UK banks and in sterling securities. The money comprised the amounts placed in Colonial Investment Funds, such as Pension Funds and Currency Funds, and in two other Funds – the Joint Colonial Fund (JCF) and the Joint Miscellaneous Fund (JMF). The management of Colonial Investment Funds, which were set up to produce returns that would be used for a specific purpose, such as the payment of pensions, is discussed in chapter three. The chapter considers the ways in which the money was invested, the reasons behind the expansion of these Funds during and after the Second World War and the various proposals put forward for reducing their size, and

19 CAOG 16/554, memo, 30 Oct. 1930; L 181, 1951. The Horticultural Society in 1966 had a turnover of £15,000 and the Refreshment Club in 1954 served 26,610 meals per year (CAOG 16/554, Knights, 13 May 1966; CAOG 16/401, memo, 6 April 1955).

20 CAOG 16/554, memo, 30 Oct. 1930; *ibid.*, Knights, 13 May 1966; *ibid.*, memo, 14 Oct. 1930; CAOG 16/401, memo, 4 Oct. 1950; L 181, 1952.

how the Agents retained clients after independence. The spotlight is then turned onto the JCF and the JMF, which largely held the sums clients kept in the UK to pay for goods purchased by the Agency. Chapter four surveys the high risk investment strategy adopted for these Funds and describes the near collapse of the JCF in 1931/2 and in 1951, and the problems it and the JMF faced in 1971 and 1974 as a result of falls in equity prices. Both this and the previous chapter also explore how the returns earned by the colonies from their various investments were reduced by the actions of the Bank of England, the Colonial Office, the Treasury, and various City institutions, all of which put their own or the British economy's interests above those of the colonies.

The third part of the monograph takes a closer look at the Agents' non-financial activities. Chapters five and six concentrate on the purchase of colonial government stores. At the start of the period, colonial regulations required administrations to buy goods that were not manufactured or produced within their own colonies or in adjacent territories from the Crown Agents. Over time, however, this requirement lapsed, and, by the late 1950s, they were free to buy supplies themselves either directly or through local merchants. Chapter five tests the colonial belief that the goods bought by the Agents were relatively expensive by considering the various factors that had an impact on the prices paid, including a bias towards articles manufactured in Britain, and the non-price costs of the goods purchased, for example inspection, packing, insurance and shipping expenses. Chapter six, meanwhile, examines the CAs' tendency to deliver goods relatively late, and explores their response to the fall in their procurement work post independence. After unsuccessfully seeking help from the UK government, they slashed their costs, searched out new customers and offered a range of new services, including the purchase of armaments and goods for international aid organisations.

The other non-financial work performed by the CAs is discussed in chapter seven. The first section describes their personnel duties, which involved recruiting expatriate technical staff and some non-technical employees, such as police officers, arranging the passage of these people to and from their country of employment, and paying some of their pensions and salaries. The Agents' engineering work is then investigated. The CAs examined designs for mechanical and engineering and electrical equipment drawn up by client Public Works Departments, designed small civil engineering structures, employed the consulting engineers and building contractors who worked on large infrastructure schemes, and provided advice on the operation of harbours, railways and other commercial projects. The chapter concludes with a short description of the other tasks they performed – the sale of their clients' stamps, the purchase or rental of London embassies, and the granting of concessions, largely land and mineral rights, to the UK private sector.

Another way in which the Agents protected themselves after independence against the loss of their traditional clients' business was to move into secondary banking and to act not as an agent but on their own account, taking all the profits of the new business and being responsible for its losses. From the mid-1960s, they began to borrow large sums of money from a variety of UK banks and their own clients, some of which they then re-lent to other financial institutions at interest rates slightly higher than those at which the funds had been borrowed. They also invested large amounts of the borrowed money in gilts, equities and property and used it to trade currencies and commodities and to purchase large and long-term equity holdings in individual companies. Unfortunately, the 1974 secondary banking crisis caused many of the firms in which they had invested to fail, and, in December 1974, the Agency itself was declared bankrupt. Two subsequent government enquiries blamed the collapse largely on the Agents themselves, finding that they had embarked on the new venture out of self-interest and with insufficient experience and inadequate internal controls, had taken unjustified risks, become involved in unethical and illegal activities and were personally corrupt.

The final part of the book investigates the motives and the operation of the CAs' secondary banking venture and the reasons for its failure. Chapter eight argues that many of the criticisms of the Agency expressed by the two enquiries were not justified. Although the Agents partly acted out of self-interest, they genuinely believed that the new venture would help their clients. The income earned would subsidise the provision of their traditional services, enabling them to be improved and extended, administrations that lent funds would earn relatively high returns, and the skills and expertise of the companies in which they invested would be directed at solving their clients' economic and social problems. Likewise, the Agents had far more experience of the City than the enquiries claimed, possessed strong internal controls, though these were sometimes not followed, and took on the same amount of risk and followed the same ethical norms as other secondary banks.

The real reason for the Agency's downfall is revealed in the final chapter, where it is shown that it succumbed to the 1974 banking crisis because it failed to call in loans and continued to lend money to a number of companies that subsequently went bankrupt. Some of the blame for these decisions lies with the Agents, who believed that the market would recover. The Bank of England, however, is equally culpable. Wishing to prevent financial meltdown, Bank officials pressured the Agents to use their own and their clients' funds to support failing institutions, even after they were aware that the Agency itself was insolvent.

1

The Public Issue of Loans

The finance required for development broadly came from four sources. The UK government and later international organizations provided aid in the form of loans and grants. The private sector invested large sums in businesses based in the colonies. Colonial governments financed projects using their own resources, and funds were obtained through the Crown Agents. Money via the Agents came from the public issue of loans in the London market, the sale of stock in the same market, inter-colonial loans and advances from the Joint Colonial Fund (JCF) and the Joint Miscellaneous Fund (JMF), investment Funds managed by the CAs. This chapter concentrates on the public flotation of colonial stock, an activity that has never previously been investigated. The various other means of obtaining development funds are discussed in the following chapter.

From 1914 to 1968, 84 public loans were floated with a total value of £267.5m and an average size of £3.2m (Figure 1.1).[1] Issues peaked in the aftermath of the two world wars, when colonies undertook development projects and maintenance that had been postponed during the war years, and in the early 1950s, when the realization that independence would reduce the appeal of their loans prompted many colonies to take advantage of their colonial status and issue stock. By contrast, few issues were floated during the inter-war slump, during which the fall in commodity prices halted the construction of public works, nor from the mid-1950s, when the approach of independence and the concurrent increase in risk reduced investor demand for colonial securities. Issuers were relatively prosperous colonies possessing easily exploitable resources and well known to the investing public, but lacking large surpluses of revenue (Appendix 2). Sixty two per cent of the stock issued was created for Africa, and, of this, 26 per cent was floated by the East Africa High Commission, 22 per cent by Nigeria and 20 per cent by Kenya. The West Indies was the second largest issuer with 21 per cent of the total, 54 per cent of which was Jamaican stock and 19 per cent Trinidadian, and SE Asia and the Indian Ocean brought up the rear, with the Federated Malay States and Ceylon accounting for 58 per cent and 66 per cent of their regions' issues respectively.

Loans were issued with the help of the Agents' brokers, J. & A. Scrimgeours Ltd, and had a fixed life, though there was usually an early repayment or conversion option, which allowed the CAs in a given year either to repay the sum owed

1 The average size of dominion loans floated in the same period was £6.38m and that of UK municipal issues £2.051m.

Figure 1.1. Publicly issued loans and JCF/JMF advances, 1914–74

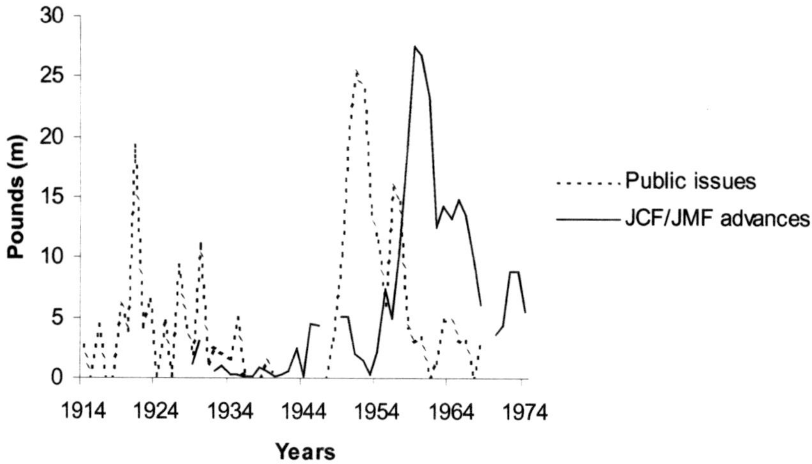

Sources. Loans: CAOG 9/33–CAOG 9/35; CAOG 9/78, memo, no date; CAOG 9/96, weeding note; CAOG 9/97, memo, 29 May 1922; CAOG 9/228; CAOG 9/276–CAOG 9/283; CAOG 9/359; CO 67/246/16, CAs to Cyprus, 30 June 1932; T 233/1425, memo, 14 May 1958; L1, finance reports, 1963 and 1964; WN 13. JCF/JMF: CAOG 1/1; CAOG 1/2; SA, JCF and JMF annual reports; SA, CA Annual reports, 1970–74.

Notes. JCF: 1931 and 1947–8 figures are missing.

or to offer investors the chance to exchange their holdings for new securities. The stock was sold for a set price that was above or below the 'par' price (100) at which it would eventually be repaid and offered a given annual rate of interest. After flotation, it was quoted on the Stock Market, which enabled investors to sell and buy holdings, with the resultant changes in supply and demand causing the quoted price to rise or fall. The initial purchasers of the stock were stockbrokers, who, in the fullness of time, sold their allocations at a profit to general investors; financial institutions, which retained their purchases as reserves; and those members of the public who 'stagged' popular issues, that is bought securities in the hope that the price would rise soon after issue, when they would be immediately re-sold.[2]

When floating loans, the Agents had two goals. First, they aimed to set as high a price as possible for stock. High prices reduced the cost of a loan to the issuing colony, as it had to float less stock to obtain the money it needed and thus paid less annual interest and had a smaller amount to repay at the end of the security's life. The Agents also had to ensure that all the stock floated was purchased and that the issuer received the sum required. The failure of a loan would prevent the issuing colony undertaking the public works project for which the money was

2 To prevent stagging, some brokers refused to allow clients to withdraw applications and requests for stock in excess of £1,000 had to be in multiples of £1,000 (CAOG 9/107, *The Economist*, 16 Oct. 1943; LA, WN 13, A055803, Scrimgeours to CAs, 4 Dec. 1962).

usually raised; reduce the Agents' income, a large part of which came from the purchase of supplies for the construction of capital works; and damage the CAs' ability to provide other colonies with short-term advances. As will be described later, the proceeds of a loan that were not to be spent immediately were placed in the Joint Colonial Fund, and a proportion then lent to other colonies.

Unfortunately for the Agents, the two goals were inter-related, with price determining demand, which, in turn, affected future prices. The setting of an excessively high price therefore would discourage investors making purchases, stock would remain unsold, and the quoted price would fall, pulling down the price of other colonial securities. Confidence in colonial loans would thus collapse, and, when floating future stock for both the issuing colony and other colonies, the Agents would have to offer more generous terms. The two goals also clashed with those of underwriters and the Bank of England. Underwriters, brokers who agreed to buy all of the stock of an issue not sold in return for a commission, were motivated by self-interest and opposed high prices as they increased the likelihood that a loan would fail and that they would be left with large amounts of unsold securities. The main objective of the Bank, meanwhile, was the smooth functioning of the market. It therefore preferred prices to be set at relatively low levels, which ensured the success of flotations, and that the Agents should take into account other issuers' needs during upturns in the market when demand was high. A failed flotation would prevent other issuing houses successfully floating their stock at a reasonable price and the mass flotation of loans during market upturns would cause the weaker issues to fail and again deflate future prices.

This chapter explores how the Agents fulfilled their goals in the face of City and Bank opposition. The first section discusses the terms of the loans issued by the CAs, paying particular attention to how prices were decided upon. Part two examines the various strategies designed to increase the appeal of the stock offered that were adopted during the issue process and how the Agents made sure that loans were repaid. The success of the Agency in maximizing subscription is then considered, and the chapter concludes with a discussion of the reasons behind the fall in the demand for colonial stock from the mid-1950s and the various solutions proposed and adopted.

Loan terms

The terms of a loan comprised the information that appeared in its prospectus. They thus included its purpose, size, length and the type of asset issued, its annual interest rate and price, the reservation of stock for colonial purchasers, and the provision of instruments that facilitated stock transfer and repayment.

Purpose, size and length of issues

To attract subscribers, issues had to finance economic development and be relatively large and of an appropriate length. Of the 66 publicly floated loans for which the purpose is known, at least some of the money of 59 (89 per cent) was raised to pay for public works, largely the construction of railways, roads and harbours. Investors understood that such projects would generate large revenues relatively quickly and improve the export potential of the issuing territory. The price of the stock bought would therefore rise over time and the issuer would have no difficulty meeting annual dividend payments or eventually repaying the debt.[3] Buyers of colonial stock were also relatively content if all or some of the loan proceeds were used to repay UK government loans or previously issued colonial stock, as was the case in 14 of the Agents' issues, or if they were lent to another colony or a municipality (8 loans), provided that they then were used to finance development. Occasionally, if a colony failed to spend all the money raised on a project, the CAs allowed the unspent balance to be used for another of the purposes listed in the prospectus, and, in the case of the 1929 Nigeria issue, permitted £550,000 obtained to finance the construction of the Lagos sewerage scheme to be used to build a railway and a college.[4] The employment of funds for purposes not stated in a prospectus was forbidden by the Stock Exchange, and, to circumvent this ruling, the Agents transferred the sum to the colony's Supplementary Sinking Fund, which was permitted, and then to the colony's Surplus Fund, from which it was spent.[5]

Ideally, loans were large, meeting the issuer's financial needs for a number of years, and were of a suitable length. Large loans attracted greater publicity and were more marketable than smaller ones, the unspent portion of their proceeds could be advanced to other colonies through the JCF, and issues of under £100,000 were not quoted on the Stock Exchange and were therefore difficult to trade.[6] The length or currency of the stock issued varied from 9 to 60 years and averaged 24.8 years, with the currency of issues floated from 1953 to 1963, when independence loomed, averaging 19.6 years, as compared to an average of 33.8 years for loans floated from 1923 to 1933. Many securities additionally possessed an option clause that allowed the issuer to repay or convert the stock early, on average after 17.7 years, from 1923 to 1933 after 23.3 years, and, from 1953 to 1963, after 16 years. Loan length was primarily determined by the purpose of the issue, the prevailing state of the market, and the currency of the colony's other debts. Loans raised for unremunerative projects or short lived capital works tended to have relatively short lives; whereas those that financed large remunerative schemes that would benefit future generations had far longer currencies. Likewise, if interest rates were unusually high, issuers tended to prefer short loans with early repayment/conversion clauses to reduce the period during which the high rates had to be paid, and, if rates were abnormally low, they sought longer currencies.[7] In order to prevent a colony having to repay a number of loans over a relatively short period, which could lead to financial difficulties, the Agents also tried to spread maturities so that repayments occurred at well spaced intervals.[8]

3 CAOG 9/324, notes for Lord Hailey's committee, 1941, p. 13.
4 WN 13, A822802; SA, S 1, A171.
5 S 1, A171.
6 L 1, Finance Dept. report, 1963; BE, G 1/202, No. 4, Norman to Hopkins, 18 Nov. 1930.
7 CAOG 9/324, notes, pp. 16, 40, 43.
8 BE, OV 44/73, No. 100, Hicks to Wilson, 29 June 1955.

Type of asset created

The Agents issued stock. At the start of the period, inscribed stock was used, the ownership of which was recorded, and, from 1952, registered stock, which was more secure, as investors additionally obtained certificates without which their holdings could not be sold.[9] Debentures, bearer securities whose ownership was not recorded, were used on only three occasions. Nigeria and Kenya, in 1915 and 1921 respectively, issued 10 year debentures convertible to longer dated stock by a given date, and, in 1966, subscribers to a Jamaican loan were given the option of buying either short-term stock or debentures.[10] Although debentures were popular with brokers, they were disliked by the public, as they were liable to theft or misappropriation, and, to obtain dividends, coupons attached to the certificate had to be sent to the issuing house.[11] They were therefore only used when public demand for a loan was expected to be weak and underwriters would only provide support if they were offered.

The stock issued was usually identical to previous securities floated by a borrower, and, in the case of Crown colony loans, had a trustee status. The flotation of loans with the same interest rate and dividend and repayment dates as previous issues encouraged existing holders of the stock to subscribe, as the security was familiar and the holdings of new and old stock could be sold together, reducing selling fees. The size of the resultant large block of stock also increased its marketability, and the identical dividend/repayment dates simplified the management of the loans, reducing the Agents' costs. Such stock, however, could only be used if it had previously been issued relatively recently, as otherwise the lifespan was too short for the sum required for repayment to be generated.[12]

Trustee status denoted that a loan could be purchased by trustees, those who managed financial trusts. Since trusts bought large amounts of securities, the status greatly increased demand and allowed higher prices to be set. Until the late 1920s, protectorates were denied this privilege, and the Agents and the Colonial Office had to adopt various stratagems to maximise price when floating their loans. Where a protectorate was closely allied to a colony, securities were issued in the name of the colony, and, in the case of the Federated Malay States (FMS) in 1921, a loan was floated by the Straits Settlements, which then lent the proceeds to the FMS. When a protectorate had no colony linkages, finance was acquired via the inter-colonial loan scheme or from the Joint Colonial Fund, or through the issue of guaranteed loans.[13] These carried guarantees from the UK government that it would repay the capital and meet the dividend payments of loans if the issuers defaulted, which had the same impact on price as trustee status. In the case of the East African Protectorate, more desperate measures were adopted. Unable to obtain help from the Treasury, because of the territory's existing debts,

9 CA (m) 60.

10 CAOG 9/324, notes, p. 2; CAOG 9/78, Scrimgeours to CAs, 12 Oct. 1921; L 2, Finance Dept. reports, Sept. 1966.

11 CAOG 9/324, notes, p. 3. The attraction of short-term debentures to brokers was that they could be easily sold to other City institutions and they could be used as collateral for advances (*ibid.*).

12 CA (m) 25, p. 10.

13 CAOG 9/88, CO memo, 1928.

Figure 1.2. Annual average yields, 1920–69

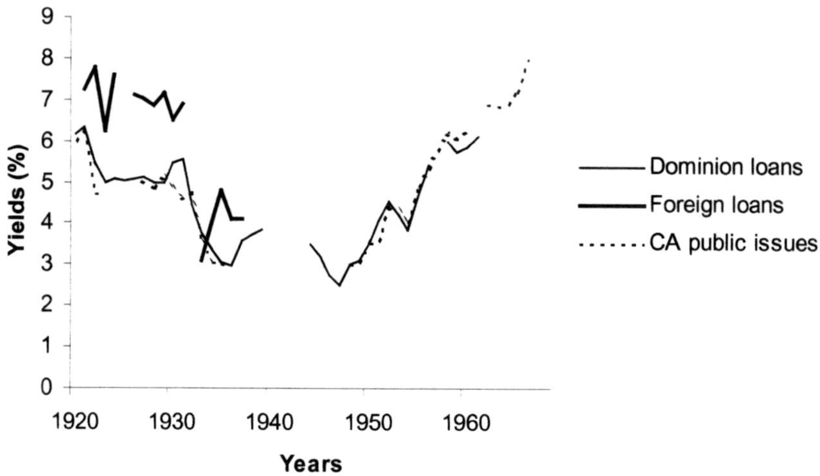

Sources. CAOG 9/33–CAOG 9/35; CAOG 9/78, memo, no date; CAOG 9/96, weeding note; CAOG 9/97, memo, 29 May 1922; CAOG 9/228; CAOG 9/276-CAOG 9/283; CAOG 9/359; CO 67/246/16, CAs to Cyprus, 30 June 1932; T 233/1425, memo, 14 May 1958; WN 13; L1, finance reports 1963 and 1964; Stock Exchange, Stock Exchange Official Intelligence, London, 1921–32, 1939, 1953, 1962.

Notes. Yield = interest rate/price x 100.

unbalanced budget and severe economic problems, and having obtained £1m of advances from the Joint Colonial Fund, the Colonial Office decided to annex the interior of the protectorate to form the Crown colony of Kenya, for which a loan was issued in November 1921.[14]

Demands by the CAs and the CO for the 1900 Colonial Stocks Act be amended to give protectorates trustee status were initially resisted by the Treasury, which feared that such a move would depreciate the value of the privilege.[15] However, aware that its intransigence was stoking antipathy towards the UK and slowing development and increasing the dependence of such territories on the Exchequer, the Treasury eventually gave way.[16] The 1929 Colonial Development Act allowed stock issued by protectorates and mandated territories to be bought by trusts provided that their governments issued orders-in-council. Over the following few years, Bechuanaland, FMS, Northern Rhodesia, Nyasaland, Swaziland, Uganda and Zanzibar all passed such ordinances. Unfortunately, the Act's provisions failed to extend to the East African Commission, a common interests authority, which had to wait until the 1948 Colonial Stocks Act before it was able to issue on equal terms with colonies.[17]

14 Stephen Constantine, *The Making of British Colonial Development Policy, 1914–40*, London 1984, pp. 49–50.

15 CO 323/839/2832, minutes, 10–19 Dec. 1919, *ibid.*, Amery to Chamberlain, 4 March 1920; *ibid.*, Chamberlain to Amery, 25 March 1920.

16 CAOG 9/88, CO memo, 1928.

17 CA (m) 25, p. 6.

Interest rate and prices

The annual yields of Crown colony loans, that is the annual dividend taking into account the price at issue, were far lower than those of foreign loans and slightly less than dominion issues (Figure 1.2). Colonial issuers thus paid relatively less for the money that they borrowed than their counterparts. The interest rate set was generally that ruling at the time of issue. After the First World War, pressure on the loan market forced rates up to 6 per cent. As demand eased, rates then fell to 4 per cent, rising to 5 per cent during the early 1930s financial crisis, but then returning to 4 per cent, followed by 3 per cent. In the aftermath of the Second World War, the government's cheap money policy prevented a repeat of the post-WW1 rate rise and rates fell to as low as 2.5 per cent, gradually rising to 6 per cent as colonial independence approached and the demand for loans fell.[18] The Agents ignored the ruling interest rate on just two occasions: in 1923 and 1952 when they set excessively low prices and rates for respectively a Nigerian and a Ugandan loan. It was believed that a combination of low prices and rates appealed to investors, such as insurance companies, who were more interested in the return they would make when a loan was redeemed at par than in annual yield, which was heavily taxed. Although alluring to insurance companies, however, the terms held little attraction to non-tax paying Pension Funds and trusts and both loans failed. The issues also generated much anger at the Treasury, which regarded them as tax dodges that sought to defraud the Exchequer and feared that they would lead to trade union disquiet.[19]

The loan prices set by the Agents were relatively high and generally were just below those of British government stock.[20] One reason was that colonial government finances were supervised by the Colonial Office and imprudent behaviour was therefore unlikely, and it was accepted in the market that the UK government would not allow any colony to default on its debts. Non-payment would reflect badly on the effectiveness of its management of the Empire and would damage the credit of all the crown colonies, making it difficult for them to raise loans and forcing them to fall back on the Imperial Exchequer for financial support.[21]

Other explanations for the high prices are the various strategies adopted by the Agents to ensure that demand for colonial stock remained high, and the purchase by the CAs of a proportion of each loan at the time of issue for the colonial investment Funds that they managed, a procedure known as 'buying firm'. The purchases were noted in the prospectus, and, by reflecting the Agents' confidence in the project to be financed and reducing the amount of stock to be sold to the public, encouraged others to subscribe. They also simplified the conversion of loans to lower interest stock, helped to attract underwriters by minimizing the risks involved in supporting loans, and cut costs. From 1928, the stock bought was not underwritten, and, when purchases occurred, Scrimgeours reduced their overriding commission (the fee they obtained for organizing underwriting) by

18 CA (mc) 60.

19 CAOG 9/324, notes, p. 14; CO 323/985/19, *The Times*, cutting, 1952.

20 CO 323/957/4, memo, Ezechiel, 1926.

21 CAOG 9/101, memo, 18 July 1935; CAOG 9/324, notes, p. 21.

20 per cent.[22] Inevitably, the Bank of England disparaged the practice, which it referred to as 'colonies taking in one another's washing'.[23] Nevertheless, the Agents bought portions of 50 loans, purchasing £41.2m of stock or 15 per cent of that issued. On average, they took 23 per cent of each loan, the amount bought being restricted by Stock Exchange rules and related to the likely public demand, the amount of money available for investment, and whether the stock was suitable for the Funds with cash to spare and likely to give a more favourable return than similar securities offered on the open market.[24]

In setting prices, the Agents followed a number of general rules. First, the price of an issue had to be below the market price of the issuing colony's existing stock. This allowed those brokers who purchased issues to make a profit, known as a 'turn', when they resold the stock onto the public.[25] Secondly, prices had to be below par (100), the price at which the stock was repaid at the end of its life. Trustees were averse to purchasing stock at a considerable premium, and, if they managed trusts with less than fifteen years to run, they were prohibited by law from buying securities priced at above par.[26] Third, the CAs had to take account of the views of underwriters, who would only underwrite a loan if the price was fixed at a level which would attract subscribers.

The prices fixed for loans were remarkably similar, despite the differing prospects of issuers. The investing public had 'little acquaintance with individual colonies and the conditions prevalent in them' and viewed the Crown colonies as a single entity to which it attached a single worth.[27] Nevertheless, when deciding on a price, the Agents did have to take some account of the circumstances of the flotation and the nature of the issuing territory. Prices tended to be set relatively low when large numbers of loans were being issued, as after the two World Wars, or when colonial stock prices were falling, for example in the early 1950s.[28] Large loans were also usually sold relatively cheaply, to avoid underwriters being left with large amounts of unsold stock, as were those issued by colonies that had not previously borrowed on the market and were therefore an unknown quantity to investors.[29] On the other hand, high prices were attached to the issues of prosperous colonies, and the competition between issuing houses for clients in the 1920s prompted the Agents to increase the prices of all colonial loans in order to prevent defections to their rivals.[30]

A further influence on price was the Bank of England, which began to seek to influence the terms set in the 1920s. Its interventions reached a peak in 1926 and 1927. In 1926, immediately before the flotation of a Nigerian loan at 99.5, the

22 CAOG 9/324, notes, p. 13; BE, ADM 14/51, No. 8, memo, 7 Oct. 1958; CAOG 9/288, memo, 'How the colonies benefited in 1934 from the CAs' financial policy'.
23 SA, IF 231/239/01, Part A, pp. 96–102.
24 CAOG 9/324, notes, p. 13; CAOG 9/105, Scrimgeours to CAs, 19 Dec. 1927.
25 CAOG 9/40, Colonial circular, 10 July 1925.
26 CAOG 9/324, notes, p. 14.
27 *Ibid.*, p. 12.
28 CAOG 9/113, memo, 19 July 1923; CAOG 9/101, memo, Scrimgeours, 5 May 1952.
29 CAOG 9/324, notes, pp. 12, 13. To reduce the loss to the issuer, first loans were relatively small (*ibid.*, p. 12).
30 CAOG 9/101, *The Times*, 25 Nov. 1925.

Bank's Governor, Montague Norman, advised the Agents that the price should not be more than 99. Not wishing to deprive the colony of the loan proceeds that would be lost if the price was lowered, the CAs postponed the issue, which eventually took place three months later priced at 100, at which it was oversubscribed.[31] A year later, the Agents fixed the price of a Kenyan loan at 95, only to be told by the Governor that they were taking 'an unjustifiable risk' and that it should be 94.5. Assured that their 'brokers ... the Bank of England's own brokers, the underwriters and the market' all disagreed with the Governor, the CAs disregarded his advice and went ahead with the issue, which was again oversubscribed. Norman, astonished that the Agents had had the temerity to ignore his instructions, made official complaints about their behaviour to both the Colonial Office and the Treasury and demanded that he be given some control over the Agency's prices.[32]

The Bank believed that such control was essential for the smooth functioning of the market. If an excessively priced Crown colony loan failed, other issuers would have difficulty successfully floating their stock at a reasonable price. The failure of the loan would reduce the credit of the market and underwriters would be left with large amounts of unsold stock. If they decided to hold their allocations until they offloaded them onto the public, they would have insufficient funds to underwrite and purchase new loans. Whereas, if they dumped them onto the market, the price of colonial stock and other securities would fall, forcing the issuers of fresh loans to set more generous terms. The resultant 'clogging' of the market would also 'queer the pitch' for Treasury issues, reducing the funds available to the UK government, and lead to the failure of foreign government flotations, encouraging them to turn to other markets for their finance.[33]

In response, the Agents argued that the prices that the Bank wished them to set were far too low and would reduce the money colonies received from issues, and that the failure of an issue would not necessarily obstruct the flotation of other loans. Colonial issues were relatively small in size and made at long intervals, large amounts of stock were bought by colonial investment Funds on a 'firm' basis, and, in the event of failure, they prevented price falls by purchasing stock from underwriters. The Agents, rather, suspected that the Bank's concern about their prices was motivated by self-interest. Many of the Bank's clients were underwriters, who would withdraw their business if it failed to protect their interests, and it was itself an issuing house.[34] The high prices commanded by Crown colony issues reflected badly on its own lower priced loans and the clogging of the market by the CAs threatened the success of its issues. The Agents also believed that Bank officials had an 'acquisitive eye for the loaves and fishes' of their loan business and that they deliberately sought to depreciate the terms of colonial loans in order to encourage colonies to abandon the Agency and move their business to the Bank.[35]

31 CAOG 9/300, CAs to Wilson, 8 Dec. 1927.

32 CAOG 9/58, CAs to CO, 14 May 1928.

33 CAOG 9/300, CAs to Wilson, 8 Dec. 1927; CAOG 9/58, CAs to CO, 14 May 1928.

34 CAOG 9/300, CAs to Wilson, 8 Dec. 1927.

35 CA (m) 61, p. 7; CA (mc) 60, p. 16, appendix 1.

In normal times, the Bank's demand for more control over prices would have fallen on deaf ears. Unfortunately for the Agents, as will be discussed in chapter three, in early 1931 poor investments led to the near bankruptcy of the Joint Colonial Fund and severely damaged the Colonial Office's confidence in the CAs' financial abilities. In 1932, therefore, the Secretary of State acquiesced to the Bank's request that the Agents inform the Governor of the intended price of each issue and seriously consider the advice proffered.[36] Thereafter, although they occasionally failed to provide details of terms, the CAs always set prices that were acceptable to the Bank, and, in 1935, declined to join UK municipal issuers who sought to reduce the Bank's influence on prices.[37]

Reservation of stock

In the early 1920s, the Agents were keen to increase the number of securities bought by residents of issuing colonies. Such purchases reduced the amount of stock that had to be disposed of in Britain and it was believed that they would encourage the development of local financial markets and enable colonial governments to issue loans in their own countries.[38] From 1922, therefore, if they suspected there was sufficient demand, the CAs began to reserve a certain proportion of flotations for those who lived in the issuing colonies. If the number of applications exceeded the amount set aside, allotments were scaled down, and, if they were less, the balance was sold to London applicants.[39] Up to 1964, 28 loans had local reservations, on average 10 per cent or £341,438 of issues was set aside, and colonial subscribers, in total, bought £9.6m of stock. The majority of applications were from local insurance companies and local government departments and officials, with a relatively small proportion coming from ordinary residents.[40] In 1964, the Agents additionally reserved £50,000 of stock of a Jamaican loan for Jamaicans resident in the UK. 'The experiment was not particularly successful' and it was not repeated.[41]

Colonial reservations had two drawbacks. There were complaints that the payment of dividends and the registration of transfers were relatively slow, largely because the stock was registered by the CAs in London. To speed up both activities, the Agents began to create local registers of locally held stock, which allowed them to transfer the performance of these services to the local Treasury.[42] A more important difficulty was that many colonial applicants failed to obtain stock, as, by the time the Agents received their applications, the flotation was over. Colonies were sent the terms of loans only a few days before a flotation

36 CAOG 9/230, meeting, 23 Feb. 1932.

37 G 1/202, No. 47, Norman to Ezechiel, 30 May 1932; CAOG 9/300, *Financial Times*, 13 June 1935; *ibid.*, CAs to Trinidad, 16 Aug. 1935; *ibid.*, CAs to Ceylon, 18 Dec. 1935.

38 CAOG 9/358, CAs to Scrimgeours, 19 Sept. 1952.

39 CAOG 9/111, CAs to Nigeria, 10 Feb. 1922.

40 For example, the Jamaica Mutual Life Insurance Society obtained 41.2 per cent of the reserved portion of the 1923 Jamaica loan, the Native Administrations bought 68 per cent of this part of the 1927 Nigeria issue, and 35 per cent of the reserved stock of the 1923 Nigeria loan was acquired by employees of the government (CAOG 9/79, Jamaica to CAs, 29 March 1923; CAOG 9/18; CAOG 9/93).

41 L 1, Finance Dept. report, 1964.

42 CA (m) 25, p. 8.

occurred and issues were generally closed as soon as sufficient applications had been received, which, in the case of popular flotations, was often within a few minutes of opening.[43] Since terms had to be determined immediately before issues, the obvious solution to the problem was to keep issues open longer for colonial applicants. The Agents, however, were reluctant adopt this practice. For allotment to take place, they needed to know the amount of stock that had been bought by a colony and the size of any unsold balance to be passed onto London applicants. If issues were kept open longer for colonial subscribers, they would not have this information until a few days after the flotation and the allotment procedure would have to be delayed. As investors had the right to withdraw their applications up to the start of allotment, such delays, if a loan was undersubscribed, would allow significant withdrawals and would increase the amount of stock that would have to be taken up by the underwriters.[44] The Agents also feared malfeasance. If issues were kept open longer for colonial investors, there was a possibility that they would delay their applications until they knew the result of the London flotation and would thus have an unfair advantage over their British counterparts. London investors, meanwhile, if the UK portion of a loan was oversubscribed, would be tempted to employ agents in the colonies to make applications on their behalf.[45]

Under pressure, the Agency gradually increased the amount of time issues were open to colonial applicants.[46] To partly solve the fraud problem, they required colonial applicants to sign a declaration that they were not applying on behalf of or as a nominee of a non-resident, with a false declaration rendering an allotment liable to cancellation.[47] To overcome the delay in allotments, they asked colonial governments to guarantee to buy for their investment Funds any of the stock reserved for colonial residents that remained unsold.[48] Inevitably, such guarantees were unpopular with administrations, which, if a loan failed, were left with large amounts of unsold stock, the price of which had plummeted. Many therefore suggested that guarantees be replaced by local underwriting, and the Agents in 1952 permitted the Kenyan government to underwrite the reserved portion of that year's loan. In the event, the local underwriters sub-contracted the underwriting to brokers in Britain, giving the issue unwelcome publicity and creating 'an atmosphere of doubt and suspicion' among the underwriters of the London portion of the loan.[49] Such was the chaos, that thereafter requests for local support were always rejected.

Transfer and repayment instruments

Two factors that discouraged people from buying loans were the payment of stamp duty when and if they sold their purchases, and a fear that, if they retained the stock bought until the end of the loan's life, the colony would default on its

43 CAOG 9/111, Kenya to CAs, 14 Dec. 1930.
44 *Ibid.*, CAs to Ceylon, 16 Dec. 1935.
45 CA (m) 25, p. 7; CAOG 9/111, CAs to Kenya, 21 Feb. 1931.
46 CA (m) 25, p. 7.
47 CAOG 9/358, CAs to Scrimgeours, 19 Sept. 1952.
48 WN 13, A1971.
49 CAOG 9/358, memo, Scrimgeours, 5 May 1952.

repayment. The Agents minimized these disincentives by paying the stamp duty on sales themselves, and, to prevent colonial default, setting up Sinking Funds. Until the 1940s, the CAs made a single payment to the Treasury at the time of issue that covered the stamp duty that would have to be paid on all the estimated future sales.[50] Thereafter, colonies met payments out of current revenue, or, after the issue of a loan, paid 1 per cent, and, from 1955, 0.5 per cent of the proceeds into an invested Stamp Duty Fund, out of which duty was paid every time stock of the issue was traded. The establishment of these Funds reduced colonial expenses, as colonial stock was largely held by institutions and trusts and rarely sold, and helped to meet repayment, the contents of the Funds being disposed off when the loan matured.[51] To further reduce costs, a number of colonies set up amalgamated Stamp Duty Funds that financed duty payments for a number of loans.[52]

To ensure repayment, unlike their British government, municipal and dominion counterparts, all CA issues had Sinking Funds.[53] A Fund was set up after a loan had been floated and received annual contributions from the issuing government, which were invested by the Agents in long-term securities. At the end of the loan's life, the contents of the Fund were then sold off and the proceeds used to pay the amount owed. The annual contributions were generally related to the length of the loan, the shorter the currency the higher the contribution, and usually only began when the project financed became remunerative.[54] Because colonies were allowed to increase contributions during periods of prosperity and some investments appreciated relatively rapidly, most loan ordinances allowed contributions to cease when the Funds became full.[55] Many colonies additionally had Supplementary Sinking Funds, into which less regular contributions were made. As their name suggests, these were used to help repay those loans whose Funds contained insufficient monies, but were often raided when the issuing government found itself in financial straits. In the 1930s, for example, some of the contents of the Nigerian and Gold Coast Funds were used to finance the construction of the Nigerian railway and Takordai Harbour respectively.[56]

Issue and management

The Agents' determination to ensure that colonies obtained the funds needed and sold their securities at a high price did not end with the publication of the loan terms. Demand and prices could be maximized through the timing of the issue and the removal of prior charges, and the failure of a loan could be over-

50 CAOG 9/324, notes, p. 20.

51 CA (m) 25, p. 11; CA (mc) 60; CAOG 9/40, Colonial circular, 21 Sept. 1955. If Funds grew too rapidly, the issuing colony was sometimes allowed to withdraw money before redemption (S 3, A723).

52 S 3, A723.

53 CAOG 9/324, notes, p. 14; CAOG 9/109, CAs to CO, 18 Jan 1931.

54 CAOG 9/324, notes, p. 20.

55 CA (mc) 60, Colonial circular, 5 Aug. 1927.

56 S 2, A306; *ibid.*, A346.

come through the employment of underwriters and by the post-issue support of stock. The manner in which the Agents managed loans, that is the efficiency with which dividends were paid and the successful repayment of debts, also influenced the demand for issues, with holders of redeemed Crown colony stock often re-investing the amount repaid in other colonial securities.

The timing of issues

Loans were issued within a few days of the publication of the prospectus, before the market conditions that had determined the terms could change; generally during winter and spring, with the tendency for brokers to take long holidays reducing the demand for stock during the summer months; and, ideally, when market conditions were favourable.[57] On a number of occasions, events in the wider world or within the issuing colony affected the state of the market, forcing issues to be postponed. In 1950, for instance, military action in Korea forced the Agents to delay a Kenyan flotation, and the announcement of the UK general election in the following year led to the postponement of a Uganda issue.[58] The Agents' autonomy as regards timing was also questioned by the Bank of England and the Treasury. In theory, the Agents, through Scrimgeours, obtained the Bank's advice as to when a loan was issued.[59] The Bank feared that without its control of issues, during upturns in the market a large number of issuing houses would float loans, and, because the supply of stock would exceed the resources of the investment community, some of the flotations would fail, damaging the credit of the City. In addition, the large amounts of unsold stock would 'clog' the market for many months or years afterwards, preventing further issues at anything other than excessively low prices.[60]

Although the Agents accepted the need for some supervision, they believed that the Bank gave other issuing houses an unfair priority, forcing colonies to float loans when market demand had cooled. By 1930, unable to meet the financial demands of colonies from the Joint Colonial Fund, the Agents were also desperate for money. In September 1930, they, therefore, floated a Ceylon loan without first contacting the Bank, and, in June and December 1931, repeated the offence when they issued a Sierra Leone and a Northern Rhodesian loan respectively.[61] Severely embarrassed by the Agents' actions, Montague Norman insisted that they toe the line, and, as with prices, the Colonial Office acquiesced to the Bank's demands and a new arrangement as regards the timing of issues was introduced.[62] Each quarter, the Agents attended a meeting with Bank and Treasury officials to discuss probable issues during the following three months,

57 CAOG 9/358, memo, Scrimgeours, 5 May 1952; CAOG 9/118, CAs to Nigeria, 1 Feb. 1927; CA (mc) 60. The 'loan season' ran from the end of September to the end of May (CAOG 9/118, CAs to Nigeria, 1 Feb. 1927).

58 WN 13, A414804/1–2, CO to Kenya, 29 Nov. 1950; *ibid.*, A866801/2, CAs to Uganda, 25 Sept. 1951.

59 G 1/202, No. 2, Philipps to Norman, 22 Sept. 1930.

60 CAOG 9/300, memo, 10 April 1929.

61 G 1/202, no. 1, Norman to Phillips, 19 Sept. 1930; *ibid.*, no. 12, Hopkins to B of E, 10 June 1931; *ibid.*, no. 16, Ezechiel to B of E, 1 Dec. 1931.

62 G 1/202, no. 17, Norman to Ezechiel, 3 Dec. 1931.

and, when a float was definitely pending, met with the Bank's staff to arrange a specific date.[63] Generally, the new arrangement worked well, though in 1932 the CAs complained that demands by the Bank for an early issue had caused a Cyprus flotation to be rushed and had led to inadequate consideration of the terms of the loan.[64]

After the Second World War, Bank and Treasury control of when issues could occur became even more stringent. Until 1948, the market was closed to all colonial loans, the issue and expenditure of which was thought to be bad for the nation. The Bank believed that their uncontrolled issue would place too heavy a strain on the resources of the market, causing loans in the national interest to fail or have to be sold at a low price, and that their expenditure would divert physical resources away from British industry, and, by increasing imports, lead to a worsening of the country's Balance of Payments deficit.[65] Thereafter, colonies could only issue if all other sources of funds had been exhausted and the necessity of the loan had been determined by the Agents and Colonial Office, a Capital Issues Committee, and the Treasury.[66] Even after being approved, issues could be long delayed, though political pressure for greater funds for commonwealth countries in 1957 prompted the Treasury to instruct the Bank to give colonial issues priority.[67]

Prior charges

A factor that depressed the demand for a colony's loan was the existence of prior charges. These were clauses in loan legislation that stated that a borrower had to pay the principal and interest of a particular debt before meeting similar payments arising from later loans. The clauses were often included in the colonial ordinances that permitted local and London issues and were in the legislation that governed the provision of loans by the Treasury and the flotation of guaranteed issues. Associated in the 'minds of investors with foreign governments of low credit, such as China or the South American republics', the charges reduced the demand for stock and forced the Agents to cut the price of subsequent loans by up to ½ per cent, which, in turn, deflated the prices of all colonial issues.[68] To eliminate the problem, the CAs checked all colonial loan ordinances for the existence of first charge clauses and strongly advised their removal.[69] If a loan with a first charge existed, the debt was paid off before the new stock was issued or the issuing colony was asked to agree to repay it from the proceeds of the new loan, which was often enlarged for this purpose.[70] When this was not possible, the

63 CAOG 9/300, CAs to CO, 14 Dec. 1934.

64 CO 67/246/16, CAs to CO, 27 June 1932.

65 CAOG 9/351, Colonial Development Finance Conference, 1951, report, p. 19, 23; CAOG 9/335, CO to Jamaica, 11 Dec. 1948. The Bank was especially fearful that there would be insufficient demand for UK government issues required to finance re-armament (T 233/933, memo, 11 May 1953; D. J. Morgan, *A Reassessment of British Aid Policy, 1951–65*, London 1980, p. 38).

66 CA (m) 25, p. 7.

67 Morgan, *A Reassessment*, p. 191.

68 CO 67/246/16, memo, 19 Jan. 1932; CAOG 9/109, CO to Waterfield, Jan. 1935 (draft).

69 For example, WN 13, A255801/1, CAs to CO, 7 Nov. 1928.

70 CO 67/246/16, memo, 19 Jan. 1932; CAOG 9/109, CAs to CO, 18 Jan. 1932.

funds required were obtained from an alternate source, or, if the debt was small and likely to have a minimal impact on demand, the charge was allowed to stand, though often mentioned on the tender form rather than in the prospectus.[71]

As regards Treasury loans and guaranteed loans, repayment of the previous debt was fraught with difficulties. Although Treasury loans that had been financed from the Local Loans Fund had depreciated in value by the 1930s, the Treasury demanded that they be repaid at par, the price at which they were issued. Despite appeals by the Agents, Treasury officials continued to 'insist on their pound of flesh' and the repayment of the debts proved relatively costly.[72] Similarly, in 1920, the Treasury refused to revalue loans made to the East African Protectorate, Nyasaland and Uganda in order to take account of the rise in interest rates that had occurred since their issue.[73]

The problem with guaranteed loans was their relatively large size. This made repayment difficult, and, if such a loan was paid back from the proceeds of a new issue, the increased amount of stock to be sold forced the new loan to carry a relatively low price. In 1932, therefore, the Agents asked the Treasury to omit the prior charge condition from Parliamentary acts that allowed the issue of these loans, or, in the case of those raised for mandated territories, to include a clause that the charges would only take affect when the mandate was terminated and the area was no longer under British rule.[74] It was argued that the charges, in addition to increasing loan prices, were 'inappropriate to the mother and daughter relationship' that existed between Britain and its colonies and were unnecessary, the repayment of the interest and principal of such loans being by definition guaranteed.[75] The Treasury turned down both requests, claiming that the clauses ensured that only governments in genuine need would issue guaranteed stock and that their abandonment would lead to Parliamentary criticism.[76]

Underwriting

All Crown Agent loans were underwritten by underwriters, who before an issue agreed to buy all the stock not sold in return for a commission of 1per cent of the value of the amount insured. The practice ensured that the issuer would still obtain the funds required if the take-up of a loan was inadequate. From 1914 to 1959, the Agents' underwriters took up at least £36.8m of the stock of 13 loans, buying on average 77 per cent of each issue. Underwriting was arranged by the Agents' brokers, J. and A. Scrimgeour Ltd, for a fee known as an overwriting commission. The firm had a small group or list of underwriters, which reduced the cost of arranging support, who were expected to underwrite all loans, both good and bad, with refusal to support an issue causing the underwriter to risk being excluded from the list.[77] The group comprised large reputable institutions

71 For example, WN 13, A055801, minute, 28 Jan. 1953; *ibid.*, A055801, Hicks to Barbados, 17 April 1956; *ibid.*, A185802/1–2, CAs to Cyprus, 30 June 1932.

72 CO 67/246/16, CAs to CO, 11 May 1932.

73 T 161/64/s4648/1, Read to Treasury, 30 Nov. 1920; *ibid.*, Meiklejohn to CO, 5 Jan. 1921.

74 CAOG 9/109, CAs to CO, 18 Jan. 1932; CO 67/246/16, memo, 19 Jan. 1932.

75 CAOG 9/109, CAs to CO, 22 June 1931; *ibid.*, CAs to CO, 18 Jan. 1932.

76 *Ibid.*, meeting, 3 Jan. 1935.

77 SA, 'Notes on the issue of loans by the Crown Agents', 1926, p. 11.

and included London and provincial banks, insurance and trust companies, and finance houses.[78] There were a number of advantages of using such institutions. First they possessed surplus capital and could be relied upon not to immediately dump any stock that they were forced to buy onto the market, which would cause the price to plummet and would damage the creditworthiness of both the issuing colony and all crown colonies. Instead, they held the stock and merely met demand until the unsold balance had been bought, often a period of several months or even years. Likewise, they could be depended upon not to sell any stock still held if the Agents announced the flotation of a further loan for the issuing colony, which would again lead to price falls and reduce demand for the new issue. The temptation to do this was great, as sales would release money that could be used to underwrite the new loan and the new issue would make it more difficult to offload the stock and force the underwriter to hold it for even longer.[79]

It was also unlikely that they would engage in sub-underwriting or would refuse to combine underwriting with applications for stock. Sub-underwriting involved underwriters reducing their risks by passing a portion of the support given to another firm, which received part of the commission. The major drawback of the practice was that there was a danger that, if the loan failed, the sub-underwriter could refuse or lack the funds to take up the unsold stock or could immediately dump it onto the market.[80] The requirement for underwriters to put in applications for the loan underwritten was designed to hide from the public any undersubscription. The underwriters' applications would increase the amount of stock they had to offload, but would disguise the extent of the failure of the loan and make the stock easier to sell to the public and reduce the severity of any price fall.[81]

Underwriting and particularly the size of underwriting and over-riding commissions, was the subject of much criticism. It was argued that underwriters got 'far too much for doing too little'.[82] When an issue was successful, they reaped large rewards from their applications for securities, and it was understood that Scrimgeours tipped them off if a loan was expected to sell at a high premium, enabling them to apply for extra large amounts of stock.[83] In the case of most CA loans, for which there was great demand, underwriting also carried little risk, and, even if they were forced to take an unsold balance, underwriters could usually sell it at prices higher than the purchase price.[84] The Agents offered issues at prices lower than the market or estimated retail price; as will be discussed

78 CAOG 9/104, memo, Abbott, 16 Oct. 1933.

79 CAOG 9/101, memo, Scrimgeours, 5 May 1952.

80 *Ibid.*, note, 15 Oct. 1923. In 1943 there was no legal obligation on principal underwriters to accept responsibility for those to whom they sub-let part of an underwriting contract (CAOG 9/107, *The Economist*, 16 Oct. 1943).

81 CAOG 9/103, memo, 31 March 1936; *ibid.*, memo, June 1936; CAOG 9/101, memo, 23 Nov. 1927.

82 CAOG 9/102, Bickersteth to Thornton, 21 July 1932.

83 *Ibid.*, Bickersteth to Gowers, 17 June 1935.

84 The West African Currency Board, when it obtained unsold stock of four of the African loans that it underwrote in the early 1920s, made an average profit of 8 pc on the sale of the securities (inclusive of underwriting and brokerage commission), and, in the case of the 1919 and 1921

below, they often supported the price of failed loans by purchasing the stock for colonial investment funds; and, over time, as the stock was gradually absorbed by the public and memories of the failure of the loan faded, prices tended to rise.[85] Underwriters made losses only in the early 1920s, when prices were set excessively high, and when the failure of a loan was followed by a prolonged general fall in the prices of gilt-edged securities, as occurred in the early 1930s.[86]

Under pressure from Parliament and the colonies, the Agents in the 1920s proposed that the underwriting commission be replaced by a sliding scale, under which underwriters would 'receive commission varying say from 1.5 per cent in the case of loans of which a large percentage is left with them to 0.5 per cent in the case of loans which are fully subscribed'.[87] Scrimgeours, however, strongly recommended that the commission should remain unchanged and the idea was dropped. They pointed out that 'if underwriters knew that they would receive commission at a higher rate in the event of a small public response' they might refrain from making applications for stock. More importantly, the introduction of a lower fee would create 'hostility' in the market and halt the underwriting of CA loans. Other brokers, fearful that their clients would follow the Agents' lead, would force Scrimgeours' underwriters to refuse to underwrite Crown colony loans by threatening to no longer give them their own underwriting. It was also likely that some underwriters would decide for themselves not to work for the Agents.[88]

Similar criticism was directed at Scrimgeours' over-riding commission, ¼ per cent of the amount underwritten, which was double that charged by the Bank of England's brokers for the underwriting of guaranteed loans, and, from 1919 to 1927, garnered the firm £132,007.[89] It was argued that the work involved in organizing underwriting was minimal, a matter of writing a small number of letters to the members of the underwriting group, and that Scrimgeours benefited in other ways from its role.[90] Like its underwriters, it used its inside information to apply for large amounts of stock expected to sell at a premium, it gained prestige, which attracted other business, and it could attract and keep customers by offering them a lucrative membership of the Agents' underwriting syndicate.[91] It also seems likely that it used the Agents' underwriting business to subsidise its less profitable support operations, giving underwriters Crown colony underwriting only if they agreed to take on riskier commitments.[92]

To reduce the cost of issuing loans, the Agents asked Scrimgeours to cut their commission, sought to employ other cheaper brokers, and attempted to abandon

Nigerian loans, profits of 10 pc and 14 pc respectively (CO 323/991/3, West African Currency Board to CO, 3 Dec. 1927).

85 CAOG 9/104, memo, Abbott, 16 Oct. 1933; SA, 'Notes on the', p. 11.

86 CAOG 9/101, *The Times*, 25 Nov. 1925; CAOG 9/104, memo, Abbott, 16 Oct. 1933.

87 CAOG 9/101, memo, 23 Nov. 1927. See also CAOG 17/21, memo, 30 July 1922; S 5, A1209; CO 323/1422/14, Ceylon to CO, 7 May 1937.

88 CAOG 9/101, memo, 23 Nov. 1927; CAOG 9/104, memo, Abbott, 16 Oct. 1933.

89 CAOG 9/40, CAs to CO, 26 Jan. 1928; CAOG 9/105, memo, 13 Oct. 1932; CAOG 9/44, amounts received by Scrimgeours, 1919–27.

90 CAOG 9/102, Bickersteth to Gowers, 17 June 1935.

91 CAOG 9/101, memo, 12 Dec. 1927; CAOG 9/102, Bickersteth to Thornton, 21 July 1932.

92 CAOG 9/102, memo, 20 Feb. 1934.

underwriting altogether. The CAs made various attempts to persuade Scrimgeours to lower their commission, and, in 1927, encouraged them to replace it with a fee of £1,000 for the first million of a loan underwritten and £500 for every additional million.[93] All the attempts failed, although, after much negotiation, the company did agree not to charge over-riding commission on the portion of loans that the Agents purchased 'firm' for colonial investment funds.[94] Scrimgeours argued that the size of the commission was fully justified. If they failed to obtain underwriters or those recruited refused to purchase an unsold balance, they themselves had to acquire the stock.[95] On a number of occasions when a loan had failed, they had encouraged underwriters to continue to hold their allocations by buying securities on the market, and, when only half of Nigeria's 1921 £3m loan was taken up, they had applied for £1.17m of the stock, reducing the extent of the under-subscription and making it easier for the underwriters to offload the remaining balance.[96] The commission also subsidised a range of services provided for no charge. These included the trading of short-term securities and the provision of advice on loan terms, investments, and the prices at which securities were to be transferred from one colonial investment Fund to another.[97]

The Agents' wish to replace Scrimgeours or to abandon underwriting was motivated by the desire to reduce overriding and underwriting costs, but also to increase the price of issues. Scrimgeours forced the CAs to set excessively low loan prices in order to reduce the likelihood that their underwriters would be left with unsold stock and to minimize the post-issue price collapse when this occurred. 'In old days', the firm had allowed the Agents to fix prices 'at such a point that the underwriters were unlikely to be left with more than half their commitments on the ground that they ought to do something for their living'.[98] But, by the 1920s, this was no longer case, and, if the Agents refused to adopt the price 'suggested' by Scrimgeours, the firm would refuse to underwrite the loan and the issue would have to be abandoned.

In 1921, encouraged by the Colonial Office, the CAs considered employing as their broker or as co-broker British Stockbrokers Trust Ltd (BST), an alliance of provincial stockbrokers, which was attempting to break London's underwriting monopoly.[99] Use of this 'first class' firm would protect them and the Secretary of State from the charge that they were countenancing the restriction of trade, lead to a reduction in over-riding commission, and would allow issues to be underwritten by non-London institutions, which would increase provincial and total demand for their loans and enable them to be issued at higher

93 CAOG 9/101, memo, 12 Dec. 1927.

94 CAOG 9/105, meeting, 23 Nov. 1927; CAOG 9/40, CAs to CO, 26 Jan. 1928.

95 CAOG 9/102, Bickersteth to Gowers, 21 June 1935.

96 CAOG 9/108, memo, no date; CAOG 9/98, memo, no date.

97 CAOG 9/358, CAs to Kenya, 18 Feb. 1955.

98 CAOG 9/101, CO to Huxham, Oct. 1938; CAOG 9/108, CAs to Stevenson, 19 Oct. 1921. The Bank of England believed Scrimgeours to be 'tenth rate' (CO 323/957/4, Niemeyer to Wilson, 29 Jan. 1926).

99 CAOG 9/108, *Daily Express*, 29 March 1922.

prices.[100] Not surprisingly, Scrimgeours opposed the use of the company. It was claimed that provincial brokers' already received their 'due share' of underwriting and that to give them more would be counter-productive, as they lacked the resources to hold stock for long periods.[101] Moreover, if BST was appointed, the colonies' current underwriters, along with their London-based counterparts, would refuse to support or to put in applications for their loans, and the London Stock Exchange would be less willing to grant them quotations.[102]

When the following year, the Agents again approached Scrimgeours with the proposition that they organize with BST the underwriting of the forthcoming Straits loan, the firm took an even harsher line. The CAs were informed that if it was required to associate with BST, even to the extent of offering the company underwriting, it would resign as their broker. On the other hand, if the Agency agreed to maintain the status quo, it would arrange underwriting of the Straits loan and one other issue at any price that the Senior Crown Agent 'within reason, might name'.[103] After due consideration, the CAs decided to remain with Scrimgeours. The company was a member of the committee of the Stock Exchange and could therefore influence decisions in the colonies' favour, it would be difficult to find another broker to deal with their investment work, and there was a danger that BST would come to an understanding with Scrimgeours and refuse to act for them. If this occurred, they would have to either return to their former broker, which would demand even harsher terms, or 'hawk our wares about the City, which would be undignified and bad for our image'.[104] In the event, this latter reason for staying with Scrimgeours proved to be prescient. The London brokers 'dragooned' the provincial underwriters into abandoning BST, and the Stock Exchange threatened to strike the company off all London underwriting lists, claiming that it had broken its regulations by opening an office within five miles of the Exchange, of which it was not member.[105] Unable to overcome its City counterparts, BST therefore came to a settlement with them, agreeing not to compete for overseas loans provided that it was given a free run at home corporation issues.[106]

The Agents considered the replacement of Scrimgeours again in the 1930s. In 1935 and 1939, the broker A. Bickerstethe, and, in 1936, the broking firm Pember Boyle offered the Agency their services. Both brokers promised lower underwriting and over-riding commissions and Pember Boyle additionally proffered membership of their own underwriting syndicate. The Agents, however, declined all the approaches, fearful that the underwriters used would dump unsold stock onto the market and that the brokers would eventually be forced

100 *Ibid.*, Stevenson to CAs, 19 Sept. 1921; *ibid.*, CAs to Stevenson, 10 April 1922; *ibid.*, CO to CAs, 22 Sept. 1921; *ibid.*, CAs to Stevenson, 19 Oct. 1921.

101 *Ibid.*, CAs to Stevenson, 10 April 1922.

102 *Ibid.*, Scrimgeours to CAs, 29 Sept. 1921; *ibid.*, Scrimgeours to CAs, 25 Oct. 1921; *ibid.*, memo, 27 Oct. 1921; *ibid.*, CAs to Stevenson, 10 April 1922.

103 *Ibid.*, CAs to Stevenson, 10 April 1922.

104 *Ibid.*, memo, no date; *ibid.*, CAs to Stevenson, 10 April 1922.

105 *Ibid.*, CAs to Stevenson, 10 April 1922; *ibid.*, memo, 24 June 1935.

106 *Ibid.*, memo, 27 April 1922.

to alter their terms by the City elite.[107] Likewise, in 1932 they examined and rejected a proposal that they should act as their own broker, recruiting their own underwriters. Such a move would have reduced costs, allowed higher prices to be set and resulted in the Office receiving preferential treatment from institutions eager to join its syndicate. But it would again have attracted the hostility of the City establishment and the Stock Exchange, which would have been concerned that other issuing houses would follow the Agents' example, and it was eventually decided that any gains would be more than offset by the retaliatory actions taken by the City to force them back into the broking fold.[108]

The possibility of abandoning underwriting altogether was raised on a number of occasions. In 1925 and 1930, the CAs considered purchasing the whole of a loan with the money they received from the colonies for the acquisition of securities for investment Funds, transferring a proportion of the stock into the Funds and then selling off the remainder on the market. The idea was dropped when the Stock Exchange made it clear that such issues would not receive an official quotation.[109] To overcome this hurdle, the Agents proposed that non-underwritten loans should be publicly issued and any unsold balance bought back, again using investment money. Attempts to adopt this course of action for the issue of the Trinidad and Ceylon loans of 1935 and 1938 respectively and those for Kenya and Grenada in 1936, however, were blocked by Scrimgeours and the Bank of England.[110]

The Bank and Scrimgeours objected both to the cessation of underwriting and the use of colonial investment Funds. The opposition of the Bank to the abandonment of underwriting was motivated by self and national interest. It seems likely that pressure was put on Bank officials to fight the CAs' plans by its clients, many of whom were underwriters, and, no doubt, feared that other issuing houses would follow the CAs' lead.[111] The Bank also predicted that the Agents' actions would result in financial meltdown. The universal abandonment of underwriting would lead to the failure of loans and the large amount of unsold stock on the market and the collapse of confidence would cause the flotation of new issues to grind to a halt.[112] The Bank thus strongly hinted that it would use its influence with the Treasury to induce the Colonial Office to over-rule them

107 CAOG 9/102, Bickersteth to Gowers, 17 June 1935; *ibid.*, Gowers to Bickersteth, 4 July 1935; *ibid.*, memo, 22 Feb. 1939; CAOG 9/103, memo, 19 May 1936.

108 CAOG 9/102, Bickersteth to Thornton, 21 July 1932.

109 CAOG 9/101, extract from CA investment committee, 1925; *ibid.*, meeting, 19 June 1935; CAOG 9/104, memo, Abbott, 16 Oct. 1933.

110 CAOG 9/101, memo, 18 July 1935; *ibid.*, memo, 6 Aug. 1936; *ibid.*, memo, no date, approx. 1936; *ibid.*, CO to Huxham, (draft), Oct. 1938. Ironically, the Bank had earlier issued a loan for the London County Council without underwriting (*ibid.*, memo, 18 July 1935).

111 *Ibid.*, CAs to CO, 22 Dec. 1937. See also CAOG 9/300, CAs to Wilson, 8 Dec. 1927. A further example of the Bank acting in response to client pressure occurred in 1927, when it objected to the Agents' wish that the West African Currency Board underwrite the Guaranteed Palestine loan and other colonial issues. After much disagreement, the CAs ignored the Bank's advice and the Colonial Office complained to the Treasury that the Bank had no right to intervene in such matters (CO 323/991/3, CO to Treasury, 22 Dec. 1927; *ibid.*, Wilson to Hopkins, 29 Nov. 1927).

112 CAOG 9/101, meeting, 19 June 1935.

if the CAs insisted on going ahead with their scheme, and, if this failed, would refuse to allot them issue dates.[113]

Scrimgeours, again acting in its own and the City's interests, warned the Agents that brokers were likely to become extremely 'unpleasant' if they went ahead with their plans.[114] The Stock Exchange would claim that they were attempting to 'corner the market' and refuse them official quotations, and, when a new loan was issued, brokers would refuse to put in large applications and discourage their clients from making purchases.[115] Normal demand for stock, meanwhile, would be decimated by brokers restricting dealings, adopting large margins between selling and purchase prices, raising questions about the financial probity of individual territories, and generally depreciating the credit worthiness of the Crown colonies. The result of these actions would be a fall in the price of colonial stock, which would leave the Agents with no alternative but to issue new loans on extremely poor terms.[116] Moreover, the City would attack the CAs' investment role. They would no longer be invited to underwrite non-colonial issues and could face difficulties in finding brokers willing to sell them securities.[117]

Arguments against the proposed use of colonial investment money were that colonial Funds would carry the same risk as underwriters, but without earning a commission; that they would be forced to buy poor quality stock, the price of which would subsequently fall; and that, if a loan failed unexpectedly, other higher yielding holdings would have to be surrendered to allow the purchase of the unsold balance.[118] Many, including some Agency staff, also doubted that the money flowing into colonial Funds would be sufficient to support new issues. It was estimated in 1937 that during the following ten years £25m of loans would be issued, but that only £13m of investment money would be available.[119] If conditions became less favourable and public demand for stock fell, the Agents would be forced to arrange the underwriting of at least some of these loans, but would find that underwriters would be reluctant to support the issues or would demand an excessively low price or a higher commission for their assistance.[120]

Faced with such an onslaught, the Agents on all four occasions dropped their decision to abandon underwriting, though not before first making their anger known to the Bank of England.[121] After the war, the high cost of underwriting, both in terms of commission and low prices/smaller loan returns, was reluctantly accepted. No attempt was made by independent brokers to break the cartel that controlled underwriting, and, more importantly, the Agents desperately needed broker support of loans. As will be described below, the possibility of colonial

113 *Ibid.*, memo, 6 May 1937.

114 *Ibid.*

115 CAOG 9/101, memo, 29 Sept. 1936; *ibid.*, memo, 6 May 1937. 'Cornering the market' involved an institution buying up a large proportion of the stock of a loan in order to manipulate its price.

116 *Ibid.*, Ceylon trade delegation to CO, 7 May 1937; *ibid.*, memo, 6 May 1937.

117 *Ibid.*, memo, 29 Sept. 1936.

118 *Ibid.*, Ceylon trade delegation to CO, 7 May 1937; *ibid.*, memo, 18 July 1935

119 *Ibid.*, memo, 7 May 1937.

120 *Ibid.*, memo, 6 May 1937.

121 CAOG 9/300, Bottomly to Gowers, 11 Aug. 1936; CO 323/1422/14, note, CO, 6 Jan. 1938.

political independence reduced the demand for colonial issues, with the result that there was a greater likelihood that flotations would fail.

Other support of loans

In the nineteenth century, the Agents supported loans both before and after issue. Several months before a flotation was to occur, securities of the issuing colony were bought for colonial investment Funds, causing their market price to increase. The rise allowed the CAs to set a relatively high price for the new loan and encouraged the public to purchase the new stock. By the 1920s, this practice had died out, largely because of opposition from underwriters, who believed that it increased the likelihood of post-issue price falls.[122] Support after issue, on the other hand, continued to occur, usually when a loan had failed. During the three months following the flotation of the 1957 Tanganyika £3m loan, for example, the Agents bought over £1m of the stock, and, between May and December of the same year, purchased £2m of the EAHC £11.5m loan.[123] The acquisitions reduced the burden of underwriters, and, by preventing a price collapse, helped them to offload stock onto the public, making them more willing to underwrite further issues. By preventing excessive price falls, they also allowed the Agents to fix a high price for future loans by the issuing colony or other territories, and the stock was bought relatively cheaply.[124]

As will be discussed in chapter three, purchases of colonial stock continued long after issue. Throughout the lifetime of a loan, the Agents bought its stock, largely for its Sinking Fund, but also for other investment Funds. By the time a loan came to the end of its life, therefore, colonial Funds could hold as much as 80 per cent of its stock, and, in 1952, out of £150m of colonial stock issued and not redeemed, Funds held £85m or 57 per cent (Figure 1.3).[125] The purchases simplified loan repayment, and, more importantly, increased demand for loans and allowed them to be issued at relatively high prices, purchasers being assured that there would always be buyers for their acquisitions and that a price collapse was unlikely.[126]

As well as purchases by the CAs, failed loans were additionally unofficially supported by Scrimgeours or the underwriters. On a number of occasions, Scrimgeours, with and without the help of the underwriters, put in one or more additional applications for stock when it became apparent that there was insufficient demand for a loan.[127] These gave the public the impression that the loan was only slightly undersubscribed and thus increased the chances that Scrimgeours and the underwriters would be able to offload the unsold stock at rela-

122 David Sunderland, *Managing the British Empire. The Crown Agents 1933–1914*, London 2004, p. 165.

123 Morgan, *A Reassessment*, p. 179.

124 CAOG 9/300, CAs to Wilson, 8 Dec. 1927; CAOG 9/101, memo, 5 May 1930.

125 T 233/934, draft report of the Working Party on Colonial Sterling Assets, 2 Sept. 1953, part 1, p. 16.

126 CA (mc) 60.

127 For example, additional applications were made after the 1949 Federation of Malaya issue and after the flotation of the 1956 British Guiana and EAHC loans (WN 13, A478802/1–2, report, 25 May 1949; *ibid.*, A087805, Seel to Lloyd, 12 April 1956; *ibid.*, A226805).

Figure 1.3. Total value of stock domiciled with the CAs and amount held by the CAs on behalf of colonial funds, 1947–62

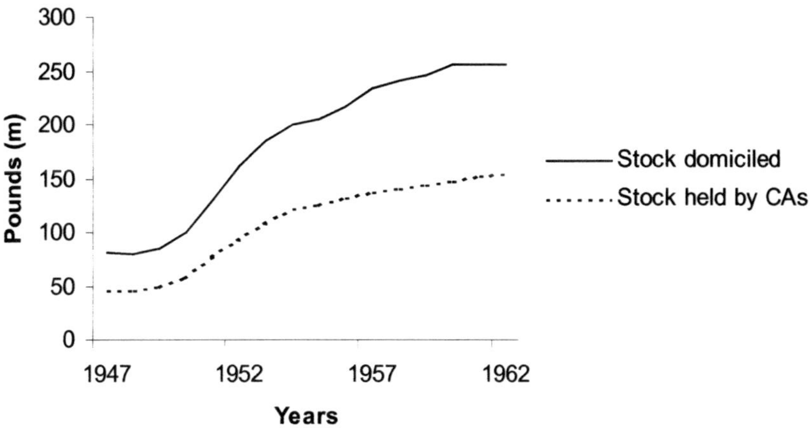

Source. CAOG 9/34; CAOG 9/31, memo, no date.

Note. All figures include inter-colonial loans.

tively high prices, and allowed the Agents to issue future loans on good terms.[128] Although highly unethical, the practice was relatively common in the City, and, from 1935 to 1937, it was adopted by the Treasury, which secretly used money from the Unemployment Insurance Fund to take up unsubscribed portions of British government loans.[129]

Management of stock

From 1924 to 1962, the amount of colonial stock managed by the Agents rose from £73.2m to £255.8m (Figure 1.3).[130] By 1939, they also supervised 724 of the loans provided by the UK government from the Colonial Development Fund, and, from the early 1960s, managed a number of World Bank loans and Commonwealth Assistance Loans.[131] Management of colonial issues involved the payment of dividends, the recording of transfers of ownership, and the repayment or conversion of stock. Dividends were paid twice yearly from funds deposited in the JCF by the issuing colonies; in 1933 to 55,394 investors.[132] Stockholders were sent warrants for the interest owed, but later the sums were paid into their bank accounts, which was more convenient for both themselves and the Agents.[133] A proposal that non-colonial holders of stock should pay local

128 WN 13, A087805, Seel to Lloyd, 12 April 1956.

129 *The Economist*, 6 Nov. 1937, p. 269; *Westminster Bank Review*, 291 (1938), p. 5.

130 CAOG 9/34; CAOG 9/31, memo, no date.

131 L 76, *Trade and Industry*, 11 May 1972, p. 226; L 1, Finance Dept. report, 1963.

132 CAOG 9/276. Because the colony had little surplus revenue, the Agents paid the first three years of dividends of the 1921 Kenya issue out of the proceeds of the loan, the size of which was increased by the required amount (Constantine, *The Making*, pp. 81–2).

133 *Crown Colonist*, 3 (1933), p. 351.

income tax on dividends in addition to UK tax was rejected by the Agents, who feared that it would discourage purchases.[134] Transfers of ownership totalled 9,527 holdings of stock in 1933.[135] To prevent losses, the Agents took out insurance against forged stock transfers and redemptions and their own negligence, and, for the convenience of brokers and to help create an 'atmosphere of trust' through 'close contact', transfers could be made at a separate office located at the heart of the City in Moorgate.[136]

Loans were repaid either at the end of their lives or at the optional date of repayment. In the case of repayment at maturity, the money required ideally came from the issuer's Sinking Fund. To prevent the market being swamped with securities, which would cause prices to fall, sales of a Fund's investments began up to a year before a loan had to be repaid and many were sold to other colonial investment Funds.[137] In some cases, disposal of the securities produced an amount greater than the sum needed, and, if this occurred, the surplus was returned to the issuer, though occasionally local legislation required it to be used for a special purpose.[138] More commonly, the sale of Sinking Fund investments failed to produce an amount sufficient to repay the loan. When this occurred, the Agents obtained the necessary money from a variety of other sources. Short-term loans were obtained from banks, local and inter-colonial loans were issued, advances made from the Joint Colonial Fund, and securities in Supplementary Sinking Funds and other investment Funds belonging to the borrower were sold.[139]

Confidence regarding the ability of principals to repay their loans remained high until the mid-1960s when the Bank of England warned that many territories would have difficulty finding the £57.3m that was due to be repaid between 1967 and 1970.[140] It was claimed that the Sinking Funds of the loans to be redeemed would prove woefully inadequate, due to the CAs' incompetent investment strategies, and that there were few other sources of finance. Many of the borrowers would be unable to repay their debts from their own resources, others would be reluctant to do so, fearful of budgetary and foreign exchange difficulties, there was little or no prospect of converting loans or raising fresh money in the London market, and banks would either refuse to lend or only provide advances at high rates of interest.[141] The Bank thus proposed that, to avoid catastrophe, the loans would have to be repaid by the UK government. If this failed to occur, the resultant defaults would damage the reputation of Britain and the London market and the debtors' credit standing, making it difficult for them to

134 CAOG 9/324, notes, p. 22; WN 13, A822802, Tanganyika to CAs, 17 March 1953.

135 CAOG 9/276.

136 S 1, A85; L 18/2, Parkin's report, 5 May 1945.

137 CAOG 9/277, 1933 report; CAOG 9/278, 1934 report.

138 Of the 15 SFs with surpluses, for which details are available, the aggregate excess amounted to £1.77m. The £100,000 surplus from the Mauritius 3pc 1940 SF, for example, had to be held for the future repayment of the colony's other loans (S 1, 182).

139 For example, S 5, A1207; CAOG 9/280, 1936 report; S 1, A118; *ibid.*, A124; *ibid.*, A50.

140 OV 44/77, no. 42f, memo, 2 Dec. 1966. It was claimed that the East African High Commission, Kenya, Sierra Leone and Uganda would have particular difficulty (*ibid.*).

141 *Ibid.*, no. 34c, memo, 29 June 1965.

raise future loans and increasing the demand for UK aid. It was also likely that they would sue the CAs for the mismanagement of their Funds and withdraw the hundreds of millions of pounds they had invested in London.[142]

Not surprisingly, the Treasury response to the proposal was one of horror and the department made it clear that it was 'adamant' that HMG should accept no responsibility for the loans. It was pointed out that the prospectuses had specifically disclaimed UK government liability, and that, 'since the bonds were freely available, no one had been forced to stay in'; an argument that the Bank believed 'reduced the problem to a party game in which it is hard luck if one is holding the parcel when the music stops'.[143] The reaction of the Agents was one of bemusement. As will be discussed in chapter three, the slow growth of Sinking Funds was wholly the result of restrictions placed on the Agency by none other than the Bank of England and the Treasury. The CAs were also convinced that the Bank's warnings of 'heavy weather', which they suspected were part of its campaign to destroy their reputation and take over their investment work, were based on false and inadequate information. A revaluation of the Sinking Funds showed that they were worth far more than the Bank had claimed, and, when informed of the possible shortfall, most of their clients were more than willing to increase their Fund contributions. Many of the ex-colonies also had valuable Supplementary Sinking Funds and held a large proportion of the outstanding stock in their own investment Funds.[144] In the event, much to the Bank's chagrin, its doom-laden prognosis failed to come about, and all the loans floated by the Agents were fully repaid on time.

Loans were repaid early if their interest rates were high relative to the prevailing rate. In the 1930s, for example, when rates averaged 3 to 3.5 per cent, the Agents used the option to pay back early the loans floated at rates of 6 per cent after the First World War. Other factors that encouraged early redemption were high gilt prices, which increased the amount that could be obtained from the sale of Sinking Funds, and the rate of interest received from the Fund investments. If the latter was higher than the interest paid on the loan then the stock would not be redeemed.[145] As with the issues repaid at the end of their lives, the money required was obtained from the sale of Sinking Funds, and, when these proved inadequate, from a variety of other sources, including the public issue of new stock.

In some cases, early repayment was combined with a conversion, which involved the Agents asking investors to exchange their holdings in the loan to be repaid for the stock of a new quoted loan, which offered a lower rate of interest.[146] In 1934, for example, the CAs offered to exchange Ceylon 3.5 per

142 *Ibid.*, no. 35l, memo, 1 Feb. 1966; *ibid.*, no. 41v, B of E to Treasury, Nov. 1966.

143 *Ibid.*, no. 41k, memo, 18 Oct. 1966.

144 *Ibid.*, no. 43j, memo, 13 Sept. 1967; *ibid.*, no. 42q, memo, 30 Jan. 1967.

145 CAOG 9/41, CAs to CO, 9 Oct. 1934; CAOG 9/300, CAs to Parkinson, 12 April 1933; CA (mc) 60, Colonial circular, 5 Aug. 1927.

146 On a number of occasions, the Agents considered offering investors voluntarily conversion i.e. asking them to convert loans that did not include an early repayment option or before the optional repayment date. Nothing came of the proposals, largely because of legal difficulties.

Figure 1.4. Conversions, loans sold to the market/placed, and Inter-Colonial loans, 1922–68

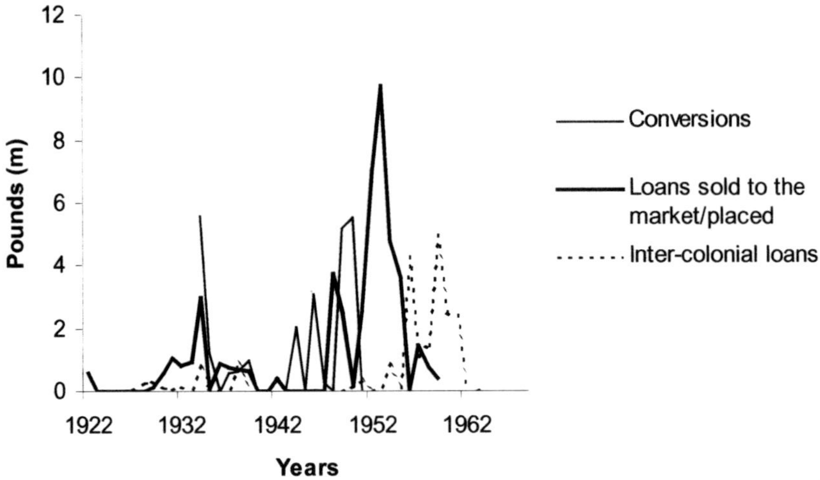

Sources. CAOG 9/33–CAOG 9/35; CAOG 9/104, memo, 16 Oct. 1933, statement B; CAOG 9/113, memo, 9 Jan. 1934; CAOG 9/138, weeding note; CAOG 9/276–CAOG 9/283; CAOG 9/359; T 233/1425, memo, 14 May 1958; WN 13.

cent 1934/59 stock for new Ceylon 3.25 per cent 1959 stock.[147] From 1916 to 1968, 24 loans were converted, which resulted in the creation of £32.6m of new stock (Figure 1.4). The advantage of conversion to issuers was that it reduced the amount of money that had to be raised to repay a loan early, and, it could leave the Sinking Fund untouched, allowing the contents to be used for general expenditure or transferred to a Supplementary Sinking Fund.[148] For investors, it allowed them to postpone the decision of where to reinvest repaid sums, and, to encourage them to participate, they received generous exchange rates and sometimes cash payments.[149]

The nature of conversions varied according to circumstances. If the CAs believed uptake would be low, they used the Sinking Fund to pay off a proportion of the loan, offering only the remainder for conversion, launched a combined conversion/public issue, using the money raised from the flotation to buy the stock not converted, or underwrote the offer, underwriters agreeing to buy the

It was also believed that excessively generous terms would have to be offered (for example, S 1, A218; *ibid.*, A219; CAOG 9/96, weeding note; CAOG 9/278, 1934 report).

147 CAOG 9/276–CAOG9/283.

148 S 1, A62; CAOG 9/278, 1934 report.

149 For example, the 1939 Ceylon conversion offered investors 101.5 new stock for 100 of old securities. Under the terms of the 1951 Mauritius conversion, investors obtained 100 new securities for 100 of their existing holdings plus a cash payment of £3 (CAOG 9/276–CAOG9/283).

unconverted residue.[150] Where they were more confident, a straight offer of conversion would be made, and, if unsuccessful, the necessary money would be obtained from the Sinking Fund or through the creation and sale of new quoted stock to the market, institutional investors or colonial investment Funds.[151] To encourage conversion, the Agents always converted the stock they themselves held in colonial Funds before the offer was made and included this amount in the prospectus.[152]

From 1933 to the end of the decade, conversion, along with the public flotation of loans for the early repayment of old issues, was unofficially halted by the Treasury, which argued that, by taking funds out of the market, such practices led to high interest rates and exchange rates and reduced the amount of cheap finance available for British government loans.[153] For colonies with financial problems, however, the Treasury eased its restrictions, fearful that the continued payment of excessive loan interest rates would increase their dependence on Exchequer funds. In 1934, it allowed public issues for British Guiana, Nigeria, and Trinidad to go ahead, though it required the CAs not to 'make any public announcement' of the relaxation of the ruling.[154] As regards other financially weak colonies, the Agents were allowed to circumvent the embargo. In 1934, they were given permission to borrow £300,000 from Barclays Bank for the purpose of completing the repayment of a Trinidad loan, and, later in the year, they were permitted to create, but not issue £306,833 and £337,143 of unquoted new stock for Sierra Leone and Trinidad respectively.[155] The new securities, for the purpose of subterfuge termed inter-colonial loans, were exchanged for the old stock held in a variety of colonial investment Funds, and a quotation only obtained by the sale of £100,000 to the market after the embargo had been lifted in 1938.[156]

Prosperous colonies found the Treasury less flexible. A complex 1936 proposal for the Straits and Ceylon to swap debts was blocked by the Treasury, and, in 1944, when the embargo was re-imposed, it insisted that the CAs repay a Gold Coast loan from the colony's Supplementary Sinking Fund and its Surplus and Reserve Funds, which were earmarked for development.[157] After much disagreement, the CAs sold investments in the Surplus Fund, only to discover that the Treasury had allowed the London County Council, for whom the Bank of England acted, to convert a £15m loan. The decision was regarded by the

150 For example, CAOG 9/41, CAs to CO, 9 Oct. 1934; WN 13, A224801/1, prospectus, 11 Aug. 1950.

151 For example, S 1, A62; WN 13, A087803, CAs to CO, 17 April 1942. The Agents bought £981,900 of the new stock for colonial Funds (CAOG 9/276–CAOG9/283).

152 Of the £32.62m of new stock created, £9.67m (29.6 per cent) was exchanged for stock held in these Funds (CAOG 9/276–CAOG9/283).

153 CAOG 9/300, Treasury to CO, 10 July 1933; *ibid.*, *The Economist*, 3 Sept. 1932. See also Howson, Susan, *Sterling's Managed Float. The Operations of the Exchange Equalisation Account, 1932–39*, Princeton 1980.

154 CAOG 9/278, 1934 report; CAOG 9/300, Treasury to CAs, 17 Feb. 1934; *ibid.*, CO to CAs, 26 April 1934.

155 CAOG 9/40, Beckett to CAs, 3 Oct. 1934; CAOG 9/115, memo, 25 Oct. 1935.

156 CAOG 9/115, note, 13 April 1938.

157 CAOG 9/101, memo, 13 Nov. 1936; CA (m) 117, A1687.

Agents as utterly unfair and a reflection of the Treasury's bias towards the Bank, and attempts were unsuccessfully made to persuade the Colonial Office to make a formal complaint to the Chancellor.[158]

Subscription

Some indication of who held colonial stock after it had been disposed of by brokers and stags is given in an analysis of the purchasers of the 1959 Barbados loan, a typical issue (Table 1.1).[159] This shows that 57 per cent of the stock was held by institutions, which on average bought £7,957 of securities, and the remainder by private investors.[160] Of the institutional purchases, 38 per cent was bought by Banks and 19 per cent by insurance companies, with the remainder acquired by local authorities, building societies, schools, churches, societies, private companies and charities.[161] The majority of private investors were male, lived in London and South East England, and, if men, were employed in law or finance, and, if female, were married.[162] On average, they bought £436 of stock, though women tended to buy more than men and there were wide regional differences in the amount acquired, with those investors living in the North on average purchasing only £253 of securities and those in the West Country £502.[163]

Of the 58 publicly issued loans for which information is available, 18 (31 per cent) were undersubscribed, 10 (55 per cent) of which were for Africa. Prior to the 1950s, issues failed when the issuer had not previously floated a loan and was an unknown quantity to the market or had issued an excessive amount of stock and had accumulated a large amount of debt, increasing the perceived likelihood of default.[164] A sudden change in the market or an unexpected development in the issuing colony after the price had been set could also dampen demand, and, over the period, there were criticisms by the Treasury, Colonial governments, the press and Parliament that the Agents had fixed prices too high.[165] As already discussed, given the pressure exerted on them by underwriters and the Bank of England, the setting of high prices was unlikely, and all of the accusations were shown to be false.

Seven of the failed loans were issued in the 1950s, when the demand for colonial stock fell precipitously and a vicious cycle developed. The failure of

158 CA (m) 117, A1687.

159 The results are based on a sample of 2,703 investors.

160 Standard deviation £20,319.

161 For example, Bedales School, Brentwood Spiritualist Church, the London Society for Promoting Christianity Among the Jews, and Trinidad Central Oil Fields.

162 42 per cent of female subscribers, for whom a marital status was given, were married, 30 per cent were widows, and the remainder were spinsters.

163 Women on average bought £475 of stock and men £416.

164 For example, CAOG 9/78, memo, 2 Feb. 1928; Morgan, *A Reassessment*, p. 181.

165 For example, WN 13, A087805, Seel to Lloyd, 12 April 1956; *ibid.*, A226804; *ibid.*, A087805, Seel to Lloyd, 12 April 1956; *ibid.*, A478802/1–2, report, 25 May 1949. For criticisms of high prices see CO 323/957/4, PHE to Read and Masterson-Smith, 9 Nov. 1923; CAOG 17/21, Parliamentary question, 24 Nov. 1925; *West Africa*, 15 July 1939, p. 1; CAOG 9/359, cutting, *The Times*, approx. 1931.

Table 1.1. Characteristics of a sample of final purchasers of the Barbados 6pc, 1971/73 Loan (%)

Private Investors

Occupations		*Residence*	
Law	14.78	SE England	29.95
Retired	14.26	London	25.75
Finance	13.22	North	11.33
Armed forces	13.02	Eastern England	9.97
Medicine	5.9	Midlands	7.79
Company directors	5.04	West Country	6.84
Retailing	3.3	Scotland, Wales & Ireland	5.23
Church	3.1	Non UK	3.63
Civil servants	2.61		
Teaching	2.61		
Farming	2.43		

Institutional purchasers (by value)

Banks	38.07
Insurance companies & private pension funds	18.56
Local Authorities	3.76
Building societies	1.07

Source. LA, Barbados 6pc stock, 1971/73 Loan Register, Vols. 1 and 2.

loans caused the market to become awash with stock, which led to price falls and reduced the demand for stock still further.[166] Perhaps the most important reason for the reluctance to purchase colonial loans was the approach of independence. Investors feared that newly independent states would become politically unstable and that the new rulers, free from Colonial Office control and lacking financial experience and expertise, would introduce unsound and imprudent financial policies and default on the payment of dividends and the repayment of loans. There were also suspicions that they would sell off many of the securities in their investment Funds, reducing the ability of the CAs to buy stock and causing prices to plummet even further.[167]

Other explanations for the fall in demand were disillusionment with the development prospects of many parts of the Empire; the Agents' disposal of securities in Currency and Savings Bank Funds, which contributed to the price falls and is discussed in the following chapter; and changes in the laws governing trusts and

166 T 233/1425, memo, Scrimgeours, 10 April 1958.

167 Gerold Krozewski, 'Finance and Empire. The dilemma facing Great Britain in the 1950s', *International History Review*, 18 (1) (1996), p. 60; CAOG 9/300, Seel to CO, 30 Sept. 1953; Morgan, *A Reassessment*, pp. 179, 191.

in the investment environment. The 1957 amendment of the Colonial Stocks Act to allow trusts to purchase the loans of ex-colonies and to require such territories to provide guarantees that dividends would be paid etc, increased demand for these stocks.[168] Much of the good generated, however, was undone by the 1959 Trustee Act, which permitted trusts to invest up to half of their Funds in equities and thus reduced the likelihood that they would opt for colonial stocks.[169] As for the investment environment, there was greater competition for market funds from the UK nationalized industries and the government, and, later, from the Eurodollar market and from countries outside the sterling area.[170] The uncertain international situation discouraged many investors from even entering the market, and post-war inflation, and, in the late 1950s, falls in commodity prices reduced the attractiveness of colonial stocks, which offered low returns and often financed projects whose revenues depended on the export of raw materials.[171]

There were a number of proposals to reverse the fall in demand. It was variously suggested that the UK government should underwrite loans, guarantee payment of interest and repayment, or give an unofficial guarantee by assuring investors in a Ministerial statement that their interests would be protected.[172] Others believed that colonial issues should have priority access to the London market, that the government should borrow sums on the market and then re-lend the proceeds to the colonies, or that the National Debt Commissioners should be allowed to invest National Insurance, Post Office Bank and Trustee Savings Bank funds in colonial stock.[173] The Agents, meanwhile, favoured the establishment of a Colonial Loans Consortium, which would represent all colonial governments. From time to time, loans would be issued on behalf of the Consortium, and the proceeds then advanced to those colonies in need of funds.[174]

All of these proposals were rejected. It was thought that any government intervention would aggravate the lack of confidence in colonial stocks and be resented by colonial governments.[175] Official guarantees would be 'bad training for independence' and unofficial guarantees would be discounted by investors.[176] There would be City opposition to government underwriting and priority market access; while the use of Debt Commissioner's funds would require additional legislation, face opposition from the National Insurance Fund trustees and harm

168 CO 1025/92.

169 CO 1025/116, Commonwealth circular, Nov. 1959.

170 OV 44/73, No. 79, memo, 11 May 1955; Gerold Krozewski, 'Sterling, the minor territories and the end of formal Empire', *Economic History Review*, 46 (2) (1993), p. 255; Gerold Krozewski, *Money and the End of Empire. British International Economic Policy and the Colonies 1947–58*, London 2001, p. 167.

171 Morgan, *A Reassessment*, p. 38; CAOG 23/5, Colonial circular, 8 July 1960.

172 L. J. Butler, *Britain and Empire. Adjusting to a Post-Imperial World*, London 2002, p. 108; T 233/1426, Draft working party report, no date.

173 T 233/1425, memo, 21 April 1958; CAOG 9/351, Colonial Development Finance Conference, report, 1951, p. 22.

174 CAOG 9/351, Colonial ..., p. 21; T 233/1425, note, Scrimgeours, 12 May 1958.

175 CAOG 9/351, Colonial ..., p. 22; Morgan, *A Reassessment*, p. 44.

176 T 233/1425, memo, 21 April 1958. Official guarantees would additionally have had an adverse effect on the demand for unguaranteed stocks (T 233/1426, note, Armstrong, 13 June 1958).

demand for UK government stock.[177] As for the Colonial Loans Consortium, when issuing its loans the CAs would act as principals rather than as agents, and they would therefore be liable for defaults on the advances to colonies, which, given their low reserves, they would be unable to meet.[178]

In the event, the Agents sought to raise demand by increasing yields and making modest changes to the issuing process. For many years, high yields were resisted. They would reduce loan proceeds, prevent the poorer colonies from venturing into the market, and, by signalling the Agents' desperation, could even reduce investor confidence.[179] Such was the need for funds, however, that the terms offered gradually improved, and, by 1968, a Jamaican loan was issued with a previously unheard of interest rate of 8.25 per cent. Among other things, the Agents also began to advertise loans more widely, dropped the requirement that investors had to apply for stock in excess of £1,000 in multiples of £1,000, and no longer retained money received in excess of allocations for the payment of the first instalment when applications were scaled down.[180] Issuers were additionally persuaded to give undertakings that they would not return to the market for a given period and to include clauses in local legislation that guaranteed that they would meet all future obligations to investors.[181]

Despite these efforts, London demand remained low and the UK was eventually forced to seek development funds elsewhere. The new sources of finance are discussed in the next chapter and included the colonies' internal resources, the UK government, international aid organisations, and the private sector. The majority of the funds came from the colonies themselves, which were encouraged to spend surplus revenues on development projects and to issue more local loans and to purchase large proportions of the stock issued themselves, raising the necessary money by selling some of the sterling securities in their investment Funds. At the same time, the UK government increased the amount of aid it provided, introducing in 1959 Exchequer loans, more applications were made for advances from the International Bank of Reconstruction and Development, and attempts were made to increase private sector investment in the colonies. The Agents also explored the possibility of issuing colonial loans overseas, and considered floating a 1956 Tanganyika loan in New York or Holland, a 1957 East African Harbour Commission issue in Switzerland, and a 1958 New Hebrides loan in Paris.[182] Apart from a small Jamaican issue, which was floated in New York in 1958 by an independent broker, however, no overseas floats occurred.[183] There was little foreign demand for colonial stock, unless it possessed a UK government

177 T 233/1425, memo, 21 April 1958. The National Debt Commissioners were large purchasers of government stock.

178 CAOG 9/351, Colonial …, p. 21.

179 T 233/1426, Draft report of the Working Party on Colonial Stock Issues; CAOG 9/351, Colonial …, p. 20; ADM 14/51, no. 7, memo, 9 Sept. 1958.

180 Morgan, *A Reassessment*, p. 188; WN 13, A055803, Scrimgeours to CAs, 4 Dec. 1962. The retention of the money deprived applicants of up to three weeks interest.

181 WN 13, A055803, Scrimgeours to CAs, 4 Dec. 1962; *ibid.*, A370806, CO to Jamaica, 28 Jan. 1963; T 233/2349, note, Phelps, 25 Feb. 1962.

182 WN 13, A1770; *ibid.*, A226805; *ibid.*, A544801. See also *ibid.*, A2483.

183 T 233/1425, Lucas to Jenkyns, 29 April 1958.

guarantee, and issuing colonies would face difficulties meeting interest payments and repayments of loans issued overseas as both would have to be made in the currency of the country in which the issues were floated.[184]

Conclusion

The Agents sought to maximize the price and subscription of colonial stock both when determining the terms of a loan and during the issue process. When fixing terms, they variously ensured that loans were of an appropriate size and length and that the proceeds would fund financially remunerative projects, arranged for stock to be purchased 'firm' and for stamp duty on transfers to be paid by the issuing colony, established Sinking Funds, and set relatively high prices. During the issue process, they removed prior charges, floated stock at times of high demand, employed underwriters, and purchased securities for colonial Investment Funds. Occasionally, they also acted or allowed others to act in a manner that could be regarded as unethical. For example, the unspent balances of at least one loan were used for purposes not stated in the prospectus, and nothing was done to prevent Scrimgeours and their underwriters making applications for stock themselves in order to give private investors the false impression that a loan was in demand.

Unfortunately, their attempts to fulfill their clients' goals were defeated, from the mid-1950s, by the fall in the demand for colonial stock, which made the failure of issues inevitable and gave them no alternative but to offer investors generous terms. They were also obstructed in the completion of their duties by the City, the Bank of England and the Treasury. Seeking to protect their high profit margins, Scrimgeours and their underwriters forced the CAs to pay excessive overriding and underwriting fees and to set relatively low loan prices. The Treasury and the Bank of England, meanwhile, required them to act in the interests of the UK economy. To ensure that funds were available for British industry, for example, the Treasury in the inter-war period halted the conversion of loans; immediately after the war, closed the market to colonial issues; and, during the 1950s, restricted florations. Where the UK's interests clashed with their goal of keeping the country's finances in order, however, Treasury officials would occasionally permit the Agents put their clients' interests above those of the domestic economy. For instance, they allowed the Agency to breach the 1933 ruling that loans should not be used for the repayment of old issues, because they feared that the payment of excessive interest rates on the old loans would cause some colonies to become more dependent on Exchequer funds.

The Agents were also forced to promote the UK economy by the Bank of England. To ensure the successful issue of loans by British institutions, the Bank required them to set relatively low prices, prevented them exploiting periods of high demand for stock, and blocked their attempts to abandon underwriting. The Bank, additionally, occasionally acted in its own interests. Bank officials, for example, partly objected to the CAs' setting high prices and issuing large

184 OV 44/74, no. 76, memo, 27 Sept. 1956; *ibid.*, no. 60a, memo, 12 June 1956.

amounts of stock during market upturns because the premium prices reflected badly on their own lower priced loans and the clogging of the market threatened the success of their own issues. Similarly, they opposed the campaign to abandon underwriting, in part, because they wished to retain the goodwill and business of underwriters, and, from the 1950s, they encouraged newly independent countries to leave the Agents in the full knowledge that they would transfer their business to the Bank.

2

Other Sources of Finance

The funds needed to finance development came from the public issue of loans, discussed in the previous chapter, but also from four further sources – private funds, other colonies, internal resources, and aid. The various ways in which the Agents extracted money from private investors and the City is the subject of the first section of this chapter, which also includes a brief discussion of corporate colonial investment. The means by which colonies lent money to other territories are investigated in part two, and the use of internal resources and the provision of aid are reviewed in sections three and four respectively. The impact these funds had on the UK economy and the manner in which they were distributed is then considered.

Private funds

In addition to publicly floating loans, the Agents tapped private funds through the sale of stock to the market, private institutions and colonial investment Funds, by borrowing from London and foreign banks, by issuing colonial treasury bills, and by providing purchasers of goods with credit, partly financed by banking and insurance companies. On top of this, colonies received the proceeds of guaranteed and municipal loans issued by the Bank of England and other issuing houses, and both British and foreign companies invested in their economies.

Sale of stock to the market/placings

From 1920 to 1969, the Agents sold to the market or placed £36.1m of stock in 45 issues (Figure 1.4). In order to gain a quotation, sales to the market had to involve at least £100,000 of securities, but, following Stock Exchange regulations, the amount sold could not exceed £250,000.[1] The stock was offered to brokers and institutions, and the Agents additionally usually purchased 'firm', that is agreed to buy at the time of issue, a proportion of the securities for colonial investment Funds. Over the period, they acquired £21.9m of stock in this way, buying between 9 and 94 per cent, and, on average, 54 per cent of the amount offered. As with public issues, sales involved the creation of a prospectus and the setting of a price, which generally allowed brokers to make a profit or 'turn' of 1 per

1 CAOG 9/101, CO to Huxham, Oct. 1938; CAOG 9/300, memo, 28 Sept. 1936.

cent when they resold the stock purchased onto the public.[2] Although the CAs believed the turn to be 'exorbitant', it was necessary to compensate brokers for the poor marketability of the loans, the result of their diminutive size.[3]

Market sales were made when a small amount of money needed to be raised or when it was difficult to judge the reception of a loan. If the latter was the case, the CAs would sell chunks of the stock to the market over a period of time, confident that any refusals to purchase would not become widely known and thus would not damage the credit worthiness of either the selling colony or the Crown colonies in general.[4] Other benefits of the sales were that they saved the seller the various costs of public flotation, involved less work for the Agents, and rarely resulted in a post-issue fall in price, as brokers could afford to hold the small amount of stock purchased until it was absorbed by the public.[5]

On twelve occasions, the Agents sold approximately £100,0000 of stock to the market to gain a quotation and to determine a price and then sold the rest of the securities in separate sales over time to colonial investment Funds at 1 per cent below the market price. The Funds thus obtained the stock at a lower price than if the Agents had applied for it 'firm' at the time of issue.[6] Another strategy was to sell stock to the market and then immediately buy it back for colonial investment Funds. The advantages of the practice were that the Stock Exchange permitted the Agents to issue more than £250,000 at any one time if such purchases occurred, and, since the brokers were assured a quick sale, the turn was generally only 1/8 per cent to 1/4 per cent.[7]

The placing of loans involved the Agents selling stock directly to one or two institutions without a prospectus and at a negotiated price. Buyers were generally banks and the loan was usually held until it was redeemed, as new stock issued in this way did not receive a Stock Exchange quotation and was not marketable.[8] The practice saved the issuing colony flotation costs and the brokers turn, and, since the City and the public were unaware of the sales, allowed it to accumulate debt with no damage to its credit rating. On a few occasions, placings were combined with market sales. In the case of a 1953 East African Railway commission loan, for example, over time £250,000 was sold to the market, £1.5m taken by the CAs for colonial investment funds, and £750,000 placed by Scrimgeours with three institutions.[9]

2 CAOG 9/324, notes, p. 31.

3 *Ibid.*, p. 2; CAOG 9/101, meeting, 7 Nov. 1933; CAOG 9/113, Ezechiel to Stevenson, 29 June 1923.

4 CAOG 9/104, memo, Abbott, 16 Oct. 1933.

5 CAOG 9/358, memo, Scrimgeours, 5 May 1952.

6 CAOG 9/101, CO to Huxham, Oct. 1938; *ibid.*, meeting, 7 Nov. 1933.

7 CAOG 9/272, memo, no date; WN 13, A850802/2, report, 19 Dec. 1951; *ibid.*, A414806/2.

8 CA (m) 25, p. 12. The £50,000 of Northern Rhodesian stock placed in 1932, for instance, was bought by West Nominees Ltd, Barclays Nominees Ltd and John Claude Russell (CAOG 9/138, CAs to Stock Exchange, 9 Feb. 1932). See also CAOG 9/133, CAs to Stock Exchange 28 Nov. 1930.

9 WN 13, A185801/2.

Bank loans, treasury bills and credit

Smaller amounts of money were borrowed from London and foreign banks, raised through the issue of colonial treasury bills, or provided as credit. Loans from London banks were rare, as they were relatively expensive and stood as a prior charge on the colony's revenues.[10] Lending by foreign banks was even less common, though, at the end of the 1960s, the Agents proposed that they be allowed to borrow from German banks and then re-lend the proceeds to colonies in need of finance. [11] The proposal, which would have solved many territories' financial problems, was rejected by the Bank of England, which believed that colonies 'ought to pay the going rate ... [and] not derive benefit by sheltering behind a first class UK name', and that such borrowing would prevent the nationalized industries obtaining funds from Germany.[12]

Colonial treasury bills were issued to provide territories with funds prior to the flotation of a loan when, for some reason, the JCF or JMF could not supply sufficient advances.[13] The bills had currencies of between three and six months, were first used in 1921, and were either placed, that is sold to particular institutions at prices based on those of British government Treasury bills, or issued by tender in multiples of usually £5,000.[14] As regards the tender sale of Tanganyika and Uganda bills in 1931, the only issues for which data is available, invitations to bid were sent to 45 firms, mostly banks, brokers and discount houses, and the bills were sold to 13 and 9 companies respectively.[15]

From the early 1930s, relatively few bills were sold by the colonies largely because the Bank of England opposed their use. As will be discussed in chapter four, the Agents' issue of bills to overcome the difficulty of floating loans on the London market in 1931 contributed to the near bankruptcy of the Joint Colonial Fund, and the trauma of this event coloured the Bank's view of the bills for the next three decades. The Bank also believed that colonial bills competed with their UK Treasury counterparts and thus damaged government finances.[16] All requests to issue bills were therefore turned down, and a 1946 proposal that the Agents issue a single low interest bill for all the crown colonies was rejected.[17] The Bank argued that the constant renewal of the bill would result in the crea-

10 For example, Barclays made loans to Barbados in 1930 and 1936 and to Trinidad in 1930, and, in 1937, Barings lent £200,000 to Iraq (CAOG 9/40, CAs to CO, 21 Feb. 1936; WN 13, A055801, Hicks to Vile, 28 Jan. 1953; L 193, Summaries of 'A' Dept. files).

11 NA, HO 268/541, b/tr/9/2, B of E to Treasury, 24 April 1969. In 1954, the Aden Port Trust, unable to obtain funds elsewhere, borrowed sums from the National Bank of India, and, in 1938, the Agents attempted, but failed, to arrange a loan for the Palestine municipality of Haifa from the London merchant bank Bensons and the Anglo-Palestine Bank (WN 13, A1770; S 5, A1392).

12 HO 268/541, b/tr/9/2, B of E to Treasury, 24 April 1969.

13 CAOG 9/40, Colonial circular, 28 June 1922.

14 S 1, A164; CAOG 9/142, CAs to Uganda, 3 Dec. 1931; CAOG 9/141, advert, 10 April 1931.

15 CAOG 9/141, Banks and firms invited to tender, 10 April 1931; *ibid.*, tenders accepted, no date; CAOG 9/142, weeding note. One of the purchasers of a later placed Uganda issue was Scrimgeours, which took £50,000 of bills (CAOG 9/142, weeding note).

16 T 233/1425, memo, 21 April 1958.

17 For example, WN 13, A478802/1–2, CAs to Malaya, 31 Dec. 1948; Morgan, *A Reassessment*, p. 190. BE, C 47/50, CO to Treasury, 20 Aug. 1946.

tion of 'a quasi-permanent floating debt' and that such a security would reduce the money available on the London market for UK investors.[18]

The demand to purchase goods by deferred payment arose in the late 1950s from newly independent territories. Prior to 1967, credit was provided by a bank or the contractor. The Agents negotiated the terms of bank credit on behalf of their clients, and, if requested, invited tenders from contractors on both a cash and a payment-by-instalment basis. The banks and contractors then obtained cover for the debts from the Export Credits Guarantee Department (ECGD), which guaranteed the repayment of loans provided to finance UK exports.[19] A drawback of this dependence on banks and contractors was that neither would provide credit to colonial governments regarded as poor risks. The colonies concerned therefore had to use private suppliers, who charged excessively high prices, and the Agents lost orders. To overcome this problem, the CAs sought to provide credit themselves, but were prevented from doing so by the ECGD, which stated that cover could only be given to banks or corporate bodies.[20]

After four years of seeking an exemption from its rules, the Agents gave in to the ECGD's demands and acquired two companies through which they could supply their own credit. In 1967, they took a shareholding in the merchant bank Sassoons, which financed the credit provided from its own resources.[21] Two years later, they established Millbank Technical Services Ltd (MTS), which supplied engineering goods and services.[22] The credit offered by MTS was financed by the Agents' clients and UK and foreign financial institutions, via the Finvest Fund, and, as ECGD cover was available only to firms with a nominal value of £1m, the Agents moved £990,000 from their Office Fund to MTS, which then relent the same amount back to the Office Fund; a manoeuvre that was arguably duplicitous, though not illegal.[23] To help those purchasers that could not conform to ECGD terms, the CAs also began to supply credit, again financed by the Finvest Fund, without ECGD backing. Owing to the risks involved, the credit provided was largely short-term and only given in return for a promissory note, and, to provide for losses, an insurance reserve was created, initially financed by the Office Fund.

Guaranteed and public body loans

Although the Agents floated ordinary Crown colony loans, they played no part in issues made by colonial public bodies or the flotation of loans with Imperial guarantees.[24] Colonial public bodies generally obtained funds from loans raised

18 C 47/50, CO to Treasury, 20 Aug 1946.

19 L 35, 1967, no. 1. On occasion, where purchases were financed by a UK Exchequer loan that had been delayed, the CAs provided credit from their own Office Fund (*ibid.*).

20 CA (m) 106, memo, approx. 1966.

21 L 36, 25 July 1967 meeting.

22 L 35, 1969, no. 8.

23 L 5, Finance Dept., April 1969; L 36, 23 April 1968 meeting. The Finvest Fund was set up by the Agents to bankroll their secondary banking venture, which is the subject of chapters seven and eight. The activities of MTS are discussed in chapter nine. Re-lending the £990,000 to the Office Fund reduced MTS's tax liability (L 36, 23 April 1968 meeting).

24 They also had no involvement in the 1922 £1m British Guiana flotation, which, as the territory had an amorphous constitution, was issued by the brokers Messrs Bernard Schelle (S 1, A167).

by their governments in London or through the inter-colonial loan scheme.[25] Requests that they issue their own stock in the UK were turned down by the Agents, who argued that their poor creditworthiness would cause the issues to fail and that this would damage the credit of their governments and of all colonies. For the same reason, the CAs also rejected a proposal for the flotation of a consolidated loan on behalf of a number of colonial municipalities.[26] The few colonial municipal loans that were issued, for example for Singapore and Nairobi, were thus handled by independent brokers or merchant banks.[27]

Imperial guarantees involved the UK government guaranteeing to repay a loan and to pay the dividends if the issuer defaulted, and were granted when, without them, a flotation would fail or stock would have to be offered at a price so high that it would damage the consolidated credit of the Crown colonies. They were therefore provided when a colony had suffered a natural catastrophe and money was needed for relief; for loans issued by protectorates and mandated territories, which, until 1929, were excluded from the Colonial Stocks Act; and, in the case of Nyasaland's 1932 and 1934 loans, because the protectorate possessed a poor credit rating.[28] As the UK government accepted responsibility for repayment, loans with guarantees were classed as government issues and were floated by the Bank of England. Fourteen were issued, raising £45.6m. Six were for the Sudan, three for Tanganyika, and the last issue was made in 1939. The loans were slightly larger than those handled by the Agents, having an average size of £3.3m, and, because of the guarantees, carried a slightly lower yield.[29]

Neither the Crown Agents nor the Colonial Office were happy that the loans were issued by the Bank of England. The Agents believed that it set excessively generous terms, which impacted on ordinary colonial loans, and suspected that it used the successful flotation of such issues in its campaign to persuade the Treasury to allow it to float ordinary colonial stock.[30] The Colonial Office, meanwhile, was aware that the domiciling of a loan at the Bank delayed its use, the Treasury 'withholding the money until it is dragged out of them'.[31] In 1926, therefore, the Colonial Office, made a concerted attempt to persuade the Treasury to allow the CAs to issue a guaranteed loan for East Africa, even raising the subject at a Cabinet meeting. It was argued that the Agency had floated colonial guaranteed loans in the past and that they were colonial rather than British government issues.[32] They were raised on the security of colonial government revenues and it was generally accepted in the market that the UK government 'unofficially'

25 For example, CAOG 9/351, Colonial ..., p. 27; WN 13, A1935/3; S 1, A247.

26 S 7, A1939. See also CAOG 9/351, Colonial ..., p. 27.

27 CAOG 9/351, Colonial ..., p. 27; S 4, A1161.

28 CO 67/246/16, memo, 19 Jan. 1932.

29 The average yield of the two guaranteed loans issued in 1921 was 4.69 per cent, as against a mean of 6.21 per cent for the CA loans issued in that year. The yields for 1932 were 4.59 per cent and 4.71 per cent respectively.

30 See CAOG 9/300, CAs to Wilson, 8 Dec. 1927. Both *The Times* and *The Statist* reported that the later 1927 Palestine loan was issued too cheaply (*ibid.*).

31 CO 323/957/4, note on Niemeyer to Wilson, 21 Nov. 1925; *ibid.*, Green to Strachey and Wilson, 30 Nov. 1925.

32 The CAs had issued the 1873 Mauritius guaranteed loan and one for Zanzibar in 1901 (CO 323/957/4, Wilson to Niemeyer, 26 Jan. 1926).

guaranteed all colonial loans. The Agents also needed the issue commissions if they were to avoid increasing the fees they charged to the colonies, and their non-involvement in the flotation of such loans caused the public to question their competence and thus affected the success of ordinary colonial issues.[33]

In response, the Treasury reiterated that the loans were British government securities and claimed that the abandonment of the practice of using the Bank 'would be regarded as so odd [in the City] that the loan might even suffer'.[34] They further pointed out that the Agents charged higher fees than the Bank and claimed that the Agency would set the price of the loan excessively high, causing it to fail.[35] Afraid that any alteration to colonial guarantee loans would damage other UK government issues, the Cabinet accepted the Treasury's case, though it did permit the Agents to manage the East African loan's Sinking Fund.[36]

Foreign and British corporate investment

Foreign corporate investment in the colonies was probably relatively low, as both the Colonial Office and colonial governments sought to restrict the operation of foreign companies. Nonetheless, during the four years from 1950 to 1954, it was estimated that £10m flowed to the colonies from this source, and it seems likely that there was a substantial increase in such investment thereafter.[37] Some indication of the money ploughed into the colonies by British companies can be obtained from figures collected by the Bank of England from 1938 to 1957 (Figure 2.1). These show that the share capital of those firms that operated in the colonies rose from £177.1m in 1938 to £197.8m in 1957 and that their loan capital fell from £29.7m in 1938 to £5.6m in 1947, before recovering to £27.6m in 1957. Africa obtained almost half of the share capital and three quarters of the loan capital, with a further third of the share capital being in Malaya and 10 per cent of the loan capital located in the West Indies.[38] The companies were involved in mining and trading, and, to a lesser extent, in the agricultural production of plantation crops, such as rubber, tea, cocoa and tobacco.[39] Greater investment in more sectors was precluded by the relative absence of infrastructure, private capital markets and local demand; in the case of mining, by insignificant known deposits of the most important minerals; in the inter-war period, by low commodity prices; and, after the war, by fears that independence would bring political instability and by Britain's Balance of Payments problem, which

33 NA, CAB 24/179/cp129 and cp130; CAB 23/52/cab14 (26) 7, minutes, 31 March 1926.

34 CO 323/957/4, Niemeyer to Wilson, 29 Jan. 1926.

35 *Ibid.*, SHW to Sect. of State, 9 March 1926; *ibid.*, Niemeyer to Wilson, 29 Jan. 1926.

36 *Ibid.*, extract from cabinet meeting of 21 March 1928.

37 CAB 130/97, note, 9 Nov. 1953. £5m was invested in the West Indies and just under £4m in West Africa (*ibid.*).

38 West Africa received 19.3 per cent of the share capital, East Africa 6 per cent, Central Africa 20 per cent, Ceylon 11.6 per cent, Malaya 34 per cent and the West Indies 9.1 per cent. As for the loan capital, West Africa obtained 1.8 per cent, East Africa 10.1 per cent, Central Africa 65 per cent, Ceylon 3.6 per cent, Malaya 9.7 per cent and the West Indies 9.8 per cent (Bank of England, *UK Overseas Investments*, London 1950, 1951, 1952, 1953, 1954, 1955, 1956, 1957).

39 Michael Havinden and David Meredith, *Colonialism and Development. Britain and its Tropical Colonies, 1850–1960*, London 1993, p. 153, 309.

Figure 2.1. Nominal share and loan capital of UK companies that operated in British Africa, Ceylon, Malaya and the British West Indies, 1938–57 and CDC expenditure 1949–65

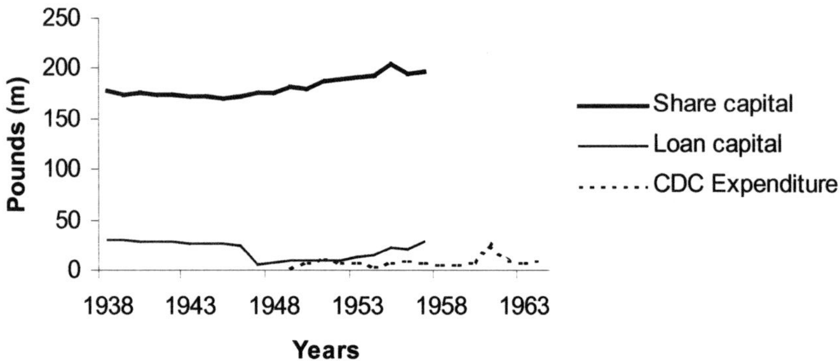

Source. Bank of England, UK Overseas Investments, London 1950, 1951, 1952, 1953, 1954, 1955, 1956, 1957; Colonial Development Corporation. Annual Report and Statement of Accounts, 1959/60–1969/70 (see bibliography).

Note. UK companies are those registered in Britain and abroad.

made the export of capital difficult.[40] Attempts to attract greater investment through the provision of incentives, such as government financial assistance or tax concessions, were generally unsuccessful.[41] Low colonial taxes, for example, were negated by the Inland Revenue, which required companies to pay UK tax if the rate was higher than that of the colony in which they operated.[42]

Funds from other colonies

Money came from other colonies via colony-to-colony loans, inter-colonial loans, and Joint Colonial Fund and Joint Miscellaneous Fund advances and overdrafts. Direct loans from one colony to another were relatively rare. In the early 1950s, there was some lending between East African administrations; from 1951 to 1961, the oil rich state of Brunei lent approximately £20m to North Borneo, Sarawak and the Federated Malay States; and, in 1975, the Urban Development Corporation of Jamaica borrowed £2.5m from Abu Dhabi. In each case, the terms were arranged by the Crown Agents and the loans guaranteed by the borrowing governments.[43]

The inter-colonial loan scheme was established in 1925 and involved the Agents creating stock for a colony requiring finance, which was then sold to one or more of the Sinking Funds under their management, and, very occasionally,

40 *Ibid.*, pp. 308–9; Butler, *Britain*, p. 108.

41 CAOG 9/351, Colonial ..., p. 25.

42 Bernard Braine, 'UK income tax and colonial industrial development', *New Commonwealth*, 17 March 1952, pp. 256–7.

43 CAOG 9/113, memo, 25 March 1953; CA (mc) 60; L 11, Finance Dept., Jan. 1975.

to other investment Funds and the JCF.[44] The stock was not quoted or traded on the market and was given the same date of maturity as the Sinking Fund(s) that bought it. The scheme benefited both borrowers and lenders. Borrowers who could not raise funds on the market, either because of their poor credit rating or the unremunerative nature of the project to be financed, could obtain money. They faced no flotation expenses or management fee, did not have to make provision for the payment of stamp duty, and could repay the loan at any time. Lenders, meanwhile, acquired suitable stock for their Sinking Funds and benefited from the savings in issue costs by obtaining a slightly higher price than that suggested by the market.[45]

In order to avoid overloading Sinking Funds with unmarketable stock and to spread the available money fairly between borrowers, the capacity of the programme was limited. From 1946, each colony could only issue £100,000 of inter-colonial (IC) loans per year, though, on a number of occasions, these limits were exceeded, and, over the period 1926 to 1964, only 108 loans worth £21.6m were provided (Figure 1.4).[46] The Agents also fought all attempts by the Colonial Office to extend the scheme to protectorates and mandated territories. It was argued that the Secretary of State's power over these areas could wane, leaving the CAs with little redress if their governments refused to repay the debts, and that many loan ordinances laid down that Sinking Funds could only be invested in securities covered by the Colonial Stock Act, which excluded protectorates. The Agents, nevertheless, made exceptions when there was no other source of money available, allowing Tanganyika, for example, to borrow from a Kenyan Sinking Fund in 1934.[47] Further restrictions came from the Treasury. From 1940 to 1948, the Agency had to obtain Treasury consent for all IC loans, and, from 1949, for issues in excess of £50,000, and, during the 1950s, the Chancellor of the Exchequer carefully monitored their use, fearing that excessive issue would deprive the London market of funds.[48]

Under pressure to provide funds, the Agents were sometimes cavalier in the way they used the scheme. They often ignored the requirement that they should obtain the permission of the Colonial Office before a loan was issued, failed to inform colonies that advances had been made from their Sinking Funds, and, on occasion, used the Funds of governments that had not agreed to participate in the programme.[49] To help borrowers, they also appear to have set relatively low prices. From 1926 to 1939, the only period for which data is available, issues on average yielded 3.87 per cent as compared to the 4.27 per cent obtained

44 CAOG 9/232, memo, 22 March 1935.

45 CAOG 9/288, 'How the colonies benefited in 1934 from the CAs financial policy', no date; CAOG 9/113, CAs to Grenada, 16 Oct. 1935; *ibid.*, CAs to St Lucia, 13 July 1943; CAOG 9/40, Colonial circular, 10 July 1925.

46 CAOG 22/30, memo, 25 June 1956. In 1956, Basutoland, Swaziland and Bechuanaland were allowed IC loans totalling £400,000 (*ibid.*).

47 CAOG 9/113, memo, 28 Sept. 1934; *ibid.*, CAs to Dominions Office, 7 Nov. 1945.

48 CO 1025/90, CO to CAs, 11 March 1955; *ibid.*, Treasury to CO, 21 Feb. 1955; CAOG 9/113, memo, 25 April 1949. The Treasury believed that SFs would invest in stock rather than UK securities.

49 CAOG 9/113, memo, 14 Feb. 1940; *ibid.*, CAs to CO, 9 Aug. 1948; *ibid.*, memo, 10 Dec. 1956.

from public issues. On the other hand, when faced with Treasury attempts to obtain cheap loans for two African railway companies in 1934, the CAs vigorously defended the lenders' interests. The Treasury's insistence that an interest rate of 3.12 per cent be set was rejected by the Agents, who demanded a rate of 4 per cent, eventually accepting 3.5 per cent.[50]

The Joint Colonial Fund was set up in 1929, and, as will be discussed in chapter four, largely contained money that the colonies kept in London to pay for their UK transactions, plus the unspent balances of loans raised on the London market. In 1951, a further Fund, the Joint Miscellaneous Fund, was established, which held similar monies, but for non-colonial and non-government clients. On average, 10 per cent of these Funds were lent to the Agents' clients, and many colonies also ran overdrafts on their accounts. Unfortunately, there is no record of the sums lent, merely the total advances provided as of 31st December in each year. For the period 1929 to 1969, these amount to £241.5m, but, as many of the loans were short-term, lasting a couple of months, the aggregate sum advanced was probably at least treble this amount (Figure 1.1). There is also no record of the amounts advanced prior to 1929 when each colony's UK surplus funds were invested and advanced on an individual basis. If these are conservatively estimated annually at half those of JCF loans in 1929, the total amount lent from 1920 to 1969 reaches £729.5m.

The sums borrowed varied according to colonial demand for finance and the quantity of money lodged in the JCF and JMF, which was influenced by the prosperity of the dependencies and the level and terms of trade, the imposition of restrictions on Fund size, and the number of loans issued on the London market. The advances from both Funds were used to meet temporary shortages of revenue, but largely to finance expenditure on public works in anticipation of a market loan.[51] The latter practice was frowned upon by the Bank of England, which believed that such advances made the Funds dangerously illiquid, but was enthusiastically embraced the Agents.[52] By delaying a public issue, the advances ensured that, by the time a loan was floated, the construction of the works was well under way and an accurate estimate of their final cost could be made. As a result, there was less likelihood that the colony would run out of money and have to return to the market, which was sure to damage its financial credibility, and the fact that a project was already underway increased public demand for the associated loan.[53] Also, if an issue was made before construction began, a large proportion of the proceeds would remain idle, earning interest at a lower rate than that payable, and the colony would have to begin making Sinking Fund contributions at an earlier date.[54]

The amount borrowed in anticipation of capital expenditure could not exceed 25 per cent of the borrower's JCF deposits or 50 per cent of the size of the eventual public issue, though this ruling was occasionally by-passed when poor

50 CA (mc) 60, appendix 1.
51 CA (m) 25, p. 2; CO 323/957/4, memo, Ezechiel, no date, approx. 1926.
52 CAOG 9/230, meeting, 23 Feb. 1932.
53 CAOG 9/40, Colonial circular, 28 June 1922.
54 CAOG 9/324, notes, p. 2; CO 323/957/4, memo, Ezechiel, no date, approx. 1926.

market conditions forced flotations to be delayed.[55] In return for the money, the borrower provided security and paid interest. Collateral took the form of permanent investments held by the Agents on behalf of one of the borrowing colony's Funds, generally its Surplus Fund, or legislative authority (or its preparation) for the CAs to issue a loan or local treasury bills and Treasury approval of the issue.[56] Occasionally, the Agents also made advances on the assurance that a grant-in-aid or similar payment was about to be made by the UK government.[57] Until 1953 and except for a short period in 1931/2, interest rate was bank rate, which was usually lower than that charged on long-term publicly issued loans, but higher than the rate that JCF monies would attract if invested short-term elsewhere.[58] Interest then fell to ½ per cent below bank rate, largely because commercial banks began to offer cheap loans to colonial governments.[59] The lower rate, however, reduced the returns to JCF depositors, causing some to withdraw their money, and interest was therefore raised to ¼ per cent below bank rate in 1957, and, in January 1959, returned to its original level.[60]

Inevitably, the Agents' difficulties in raising loans on the London market from the mid-1950s had an impact on the demand for advances, which increased dramatically. At the same time, as will be discussed in chapter four, there were fears of a fall in the amount of money deposited in the JCF and JMF once clients became independent. In their response to the crisis, the Agents were placed under pressure by both the Bank of England and the Treasury. The Bank urged that advances in anticipation of the issue of new loans be discontinued or at least limited in amount and length. It argued that it was unfair that the Agents' clients, unlike UK institutions, should have access to such advances, and that excessive lending would prevent the two Funds covering temporary revenue shortfalls during a World recession.[61] The Treasury, on the other hand, was in favour of the Funds meeting all demands for finance, regarding the advances as 'an alternative to Exchequer loans or other emergency devices'.[62] In the event, the Agency, followed the Bank's advice, and, in 1957, capped total advances at £15m and refused to provide loans in anticipation of public flotations, though, in the early 1960s, an exception was made for the West Indies.[63] They also began to advise clients in need of finance to sell their short-term investments when the return was less than the advance interest rate, and considered directing them to sell longer-term securities, but dropped the idea on fears that the heavy sale of

55 CAOG 9/227, memo, Beresford-Stooke, 23 Nov. 1953; CO 67/246/16, CAs to CO, 15 April 1932.

56 CA (m) 25, p. 3; CO 323/1623/19, CAs to CO, 26 Oct. 1939; CAOG 9/113, CAs to Aden, 23 May 1939; CAOG 9/230, meeting, 23 Feb. 1932.

57 CAOG 9/226, CAs to CO, 1 Dec. 1955.

58 CAOG 9/230, meeting, 23 Feb. 1932.

59 CAOG 9/227, memo, Hicks, 19 Nov. 1953

60 *Ibid.*, memo, 20 March 1956; *ibid.*, Colonial circular, 25 Feb. 1957; *ibid.*, CA circular, 4 Dec. 1958

61 OV 44/75, no. 1, memo, 13 Nov. 1957.

62 ADM 14/50, no. 28, memo, 19 Dec. 1957.

63 CAOG 9/227, CAs to CO, 12 Nov. 1957; *ibid.*, CAs to CO, 27 June 1962; ADM 14/50, no. 28, memo, 19 Dec. 1957.

colonial stock would damage the credit of both the seller and others in financial difficulties.[64]

The tendency for principals to run overdrafts on their JCF and JMF accounts was a persistent problem for the Agents. Average monthly overdrafts totalled £500,231 in 1967, £636,333 in 1969, and, during the 1974 economic slump, reached £8m.[65] The main culprits were public bodies; in the 1930s and 1950s, British Guiana; in the 1950s, Malta; and, in the 1960s, Jordan, Libya, Nigeria and Sierra Leone.[66] British Guiana's 1930s overdrafts were the result of overspending by the governing body, the Combined Court, over which the Colonial Office had little control, and its 1950s debts were related to an ambitious development programme, the colony's inability to raise funds in London, because of market suspicion of its creditworthiness and political stability, and delays in the provision of an HMG Exchequer loan.[67] Malta's difficulties, meanwhile, arose from heavy wartime expenditure and the cost of repairing public works damaged during the war and its unstable government, which made the Treasury reluctant to provide UK government aid.[68] As for the increase in overdrafts in the 1960s, this was largely the result of independence. The new governments lacked funds and financial control mechanisms, suffered chronic shortages of sterling, and behaved irresponsibly, investing in grandiose capital projects that they could ill-afford and building up large defence forces.[69]

The Agents sought to reduce overdrafts in a number of ways. To overcome Nigeria's shortage of sterling, the CA representative in the country accepted local funds for services provided by the Agents in London.[70] The CAs also put pressure on the Colonial Office to improve colonies' financial management systems and kept 'a very close watch' on principals' Fund balances, in 1966 placing clients into various categories that ranged from 'most reliable' to the closely monitored 'thoroughly unreliable'.[71] If overdrafts, nevertheless, occurred, CA staff visited the appropriate government departments, giving officials advice on how such debts could be repaid and avoided in the future.[72] Solutions included the issue of a loan, the sale of investment Fund securities, and appeals to the Colonial Office and Treasury for UK government aid.[73] The latter was often ineffective and the Agents sometimes had to go to extreme lengths before action was taken. In 1966, for example, to force the Overseas Development Ministry to help Sierra Leone they had to threaten to suspend the territory's pension and loan interest payments.[74] On occasion, more esoteric sources of funds were tapped. Sierra

64 CAOG 9/227, CAs to CO, 12 Nov. 1957; CAOG 9/227, CAs to Sarawak, 28 Dec. 1956; *ibid.*, CAs to Aden, 28 Nov. 1956; WN 13, A1770.

65 L 1–11, Finance Dept. monthly reports to Board; L 10, Banking Dept., July 1974.

66 CAOG 17/137, memo, 20 May 1954; S 2, A459; *ibid.*, A463; 'Notes for Office history, 1958–65', p. 8; L 4, F Dept., Feb. 1968.

67 L 193, Summaries of 'A' Dept. files; S 2, A459.

68 S 2, A463.

69 L 36, 20 Dec. 1965 meeting; L 38, No. 75; L 4, Finance Dept., April 1968.

70 L 5, Finance Dept., March 1969. See also L 4, Finance Dept., June/July 1968.

71 S 2, A459; L 36, 20 Dec. 1965 meeting; 'Notes for Office', p. 8.

72 For example, L4, F Dept., April 1968; L 35, 25 Jan. 1972 meeting.

73 For example, S 2, A459; S 3, A765; *ibid.*, A743.

74 S 3, A765.

Leone's difficulties were partly solved in 1966 by a loan from the diamond corporation DICORP, and, in 1950, the Agents lent the Iraq Railway Administration money from their own Office Fund, an act that resulted in a stiff Colonial Office reprimand.[75]

For those clients that were persistently in debt, the Agents adopted a less helpful approach. Officials were sent warning letters and penalties were imposed.[76] In the 1930s, British Guiana was forced to pay a special overdraft interest rate, in the 1950s public bodies that rarely made payments to the JMF were charged interest of 2 per cent above bank rate, and, in 1967, a universal charge of not less than 1 per cent above bank rate was imposed.[77] As a last resort, work was suspended on orders for goods until money was remitted to the appropriate Fund, though an exception was usually made for medical and sanitary supplies and sometimes for urgent indents.[78] In 1958, the Agents refused to handle new orders for Malta, and, in the 1960s and 1970s, the East African Railway, Nigeria, Sierra Leone and Uganda all suffered delays in receiving goods.[79]

Internal finance

Money for development was obtained from within the colonies themselves via the local issue of treasury bills and loans, the provision of advances from local banks, and the expenditure of Surplus Funds.

Local issue of Treasury bills and loans

The local issue of treasury bills suffered the same fate as the London sale of these securities. The Bank of England feared that their use in the finance of capital expenditure could lead to repayment difficulties and successfully put pressure on the Treasury to block sales. Consequently, up to the early 1950s, relatively few bills were issued, and, thereafter, this form of borrowing halted.[80]

Over the period, at least £78.9m of loans were issued locally.[81] They were floated when the proceeds were to be spent internally rather than on purchases from the UK, if the money was required by public bodies, which were effectively barred from the London market, or when a UK flotation was likely to prove difficult, either because the colony was not regarded as creditworthy or the money was to be used for unremunerative purposes. The loans were largely issued by colonies that possessed a local securities market, which allowed the stock to be traded; a large number of wealthy European residents; an unstable exchange rate, which reduced the value of loans raised in London; and a strong banking

75 *Ibid.*, A765; CA (m) 64, memo on past CAs, no date. The Agents were confident that money for the Administration would be obtained from the ECGD (*ibid.*).

76 For example, L 10, Banking Dept., Feb. 1974.

77 S 2, A459; CAOG 17/137, memo, 20 May 1954; L 36, 23 May 1967 meeting.

78 S 3, A765; L 35, 26 Oct. 1971 meeting.

79 S 2, A463; L 10, C Dept. report, Feb. 1974; L 35, 26 Oct. 1971 meeting.

80 C 47/50, memo, Malta, 6 Feb. 1952; T 233/959, memo, Granger-Taylor, 21 April 1951.

81 No list of local issues survives.

system.[82] Banks benefited from the expansion of local securities markets, and, therefore, did all they could to encourage local issues. In many colonies they organized flotations, provided underwriting, often for no charge, helped to form a market for the loan by allowing it to be bought and sold at their counters, encouraged customer support, and bought stock themselves.[83] Of the £59.4m of local loans outstanding in December 1952, £22.3m or 37.51 per cent was held by local banks. The main issuing colonies were thus located in the Far East and SE Asia, which raised 52 per cent of the local loans for which there are records, in the West Indies, which floated 19.2 per cent, and in the Indian Ocean, which accounted for 15.4 per cent of the stock sold.[84] Other important issuers included Kenya, Northern Rhodesia, Sierra Leone, Tanganyika and Uganda.

The loans did not carry trustee status nor were they quoted in London. Requests to receive a London quotation were blocked by the Stock Exchange, and proposals that loans should be simultaneously issued locally and in the UK, which would ensure a quotation, were rejected by the Bank of England.[85] It was claimed that such local/UK floations would reduce the money available in the London market for British needs, since London investors would be encouraged to apply for the local portion of issues, and that local purchasers would offload their holdings in the capital, where they would command a better price.[86]

The majority of the loans issued were small, those floated from 1920 to 1941 averaged £966,283, and had short lives.[87] Local securities markets could not absorb large issues, which local governments, in any case, found difficult to manage, and banks, the main buyers, disliked securities with maturities of more than ten years.[88] To increase demand, many colonies floated premium bonds, which avoided the danger of capital depreciation and attracted small investors, appealing 'to the gambling element prevalent in certain colonial peoples'.[89] Others offered investors a choice of stocks.[90] A 1944 Jamaica loan, for example, gave subscribers the choice of purchasing a stock paying 2.5 per cent interest for 5 to 7 years, a 2.75 per cent 10 to 12 year stock, and one giving a return of 3 per cent over 15 to 20 years.[91]

Issues were organized by the local government, local bank, or London brokers

82 CAOG 9/324, notes, pp. 33–4; OV 44/73, no. 39d, memo, 16 July 1954.

83 CAOG 9/329, CAs to Gold Coast, 31 Aug. 1944; CAOG 9/257, Hong Kong to CO, 15 July 1940. See also OV 44/73, no. 39d, memo, 16 July 1954.

84 OV 44/72, no. 39d, table 1.

85 For example, S 4, A1135; WN 13, A414802, memo, Treasury, 11 April 1945; *ibid.*, A866801/2, Uganda to CAs, 8 March 1951; *ibid.*, A414806/2, memo, Scrimgeours, 28 Sept. 1953.

86 OV 44/70, no. 42, memo, 6 April 1950.

87 CAOG 9/324, notes, pp. 33–4.

88 OV 44/73, no. 79, memo, 11 May 1955. The Agents generally advised against the issue of stock with very short maturities, arguing that it was unsuitable for the finance of long-term development projects and was difficult to repay, as the SFs generally showed a considerable shortfall on redemption (CAOG 9/335, CO to Jamaica, 29 April 1948).

89 OV 44/73, no. 79, memo, 11 May 1955.

90 *Ibid.*, no. 39d, memo, 16 July 1954.

91 *Ibid.*, report on the raising of the general purposes loan authorized by law 1 May 1947, Jamaica Treasury.

– in the case of Kenya by Scrimgeours.[92] To maximize demand, most loans had Sinking Funds, investors were given a few days to put in subscriptions, and allocations of oversubscribed loans were often biased in favour of first time buyers and private investors.[93] Failure was prevented by underwriting issues and the government buying stock on a 'firm' basis for investment Funds. The largest purchasers were therefore usually the government, local banks, and, in the 1950s in West Africa and Uganda, local Marketing Boards. Established to iron out fluctuations in World commodity prices, the latter had large reserves, which were partly used for local investment.[94] The Agents role in issues was the provision of advice on legislation, loan terms, and the issue process.[95] They also arranged the printing of security certificates, ensured that investment Funds had sufficient cash for the purchase of stock, and managed the Sinking Funds.[96]

From the early 1950s, there was much debate between the Agents, Bank of England, Colonial Office, and Treasury regarding the extent to which colonies should raise funds locally.[97] Bank of England and Treasury officials generally believed that an increase in local issues would benefit both the UK government and the colonies. Market resources would be released for UK needs and colonial demands for British aid would fall.[98] As for the colonies, local issues would replace the funds that could only be raised with difficulty on the London market, and, by floating fewer loans in the UK, they would improve their creditworthiness, increasing the likelihood that future London issues would be a success.[99] An expansion of local issues would also have a beneficial effect on their economies. It would encourage the development of local capital markets and thus promote local enterprise.[100] The payment of interest to colonial residents in the local currency would avoid the need to remit sterling to Britain, strengthening Balances of Payments accounts and easing sterling shortages, and the incident of local taxation on dividends would increase government revenues.[101] The ability to raise short-term finance, meanwhile, would reduce the amount of money languishing in Reserve Funds, and the investment of surplus cash in local securities would take money out of economies, minimizing the inflationary effects of development expenditure.[102]

Not everyone, however, was convinced that local issues were the general

92 WN 13, A414807.
93 CAOG 9/335, report on the …; *ibid.*, CAs to CO, 1 July 1947.
94 E. K. Hawkins, 'Marketing Boards and economic development in Nigeria and Ghana', *Review of Economic Studies*, 26 (1958), pp. 51–62.
95 See, for example, WN 13, A1979; *ibid.*, A414807; S 1, A56; CAOG 9/280, 1936 report.
96 S 1, A173; WN 13, A1770.
97 The discussions largely took place within the 1951 Colonial Development Finance Conference and the 1953 Working Party on Colonial Sterling Balances.
98 T 233/1425, O'Brien, 20 Feb. 1958.
99 OV 44/74, no. 33c, memo, 31 Jan. 1956.
100 T 233/934, draft report of the Working Party on Colonial Sterling Assets, 2 Sept. 1953, part 1, p. 8.
101 OV 44/74, no. 33c, memo, 31 Jan. 1956; CAOG 9/324, notes, p. 33.
102 T 233/934, draft report …, p. 7; D. J. Morgan, *Developing British Colonial Resources, 1945–51*, London 1980, p. 47. The Funds usually held 4 to 6 months of revenue (T 233/934, draft report …, p. 7).

panacea claimed. There were doubts that there would be sufficient local demand for the extra stock issued. Poverty and narrow export bases made capital accumulation in the colonies difficult and the colonial branches of British banks invested most of their surpluses in the London money market. Indeed, from the mid-1950s, it appeared that demand was likely to fall. Commodity prices were declining, larger proportions of London loans were reserved for colonial investors, and the movement towards independence led to fears of political instability.[103] Even if more loans were issued, the UK and the colonies would not necessarily benefit. The development of local capital markets would reduce the importance of London as a financial centre, and increase the likelihood that colonies on reaching independence would withdraw their investments from the City.[104] For the colonies, local loans would generate fewer funds than their London counterparts, owing to the tendency for colonial governments to set excessively low prices, and the loss of the need to maintain their creditworthiness in the London market could lead many administrations to act irresponsibly.[105] Colonies could also find it more difficult to raise money in the UK. Absence from the London market would cause their name and financial strengths to rapidly fade from investors' memories, the failure of local issues would damage their creditworthiness, and the local debt would constitute a prior charge on their finances, and, unless paid off, discourage the take-up of loans.[106]

In the event, in 1956 it was decided that the flotation of local loans should be encouraged and a range of ideas were put forward for raising colonial demand for the stock. It was suggested that dividends should be exempted from local taxation, that Stabilisation Funds should be established to support the price of previous loans by purchasing surplus stock, that local governments should guarantee the re-purchase of stock on request, and that loans should carry high interest rates.[107] All of the proposals were rejected and it was eventually decided that issuing governments should be allowed to use some of the money in the investment Funds managed by the Agents to purchase a proportion of the stock issued. Use of the Funds would be politically beneficial to the UK government, weakening accusations, discussed in chapter three, that it forced colonies to invest large sums in London.[108] It was also believed that it was better for the colonies to spend these Funds while they were under British rule than later when they were independent, since the monies would be expended on worthwhile development schemes rather than frittered away on inconsequential projects.[109] Many government officials were convinced that political power would be placed in the hands

103 Havinden and Meredith, *Colonialism*, pp. 158, 264–5; OV 44/73, no. 79, memo, 11 May 1955.

104 T 233/934, draft report ..., pp. 4–6.

105 For example, CAOG 9/257, telegram, Hong Kong to CO, 20 Nov. 1939. T 233/1426, draft report of working party, no date.

106 T 233/934, draft report ..., pp. 4–6; CAOG 9/329, CAs to Gold Coast, 31 Aug. 1944; WN 13, A1770.

107 CAOG 9/351, Colonial ..., pp. 13, 14; OV 44/73, No. 79, memo, 11 May 1955; OV 44/72, no. 99, CO to B of E, 16 Sept. 1953.

108 Catherine R. Schenk, *Britain and the Sterling Area. From Devaluation to Convertability in the 1950s*, London 1994, pp. 39–40.

109 T 233/933, memo, 11 May 1953.

of inexperienced left wing politicians on independence, who would inaugurate impractical and unremunerative schemes and that the loss of expatriate officials would cause administrative standards of efficiency and honesty to fall precipitously.[110]

The two investment Funds chosen to accommodate local securities were Savings Bank Funds, which contained investments equal in value to the sums lent by the banks for which the Funds were established, and Currency Funds, which guaranteed the value of local currencies. Colonial governments were encouraged to use their powers to invest up to a third of Savings Bank Funds in local securities, and financially secure territories were permitted to invest up to half, and, in some cases, two thirds of these Funds in such investments.[111] Currency Commissioners, meanwhile, who had always been required to maintain sterling investments equal to 110 per cent of the currency in circulation, were allowed to keep up to 20 per cent of their Fund holdings in local securities.[112] To encourage the use of the Funds, those colonies that purchased local stock, for example Kenya, were given access to the London market and UK aid, and those that refused, such as the Gold Coast, were prevented from issuing loans and received little or no aid.[113]

In fact, relatively few colonies actually took advantage of the relaxation of Fund regulations, partly because of the Colonial Office's unenthusiasm for the new policy.[114] Territories that did respond include Jamaica, Kenya, Nigeria, Sierra Leone and Uganda.[115] Governments feared that the purchase of local securities for Savings Bank Funds would reduce public confidence in and use of the banks. The widespread withdrawal of Savings Bank deposits was most likely to occur when the local securities market was depressed, and a government would therefore have difficulty realizing these investments or would have to sell them at a loss.[116] Likewise, the argument that at least 40 per cent of Currency Funds would never be needed to be redeemed, however bad the currency crisis, was met with suspicion by many Currency Commissioners.[117] There was also a fear that a lowering of sterling coverage would weaken public confidence in their currencies, reducing foreign private sector investment, demand for London loans and access to foreign aid, and that coverage reductions would set a bad example to those politicians that attained government on independence, who would be encouraged to use the Funds to finance budget deficits.[118] In addition, there was a reluctance to sell colonial securities at the heavy discounts then prevailing, and a general belief that the use of investment Funds for development purposes would

110 OV 44/74, no. 63a, memo, 20 June 1956.

111 T 233/934, draft report ..., p. 10; T 233/1425, memo, 21 April 1958.

112 T 236/4253, memo, Dunn, 6 Jan. 1955. The East African Currency Board was allowed to devote 30 per cent of its Fund to local securities (T 233/1425, memo, 21 April 1958).

113 Krozewski, 'Finance', pp. 63, 65; Krozewski, *Money*, p. 115.

114 Krozewski, *Money*, p. 122.

115 S 2, A345; *ibid.*, A364; Havinden and Meredith, *Colonialism*, p. 264.

116 CAOG 9/351, Colonial ..., p. 17.

117 T 233/934, draft report ..., p. 13.

118 *Ibid.*, draft report ..., p. 13; CAOG 9/149, Conference on the technique of development finance, 10th meeting, 14 June 1951.

give the UK government an excuse to reduce government aid, and scupper the issue of loans in London.[119] The Agents would be unable to purchase stock 'firm' at the time of issue, increasing the likelihood that loans would fail, and the sale of the securities would mop up money in the market that would otherwise be used to purchase colonial loans, and, in the case of the disposal of colonial securities, would cause colonial stock prices to fall, again making it more difficult to make fresh issues.[120]

Local bank advances and the use of Surplus Funds

Borrowing from local banks took the form of overdrafts or short-term advances and involved relatively small sums of money. Generally, the Agents advised against such loans because of the high rates of interest charged and suggested that colonies instead should borrow the sums needed from the JCF or inter-colonial loan scheme.[121] Exceptions to this policy occurred in the 1920s and in the 1950s. In the 1920s, poor relations between the Crown Agent Sir Percy Ezechiel and the Permanent Under Secretary Sir George Grindle resulted in the Colonial Office failing to inform the Agency of a number of loans.[122] In 1925, the Agents were told nothing about an advance from the Hong Kong Bank to the Hong Kong government, and, in 1928, were unaware of a £200,000 loan from the local branch of the Ottoman Bank to the Cyprus Agricultural Bank.[123] After protests from the Agents and the retirement of Ezechiel and Grindle, relations improved, and, from the early 1930s, the CAs were involved in all decisions to use local banks. In the 1950s, there was a growing tendency for colonies to insist that advances be obtained locally. Banks began to offer better terms, there was no remittance cost for transferring the funds to the colony, the interest paid was subject to local income tax, and, with the approach of independence, governments wished to form closer relationships with their local financial institutions.[124] In response, the CAs reduced the interest charged on JCF advances, but accepted that when the rate offered by banks was below that of the JCF, after taking into account local income tax and remittance costs, colonial governments should obtain funds locally, particularly when the money was to be spent within the colony.[125]

In the inter-war period, a few colonies, such as Hong Kong and the Seychelles, financed public works entirely from Surplus Funds, which contained excess revenues, and a larger number obtained small temporary advances from the Funds to finance capital expenditure until a loan could be issued on the London market. The advances were borrowed at bank rate and repaid from the loan proceeds. In the decade after the war, the use of Surplus Funds as a source of development

119 OV 44/74, no. 63a, memo, 20 June 1956.

120 Schenk, *Britain*, p. 41; OV 44/72, No. 25a, memo, 5 May 1952; T 233/1425, O'Brien, 20 Feb. 1958. 13 per cent of the Currency Funds held by the Agents were invested in colonial sock and 6 per cent of the Funds held by Currency Boards (T 233/934, draft report ..., p. 13).

121 For example, WN 13, A544801; *ibid.*, A739801/1, CO to CAs, 1 March 1949; S 7, A2079.

122 S 1, A233.

123 *Ibid.*, A233; *ibid.*, A2672.

124 CAOG 9/227, Jamaica to CO, 27 Jan. 1954.

125 *Ibid.*, CAs to CO, 3 May 1954.

finance increased.[126] Having spent little on public works during the war years, colonies in 1946 had £30.5m in these Funds, which grew rapidly due to the rise in commodity prices and increased local taxation, largely higher indirect taxes on imports, and, to a lesser extent, on exports.[127] There was also a belief within the Treasury that, where possible, colonies should finance development with local resources. In the event, from 1946 to 1964 colonial development plans proposed that £717.4m of the cost of development should come from local resources, a figure that included locally issued loans. The use of Surplus Funds, however, declined from the mid-1950s, when commodity price falls slowed revenue growth, and only the richer territories, such as the Gold Coast and Northern Rhodesia, were able to finance projects wholly from this source.[128]

UK Government aid to colonies and independent territories

The Agents had no involvement in the provision of aid. Nevertheless, it is important for comparison purposes to summarise the assistance given. Aid can be split into UK government help to colonies and to independent territories and foreign aid. UK government aid to the colonies largely comprised grants-in-aid and loans-in-aid, development and welfare grants and loans, and Exchequer loans.[129] The Treasury also lent sums, £92m by 1962, to the Colonial Development Corporation, and, as already discussed, during the early 1920s, the government guaranteed a number of loans issued on the London market. Colonial grants-in-aid and loans-in-aid were given to colonies whose budgets could not cover their administration costs or had suffered a natural disaster or civil emergency and needed funds for relief and reconstruction.[130] The money had to be approved by Parliamentary vote, and, from 1920 to 1965, the aid provided amounted to £315.4m (Figure 2.2). A similar amount, £312.7m, was given to the colonial governments in development and welfare loans and grants. These first became available in 1929 when the Colonial Development Act established the Colonial Development Fund, from which up to £1m could be advanced to colonies in any one year in the form of grants, loans and the payment of interest on loans raised elsewhere. The distribution of funds was managed by a Colonial Development Advisory Committee, which considered schemes put forward by colonial governments that would help the development of agriculture and industry in their own countries, but would additionally help the British economy and contribute to a

126 Constantine, *The Making*, p. 294; CA (m) 25, p. 9.

127 Havinden and Meredith, *Colonialism*, p. 259. Direct taxes were often inappropriate, as individual incomes were low, a large and expensive collection system would have to be established because of the scattered populations, and it was believed that they would discourage private enterprise and lead to higher wages, stoking inflation (CAOG 9/351, colonial …, pp. 9–10)

128 Havinden and Meredith, *Colonialism*, p. 259; Overseas Development Institute (ODI), *British Aid. Volume 5: Colonial Development*, London 1964, p. 58.

129 The grants-in-aid and loans-in-aid figure is taken from the colonial services section, and, where appropriate, the commonwealth services section of the Civil Appropriation Accounts. See also Constantine, *The Making*, p. 268.

130 ODI, *British Aid. Volume 2: Government Finance*, London 1964, p. 15.

Figure 2.2. UK government aid, 1919/20 to 1964/5

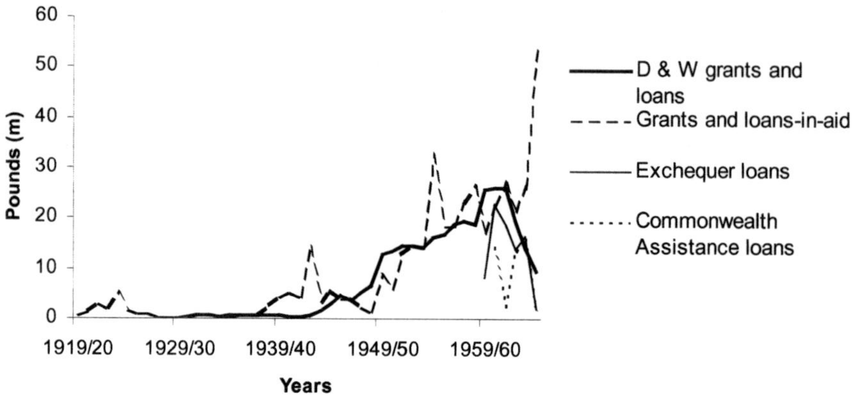

Source. Civil Appropriation Accounts, 1920–65 (see bibliography); Wicker, 'Colonial development', p. 176; Overseas Development Institute, British Aid. Volume 2, pp. 138–9; PP 1970–71, 8, Colonial Development and Welfare Acts, 1929–70, p. 50, table 4; PP 1970–71, 8, Colonial Development and Welfare Acts. Final Return, p. 22.

Note. ECGD Figures are for calendar years.

reduction in UK unemployment.[131] Drawbacks of the Act were that the amount of money available was determined by Parliament and therefore tended to fall in years of poor trade when colonial needs for funds were at their greatest, the money furnished often failed to cover the full cost of projects, and the schemes financed did not significantly reduce UK unemployment.[132] By 1940, Parliament had permitted just £8.8m of expenditure, half in the form of grants, of which £6.5m was actually spent.[133] Since colonial governments lacked the expertise to develop suitable schemes, only 617 projects were supported, each on average obtaining a meagre 46 per cent of their finance from the development Fund.[134]

A new Development and Welfare Act was passed in 1940 and increased the assistance available to £5.5m per year for the following ten years for 'any purpose likely to promote the development of the resources of any colony or the welfare of its people'.[135] Although the aid was no longer partly intended to help the UK economy, its provision was far from altruistic. The British government wished to halt growing criticism of its administration of the Empire at home, abroad and in the colonies and thus legitimize the perpetuation of colonial rule, and it was believed that the promise of future help would improve colonial morale and make it easier to extract those resources needed for the war effort.[136] In fact few schemes were financed by the Act owing to shortages of personnel and supplies, Treasury reluctance to provide funds, and difficulties in formulating development

131 PP 1970–71, 8, p. 6.
132 Constantine, *The Making*, p. 220.
133 PP 1970–71, 8, p. 6.
134 Butler, *Britain*, p. 21; Havinden and Meredith, *Colonialism*, p. 160.
135 PP 1970–71, 8, p. 7.
136 Constantine, *The Making*, p. 259; Butler, *Britain*, p. 51.

plans.[137] Indeed, such was the failure of the legislation that the government was forced to pass another Act in 1945, which made £120m available for the period 1946 to 1956 and required colonial governments to submit ten year development plans. Material shortages and planning problems, again, slowed the progress of projects, but more money flowed to the colonies. In 1955 and 1959, further sums were allocated for development, and, in 1955, assistance was directed to those colonies that were least able to find funds from other sources.[138]

Exchequer loans were first issued in 1959, and, from that year to 1965, £82m was lent. The loans carried interest equal to the current cost of government borrowing, plus an additional 1/4 per cent, had lives of up to 30 years, and were provided only to colonies and colonial public bodies that were unable to raise funds on the London market and for projects approved by the Secretary of State and able to generate sufficient revenue to meet the interest due.[139] Although recipients did not have to use the funds received to purchase British goods, it was anticipated that the loans would 'have a valuable effect on the orders coming forward for UK industry'.[140] Needless to say, their introduction was opposed by the Treasury, which refused to accept that an additional source of finance was required and feared that they would strain UK government resources and that their administration would damage relations with newly independent governments.[141]

The two colonial public corporations, established in 1948, were quangos. The Overseas Food Corporation rapidly disappeared after its scheme to grow groundnuts in Tanganyika collapsed with the loss of £40m of government funds.[142] The Colonial Development Corporation (CDC), renamed the Commonwealth Development Corporation in 1963 when it was allowed to operate in newly independent territories, was far more successful, and, from 1949 to 1965, invested £132.7m in the colonies (Figure 2.1). Financed by the UK government, private sector funds and its own revenues, it invested in schemes that would have been operated by the private sector but for their low profitability. It ran or owned its own projects, invested in enterprises in partnership with private or government concerns or both, and made loans to governments and public bodies.[143] If a 1958 Treasury proposal had been accepted, it would also have taken over the public issue of colonial loans from the Crown Agents. After consideration, the plan was abandoned, as, although it was believed that CDC flotations would increase the demand for stock, the Corporation lacked the necessary finance house experience

137 E. R. Wicker, 'Colonial development and welfare, 1929–57. The evolution of a policy', *Social and Economic Studies*, 7 (4) (1958), p. 190; Butler, *Britain*, p. 35.

138 Havinden and Meredith, *Colonialism*, p. 253; Butler, *Britain*, pp. 83, 108; OV 44/73, no. 72, finance of the colonies, approx. July 1954.

139 Morgan, *A Reassessment*, pp. 194, 202–3.

140 PP 1958/9, 10, p. 9.

141 T 233/1425, memo, 21 April 1958; J. M. Lee, *Colonial Development and Good Government*, Oxford 1967, p. 124.

142 Butler, *Britain*, p. 83.

143 ODI, *British Aid. Volume 2*, p. 40.

and expertise, its issue costs would be relatively high, and the UK government would have less control over which colonies entered the London market.[144]

UK government aid to independent territories primarily consisted of Commonwealth grants-in-aid and loans-in-aid and Commonwealth Assistance Loans. In addition, ex-colonies obtained technical assistance, that is expert advise, equipment and training of personnel, under various regional development programmes, such as the Colombo Plan and CENTO, and, to enable them to retain the services of expatriate experts until their own staff could take over, the British government, via the Overseas Service Aid Scheme, contributed about half the cost of employing expatriate officers.[145] Like their colonial counterparts, Commonwealth grants-in-aid and loans-in-aid were issued annually after approval by Parliament and helped to cover administration costs and provided badly needed finance during emergencies. On independence, Britain also gave all new governments a grant equivalent to the balance of any development and welfare aid that had been allocated but not spent, and usually agreed to provide mutually acceptable sums for use in developing the new country.[146] In total, from 1949 to 1965, £101.5m of grants and loans were distributed.

Commonwealth Assistance Loans were issued by the Export Credits Guarantee Department of the Board of Trade, which, in 1949, was permitted to make such advances to any overseas government in need of economic assistance. The first loan to an ex-colony was made in 1963, and, by March 1964, ten newly independent territories had received 13 advances worth £51.6m. The loans had to be used to purchase British goods, carried an interest rate equal to the government's borrowing rate plus ¼ per cent, were generally for periods of 15 years or more, and were normally repaid in equal half yearly instalments spread between the end of a grace period, during which no repayments had to be made, and the date of final maturity.[147]

Loans and grants from international organizations and foreign governments amounted to over $100m by 1964.[148] A large proportion of the money came from the International Bank of Reconstruction and Development, later renamed the World Bank, which was established in 1944 to supply funds to the less developed World and those countries whose industries had been devastated by the war. Colonies were permitted to obtain loans from 1949, but initially none put in applications.[149] The rates of interest, along with the Bank's 1 per cent commission, made the advances more expensive than those raised on the London market, and, in the first few years of existence, loan proceeds had to be used to purchase goods manufactured in the USA, which were subject to long delays, and, thereafter, could not be used to purchase supplies valued in the local currency of the loan holder or sterling.[150] Over time, however, as the margin between World Bank loans and those raised in London narrowed and restrictions

144 T 233/1425, memo, 21 April 1958.
145 ODI, *British Aid. Volume 2*, p. 79.
146 *Ibid*, pp. 58, 65.
147 *Ibid.*, pp. 48, 73, 75–6.
148 L 13, minutes, SEVL to Morris, Sept. 1964.
149 Lee, *Colonial*, p. 124.
150 CAOG 9/351, Colonial ..., pp 21, 22; Morgan, *Developing*, p. 97.

on the use of proceeds were lifted, more colonies and newly independent territories approached the Bank and succeeded in winning funds. By late 1964, loans totalling $65.5m had been obtained by the East African railway, the Malayan and Mauritian Electricity Boards, the Nigerian Ports Authority and the Nigerian railway.[151] Other sources of international aid were the USA's International Co-operation Administration, superseded in 1961 by the Agency for International Development, the aid organizations of various commonwealth countries, the United Nations, and, from the late 1960s, various development banks.[152]

Extent and direction of finance

Throughout the period, the Bank of England feared that the finance of colonial development by the Agents, the UK government, and corporate investors diverted funds away from Britain and that the stimulation of colonial growth was at the expense of the expansion of the UK economy.[153] In reality, a relatively small proportion of the funds that flowed to the colonies through the Crown Agents came from UK investors (Table 2.1). From 1920 to 1965, the public issue of colonial loans, the sale of stock to the market and conversions raised £328.3m. But, of this amount, £85.7m or 26 per cent came from colonial investment Funds, and, during the lives of loans, the Agents bought more stock for the colonies, until, in some cases, they held as much as 80 per cent by the time a loan came to the end of its life. As the size of the colonies' investment Funds expanded, the proportion of the total amount of stock issued held by them grew. In 1924, 21 per cent of all the stock floated was in the hands of the colonies, and, by 1962, this figure had risen to 60 per cent (Figure 1.3). On top of this, 3.7 per cent of the stock held by private investors was in the hands of people resident in the colonies or colonial financial institutions. Consequently, by the end of the colonial era, only 36.3 per cent of market debt accumulated during the previous forty or fifty years was held by Britain.

Moreover, even the finance that derived from the UK did not constitute a loss. Nine per cent of the stock issued (£21.96m) was converted from older higher interest securities and therefore involved no new expenditure, and the outflow of funds was matched by inflows in the form of interest and the repayment of old colonial loans. Investors recouped over half (54.1 per cent) of their investments in the form of interest payments, which from 1926 to 1962 totaled £188m. Unfortunately, no record of redemptions survives. However, 33 loans floated prior to 1914 worth £25.4m and 32 issued from 1914 to 1934 worth £60.5m had final redemption dates of between 1914 and 1960 and another three worth £8.75m floated prior to 1914 and 31 worth £35.58m issued from 1914 to 1939 could be

151 L 13, minutes, SEVL to Morris, Sept. 1964.

152 *Ibid.*; Miller, *Survey*, p. 305; L 38, 1975, no. 48. The development banks included the African Development Bank, established in 1967, which, by May 1975, had lent $220m to 33 African states; the Asian Development Bank, set up in 1968, which had $1,925 dollars of loans outstanding in May 1975; and the Caribbean Development Bank, formed in 1969, which had committed $44m dollars to projects by 1973 (L 38, 1975, no. 48).

153 Butler, *Britain*, p. 108.

Table 2.1 Finance of development, 1920–65 (£m)

	Amount	Colonial finance	Publicly issued stock reserved for colonial investors
Non-aid finance			
Raised by CAs			
Public issues	248.5	42.1	9.6
Stock sold to the market	36.1	21.9	
Stock sold to colonial funds	11.0	11.0	
Conversions	32.6	10.6	
Inter-colonial loans	24.6	24.6	
JCF and JMF advances	729.5	729.5	
TOTAL	1082.4	839.9	
Other			
Guaranteed loans	45.6		
Local resources (including local loans)	717.4	717.4	
CDC (excluding UK government loans)	40.7		
UK Government aid			
D & W grants and loans	312.7		
Grants and loans-in-aid	417		
Exchequer loans	82		
Treasury loans to CDC	92		
Government funds lost on collapse of Overseas Food Corporation	40		
ECGD loans	51.6		
TOTAL	995.2		
International aid	100 ($)		

Source. See Figures 1.1, 2.1, 2.2 and 2.3; PP 1954/5, 4; PP 1956/7, 10; PP 1961/2, 11; Overseas Development Institute, British Aid. Volume 5, p. 47; Butler, Britain, p. 83; L 13, minutes, SEVL to Morris, Sept. 1964.

redeemed between these dates at the option of the Agents.[154] Therefore, from 1914 to 1960, taking into account conversions, between £63.9m and £108.22m was returned to investors in the form of loan repayments.

In addition to the sums raised via the London market, the colonies received money from the inter-colonial loan scheme, the JCF and the JMF. All of this money came from the colonies themselves. The IC scheme raised £24.6m, and, if the annual totals are summed, the JCF and JMF gave advances worth £211.9m. Because of the lack of information, however, the latter figure is an underestimate. As already discussed, it does not include JCF and JMF overdrafts, the advances made to the colonies before 1929 and the formation of the JCF, and

154 Pre-1914 figures from Sunderland, *Managing*, appendix 1, table 2.

assumes that JCF and JMF advances were long term, when, in fact, they were for short periods. If these factors are taken into account, the JCF and JMF contributions to the colonies can be estimated at £729.5m. Taking into account market loans, the Agents therefore raised for their clients at least £1082.4m, of which £839.8m or 77 per cent came from the colonies' own resources.

Turning to the other sources of development funds, UK government aid amounted to £995.32m, the colonies contributed £717m from their own resources, international aid totaled $100m, and the UK corporate sector invested an unknown sum, which was probably more than covered by its profits - from 1938 to 1957 companies operating in the colonies produced £1,148m of share dividends and £134m of loan interest.[155] Apart from UK aid, none of these sources were a drain on UK finances, although it could be argued that international aid was effectively financed by Britain; the UK government from 1945/6 to 1962/63 gave £98.9m to the IBRD and its affiliates and £57.7m to the agencies of the United Nations.[156] All in all, therefore and excluding corporate investment and international aid, Britain's contribution to colonial development appears to have been approximately £1,324m, slightly less than the £1,567m which came from the colonies themselves. Although, as discussed in the following chapters, far more than £1,324m came back to Britain in the form of expenditure on UK goods, contractors, consulting engineers and expatriate staff, and colonial administrations invested even greater sums in UK banks and securities.

As regards the geographical distribution of the money raised, the Agents' various financial activities, UK government aid and corporate investment complimented one another. The Agents various ways of financing the colonies ensured that both the very richest and the very poorest obtained funds and allowed the former to subsidize the latter (Appendix 2). Prosperous colonies with a great deal of development potential obtained money through the public issue of loans on the London market; a comparison of public revenues in 1950 and total public issues giving a correlation co-efficient of 0.62.[157] Amongst these territories there was a pecking order that was clearly reflected in the price of the loans floated. The most prosperous colonies could issue at relatively high prices, whilst the less prosperous had to offer stock on more generous terms. The sale of stock to the market, similarly, benefited the richer territories, though second league colonies that had difficulty making public issues also gained from this method of obtaining finance; 14 per cent of the countries that sold stock having never publicly issued. These second leaguers largely obtained their funds from the inter-colonial loan scheme, with ten of the 25 countries (40 per cent) that acquired these loans having neither publicly issued nor sold stock on the market. The Agents' reluctance to accept into Sinking Funds the stock of those that had little chance of meeting the interest payments or repayments, however, excluded the very poorest colonies from the scheme. These territories, which required little

155 B of E, *Overseas.*

156 ODI, *British Aid. Volume 2*, p. 83.

157 The Pearson Product Moment Correlation measures the strength of the association between two variables. The higher the co-efficient up to 1 the stronger the correlation.

finance, obtained funds in the form of advances and overdrafts from the JCF and JMF.[158]

The subsidization of poor colonies by their richer compatriots occurred in a number of ways. The prosperous colonies, via their Sinking Funds financed the inter-colonial loan scheme, and the monies they held in the JCF and JMF, including unspent loan proceeds, allowed the CAs to provide advances from these Funds.[159] Their large revenues and ability to float local loans also enabled them to finance development from local resources and thus allowed others to venture into the London market, their high credit rating increased the creditworthiness of all colonies, and their large investment Funds permitted the Agents to purchase stock, which allowed high loan prices to be set. Development in these colonies, therefore, effectively helped to finance development elsewhere.

The Agents' activities, in turn, were complemented by corporate investment and UK government aid (Appendix 3). Prosperous colonies with development potential were the main recipients of corporate investment, and, when they were unable to issue on the market in the early 1960s, they had a good chance of obtaining an Exchequer loan.[160] Second league colonies, likewise, obtained funds from the Exchequer and also through the Colonial Development and Welfare Scheme, with 35 per cent of recipients of Exchequer loans and 53 per cent of those that benefited from the CD & W acts having never issued on the market. The very poorest colonies, meanwhile, received a large amount of their finance from grants-in-aid and loans-in-aid.[161]

Conclusion

As well as issuing public loans, the Agents raised external funds for their clients in a large number of other ways, seeking to provide the maximum amount of finance at the lowest cost. In order to succeed in this mission, they occasionally acted in a manner that could be interpreted as unethical. For example, they issued inter-colonial loans without first obtaining the permission of the Colonial Office, and, to ensure that MTS received ECGD cover, circumvented that department's rules. They also sometimes took what the Bank of England regarded as excessive risks, and placed the interests of territories in need of money above those of lending colonies. The Bank of England, for instance, believed that the provision of JCF/JMF advances made these Funds dangerously illiquid, and, when providing inter-colonial loans, the Agents from time to time used the Sinking Funds of governments that had not agreed to participate in the programme and set relatively low interest rates.

Unfortunately, their attempts to act in the interests of their clients were

158 As discussed, the IC scheme and the JCF and JMF also helped out the more prosperous colonies whilst they awaited opportunities to issue market loans.

159 Seven colonies with no investment funds received IC loans or had stock issued in London purchased firm by the CAs.

160 65 per cent of territories that received an Exchequer loan had also issued or sold stock on the London market.

161 ODI, *British Aid. Volume 2*, p. 92.

hindered by the Bank of England's and the Treasury's wish that they promote the UK economy. The Bank, for example, blocked the issue of colonial Treasury bills, because it believed they competed with the UK Treasury counterpart; stopped the Agents borrowing from German banks, maintaining that this source of funds should be reserved for the nationalized industries; and turned down proposals that that local loans should be simultaneously issued locally and in London, claiming that dual flotations would reduce the money available in the London market. Treasury officials, meanwhile, were reluctant to permit any alteration in colonial guarantee loans that could damage other government issues, and, to ensure that the market was not deprived funds, from 1940 to 1948 required the Agents to obtain their consent before issuing all inter-colonial loans, and, from 1949, those IC issues in excess of £50,000. Where the UK's interests clashed with their goal of protecting the country's finances, however, Treasury officials would occasionally permit the Agents to put their clients interests above those of the domestic economy. In the mid-1950s, for instance, they strongly opposed a Bank of England proposal that JCF/JMF advances should no longer be issued in anticipation of new issues, arguing that the colonies deprived of these advances would make greater calls on the Imperial Exchequer.

All in all, the Crown Agents, along with UK aid, ensured that the colonies obtained large amounts of finance. Inevitably, the most prosperous colonies, whose existing wealth reflected their economic potential, most benefited from the help given. Comparisons of public revenues in 1950 and total market sales/ issues and aggregate aid give correlation co-efficients of 0.66 and 0.53 respectively. Nonetheless, the poorer territories through the inter-colonial loan scheme, JCF and JMF advances and grants-in-aid and loans-in-aid also received funds, and the Agents' organisation of colonial financial affairs transformed a disparate group of colonies with differing needs and prospects into a single co-operatative entity, the most prosperous members of which partly financed the development of their less wealthy brethren.

The system began to fail in the run up to independence. As discussed in the previous chapter, the Treasury sought to restrict access to the London market and demand for colonial stock gradually fell. The decline in the issue of loans and the fall in the number of Sinking Funds, in turn, reduced the number of inter-colonial loans that could be issued and the tendency for territories to withdraw funds from the JCF and JMF on gaining political freedom forced the Agents to cut the advances from these two Funds. By the mid-1960s, the system had collapsed completely. Although the CAs' clients continued to obtain JCF and JMF advances and credit, the vast majority of their development funds came from aid, and, in the 1970s, from commercial banks. Regrettably, in Africa much of the finance was squandered. Prior to independence, the wastage of development funds was prevented by Colonial Office supervision of expenditure, the fact that much of the money came from the colonies' own resources or from the revenues of other territories, and the understanding that neither the market nor the CAs would be prepared to provide further funds if loans, IC or JCF/JMF advances were misspent. The adequate operation of capital schemes, meanwhile, was assured by the need to pay competitive interest rates on loans and the knowledge that default would halt future inflows of funds.

In the post-colonial World, all of these controls disappeared. Wishing to demonstrate progress, reward supporters, and employ growing populations, new governments often used aid and later bank loans to finance a massive increase in expenditure on welfare services, education, military forces, prestigious buildings, and capital projects. The latter, however, were often ill conceived, based on widely over-optimistic projections, and poorly operated, as the relatively low interest rates demanded by aid organizations and banks placed little pressure on governments to run them effectively. Rather than increasing productive capacity and providing funds for subsequent development expenditure, such projects therefore generated no or few profits and merely stoked inflation.[162]

162 D. K. Fieldhouse, *Black Africa 1945–1980. Economic Decolonisation and Arrested Development*, London 1986, pp. 238, 243; D. K. Fieldhouse, *The West and the Third World. Trade, Colonialism, Dependence and Development*, Oxford 1999, p. 23.

3

The Management of Colonial Investment Funds

During the period under review, the number and size of colonial Investment Funds managed by the Agents grew dramatically. In 1930, they supervised 320 worth £115m, in 1962 over 1,000, which contained cash and securities valued at £908m, and, in 1974, 700, belonging to 100 clients, that held £856m (Figure 3.1 and Appendix 4).[1] The largest Funds were those owned by colonial Currency Commissioners, which, in 1939, contained slightly over a quarter, and, in 1958, around one third of the investments held by all capital reserves.[2] Each Currency Fund contained sterling securities equal to 110 per cent of the value of the currency in circulation in the holding colony, and allowed residents to redeem notes and coins for sterling at any time. Like the amount of money in the economy, the size of the Funds changed over time, increasing when the volume of currency rose and declining when it fell.[3]

The next largest capital reserves were Sinking Funds and Surplus Funds, which, in 1939, accounted for 14 per cent and 18 per cent of investments respectively.[4] The former, discussed in detail in chapter one, held securities that would eventually be used to repay the associated loan; whilst the latter contained revenue surpluses not immediately required by colonies, which were used to finance development and incidental expenditure and provided security for advances from the JCF, the JMF and local banks.[5] Other sizable Funds were those set up by Savings Banks and those created as revenue reserves. Saving Bank Funds contained investments equal in value to the sums lent by the banks for which they were established. Reserve Funds, meanwhile, were instituted in times of prosperity and generally contained the equivalent of four to six months of the holding government's annual revenue. Their contents were sold and the proceeds used only when the terms of trade turned against the colony, causing its export returns and tax receipts to fall, and when the deficit could not be plugged with a bank loan or the issue of treasury bills.[6]

The chapter investigates how the Agents managed all these and other smaller

1 L 38, 1975, no. 44.

2 CO 323/1623/19, CAs to CO, 26 Oct. 1939; T 233/1425, memo, 5 May 1958. The Currency Funds established for West and East Africa and Palestine were supervised by Boards, on which the CAs were represented.

3 CO 537/7673, memo, 'Colonial sterling balances', approx. 1952.

4 CO 323/1623/19, CAs to CO, 26 Oct. 1939.

5 CAOG 9/201, memo, Ezechiel, 15 June 1922; CO 323/1623/19, CAs to CO, 26 Oct. 1939.

6 T 236/3562, working party report, 4 Sept. 1953; CO 537/7673, memo, Aug. 1952.

Figure. 3.1 Value of Colonial Investment Funds and JCF/JMF at year ends, 1920–74

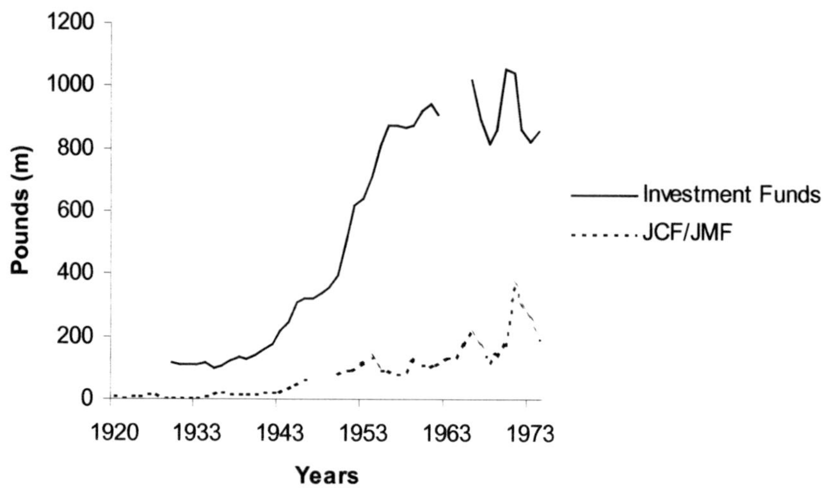

Source. JCF: CAOG 1/1; CAOG 9/228; JMF: CAOG 1/2; Floating balances: CAOG 9/234, memo, March 1924; CAOG 9/234, note, 8 March 1928; Funds: T 233/959; OV 44/72–OV 44/77; L 1–11; L 188, file 1, memo, no date.

Notes. JCF/JMF prior to 1929 represent floating balances. 1925–27 floating balance figures and 1963–5 Investment Fund figures are missing. JCF/JMF 1970–73 are maximum holdings for each year.

capital reserves.[7] Sections one and two consider how the monies remitted by the colonies were invested, the peculiarities involved in the supervision of Sinking Funds and Currency Funds and the trading of securities, both in the market and between Funds. There is then an examination of the reasons behind the expansion of Funds during and after the Second World War and of the various proposals put forward for reducing their size. The chapter ends with an investigation of why some colonies abandoned the Agency on independence and how the CAs retained clients through the provision of better relations and the diversification of investments into UK and overseas equities and property.

Investment of Funds

General investment rules

The contents of Funds were invested in London, largely because the colonies lacked well developed capital markets of their own, the City could provide

7 Other capital reserves included Development Funds, which financed development projects; Pension Funds; Endowment Funds that provided the income necessary to support the operation of a particular institution, such as a school or a hospital; and Investment Reserve Funds, which covered losses that resulted from the depreciation of security prices (S 3, A735; CAOG 9/202, CO circular, 22 Nov. 1919).

relatively high returns, and, as discussed below, their presence helped the UK economy.[8] In order to meet urgent demands for money, which, for example, could arise from a run on a bank or on a currency, on average 7 per cent of the total invested was kept liquid, that is placed in investments from which it could be retrieved rapidly and with little loss of capital. Liquid investments comprised UK Treasury bills, which could be sold at any time, though at a slight discount to the purchase price, and bank accounts, either current accounts, from which cash could be withdrawn immediately, or deposit accounts, where money was placed for a fixed period of up to a year (Figure 3.2). The amount of a Fund that was kept liquid largely depended on its purpose. Currency and Savings Bank Funds, the contents of which could be required at short notice, maintained a high rate of liquidity, whereas Sinking Funds, which were only sold at the end of the associated loan's life, had only a relatively small amount of monies placed in banks and Treasury bills.

The non-liquid contents of Funds were used to purchase long-term securities. When buying stocks, the Agents took account of their maturities (the length of time they had to be held before the money used to purchase them was repaid or redeemed) and the requirements of the various Trustee Acts. The maturity of the investments bought again depended on the Fund for which they were purchased. In the case of capital reserves that were to be realized by a fixed date, such as Sinking Funds, the Agents acquired securities that would be redeemable slightly before or up to two years after that date. So, for example, for a Sinking Fund for a colonial loan that was to be repaid ten years hence, investments with maturities of either nine years or eleven to twelve years would be acquired. The advantage of buying securities that matured slightly before the contents of the Fund needed to be realised was that the colony avoided the cost of selling the investment, obtained the par price (£100 per stock) rather than a possible depreciated price, and evaded the drop in value that sometimes occurred if a Fund was selling large amounts of a particular stock for which there was little demand. Drawbacks were that the proceeds of sales had to be placed on deposit at a bank or invested in short-term securities until needed, both of which paid relatively low interest rates, and the colony missed the price appreciation of securities that occurred towards the end of their maturities. By buying stock that matured slightly after a Fund's realization date, the CAs captured for the colony this price rise, which was caused by the increased attractiveness of such stock to City institutions that wished to invest money for a relatively short time period. On the other hand, the colony had to absorb the cost of selling the investment and ran the risk of a small price fall if large amounts had to be disposed of or market conditions were poor at the time of sale.[9]

In the case of Funds that had no date for realization and could be called upon to provide money at any time, such as Savings Bank Funds, the Agents bought investments that matured at set intervals. So, for instance, for a Currency Fund, whose investments would have to be sold if there was a run on the currency it

8 T 233/1425, memo, Armstrong, 26 Feb. 1958.

9 L 266, memo, 16 July 1921; *ibid.*, CAs to Scrimgeours, 24 May 1951; CAOG 9/186, CAs to CO, 9 Aug. 1927.

Figure 3.2. Distribution of Colonial Investment Fund and JCF/JMF investments, 1930–62 (percentage of total)

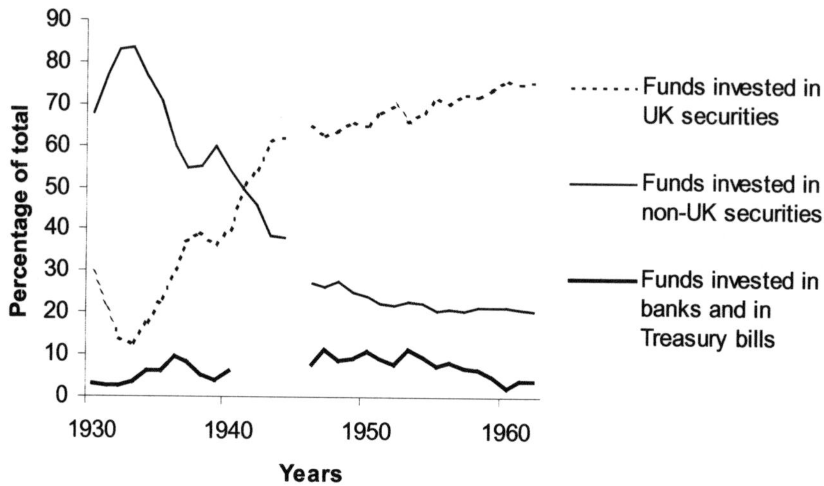

Source. T 233/959; OV 44/72–OV 44/77.

backed, stock would be bought that matured in 1 year hence, 2 years hence, 3 years hence and so on. If the Fund had to meet cash demands when security prices were depressed, therefore, it would contain at least some stock about to be redeemed at the par price and some securities close to the end of their lives, which could be sold at an appreciated price.[10]

Since the Funds were essentially trusts, the Agents were required by the Secretary of State to abide by the various Trustee Acts. They could thus only buy securities listed in this legislation as appropriate for purchase by trustees and were restricted as regards the price they could pay for these investments. The securities that could be purchased by Funds comprised colonial and dominion government loan stock, securities issued or guaranteed by the UK government, and Local Authority stock.[11] As can be seen in Table 3.1, the distribution of investments over these categories varied both between Funds and over time. British government securities generally had shorter maturities than colonial and dominion stock, and, owing to the amounts issued, were more marketable. Large amounts of such stock were therefore bought for those Funds that could need to be liquidated relatively rapidly, and, to ensure that such purchases always occurred, the Agents in 1935 ruled that UK government securities should make up at least 15 per cent of the holdings of Surplus, Currency and Savings Bank Funds, and up to 10 per cent of the contents of Reserve and Opium Funds.[12]

From 1930 to 1962, on average, just over half of the contents of Investment Funds, the JCF and the JMF, was placed in UK investments, largely UK govern-

[10] L 266, memo, 16 July 1921; CA (m) 25, p. 4.
[11] CAOG 9/197, memo, 14 Jan. 1937.
[12] CAOG 9/232, memo, 15 April 1935.

ment securities, and, to a much lesser extent, Local Authority stock, and 41 per cent was invested in colonial and dominion securities (Figure 3.2).[13] Colonial stock mostly comprised the loans floated by the colonies in the London market, inter-colonial issues and stock floated in the colonies themselves, and dominion securities were the London issues of Australia, Canada, India, New Zealand, and South Africa.[14] Over time, the percentage of Funds held in colonial stock fell, from 49 per cent in 1935 to 16 per cent in 1958, whereas holdings of UK government securities rose – from 11 per cent in 1935 to 74 per cent in 1962 (Table 3.1).

In the 1920s, the Agents gave preference to colonial government loan stock, which they bought 'firm' at the time of issue, immediately after flotation, and at other times. As discussed in chapters one and two, the purchases increased the demand for colonial loans and allowed them to be issued at a relatively high price, and encouraged the underwriting of flotations. In addition, the stock had relatively high interest rates, and, until 1931 and unlike most UK government securities, the dividends were not taxed.[15] In 1939, Colonial government stock gave an average dividend of 4.32 per cent, whereas dominion securities paid out 4.29 per cent, municipal investments 4.06 per cent, and UK government stock only 3.71 per cent.[16]

The proportion of Funds invested in UK government securities began to increase during the war when the Agents sold large amounts of Fund investments, £3.3m from 1941 to 1943, and reinvested the proceeds in government stock, and placed most of the money remitted for investment in Funds in these securities. By 1945, colonial Funds held £72.75m worth of war loans, mainly 3 per cent Savings Bonds and 2.5 per cent National War Bonds.[17] Although the stocks had relatively low interest rates and were inappropriate for many Funds, offering only two maturity dates, they were purchased because the Agents felt that they had 'a patriotic duty' to support the war effort, and because the government had halted the issue of all other stocks.[18] Attempts by the Bank of England in 1941 to force them to use the cash that Funds deposited at banks to buy yet more of the stock, however, were strongly resisted. It was argued that the withdrawal of deposits would reduce the liquidity of Funds; further reduce returns, bank deposits paying a slightly higher interest rate than government securities; and damage their relationships with their banks, which offered them favourable rates.[19] After much negotiation, a compromise was reached and the Agents agreed to invest some of their cash in Ways and Means Advances, which paid an

13 In 1935, 5 per cent of investments were in municipal stock (CAOG 9/232, memo, 22 March 1935).

14 In 1935, of the dominion stock held by the CAs, 31 per cent was issued by New Zealand, 23 per cent by Australia, 19 per cent by South Africa, 16 per cent by India and 9 per cent by Canada (CAOG 9/232, memo, 22 March 1935).

15 CAOG 9/197, CAs to CO, 8 May 1922; S 2, A428.

16 CO 323/1623/19, CAs to CO, 26 Oct. 1939.

17 CAOG 9/207, memo, 28 May 1943.

18 *Ibid.*; CAOG 9/249, memo, 31 Oct. 1930.

19 T 233/959, memo, 21 Oct. 1941; *ibid.*, CAs to B of E, 26 Jan. 1942.

Table 3.1. Distribution of Fund investments, 1935 and 1958 (%)

	Currency and Saving Bank Funds		Sinking Funds		Surplus and Reserve Funds		Other Funds		Totals	
	1935	**1958**	**1935**	**1958**	**1935**	**1958**	**1935**	**1958**	**1935**	**1958**
British government securities	22	75	1.1	39.4	8.7	82.1	5.5	71.6	10.8	74.4
Other UK securities	1.8	3.9	4.3	9.1	9.7	1.9	3.1	1.8	5.5	3.3
Dominion securities	48.5	6.2	21.5	10.4	33.4	4	30	6.9	35	5.7
Colonial securities	27.7	14.9	73.1	41	48.2	11.9	61.5	19.7	49	16.5

Source. 1935: CAOG 9/232, memo, 22 March 1935; 1958: T 233/1425, memo, 10 April 1958; Morgan, *A Reassessment*, p. 176.

interest rate comparable to that offered by banks, but continued to keep the bulk of the money on deposit.[20]

After the war, Fund holdings of colonial stock fell even further. The Agents bought fewer colonial securities, as, from the mid-1950s, the number of loans issued on the London market fell and there was a decline in stock prices. The failure of those issues that did occur left the market awash with stock, and investors began to sell their holdings, fearing that newly independent administrations would default on the payment of dividends and the repayment of loans and would begin to off-load their colonial securities, using the proceeds to finance development or buy non-sterling investments. Great pressure was also placed on the Agents to diversify out of colonial stock and into UK government securities by the Bank of England, which believed such transfers would assist the British economy. The purchase of UK government investments would increase State finances, and, as the securities paid relatively low rates of interest, it would reduce the flow of monies out of the country, benefiting the Balance of Payments and increasing the finance available to industry. As discussed below, the Bank required a large proportion of Currency Funds to be invested in short-term government stock, and regularly alerted the Agents and Treasury of the dire consequences of over-investment in colonial securities. These warnings reached their height in 1958, when the Bank predicted that the imminent sale of stock by Ghana, Kenya, Malaya and Nigeria could trigger the 'complete disintegration' of the colonial securities market, which, in turn, could set in motion a meltdown of the UK's financial system.[21]

The Bank argued that the Agents' long-term purchase of colonial stock had caused its price to become 'wholly artificial', and that the sale of relatively small

20 *Ibid.*, B of E to Bottomley, 16 Jan. 1942; *ibid.*, CAs to B of E, 26 Jan. 1942.

21 T 233/1425, memo, O'Brien, B of E, 20 Feb. 1958.

quantities would elicit a wholesale collapse of prices.[22] If this occurred, colonial credit would crumble, flotations on the London market would cease and development projects would have to be abandoned. The colonial stock held in Funds, meanwhile, would only be able to be sold at 'catastrophically low prices', and, as a result, loans would fail to be repaid and runs on currencies or banks would not be halted.[23] On a wider scale, the collapse in colonial stock prices would elicit falls in the price of other securities, and the 'severe capital losses' suffered by Fund holders would encourage colonies to seek independence and independent countries to transfer their monies out of sterling investments.[24]

To avoid such a catastrophe, the Bank proposed that the CAs halt all purchases of colonial stock and increase their holdings of UK government securities and that a working party be established to further investigate how a sell-off could be avoided.[25] In the event, much to the Bank's embarrassment, the working party concluded that the collapse of colonial stock prices was highly unlikely. It was discovered that only Ghana and Malaya were likely to sell their investments and that neither owned large amounts of colonial securities. Moreover, well aware of the danger of sales, the Agents, over the previous few years, had reduced the amount of colonial stock they purchased, bought such securities only for Funds, such as Sinking Funds and Pension Funds, which were unlikely to be sold, and had 'for some time' been rearranging their investments. Colonial securities held in Savings Bank Funds and Surplus Funds that could be relinquished at any moment had been transferred into Sinking Funds and Pension Funds or quietly sold in the market and replaced by UK government securities.[26] By 1958, therefore, the CAs held only 59 per cent of the colonial stock in the market, the rest being owned by long-term holders, such as insurance companies and private pension funds; these securities accounted for only 17 per cent of the Agency's investment Funds; and only a small proportion of the stock was lodged in what was termed 'vulnerable' Funds.[27]

The price restrictions laid down by the Trustee Acts were that the CAs could only buy the securities listed if the price was less than £115, or, in the case of stocks with maturities of less than 15 years, when it was below £100.[28] Although they were content to comply with the Acts' stock restrictions, the Agents bridled at following the price constraints. In 1922, they asked the Colonial Office for permission to purchase stocks at higher prices than those specified, arguing that there was no legal reason for them to be bound by the legislation.[29] The large demand for money after the war had caused all security prices to rise and had put high interest bearing stock, and particularly that issued by colonial governments, out of their reach. As a result, they had been forced to place some sums in low interest bearing bank deposits and to buy poor quality stocks, which had

22 *Ibid.*
23 *Ibid.*; *ibid.*, memo, Armstrong, Treasury, 26 Feb. 1958.
24 *Ibid.*, memo, Armstrong, Treasury, 26 Feb. 1958.
25 *Ibid.*, memo, O'Brien, B of E, 20 Feb. 1958; ADM 14/50, no. 34, memo, 20 Feb. 1958.
26 T 233/1425, note for working party, 15 April 1958; *ibid.*, memo, 10 April 1958.
27 *Ibid.*, note for working party, 15 April 1958; T 233/1426, draft working party report.
28 CAOG 9/186, CAs to CO, 21 Sept. 1928.
29 CAOG 9/113, CAs investment committee, Jan. 1923.

artificially high prices because of the demand from trusts, paid low returns, were unlikely to appreciate in value, and, in many cases, had maturities that were unsuitable for the Funds for which they were purchased. The CAs' inability to buy stocks above £100/£115, furthermore, had caused them to miss out on a number of bargains, as the slump in demand for such stocks from trusts had depressed their prices below their true value.[30]

Unfortunately, Colonial Office officials were unconvinced that the price rises were anything more than a temporary aberration. To ease the situation, in June 1922 they therefore only allowed the CAs to invest up to £500,000 in higher priced stock. A request by the Agents the following year to spend more on such securities was turned down, but in 1925 they were permitted to invest an additional £500,000, in 1927 a further £500,000, and, in 1928, yet another £500,000.[31] To provide further relief, the Agents also partly circumvented the Colonial Office's instructions by deliberately misinterpreting its authority for them to buy 'self stock' for Sinking Funds 'at a reasonable price'. Although Colonial Office officials undoubtedly intended the price to conform to the Trustee Act restrictions, the 'point was not actually mentioned in the correspondence' and the Agents therefore assumed that they had been allowed to breach the limits for these Funds.[32]

By 1932, it was obvious to all that the high prices were a permanent feature of the market and the Agents, therefore, again requested permission to buy more expensive stocks.[33] The Colonial Office remained wary. There was a fear that they would 'appear to be amending the act on [their] own account', and that giving the Agents greater freedom would somehow result in a repeat of the collapse of the Joint Colonial Fund the previous year, and that, if this occurred, much of the blame would be directed at the Secretary of State.[34] After consultation, however, the Colonial Office eventually gave way, allowing the Agents to breach the Acts' limits, though only if they were satisfied that the prices were 'reasonable' and that the stock was suitable for the Fund for which it was purchased.[35]

Sinking and Currency Funds

The investment rules followed by Sinking Funds and Currency Funds were slightly different from those that applied to other capital reserves. At the start of the period, Sinking Funds could not be invested in the stock of the loan to which they were associated nor in any other securities issued by holding colonies. So, for example, the Sinking Fund set up for the Nigeria 6 per cent loan issued in 1919 could be invested neither in the stock of this issue nor in any other loan floated by the colony. The Colonial Office argued that if a colony became insolvent, the price of its stock would collapse, and that, if a Sinking Fund held such

30 *Ibid.*; CAOG 9/197, memo, 8 March 1922; *ibid.*, CAs to CO, 21 April 1922.

31 CAOG 9/197, CO to CAs, 6 June 1922; *ibid.*, CO to CAs, 26 June 1923; *ibid.*, CO to CAs, 7 Sept. 1925; *ibid.*, CO to CAs, 23 Aug. 1927; *ibid.*, CO to CAs, 8 May 1928.

32 *Ibid.*, memo, 23 Oct. 1930.

33 *Ibid.*, CAs to CO, 24 Oct. 1932.

34 CO 323/1202/11, memo, Vernon, 29 Sept. 1932.

35 CAOG 9/197, CO to CAs, 20 Dec. 1932.

securities, it would be unable to repay its associated loan, which would damage the creditworthiness of both the territory and all the CAs' other clients.[36]

The Agents disagreed, and, in 1919, unsuccessfully, requested that the rule be dropped, and, in 1927, asked permission to acquire for Sinking Funds only the stock of the loans for which the Funds were established. It was pointed out that it was highly unlikely that a colony would become insolvent, given the Colonial Office's close control of colonial finances, or that the Imperial Government, wishing to maintain colonial creditworthiness, would allow a territory to default on its debts. More importantly, the purchase of such stock would relieve the difficulty of finding securities for Sinking Funds that were of the correct maturity and price and would cause the price of the stock to rise, which would benefit the general investor and improve the credit of the colony.[37] The Colonial Office was not wholly convinced, but eventually relented, though it only allowed the self-stock to be bought at 'a reasonable price,' and, despite countless requests, Sinking Funds were never allowed to invest in other loans floated by their holding colonies.[38]

The two investment issues that were most important to Currency Funds were coverage and liquidity. To ensure that colonial residents could always exchange currency for sterling, the Funds were required to maintain sterling investments equal to 110 per cent of the currency in circulation, the additional 10 per cent being needed to cover fluctuations in the value of the assets. At the start of the period, the Bank of England and the Treasury regarded such coverage as essential to the economic well being of colonies, arguing that it ensured confidence in their currencies without which they would have difficulty attracting investment.[39] Any attempt to alter the coverage was therefore strongly resisted. In 1933, the Agents' policy of allowing Funds to hold less than 110 per cent cover when a new currency was introduced and using the profits generated by investments to gradually increase ratios was severely criticized.[40] Likewise, all requests to invest Funds in locally issued stock were turned down for fear that during an economic downturn, when a run on a currency was most likely to occur, the holdings would be unmarketable or saleable only at a heavy discount.[41] In the late 1950s, however, when it became advantageous to the UK economy for coverage to be lessened, both the Treasury and Bank performed a volte face, and, as discussed in chapter two, strongly supported the proposal that colonies should be actively encouraged to keep up to 20 per cent of their Currency Funds in local securities.

Concern was first expressed about the liquidity of Currency Funds in 1938. The Bank of England complained that an excessive proportion of the Funds was invested in long-term securities, which could lead to difficulties in a financial crisis. Demands for the redemption of currency in sterling would be unable to be met from the liquid reserves, forcing the sale of the securities, which could

36 CAOG 9/186, memo, 17 Oct. 1919.

37 *Ibid.*; *ibid.*, CAs to CO, 9 Aug. 1927.

38 *Ibid.*, memo, 16 July 1928; *ibid.*, CO to CAs, 19 June 1929; *ibid.*, memo, 11 Sept. 1930; *ibid.*, CAs to CO, 8 Aug. 1956; L 266, memo, 15 Oct. 1950.

39 CAOG 9/151, CO circular, 10 Sept. 1954.

40 CO 83/201/2, CO currency committee, treatment of revenues of note guarantee funds.

41 CAOG 9/151, CO circular, 10 Sept. 1954.

be problematical, and, if the emergency had an impact on the London Stock Market, could involve significant losses. The Bank, therefore, suggested to the Colonial Office that the Agents replace long-term securities with more short-term stock.[42] After obtaining the CAs' reaction, the Colonial Office replied that such a re-arrangement was not desirable and the Bank decided to take no further action. The Agents' pointed out that a colonial emergency would not necessarily lead to a run on a currency, and that, even if this occurred, their Funds contained sufficient liquid reserves to meet any increase in demand. It was also highly unlikely that a colonial crisis would affect the London market, and, if one did, any resultant depreciation in the price of colonial stocks would be slight. Moreover, there was a shortage of short-term securities and any reorganization of their portfolios would involve the sale of stock at below-cost prices.[43]

The Bank of England launched its next attack in 1943, when it proposed that 10 per cent of the Funds should be held in cash and that the Agents should replace a significant proportion of longer dated stock with securities with shorter maturities.[44] An ulterior motive of this request was probably a wish for the colonies, through their Fund investments, to aid the war effort. An increase in liquidity would reduce the outflow of money from Britain and increase purchases of UK government stock. Officially, however the argument put forward was that, unless there was an immediate rearrangement of investments, many Funds would collapse after the war. There was some evidence that colonial residents were hoarding currency notes and that they would 'dehoard' and demand redemption in sterling at the end of hostilities. If the CAs were unable to meet this surge in demand from their liquid reserves, they would be forced to sell their long-term securities, which would cause 'something of a headache', as there would be little market demand and the price would have significantly depreciated.[45]

The Agents again rejected the proposal. The hoarding/dehoarding theory appeared distinctly weak and colonial stock rather than depreciating after the war was more likely to appreciate, since the Bank rate would be kept relatively low in order to encourage recovery.[46] Even if the Bank was correct, most Funds were sufficiently liquid to meet any demands for redemption, cash could be advanced from the JCF or taken from the money received for investment into other Funds, and, if long-term securities had to be disposed off, they could be easily sold to Sinking Funds.[47] The Bank, however, was unwilling to admit defeat, though, after a meeting between the Agents, the Bank, the Colonial Office and the Treasury, a compromise was reached – the CAs agreed to place 50 per cent of all new money going into the Funds in securities with maturities of one to ten years and to keep the balance in the Joint Colonial Fund. Aware that some Currency Commissioners could object to this misuse of their monies and that, in many cases, they possessed statutory control over the investment of their Funds, the meeting also decided that the agreement should be informal and not commu-

42 CO 852/156/6, Burns to CO, 8 Sept. 1938.
43 *Ibid.*, memo, Clauson.
44 CO 852/360/16, Treasury to CO, 19 Aug. 1942.
45 CAOG 9/150, B of E to CO, 5 Aug. 1942.
46 CO 852/360/16, CAs to CO, 29 Dec. 1942.
47 *Ibid.* CAs to CO, 4 Sept. 1942; CAOG 9/150, meeting, 6 Jan. 1943.

nicated to the colonies.[48] In the event, a number of the more perceptive Commissioners began to notice the Agents' irrational use of their money and complained to the Colonial Office, which sought to assuage their anger by explaining the dangers posed by hoarding. Apart from Cyprus, Malaya, Malta and Trinidad, which successfully insisted that the former investment policy be readopted, most of the complainants accepted the justifications.[49]

At the end of the war, the Agents and those Currency Commissioners in the know awaited the expected run on currencies. When this did not occur, the CAs demanded that the new policy be abandoned and that they be allowed to reduce the liquidity of the Funds. The Bank and Treasury refused to back down. Unable to fall back on the dehoarding argument, they admitted that they opposed lower liquidity ratios because the higher interest earned would increase the outflow of monies from the UK and 'add infinitesimally to the adverse Balance of Payments, which is the constant nightmare of the Treasury'.[50] Furthermore, less liquidity would force the London market and British industry to pay more for the colonies' funds, and, via the sale of government securities, damage UK government finances.

Representing the colonies, the Agents rejected these arguments, but initially received little support from the Colonial Office, which advised them to 'let sleeping dogs lie', contending that a campaign to reduce liquidity would only prompt the Bank to impose stringent investment regulations on the Funds.[51] Gradually, however, Colonial Office officials came round to the Agents' way of thinking. More and more colonies began to complain about the way their Funds were invested, angry that they were forced to borrow money in London at a higher rate than they received on their own investments in the capital, and it became clear that the issue could benefit the independence movement.[52]

In 1948, the Colonial Office finally confronted the Treasury, which was informed that the existing instructions were 'absurd and incomprehensible'. Not only were they inconsistent with the government's development policy, which was to encourage territories to finance schemes using their own resources, but they served no practical purpose, as there was no indication that currencies would contract.[53] Asked to comment, one Bank of England official declared the letter to be 'stupid', 'bordering on the impertinent', and written by a person who saw 'himself as the champion of misdirected colonies rather than as representing one side of Whitehall, which is collectively responsible for HMG's general policy'.[54] Although some at the Bank urged that the Agent's Currency Fund investment role be taken away from them and passed to an advisory committee or investment board, it was eventually decided that some form of compromise should be

48 OV 44/69, no. 23, Bourdillon to Treasury, 30 Sept. 1948.

49 *Ibid.*; CO 852/360/17, CAs to CO, 23 Jan. 1943; *ibid.*, CAs to CO, 31 March 1943; *ibid.*, CAs to CO, Aug. 1943; *ibid.*, CO to Jamaica, 8 May 1943; *ibid.*, CO to Gibralter, 24 June 1943.

50 CAOG 9/150, CO to Caine, 11 March 1948.

51 *Ibid.*, Co to CAs, 19 Feb. 1947; *ibid.*, CO to Fellows, 6 April 1948.

52 For example, CO 852/682/3, Hong Kong to CO, 29 April 1948; *ibid.*, Seychelles to CAs, 22 Dec. 1947; *ibid.*, telegram, Jamaica to CAs, 6 July 1948.

53 CAOG 9/150, Bourdillon to Treasury, 30 Sept. 1948; *ibid.*, CO to Powell, 25 Oct. 1948.

54 OV 44/69, no. 27, 5 Nov. 1948.

sought.[55] A meeting with the Colonial Office, the Agents and the Treasury was therefore arranged, at which it was agreed that action should be taken to reduce the liquidity of Funds only if a colony expressly requested it, and then only after the Colonial Office had attempted to make them see the error of their ways.[56]

Since the Colonial Office had no intention of persuading colonies to maintain the status quo, this represented a victory of sorts, but, for the Agents, did not go far enough.[57] In 1949, therefore, the Colonial Office proposed that the Bank allow 30 to 40 percent of Funds to be placed in investments of over ten years.[58] A year later, it had received no response to the proposal, a silence that the Agents interpreted as approval, arguing that 'the Treasury see nothing to take objection to, but [are] reluctant to commit themselves to agreement in case this should be brought up in evidence at a later date'.[59] Convinced, the Colonial Office permitted the Agency to reduce liquidity, and, thereafter, with the Treasury's unofficial blessing, up to forty per cent of Funds was placed in stock with maturities of over 12 years, of which up to 15 per cent could have lives of over 20 years.[60]

Trading of securities

The Agents' trading activity involved two tasks. They firstly bought new stock for Funds, using the money the colonies remitted to them for this purpose, and sold the securities of Funds that were being realized. So, for example, each year they purchased stock for Pensions Funds using that year's pension contributions, and, when a loan had to be repaid at the end of its life, sold the stock of the associated Sinking Fund. These purchases and sales were made in the market, but ideally between Funds.[61] Occasionally, stock was also sold or bought directly to and from City institutions or to and from the National Debt Commissioners, though the Commissioners convoluted procedures discouraged such trades.[62]

The advantage of transferring securities between Funds was that the expense of market trades was avoided. In return for selling or buying stock on the market, brokers charged a brokerage fee of ¼ per cent of the value of the securities bought or sold, half of which, and, from 1941, a third of which was passed to the Agents in payment for their work on the trades.[63] To ensure that dealers made a profit, securities was also bought or sold at a premium known as 'a jobbers turn'.

55 *Ibid.*, no. 30, memo, 10 Nov. 1948.

56 CO 852/682/3, Bourdillon to Hullond, 14 Feb. 1949.

57 CAOG 9/150, CAs to Young, Treasury (draft), 18 May 1949.

58 *Ibid.*, memo, Hulland, 21 May 1949.

59 CAOG 9/151, CAs to CO, 12 June 1950.

60 L 266, memo, 15 Oct. 1950; T 233/959, memo, Granger-Taylor, 21 April 1951.

61 In 1934, 53 per cent of the £12.6m of new investments bought and 75 per cent of the £7.5m sold by the Agents came from other Funds (CAOG 9/288, memo, 'how the colonies benefited ...').

62 CAOG 9/358, CAs to Kenya, 18 Feb. 1955; CAOG 9/306, weeding note.

63 L 266, CAs to Brunei, 28 Sept. 1950; L 178, memo, Abbot, May 1969. Brokerage rates were reduced if large amounts of stock were bought or sold or the securities only had a short remaining currency (L 266, CAs to Brunei, 28 Sept. 1950).

Stock was sold to dealers at a price slightly lower than that at which they would sell it and bought at a price slightly higher that that at which it had been bought. Trading through Funds thus saved both this premium, plus the broker's share of brokerage.[64] Securities were transferred between the Funds at cost price, and, after 1929, at the market price.[65] If a Fund selling stock did not hold securities suitable for the purchasing Fund, the CAs involved a third Fund that did hold appropriate stock. This Fund would buy the realizing Fund's unsuitable securities and raise the money needed to make these purchases by selling its more appropriate stock to the buying Fund.[66]

The Agents' second trading activity was the switching of investments. This involved selling stocks held in Funds to the market and using the proceeds to buy other stock that had a higher yield or was more suitable for the Fund than the security sold. The increase in yields maximised Fund returns, and the sale of unsuitable stock, bought when more appropriate securities were not available, enabled Funds to better serve their function. Before 1923, the Agents had to obtain the permission of the Colony that owned a security before it could be switched. This reduced the number of exchanges that occurred, as, by the time permission had been obtained, the advantages of the trade had often disappeared, and many colonial administrations were reluctant to allow switches, particularly if the stock was sold at below the original purchase price. Colonial accounts recorded investments at the cost price and the sale of a security at below this level forced the loss to be written off, and, in some cases, required the sanction of the local legislature.[67] The Agents therefore asked the Colonial Office to give them complete discretion to make advantageous trades. After consideration, the Secretary of State in 1923 allowed them to undertake such exchanges for Sinking Funds and later for all Funds, unless a colony specifically ruled them out, and, to facilitate trading, required administrations to provide the Agency with more information about their Funds.[68]

Able to switch at will, the Agents began to regularly examine the contents of Funds, and, along with their brokers, to monitor the market. Switching to increase effective yield was highly complex, but basically took account of two factors - currencies and price. Stock with short remaining maturities were exchanged for those with more years to run, thus increasing the amount of time a given rate of interest would be earned. So, for example, a 3 per cent stock at a price of £80 with 10 years remaining would be traded for a similar stock with 20 years to run and that would pay an additional ten years of interest. Such exchanges would occur even if the security with the longer currency was slightly more expensive than the stock held, as over time the purchasing loss would be offset by the additional interest earned. Exchanges based on currencies also took account of forecasts of future interest rates. If it was believed that rates would rise, long dated stock would be exchanged for a short dated equivalent. For instance, if rates were

64 CAOG 9/288, memo, 'how the colonies benefited ...'.
65 CAOG 9/202, CO circular, 9 Jan. 1929.
66 CAOG 9/288, memo, 'how the colonies benefited ...'.
67 CAOG 9/201, committee report, 29 Jan. 1923.
68 CAOG 9/288, memo, 'how the colonies benefited ...'; CAOG 9/186, CO circular, 9 July 1925.

expected to rise to 4 per cent in two years hence, the Agents would exchange a 3 per cent stock with ten years to run for a 3 per cent security with only two years to run, enabling them to take earlier advantage of the availability of higher interest stock. On the other hand, when interest rates were forecast to fall, the reverse occurred – short dated stock was exchanged for longer dated securities, allowing the Agents to benefit from the existing relatively high interest rates for a longer period.[69]

As regards price, exchanges took place when, all things being equal, the stock to be bought had a lower price than the one being sold, which allowed the Fund to increase its holdings at no extra cost. In 1950, for example, the Agents sold 20,000 units of 3 per cent NZ stock with 10 years to run for £100 per stock and with the proceeds bought 25,000 units of Australian securities with 10 years to run for £80 per stock, thus gaining for the purchasing Fund an additional 5,000 stock.[70] Price switches especially involved the purchase of new issues, the price of which tended to fall immediately after flotation and then slowly recover over time. To benefit from the price falls, the Agents after a new issue, and, in particular, after the flotation of Local Authority stock, the price of which regularly fell to a deep discount, tended to sell existing stock and with the proceeds buy some of the new discounted issues. The amount bought was then either retained or sold after the price had risen, and, if the latter was the case, the proceeds would be used to purchase part of another new issue. A further strategy was the reverse switch, which took advantage of the tendency for stock prices to fall and then to recover when market sentiment changed. If the Agents suspected that the price of a stock was about to fall temporarily, they would sell the stock, use the proceeds to buy a security with the same or lower price and then sell this stock and repurchase the original stock if its price actually fell. Such reverse switches, though risky, could be highly lucrative, with a reverse switch for the Hong Kong Exchange Fund involving UK Government conversion stock in 1937 increasing the Funds' holdings by £20,000.[71]

From 1924 to 1943, an average of £42m stocks were switched per year, equal to 35 per cent of total investments.[72] The number of transfers made was dependent on a range of factors. Until 1932, exchanges were restricted by the Colonial Office's refusal to allow the Agents to buy stocks at prices outside the trustee limit.[73] Trades, similarly, fell when the Agency was issuing a large number of loans or involved in conversions and staff could not be spared to monitor the market, and during the realization of large Sinking Funds when switches were made with the stock being sold.[74] Exchanges were also heavily influenced by changes in the market environment. In the run up to the Second World War, for example, activity fell as there was a shortage of stock, and, to minimize the risk of losses, dealers began to quote bigger turns, which narrowed price anomalies,

69 CAOG 9/196, memo, 27 April 1939.
70 *Ibid.*
71 CAOG 9/ 281, 1937 report.
72 CAOG 9/276–CAOG 9/287.
73 CAOG 9/276, 1932 report.
74 CAOG 9/278, 1934 report; L 36, 1965/6, 19 April 1966.

and were less willing to handle large amounts of stock.[75] During the war years, meanwhile, exchanges ceased completely since there were no new public issues and the Agents lacked the staff to monitor the market, and, as discussed, were encouraged to keep a large proportion of their investment Funds permanently in British government securities.[76]

From the late 1950s, the Agents' switching operations were the subject of much criticism from the Bank of England, which was particularly concerned by the small number of exchanges made for Currency Funds. Bank officials 'had the strong impression that the CAs [did] little if anything in the way of day-to-day scrutiny of the market and consultation with brokers', and, in 1956 and 1958, they considered asking the Colonial Office to transfer the management of Currency Funds to the Bank, and, in 1958, to pass their supervision to an individual or committee.[77] In 1962, the possibility of moving them away from the Agency was again discussed, as was persuading the Colonial Office to force the CAs to segregate them from other Investment Funds and to manage them more intensely, ideally with advice from the Bank or an external broker.[78] If the Colonial Office proved resistant to persuasion, it was suggested that the Bank could perhaps ask the Malaysian Currency Board or the Malaysian Central Bank to put direct pressure on the Agency to improve its performance.[79] Yet more criticism was rained down on Agents in 1969 and 1971, when it was noted that they possessed 'an almost complete lack of initiative in managing portfolios' and that their attempts at supervision were 'grossly inefficient'.[80]

By the late 1960s, the Bank's concern at the inadequacies of their switching operations was shared by the Agents themselves. Lack of staff meant that they actively managed only the 'larger and more important Funds'.[81] Others received a lower standard of supervision than that given by corresponding commercial organizations and failed to receive 'a proper service for the revenue received'.[82] Realising that the only way to retain politically independent clients was to increase Fund returns, the Agents in 1967 extended their portfolio management service to all Funds, and, for this purpose, transferred more staff to the Finance Department and recruited people with financial knowledge from outside the Agency.[83]

Use of Scrimgeours

To the outside world, the Agents bought and sold stock through their broker, J. & A. Scrimgeours Ltd. In reality, from 1929 to 1941, approximately half of their trades were made by the broker Edward Bickerstethe, who worked for London Standard Investment Trust and subsequently for Triton Labouchere &

75 CAOG 9/280, 1936 report; CAOG 9/282, 1938 report.
76 CAOG 9/284, 1940 report; SA, Folders 119/120, memo, 2 July 1941.
77 OV 44/77, no. 1b, memo, no date 1958; OV 44/74, no. 69d, memo, 20 July 1956.
78 OV 44/77, no. 2c, memo, 27 July 1962.
79 *Ibid.*, no. 16, memo, 19 July 1963.
80 HO 268/327, memo, 1 Oct. 1971; HO 268/341, memo, 3 April 1969.
81 L 35, 1967, no. 4.
82 L 36, 24 Jan. 1967 meeting.
83 *Ibid.*, 21 March 1967 meeting; L 35, 1967, no. 18.

Caro.[84] To keep their use of the broker secret, the CAs conducted all transactions through a third party, Martins Bank Ltd. When stock was to be bought, the bank transferred the necessary funds from the Agent's account to the one held by Bickerstethe, and, when securities were sold, the proceeds moved in the opposite direction from Bickerstethe's account to the CAs' account.[85]

This curious arrangement, which, though not illegal, was certainly unethical and would have led to protests from the Stock Exchange and in Parliament if it had been discovered, occurred for a number of reasons.[86] The Agents strongly believed that Bickerstethe provided a better service than Scrimgeours. A comparison of trades through the two brokers had discovered that Bickerstethe could buy and sell stock at more favourable prices. Unlike Scrimgeours, he did not 'let drop a deal, but persist[ed] in refreshing it until successful' and was prepared to 'engage in prolonged haggling'.[87] He also offered suggestions for advantageous purchases and exchanges of stock, of which his rival appeared unaware, and provided clients with a daily intelligence sheet far superior to the one produced by Scrimgeours. The information was recorded in a more convenient form and in greater detail and was more up-to-date, the sheet being updated between 10am and 11am each morning.[88]

Other reasons for the employment of Bickerstethe were that he used his considerable influence in the City to encourage institutions to purchase colonial stock, both during and after issue, and, as will be discussed in the following chapter, during the collapse of the Joint Colonial Fund in 1931 his organisation of bank loans saved the Fund from bankruptcy.[89] The Agents may also have wished to punish Scrimgeours for its refusal, discussed in chapter one, to reduce its over-riding commission when underwriting colonial loans.

The new arrangement, at first, was kept secret from Scrimgeours, but, in 1930, a decision was made to inform the firm, which was asked not to divulge Bickerstethe's trades to its fellow brokers or to dealers. Although 'saddened' by the Agents' actions, it agreed to the request, aware that the knowledge that it was no longer the CAs' sole broker would damage its business.[90] Among the reasons put forward for the secrecy were that, if it was discovered that the Agents were employing two brokers, one of which was relatively low in the City's pecking order, market confidence in them would fall and their ability to issue high priced loans would be jeopardized. They would also be 'bombarded' with applications from other brokers wishing to act for them, the rejection of which would lead to bad feeling; the arrangement could be terminated at any time without the intervention of the Stock Exchange; and it offered them some protection if Bickerstethe went bankrupt – any money held by Martins Bank would be safe from the receivers.[91] A more important explanation for the subterfuge, however,

84 Folder 119/120, memo, 14 Jan. 1938; *ibid.*, memo, 5 Oct. 1934; *ibid.*, memo 14 Jan. 1938.
85 *Ibid.*, memo, 5 Oct. 1934.
86 *Ibid.*, memo, 1 Nov. 1930.
87 *Ibid.*, memo, 14 Jan. 1938.
88 *Ibid.*, memo to Ezechiel, 16 Oct. 1930; *ibid.*, memo, 14 Jan. 1938.
89 *Ibid.*, memo 14 Jan. 1938.
90 *Ibid.*, memo, 8 Jan. 1931; *ibid.*, memo, 1 Nov. 1930.
91 *Ibid.*, memo to Ezechiel, 16 Oct. 1930; *ibid.*, memo, 1 Nov. 1930.

was that the Agents strongly suspected that dealers sold stock to them at a relatively high price and bought their securities at a relatively low price, and, in both cases, pocketed the difference. Secret sales through Bickerstethe thus allowed the Agency to obtain ordinary market prices.[92]

The arrangement with Bickerstethe lasted for ten years, during which time the broker earned £70,860 in brokerage fees.[93] It came to an end, partly because the Agents' Finance Department staff had acquired extensive experience of the market and could identify advantageous deals themselves, and, partly because Bickerstethe became seriously ill and retired from business.[94] Thereafter until the late 1960s, the Agents traded exclusively through Scrimgeours, using their in-house expertise to monitor dealing prices.

Colonial sterling balances

From 1945, there was much concern at the size of colonial sterling balances, money held in sterling investments in the UK. These comprised the colonies' Investment Funds, which in 1950 made up 59 per cent of the balances, and the London holdings of local banks and Currency and Marketing Boards (39.2 per cent of the total) and colonial loans and gifts to the UK government (1.8 per cent).[95] During the war, the balances had increased significantly, reaching £563m in 1945.[96] The most important cause of the rise was the decline in colonial imports, particularly from the non-sterling area, which reduced expenditure and increased savings and led to the growth of Savings Bank Funds. Although partly caused by the shortage of shipping space and the transfer of British manpower from the export industries to those engaged in the war effort, the fall was largely planned.[97] The UK government wished to limit the expenditure of foreign currencies needed to finance the purchase of munitions and other materials, save shipping space, and direct a greater share of the country's productive capacity to the war effort.[98] It thus imposed controls on shipping, rationed certain raw materials, such as petrol and newsprint, and encouraged colonies to introduce import controls and to damp down consumer demand by raising taxes and launching savings campaigns.[99] More significantly, it required all foreign currencies earned by the colonies to be sent to London, where they were exchanged for sterling, placed in an Exchange Equalisation Account and doled out to pay for non-sterling imports only if the requesting colonial administration could prove that the goods were essential.[100]

92 *Ibid.*, memo, 5 Oct. 1934.
93 *Ibid.*, memo, 14 Jan. 1938.
94 *Ibid.*, memo, 14 Jan. 1938; *ibid.*, Mrs. Kerby to CAs, 2 May 1941; *ibid.*, memo, 8 May 1941.
95 T 233/1426, working party report, table 1.
96 CO 537/4466, memo, 37826a.
97 Paul Bareau, *The Sterling Area*, London 1948, p. 10.
98 CAOG 9/308, circular, 5 Sept. 1941.
99 Paul Bareau, *The Sterling*, p. 9; CO 537/1378, memo, 1 Aug. 1946; CAOG 9/308, circular, 5 Sept. 1941.
100 Butler, *Britain*, p. 31.

Other reasons for the expansion in balances were relatively high export earnings, military expenditure, and the provision by colonies, via the CAs, of gifts and loans to the UK government. By 1945, gifts from colonial residents, private bodies and governments totalled £24m and loans amounted to £48.8m.[101] From March 1941 to March 1945, 766 loans were made, only 54 per cent of which bore interest, which was generally fixed at relatively low local rates (Appendix 4).[102] The advances were provided from colonial governments' own funds or raised from the local population through the flotation of special loans and the sale of war bonds or saving certificates similar to those issued in Britain.[103] Generally, the Treasury preferred loans to gifts, which it was feared could generate colonial discontent, and strongly suggested that the terms of bonds, certificates and loans be less generous than those of ordinary local issues, as, in effect, the investor was lending money to and receiving the security of the UK government.[104]

Balances continued to rise after the war, reaching £620m in June 1947, £977m in 1951 and £1,454m in 1956.[105] At the end of hostilities, the export revenues of colonies soared, increasing the circulation of currencies and the size of Currency Funds, and, via higher tax returns, enlarging Surplus Funds. Demand for their raw materials rose, due to post-war reconstruction and British promotion of those exports that earned or saved dollars, and the increased demand, along with the later outbreak of the Korean War, caused commodity prices to surge.[106]

Whilst export returns grew, however, imports stayed low and the money earned remained unspent. Imports were depressed partly because there was little colonial development, the result of a shortage of technicians and materials, and partly because the lack of shipping space and reconstruction and rearmament restricted the supply of goods from Britain.[107] More important reasons were that the UK government needed to retain colonial dollar earnings to pay for reconstruction materials from the USA and wished balances to remain high. The balances, along with non-colonial UK sterling investments over which the UK government had little control, enabled Britain to retain a positive Balance of Payments account, without which confidence in and the value of the pound would fall, damaging industry, and, by weakening London's position as an international financial centre, leading to a fall in invisible earnings.[108] To ensure dollars were retained and balances remained high, in the immediate post-war period the exchange and import controls introduced at the start of the war were therefore preserved.[109] At the same time, the UK government continued to encourage territories to restrict domestic consumption through high taxes,

101 PP 1947, 162; T 233/959, Loans to HMG, 1942–45.

102 CAOG 9/318, Loans to HMG; CAOG 9/308, Weeding note.

103 *Ibid.*, Summary of procedure re gifts; *ibid.*, colonial dispatch, 21 June 1940.

104 *Ibid.*, circular, 5 Sept. 1941; *ibid.*, colonial dispatch, 21 June 1940. In fact, given that the UK was fighting for its very existence, this security was worth very little.

105 CO 537/4466, memo, 37826a; Morgan, *A Reassessment*, p. 159; WN 13, memo, 29 July 1957.

106 Krozewski, *Money*, p. 191; T 233/934, working party report (draft), part 2, p. 2; T 236/4253, memo, Littler, 14 March 1955.

107 T 233/934, working party report (draft), part 2, p. 4; Havinden and Meredith, *Colonialism*, p. 271.

108 Havinden and Meredith, *Colonialism*, p. 270; Butler, *Britain*, p. 190.

109 Bell estimates that, from 1946 to 1952, the colonies made a net contribution to the Exchange

additionally motivated by the belief that development should be financed from internal resources, that reserves needed to be built up in case the terms of trade suddenly turned and raw material prices fell, and that the increase in revenues would otherwise stoke inflation.[110]

Unfortunately, the advantages in keeping substantial balances were matched by drawbacks, which, as the 1950s progressed, grew in importance. The most significant problem was the danger of very sudden withdrawals of funds from the London market as colonies became independent. It was generally believed that, on independence, administrations would sell their sterling balances in order to advertise their new political status and to purchase US dollars and acquire American goods.[111] The sales would plunge the Balance of Payments account into deficit and cause confidence in sterling to plummet, especially as the territories would continue to be long-term borrowers from Britain. Indeed, there was a danger that even before the flight from sterling began, the very possibility of it occurring could damage confidence in and the value of the pound.[112] It was also suggested that sales would lead to a collapse in security prices, that the Agents would no longer be able to support new colonial London issues, forcing loans to be floated at a higher interest rate or the money to be found from the coffers of the Treasury, and that territories could use the threat of a pull-out from sterling as a way of gaining political advantage.[113]

Over time, however, the Treasury and the Bank of England became less concerned about the consequences of withdrawals largely because the increase in the UK's reserves and the London investments of Middle Eastern oil producing members of the sterling area lessened the importance of the colonial balances as a prop to sterling.[114] Withdrawals, in any case, were highly unlikely. There were few advantages in buying dollar investments, as by the end of the 1950s, the US dollar was under considerable pressure in the international payments system, US investors had no interest in providing funds to ex-colonies, and most public sector goods were purchased in Britain using sterling. In addition, unless they were spread over a very long period, sales of sterling investments would have resulted in losses and would have damaged the private sector's confidence in the financial competency of newly independent administrations, reducing their chances of gaining future development capital.[115]

A further downside was the belief that the possession of balances promoted the movement towards independence. Such assets would greatly simplify the administrative task of the leaders of newly independent countries and their existence led to charges that the UK government was exploiting the colonies,

Equalisation Account of $1,830m (Philip W. Bell, *The Sterling Area in the Post War World*, Oxford 1956, p. 56).

110 T 233/934, working party report (draft), part 2, pp. 4, 6.

111 *Ibid.*, p. 6; T 236/4253, Wilson, CO to Hillis, Treasury, 7 Feb. 1955, enclosure.

112 T 233/934, working party report (draft), part 2, p. 6; *ibid.*, part 1, p. 1.

113 *Ibid.*, part 1, p. 1; T 233/1425, Armstrong, Treasury, 26 Feb. 1958; T 236/4253, Wilson to Hillis, 7 Feb. 1955, enclosure.

114 Krozewski, 'Finance', p. 53.

115 Catherine R. Schenk, 'Finance and Empire: confusions and complexities: a note', *The International History Review*, 18 (4), (1996), pp. 870–71.

which fuelled demands for political freedom.[116] It was accurately pointed out that the rate of interest territories earned on their sterling investments was far lower than that charged on their London loans, and many claimed that the colonies were forced to keep their funds in the UK and that these were used to finance the rearmament programme, the establishment of the welfare state, and capital flows to countries in the independent sterling area, such as Australia, India and South Africa.[117]

Although these latter allegations were untrue, they were widely believed and went some way in influencing the actions of the United States government, which put great pressure on the UK to cancel the balances.[118] Apart from the understanding that they were exploitative, the US also argued that that they stood in the way of sterling becoming freely convertible to dollars and that it was inequitable that the balances should remain when the US had written off large sums in lend-lease. Further discontent arose from the fact that the balances could only be spent in the sterling area and would therefore not help the US economy and that the dollars lent to the UK, in effect, were being used to pay interest on the investments.[119]

Numerous policies to reduce the balances were discussed. The most extreme was the proposal that up to £100m of the monies be cancelled, which was strongly opposed by both the CAs and the Colonial Office.[120] Their main arguments against cancellation were that it would be difficult to devise a common formula of appropriation given the different circumstances of the colonies, and that the wartime rise in the balances had resulted from low imports and not, as in the case of some dominions, from military expenditure and profiteering. The military had spent relatively little in the colonies, and, during the war years, export prices had actually risen to a lesser extent than the prices of imports.[121] It was also maintained that cancellation would lead to greater calls for independence and harm the UK economy. Unilaterally seizing large portions of colonial Investment Funds would constitute a 'gross breach of faith to governments', which had been officially encouraged to build up balances, and make a mockery of the government's development policy, which was to assist territories in large scale development projects.[122] Whilst such perfidy would encourage some colonies to move more rapidly towards independence, others would withdraw their remaining funds from the London market, fearing that they too would be seized, or simply make up their losses by raising raw material prices.[123]

Another proposed method of eliminating the problem was the conversion of

116 T 236/4253, Wilson to Hillis, 7 Feb. 1955, enclosure.

117 *New Commonwealth*, 21 Jan. 1952 pp. 61–2; *The Nation*, 23 Feb. 1952; *The Economist*, 15 Oct. 1955; J. Polk, *Sterling: its Meaning in World Finance*, New York 1956, p. 229.

118 T 233/934, working party report (draft), part 2, p. 5; Schenk, *Britain*, p. 106.

119 Bareau, *The Sterling*, p. 12; CO 537/4466, Brief on the American financial agreement of 1945.

120 CO 537/1378, memo, 1 Aug. 1946.

121 *Ibid.*; CO 537/4466, memo, Newsam, 9 Nov. 1950.

122 CO 537/1378, memo, 1 Aug. 1946; CO 537/4466, Brief on the American financial agreement of 1945.

123 CO 537/4466, memo, Newsam, 9 Nov. 1950; CO 537/1378, memo, 1 Aug. 1946.

up to 80 per cent of Currency Funds and a substantial portion of Surplus Funds into interest free loans to the UK government, which would be repayable only when there was a run on a currency or the Surplus Funds were required to meet a deficit or to finance development. Needless to say, the proposal received short shrift from the Colonial Office and the Agents, who argued that it was impracticable and would again lead to colonial discontent.[124]

Eventually, it was decided that the colonial governments should be encouraged to gradually run down their balances and use the proceeds to finance development. Such a strategy would prevent a sudden sell-off on independence, ensure that the money was spent on worthwhile development schemes rather than frittered away on inconsequential projects, aid UK industry by creating a demand for British imports, and partially solve the difficulties of financing development.[125] As discussed in chapter two, colonies were urged to sell part of the sterling assets of their Saving Bank Funds and Currency Funds and to use the proceeds to purchase locally issued government development loans. In the event, although a number of territories participated in the scheme, most proved highly resistant to the government's entreaties.

Independence and Funds

In fact, few countries withdrew their balances from London on independence, though a few did embark on extended spending sprees financed by the sale of Reserve Funds.[126] Their loyalty to sterling, however, did not extend to the Crown Agents, and, from 1953 to 1972, at least twelve former clients transferred control of their London investments to a Central Bank, which passed day-to-day management to the Bank of England, a British commercial bank, or a foreign bank.[127] The abandonment of the Agents was an integral part of throwing off the economic shackles of colonialism and earned new administrations political kudos, both internally and with other newly independent states. [128] There were also practical reasons for the change. Hong Kong believed that its Funds were too large to be kept with one organisation and that transferring a portion to the Bank of England would allow it to compare the Agents' and the Bank's performances.[129] Bahamas took its balances to the Royal Bank of Canada because it wanted to link its economy more closely with North America, and those former colonies that employed commercial banks often wished to keep the size of their sterling balances secret from the British government.[130]

124 CO 537/2974, memo, 20 Feb. 1947; CO 537/4466, memo, 26 Aug. 1949.

125 T 236/4253, Wilson to Hillis, 7 Feb. 1955, enclosure; T 233/933, memo, 11 May 1953.

126 HO 268/327, memo, 1 Oct. 1971.

127 Former colonies that moved some or all of their Funds include Bahamas, Ceylon, Cyprus, Kenya, Malaya, Singapore, Tanzania, Uganda and Zambia (CAOG 9/330, Ceylon to CAs, 12 March 1953; L 1, Finance Dept., 1965; L 2, Finance Dept., Jan. 1966; L 7, Investment Dept., April 1971; *ibid.*, Sept. 1971; L4, Finance Dept., Feb. 1968).

128 L 18/11, Savage report, March 1962, p. 1.

129 L 215, Hong Kong to CAs, 4 Nov. 1971; *ibid.*, Alan to John, 27 Nov. 1971.

130 L 2, Finance Dept., Jan. 1966; CO 537/2974, Sayers, CAs, to Caine, CO, 6 May 1948.

A further motivation was dissatisfaction with the Agents' past and current performance of its duties. The various restrictions on Fund investments had, for many years, led to low returns, and the purchase of colonial stock had left most newly independent countries with 'a rag bag' of securities for which there was little demand.[131] Many believed that the Agency's post-independence service was little better. As discussed, smaller funds were left unmanaged, and, according to the Bank of England, there was 'no real attention to the underlying purposes of the different funds...and...the right type of investment', personal contact between the Agents and their clients was minimal, and there were long delays in the provision of accounting information.[132] There was also concern among clients about the Agency's move into secondary banking, its financial viability and independence from the UK government.[133]

The views of the Bank of England, of course, were not unbiased. It stood to gain from the Agency's losses and there is much evidence that its officials actively encouraged administrations to dispense with the CAs, arguing that the control of overseas assets was the proper function of a central bank, expressing doubts about the efficiency of the service provided, and offering to do the work for a lower fee.[134] The Bank even supported transfers to commercial banks, which again put pressure on administrations to ditch the Agency.[135] It was claimed that City banks possessed advantages as investment managers and that their sale of colonial stock would have less impact on the market than disposals by the Agents.[136] There was also a belief that the transference of the CAs' work, whether to the City or the Bank, would cause their inadequacies to 'come under the spotlight thus exposing [them] to public criticism in political and other circles in the UK' and lead to their downfall.[137]

Not all newly independent colonies deserted the Agents. Many remained loyal. Some clients that had abandoned the Agency in the first flush of independence also later regretted their hasty decisions and returned to the fold and the Agents

131 HO 268/327, memo, 1 Oct. 1971.

132 HO 268/341, memo, 3 April 1969; HO 268/327, memo, 1 Oct. 1971; OV 44/77, 3a, memo, 2 Aug. 1962.

133 L 215, memo, meeting, 27 Nov. 1970. In 1964 the Commonwealth Office ordered the Agents to ignore a request from the new Communist government of Zanzibar to sell all of that country's investments, as the administration was not recognized by Britain and repayment would suggest to the rest of the World that the UK's stance was weakening (Folder 117, o/conf 321, Luke to CO, 24 Jan. 1964; *ibid.*, Luke to Zanzibar, 31 Jan. 1964). Ten years later, the Foreign Office, via the High Commissioner of Brunei, put great pressure on John Shuter, the CAs' Head of Investment, not to advice the Sultan to diversify his investments away from the UK, arguing that, although this would increase the Kingdom's income, it would severely damage the London market (Author's interview with John Shuter, 20 October 2004. See also OD 59/33, meeting, 6 March 1975).

134 HO 268/327, memo, 1 Oct. 1971; L 38, no. 66. See also ADM 14/50, no. 17, memo, 4 Dec. 1957; SA, Croom-Johnson Tribunal. Evidence, b/be/5/1, p. 164, memo, 22 Dec. 1971.

135 For example, in 1949, the City figure Lord Rennell attempted to persuade Kenya to 'emancipate' the Transport Commission from the Agents (S 7, A1871).

136 ADM 14/50, no. 17, memo, 4 Dec. 1957; *ibid.*, no. 18, memo, 5 Dec. 1957. City institutions possessed closer touch with the market and lacked a 'past' and the CAs' 'family responsibilities' (*ibid.*, no. 17, memo, 4 Dec. 1957).

137 *Ibid.*, no. 17, memo, 4 Dec. 1957.

gained some new portfolios, including the assets of the East and West African Currency Boards and various Funds belonging to the oil rich Abu Dhabi and Brunei.[138] Clients remained loyal for a number of reasons. For the 'small unsophisticated' territories, the Agency provided 'a convenient and familiar source of financial advice'.[139] Socialist states were reluctant to employ either the Bank of England, believed to be excessively close to the UK government, or commercial banks, regarded as corrupt profiteers and lackeys of the capitalist system.[140] Others found it difficult to dispense with the Agents, as the statutes that established their Funds, in particular their Currency Funds, specifically required their employment.[141] Their retention was additionally encouraged by the Foreign and Commonwealth Office (FCO), which believed that they ensured the 'prudent and profitable management' of investments, and, compared to the Bank of England and commercial banks, were more susceptible to FCO influence and far more willing to assist clients who found themselves in financial difficulty.[142]

The Agency sought to halt the loss of portfolios through the establishment of better relationships with its clients and the provision of higher returns. Relations with clients were improved through more regular meetings with their finance officers, the 1968 appointment as Head of Finance of Alan Challis, who possessed better people skills than his 'staid' predecessor, and the provision of training courses for the staff of principals.[143] To maximize returns, the Agents managed all of their Funds more actively and diversified into property, and, to a far greater extent, UK and overseas equities.[144]

In 1973, less than one per cent of Investment Funds were invested in UK and overseas property.[145] The most important holding was held by Singapore, which, in 1969, lent Abbey Orchard Property Investments, the Agents' Australian property company, A$15m, and, in return, received interest of 7.5 per cent per annum, 15 per cent of the equity of the company, and a cut of the profits.[146] To prevent disagreements with the Singapore government, the Agents 'discreetly edited' the minutes of the firm's Board minutes that were passed to officials of the administration, 'exercis[ing the] bits which are better not transmitted'.[147] In the event, the government withdrew from the scheme in 1975, as its other property investments had performed poorly and the events of the previous year had damaged its confidence in the Agency's effectiveness.[148]

The Agents first attempted to move into UK shares in 1957, when they

138 L 7, Investment Dept., April 1971; L 9, Investment Dept., Aug. 1973.

139 HO 268/327, memo, 1 Oct. 1971.

140 SA, Hayes' Fay committee notes. In 1957 there were rumours that London brokers had 'taken [Malaya] for a ride' (WN 13, A1866).

141 HO 268/327, memo, 9 Dec. 1971.

142 FCO 86/30, memo, Huijsman, 20 April 1972.

143 L 35, 1967, no. 18; PP 1977–8, 8, p. 16; L 2, Finance Dept., April 1966.

144 L 35, 1967, no. 18. Equities are the shares of industrial and service companies. They pay a variable dividend and their price, recorded on share market indices, rise or fall depending on demand and supply.

145 CAOG 22/23, five year review, 1968/73.

146 CAOG 24/16, Hewins to Singapore, 13 Nov. 1969; *ibid.*, Singapore to CAs, 18 Nov. 1970.

147 *Ibid.*, Hewins to Walter, 21 Dec. 1970; *ibid.*, Hewins to Walter, 8 March 1972.

148 Johns to Sunderland, 12 Oct. 2005.

proposed that they be allowed to place up to a quarter of each Fund in non-fixed interest stock, concentrating holdings in Pension Funds and other Funds that were unlikely to be realized at short notice. It was argued that a change in the law that would permit trusts to invest in the share market was imminent and that equities would appreciate to a greater extent than fixed price securities and keep better pace with inflation – holders directly benefiting from economic growth through rises in both prices and dividends.[149]

Not surprisingly, the Bank of England and the Colonial Office strongly opposed the proposal and the request was turned down, though in 1958 and 1960 the Agents were allowed to buy shares for the Overseas Superannuation Fund and the Aden Widows and Orphans Fund.[150] Opposition centered around the high risks involved and the likely impact on the demand for colonial loans. A move into equities would weaken investor confidence in colonial stock and the Agents would be less able to support London flotations during and after issue.[151] Investment in the share market would also set a bad example for the central banks of newly independent territories and encourage the CAs' clients to demand the purchase of local equities, which were even more speculative and much less marketable.[152]

In 1960, the Agents raised the subject again, pointing out that a failure to place at least a small proportion of Pension and Provident Funds in equities made them 'seriously vulnerable to criticism' from both clients and the liberal press.[153] Perturbed, the Colonial Office compromised. It was decided that the CAs should set up a unit trust through which investments could be made with less risk, but, in the meantime, that they could buy shares for Pension Funds.[154] In the event, the unit trust scheme collapsed, owing to taxation changes introduced in the 1965 Finance Act, which made such an arrangement disadvantageous to overseas tax-exempt investors, and all equity investments were thus made directly for Funds; the Agents in 1963 having obtained permission to buy shares for those colonies that specifically requested their purchase.[155]

By June 1968, the Agents' clients had £26m in the London share market, and, by December 1973, £43m. From 1966 to 1968, the holdings generated a realized profit of £2.75m and an unrealized gain of £5.75m, and, in the following year, performed better than the All Shares Index.[156] The investments were broadly split between two portfolios. A safe 'anchor' group of sixty to eighty shares selected from approximately 180 companies with large capitalisations, which were kept for relatively long periods, and an 'active' portfolio, the contents of which were smaller company shares that were 'ruthlessly' traded in order to make short-term

149 D. Johns to D. Sunderland, 6 Dec. 2004, enclosure, p. 1; CAOG 23/5, draft circular, Oct. 1958.

150 CAOG 23/5, memo, no date, approx. 1960.

151 ADM 14/51, no. 8, memo, 7 Oct. 1958; CAOG 23/5, CO circular, 8 July 1960.

152 CAOG 23/5, CO circular, 8 July 1960; OV 44/76, no. 9b, memo, 9 Feb. 1960.

153 CAOG 23/5, Luke to CO, 4 Jan. 1960.

154 *Ibid.*, CO to CAs, 20 Dec. 1961; L 18/24, Coopers and Lybrand report, p. 5.

155 CAOG 23/5, CAs to CO, 3 Jan. 1966; *ibid.*, CO to CAs, 12 Feb. 1963.

156 L 5, Finance Dept., Jan. 1969; *ibid.*, Oct. 1969; L 1–11.

gains.[157] The former portfolio included extensive shareholdings in firms in which the Agents' company Four Millbank Investments Ltd had interests and in the Provident Clothing Co. Ltd, a firm operated by Ralph Yablon, with whom they jointly owned Sassoons Bank.[158] The holdings, of which the investing public and the two government inquiries were unaware, helped to prop up the share price of these firms, and, to the extent that they benefited the Agents more than their clients, were unethical.

To aid them in their choice of shares, the CAs made use of the research papers published by their stockbrokers, picked up tips through their 'frequent informal contact with brokers and other institutions', undertook their own in-house research, and established an Equity Advisory Panel.[159] The Advisory Panel met quarterly and later monthly and comprised a leading stockbroker, an investment fund manager, and a merchant banker.[160] Unfortunately, the advice provided was of poor quality; an assessment of the Panel's performance in the ten years to 1974 discovered that only half of its recommendations had increased in value.[161] There were also suspicions that Panel members acted in their own interests. It was suggested that some passed information on the CAs' activities acquired at meetings to institutions to which they were connected and which competed with the Agency in the secondary banking sector. Others were thought to advocate the purchase or advise against the sale of shares in which they had an interest or to indulge in insider trading, buying the shares that had been recommended at meetings in the knowledge that CA purchases would cause their price to rise.[162] Although it regarded the Panel as a useful piece of 'propaganda', increasing client and Bank of England confidence in their dealings, the Investment Department thus sometimes ignored its advice – much to the anger of both the Senior Crown Agent and the Panel members, who argued that any major losses on equities would reflect badly on their reputations.[163]

The Agents began to buy overseas equities and bonds in the late 1960s, using colonial Investment Fund money, foreign currency lodged in the Joint Colonial Fund and Joint Miscellaneous Fund, and the deposits held in Finvest, their secondary banking Fund. By 1972, the Agency's total portfolios were worth £55m, of which £10m was invested on behalf of the JCF and JMF and £5m for Finvest.[164] Colonial investment Funds and the JCF and JMF held European equities quoted on the Belgium, Dutch, French, German, Italian and Swiss stock markets, and, along with Finvest, had extensive holdings in Canada and the USA,

157 L 4, Finance Dept., Aug. 1968.

158 On 31 Dec. 1970, 11 Funds held 4.038m First National Finance Corporation Ltd shares and a further Fund had £12,000 deposited at the bank; 1 Fund held 10,000 Stanley Gibbons Ltd shares; 9 Funds held 360,000 Inter City Investment & Holding Co. Ltd shares; 1 Fund held 9,900 Metro Industries Ltd shares; and 5 Funds held 17,500 Provident clothing Co Ltd shares (CAOG 21/67–8, CAOG 21/71).

159 CAOG 23/5, circular 1967; L 38, no. 74.

160 L 4, Finance Dept., Oct. 1968; PP 1981–2, 364, p. 142.

161 L 38, no. 74.

162 *Ibid.*; Author's interview with John Shuter, 20 October 2004..

163 CAOG 22/28, Hayes, 16 July 1974.

164 L 227, Objectives for overseas investment branch, 1 Feb. 1972.

and, in the case of SE Asian Funds, in Australia, Hong Kong and Singapore.[165] All the Funds also had large sums invested in foreign bonds, £12m and £34m in respectively 1971 and 1974, and Finvest and some colonial Investment Funds participated in at least one placing of company shares. In November 1969, £2m of equities issued by the Australian mineral company, Eastern Copper Ltd were purchased, the total cost being recovered one week later when 15 per cent of the holding was sold.[166]

Investment was co-ordinated by the Overseas Investment Branch, which sought to generate profits by holding shares that were likely to rise in price in the long-term, and, in the case of the JCF and JMF, short-term trading in active stocks. Generally, the Branch had full discretion as regards investment decisions, though in the case of certain Funds, such as those belonging to Singapore, permission had to be obtained before deals could go ahead.[167] It also had to conform to self-imposed market ceilings, maximum amounts that could be invested.[168] To ensure high returns, in each market the Branch appointed one or two premier local banks to act as managers, in some cases, for a performance-based commission.[169] The US portfolio, for example, was jointly operated by the bank Continental Illinois and the finance house Kuhn Loeb & Co, the French investment programme by Credit Lyonnais and the Banque de Paris, and the German and Japanese portfolios by Deutsch Bank and Daiwa Securities respectively.[170] Independent advice was obtained from other leading institutions and from local contacts. Senior officials made regular visits to countries in which Funds were invested, received representatives of foreign banks and stockbrokers at their offices in London, and attended European investment symposiums.[171]

Conclusion

The Agents' management of Investment Funds was blighted by intervention from the Colonial Office, the Treasury, the Bank of England and the City, all of which had their own interests that often clashed with those of colonial governments. The Colonial Office wanted the colonies to prosper, but at the same time needed to protect its own position in the government hierarchy. Fearing a financial crisis that could damage its own reputation and standing, it was thus highly risk averse and opposed the Agents' wish to exceed the price restrictions laid down in the Trustee Acts, the investment of Sinking Funds in the stock of the loan to which they were associated, and the mid-1960s move into equities.

165 *Ibid.*; L 188, file 1, memo, Asquith, 30 June 1971. Finvest was not allowed to invest in European equities (*ibid.*).

166 L 5, Finance Dept., Nov. 1969.

167 L 188, file 1, memo, Asquith, 30 June 1971.

168 L 7, Investment Dept., Jan. 1971.

169 L 8, Investment Dept, Feb. 1972.

170 L 4, Finance Dept., Sept. 1968; L6, Finance Dept., Feb. 1970; *ibid.*, Investment Dept., June 1970; L 7, Investment Dept., Nov. 1971.

171 For example L 4, Finance Dept., Oct. 1968; L 8, Investment Dept., April 1972; L 7, Investment Dept., June 1971.

The Treasury and the Bank of England, meanwhile, primarily cared about the home economy. They therefore encouraged the purchase of British securities, and, in particular, UK government stocks at the expense of colonial investments. The finance of central and local government was thus facilitated and the outflow of monies from the UK slowed, but colonies' returns were lower and colonial governments found it more difficult to successfully issue loans at high prices. Similarly, during and immediately after the war, policies were adopted that helped the war effort and post war recovery, but limited development expenditure, and, in the 1950s, the need to appease the USA, curtail the independence movement and avoid the economic consequences of a rapid withdrawal from sterling prompted the discussion of proposals that would have severely damaged colonial prosperity had they been adopted. Pressure was also placed on the Agents to increase Currency Fund liquidity, which reduced colonial incomes, but avoided the danger of calls on Treasury coffers during future currency crises, and again stimulated the purchase of UK government stock.

The Bank, furthermore, acted in its own interests. Aware that it stood to gain from the decline of the Agents' investment role, it took every opportunity to criticise them, and, in the early 1960s, actively encouraged the central banks of newly independent countries to abandon the Agency. Its self-interest was shared by other City institutions with which the CAs were involved. Dealers set artificially high and low prices when respectively buying and selling stock on behalf of colonies, and, in the late 1960s and 1970s, members of the Agents' Equity Panel used information gathered at meetings for their own advantage.

The Crown Agents represented the interests of the colonies and thus sought to increase colonial returns through careful investment, the exchange of securities, and by fighting any attempt by the Colonial Office, the Treasury, the Bank or the City to limit or prevent the appreciation of yields, if necessary resorting to unethical practices to achieve this goal. Only during the war did they allow the interests of the UK to take precedence, and even then there were limits to their patriotism. Although they were willing to increase purchases of UK government stock during the hostilities, they strongly resisted the use of the colonies' cash funds for this purpose. The Agents, of course, were not immune to self-interest, and, by promoting their clients' interests, they often furthered their own. Active switching boosted their brokerage earnings and high investment returns increased their clients' ability to use their other services and reduced the likelihood that they would be abandoned on independence. However, as discussed in the Introduction, the culture of the Office ensured that its staff genuinely identified with their principals and their actions on behalf of colonies were often purely altruistic.

Despite the CAs' stiff resistance, the Colonial Office, the Treasury, the Bank and the City succeeded in limiting the returns earned by their clients. The purchase of UK government stock, the price restrictions imposed by the Trustee Acts and dealer dishonesty all reduced yields, as did the Agents' trading inadequacies of the late 1950s and early 1960s. Obviously, it is impossible to determine accurately the sum lost. However, if it is assumed that investment Funds earned just half a per cent per annum less than they would otherwise have done, a conservative estimate, Funds will have forfeited from 1930 to 1960 £68.41m.

For the Agents, the constant disagreements with the Bank of England also had a further drawback. The resultant poor relations meant that they received little support in times of crisis, and, as will be discussed in chapters four and nine, in the early 1930s and in 1974, the Bank refused to provide the Agency with monies necessary for its survival.

4

The Management of the Joint Colonial Fund and the Joint Miscellaneous Fund

Throughout the period, the Agents' clients held funds in the UK to pay for goods purchased by the Agency and to meet salary, pension, loan interest and other commitments. The money, known as floating balances, was remitted to Britain, and also comprised the unspent proceeds of loans raised in London and the colonies, money from realized Sinking Funds that had yet to be used to repay associated loans, monies about to be invested on behalf of other Funds, unused British government aid, and, from around 1937, a portion of colonial Currency Funds.[1] Before 1924, each colony's floating balances were invested separately for very short periods. Sums likely to be required immediately were placed in the Agents' Bank of England current account. Because this paid no interest, as little as possible was deposited here, and, to ensure this was the case, the anticipated cash requirements of each colony were studied on a daily basis.[2]

Depending on when they would be needed, the remaining balances were either deposited at call or for fixed periods, advanced to other colonies, or used to buy UK Treasury bills or securities with slightly longer maturities, such as National Bonds. Money deposited at call was usually entrusted to the Westminster Bank, which, 'jealous of their position [as] … the CAs bankers', paid interest ¼ per cent above the normal deposit rate.[3] Fixed deposits, on the other hand, were lodged with a number of banks and also with discount houses. The sums were placed for periods of a few days to a year, though more commonly for three months, and earned a slightly higher interest rate than callable deposits.[4] An even bigger return was realized if the money was advanced to colonies or used to buy Treasury bills or other short-term stock, though the latter incorporated a degree of risk, in that, if the bills or stock had to be sold before maturity and market prices were low, sales could involve a capital loss.[5]

From 1920, the Agents sought to increase the returns earned by the balances. Owing to the issue of post-war loans, their size had increased from an annual

1 CAOG 9/280, 1936 report; CAOG 9/252, note, 28 Dec. 1931. From 1946 to 1962, 13 per cent of Currency Funds were placed in the JCF.

2 CAOG 9/113, memo on the employment of floating balances, March 1924.

3 *Ibid.*; CAOG 9/232, CAs to Nigeria, 6 Nov. 1935.

4 In 1922, there was 'a rather acid exchange of letters' with the Colonial Office, which queried the lowly status and safety of deposits placed with the P & O Banking Corporation (S 2 A557).

5 CAOG 9/113, memo on …, March 1924.

average of £2.3m in 1914/18 to £10.4m in 1919/23, and it was thought ridiculous that such large sums of money should earn low rates of interest.[6] In 1924, therefore, it was decided to invest up to 20 per cent of the balances in securities of up to five years maturity. To guard against price falls, a Depreciation Fund was set up, which received 2 per cent of all the money remitted to London, and, if a colony needed the balances so invested before the stock matured, the investments were sold to another colony at the maturity price.[7] As the depreciation Fund grew, more money was placed in long-term securities, and, by 1928, they accounted for 32 per cent of total balances and average returns had increased from 3.5 per cent in 1924 to 4.5 per cent.[8]

To raise returns still further, the CAs proposed that all the separate floating balances be pooled into a single Fund. Because they would be able to draw on a larger amount of money to meet colonies' immediate needs, this would allow more funds to be safely invested in long-dated stock and a small proportion of the balances to be placed in securities with even longer maturities, which offered even better rates.[9] Moreover, all colonies would receive the same rate of return; the earnings of the poorer colonies, which kept relatively small sums in London that were largely deposited for fixed periods, would rise; and the Agents would have a lighter workload.[10] Initially, some at the Colonial Office had doubts about the scheme. It was believed that the Fund would transform the Agents' role from one of trustee to banker, encourage them to engage in 'ingenious financial operations', and could give rise to misunderstandings and have 'undesirable political consequences'.[11] After consideration, however, the Secretary of State eventually in 1929 gave his blessing to the pool, which was named the Joint Colonial Fund, and, from 1956, the Joint Consolidated Fund.

From 1929 to 1969, the Fund grew from £5.7m to £129m, though, in the short term, deposits rose and fell according to the number of loans issued, Sinking Fund redemptions, changes in the terms of trade, and the size of the Fund's dividend (Figure 3.1). A comparison of the deposits and the interest rate paid gives a correlation co-efficient of 0.58 from 1929 to 1960 and 0.18 from 1960 to 1969.[12] On average, 42 per cent of the Fund was invested in securities, 22 per cent placed in bank deposits, 16 per cent lent to Local Authorities, 11 per cent used to buy UK Treasury bills, and 8 per cent advanced to colonies. The Agents also used the contents of the Fund to underwrite non-colonial loans.

The portion of the Fund held in bank deposits fell from the early 1950s to the mid-1960s, but then rose, accounting for 66 per cent of the Fund in 1974 (Figure 4.1). Before the war, the Agents used only five banks, and, as a reward for their

6 CAOG 9/234, memo, 26 Oct. 1923.
7 CAOG 9/113, memo on …, March 1924
8 CAOG 9/234, note, 8 March 1928.
9 CO 323/1019/8, circular, 26 July 1928.
10 CAOG 9/234, memo, 4 March 1924; A. W. Abbott, *A Short History of the Crown Agents and their Office*, London 1959 (privately published), p. 40.
11 CO 323/918/10872, note, Grindle, 1 April 1924; CAOG 9/234, CAs to CO, 22 March 1927; *ibid.*, meeting, 22 Dec. 1924.
12 The Pearson Product Moment Correlation measures the strength of the association between two variables. The higher the co-efficient up to 1 the stronger the correlation.

Figure 4.1. JCF monies at banks, in securities and lent to colonies, 1929–69 (percentage of total JCF deposits)

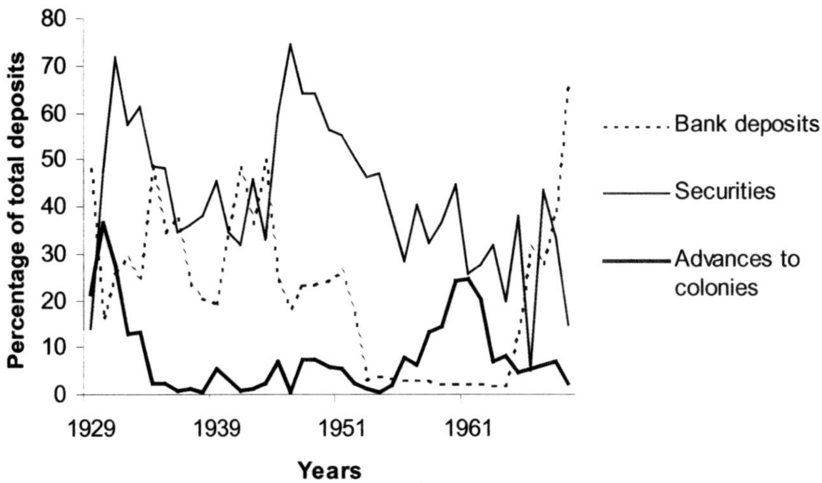

Source. CAOG 1/1; CAOG 9/228; T 233/959, memo, 15 March 1951.

loyalty, received favourable interest rates, and, in the case of fixed deposits, were allowed to withdraw a proportion of their money 'at any time'.[13] Investment in securities, meanwhile, peaked in 1931 and 1945, when they accounted for 72 per cent and 75 per cent of the Fund respectively. The type of stock held was dependent on the market price and varied considerably. From 1946 to 1962, 53 per cent of the Fund was in 'UK securities', the proportion ranging from 43 per cent in 1958 to 62 per cent in 1952, and 16 per cent was held in 'other securities', 4 per cent in 1954 and 33 per cent in 1949. 'UK securities' largely comprised government stock, and Local Authority securities, whereas 'other securities' consisted of dominion stock, particularly that of Australia, India, New Zealand, and South Africa, and, to a lesser extent, colonial stock issued on the London market.[14]

Prior to 1925, the Agents obtained their underwriting from Scrimgeours, who had added them to their list of underwriters. Thereafter, they also underwrote loans for other brokers, generally providing backing of up to £50,000, and, like their colleagues, agreeing to put in applications for stock in order to increase the impression that there was a large demand for the issue underwritten.[15] From 1928 to 1933, the only period for which there are full figures, they underwrote £3.04m of 48 issues floated for dominions, UK Local Authorities and public bodies, and took-up £544,750 of unsubscribed securities (18 per cent).[16] Any

13 T 233/959, CAs to B of E, 26 Jan. 1942; *ibid.*, memo, 21 Oct. 1941.

14 In 1940, 46 per cent of JCF securities were dominion stock and 11.5 per cent Crown colony stock (JCF Annual report 1940).

15 CAOG 9/104, memo, 16 Oct. 1933; CAOG 9/103, memo, 19 May 1936.

16 CA (m) 60; CAOG 9/104, memo, 16 Oct. 1933, statement A.

stock acquired was initially held by the Fund, but then sold to other colonial Investment Funds that had money to invest. Strangely, from 1925, the commission earned was kept by the Agents and placed in the Office Fund; a Colonial Office instruction of that year having been deliberately misinterpreted.[17] Aware that this was unfair and perhaps fearing that the Colonial Office would discover the sleight of hand, from 1947 all commissions were placed in the JCF, whether or not stock had been taken up.[18]

The return provided from the Fund's investments and underwriting was calculated quarterly, and, from 1960, half yearly, and divided pro-rata among the depositors according to their daily balances during the preceding three or six months.[19] Although it was always below the average yield on 2.5 per cent consols, the dividend consistently remained above the bank deposit rate, and, until the early 1950s, exceeded and thereafter was equal to or just slightly below the Treasury bill discount rate (Figure 4.2). Any surplus left over after crediting the dividend was paid into a reserve Fund, which was designed to meet any depreciation of investments, and, by 1955, stood at £1.52m.[20]

1931/2 crisis

The Fund faced its first test in 1931, when it teetered on bankruptcy. Its collapse was caused by an abnormally high demand for advances and a lack of liquidity. The demand for advances was primarily due to the inability of the Agents to issue a loan for Northern Rhodesia and the Bank of England to float Tanganyika and Ugandan guaranteed stock. The loans could not be issued because the Colonial Office had underestimated the time that it would take to lay before Parliament the orders-in-council that permitted Northern Rhodesia and Uganda to enter the London market, and the Treasury had failed to notice that the legislation enabling the Tanganyika loan to be floated was flawed. When, at last, the loans were ready for issue, the September 1931 suspension of the Gold Standard had forced the Treasury to close the London market to all new flotations.[21] Unable to obtain funds from the market, the three territories financed the construction of the public works for which the loans were to be raised from the Joint Colonial Fund. By November 1931, advances to Northern Rhodesia stood at £750,000, those to Uganda had reached £500,000 and Tanganyika owed the Fund £960,000.[22] At the same time, the World trade depression caused other colonies to make demands on the Fund, either via requests for advances or the accumulation of overdrafts.[23]

17 CAOG 9/101, memo, 17 Sept. 1956.

18 CAOG 9/225, memo, 26 June 1947.

19 CO 323/1019/8, circular, 26 July 1928; JCF annual report, 1960.

20 CO 323/1079/18, JCF annual report, 1930; CA (m) 25, p. 2.

21 CAOG 9/252, CAs to CO, 19 March 1951; *ibid.*, note, approx. early 1932; CAOG 9/141, CAs to CO, 26 March 1931.

22 S 1, A270; CAOG 9/142, CAs to CO, 30 April 1931; CAOG 9/141, CAs to CO, 26 March 1931.

23 CAOG 1/1, JCF annual report, 1932.

Figure 4.2. JCF dividend rates relative to comparable investments, 1929–71 (%)

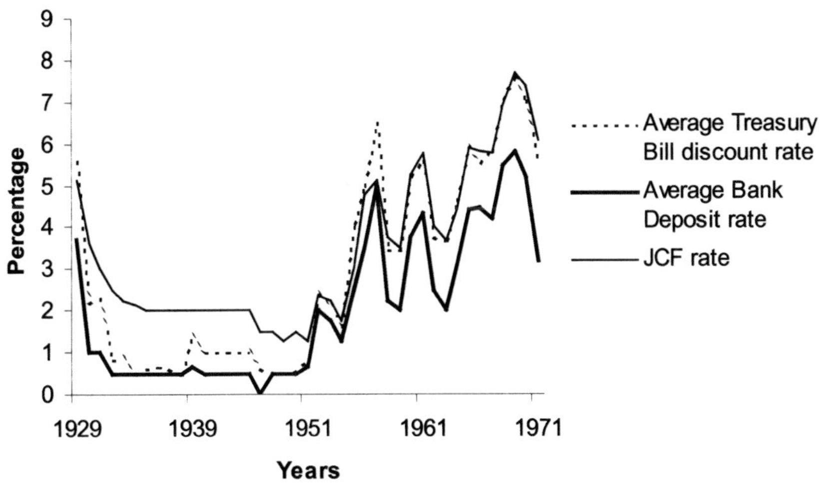

Source. CAOG 1/1; CAOG 9/228; SA, CA Annual Reports 1970, 1971.

Unfortunately, from the start of the year, the Fund found it increasingly difficult to meet these demands, partly because remittances from depositors had declined, owing to the trade depression, but largely because over the previous year the Agents had invested massive amounts of the Fund in long-term securities.[24] Reductions in Bank rate from September 1929 to March 1930 had caused the rate of interest on short-term investments to fall far below that on longer term stock, the price of which also rose. Wishing to earn the highest return possible for the colonies and naïve in the ways of the market, the Agents sold a large portion of the Fund's short-term securities, placing the proceeds in long-term investments, which, by April 1930, represented 74 per cent of the Fund.[25] In normal circumstance, this sudden change of policy would have been regarded as a good business decision, albeit, given the small size of the reserve, highly risky. However, as the Agents should have known, World economic conditions were far from normal, and, over the next year, the price of long-term securities plummeted, and, by September 1931, the value of the Fund's holdings had declined by over £300,000.[26]

Ideally, the Agents should have sold a portion of the Fund's investments early in 1931, reducing the losses through the use of the £4.3m depreciation reserve. Instead, confident that prices would rapidly recover and aware that a permanent loss would lead to severe criticism from the Treasury, they halted the distribution of the Fund dividend, persuaded colonies such as Nigeria and the Straits to finance their London commitments through the sale of investments in their

24 CAOG 9/252, CAs to CO, 19 March 1951.
25 CAOG 1/1, JCF annual report, 1930.
26 *Ibid.*, JCF annual report, 1932.

Surplus Funds, and obtained money from the sale of colonial treasury bills and from banks.[27]

In April 1931, the Agency issued £1.25m Tanganyika Treasury bills and £500,000 Uganda bills, and, in the following month, a further £500,000 was sold for Northern Rhodesia. Bills were also issued for the Federated Malay States and Nyasaland, and, by June 1931, a total of £3.3m had been sold.[28] On discovering the Agents' profligate use of bills, the Bank of England was aghast. The finance of long-term capital works with short-term loans was bad financial practice and it feared that a failure by the Agents to repay the bills on maturity would force holders to call in other debts, causing the market to enter a spiral of decline.[29] The Bank therefore ordered the Agents to halt all bill issues, and when, in December, it was revealed that they had ignored this instruction, the Bank's governor, Montague Norman, wrote a strong letter to the Senior Agent demanding that sales be stopped.[30]

Faced with the Bank's June 1931 embargo on the sale of bills, the Agents turned to the banks. By March 1931, the Westminster bank had lent the Fund £530,000, and, by September, £740,000. It then limited lending to £750,000 and the Agents were forced to approach other commercial banks, all of which expressed an extreme reluctance to lend.[31] Salvation came in the unlikely form of Edward Bickerstethe, the Agents' secret broker, who used his connections to arrange loans from Martins bank and Barclays bank, with whom 'he was in a particular favourable position'.[32] Martins agreed to lend the Fund £150,000 at the relatively high interest rate of 5.25 per cent and Barclays provided £600,000 at a generous 1 per cent below Bank rate.[33]

Crisis point was reached in December 1931. Colonial advances stood at £3m and were estimated to reach £5.65m by March the following year.[34] However, there appeared little hope that the Fund would be able to provide the extra £2.65m. The Treasury indicated that public issues would have to be severely rationed for at least three months, security prices had failed to recover and sales of securities could therefore only be made at a loss, Banks were reluctant to lend more money and could even begin to call in loans, and remittances to the Fund had slowed to a trickle, total deposits having fallen from £10.3m in April 1930 to £4.8m.[35] During December, the Agents discussed the Fund's parlous position with the Bank of England, the Treasury, and the Colonial Office. A Bank sugges-

27 *Ibid.*; CAOG 9/252, note, 28 Dec. 1931.

28 CAOG 9/141, advert, 10 April 1931; CAOG 9/142, CAs to CO, 30 April 1931; CAOG 9/230, meeting, 23 Feb. 1932; C 47/50, Norman to Hopkins, 4 June 1931.

29 C 47/50, Norman to Hopkins, 4 June 1931.

30 G 1/202, no. 17, Norman to Ezechiel, 3 Dec. 1931.

31 Folders 119/120, memo, 5 Oct. 1931.

32 *Ibid.* Arthur Abbott, the Agents' Secretary and later Archivist, claimed that the loans were arranged by the Crown Agent Sir William Gowers, who 'called a crony in the City (the eminent Chairman of one of the clearing banks)' (CA (m) 64, memo on past CAs, Abbott, no date). However, Gowers only became an Agent in 1932 and there is no contemporary record of his intervention.

33 Folders 119/120, memo, 5 Oct. 1931; *ibid.*, Ezechiel to Barclays, 2 Oct. 1931.

34 CO 323/1079/18, CAs to CO, 24 Dec. 1930; CAOG 9/252, note, 22 Dec. 31.

35 CAOG 9/252, note, 22 Dec. 31; CAOG 1/1, JCF annual report, 1930.

tion that the government bail out the Agents was rejected by the Treasury, and a CA request for a Bank of England loan was refused, even though the Bank had agreed to advance £5m to the Central Electricity Board, and, if necessary, had promised to help other issuers.[36] Norman 'considered that the Crown Agents themselves were responsible for the difficulties of their position' and should therefore 'stand the consequences of their actions' and sell the Fund's long-term investments, starting with its UK Treasury bonds.[37] As Norman well knew, the resultant losses and damage to depositors' confidence would mark the end of the Fund and the Agents feared that sales would further depress the London stock market.[38] They thus rejected the suggestion and put forward two counter-proposals – the issue of more Treasury bills and more short term borrowing from banks – both of which Norman turned down.[39]

It was eventually agreed that the CAs should create a small amount of stock for each of the colonies in need of funds, which would be sold to the market to gain a quotation. As money was required, they would then create more of this stock, up to £3.5m, which would be bought for Sinking Funds, using annual SF contributions and the proceeds of sales of SF securities.[40] Unbeknown to the holding colonies, security sale losses would thus be absorbed by the Sinking Funds, enabling the JCF investments to be retained until the market recovered. At the same time, the Colonial Office acceded to a CA request to send cautionary telegrams to colonies asking them to minimize their expenditure of JCF deposits, and the Agents increased the interest rate on advances from the Fund from Bank rate to 1 per cent above this rate.[41]

In the event, Sinking Funds bought only £400,000 of Northern Rhodesian stock and £29,307 and £155,356 respectively of Fiji and Grenada securities.[42] More purchases were not made because, from January 1932, the market began to recover and it became possible to issue some of the long overdue loans. During the following months, the Agents floated a £2m Uganda loan, £600,000 of which it bought firm, and the Bank of England issued a total of £3.1m of guaranteed stock for Mauritius, Nyasaland and Tanganyika.[43] The economic recovery also reduced the forecast demand for advances, increased remittances to the Fund, and led to a rise in the market prices of long-term securities, allowing some of the Fund's investments to be sold at satisfactory prices.[44] In March 1932, nine months of unpaid Fund dividends were distributed and the advance interest rate was again reduced to Bank rate, and, by the end of the year, the crisis was over.[45] Its repercussions, however, were to have an impact on the Agents' investment policy for the next three decades.

36 G 1/202, no. 24, Norman to Hopkins, 11 Dec. 1931.
37 *Ibid.*, no, 29, memo, 18 Dec. 1931; CAOG 9/252, note, 6 Jan. 1932.
38 CAOG 9/252, note, 28 Dec. 1931.
39 G 1/202, no. 29, memo, 18 Dec. 1931; CAOG 9/252, note, 6 Jan. 1932.
40 CAOG 9/252, note, 22 Dec. 1931; *ibid.*, note, 30 Dec. 1931.
41 *Ibid.*, CAs to CO, 4 Feb. 1932; CAOG 1/1, JCF annual report, 1932.
42 CAOG 9/276–CAOG9/283.
43 *Ibid.*; CAOG 1/1, JCF annual report, 1932.
44 CAOG 9/252, CAs to CO, 4 Feb. 1932; CAOG 1/1, JCF annual report, 1932.
45 CAOG 1/1, JCF annual report, 1932.

The liquidity of the Fund

Determined that there would be no recurrence of the disaster, the Treasury proposed that a committee of enquiry be established to investigate the banking operations of the Agency and that an advisory committee or board of bankers be formed to monitor and contribute to its investment decisions. Both proposals were strongly opposed by the Agents and were eventually dropped.[46] The cudgels, however, were taken up by the Bank of England, which demanded that the Fund be kept liquid and invested exclusively in UK Treasury bills, and, to a very limited extent, in trustee securities that had less than 12 months to run. It further required that no recourse should be made to either colonial treasury bills or bank loans and that the provision of advances to colonies should cease.[47] The Agents again objected, pointing out that the joint stock banks held up to a quarter of their deposit liabilities in long-term investments, and, after much negotiation, the Bank compromised.[48] It was agreed that the 'bulk' of the money held in the Fund should be liquid and placed in call or short notice bank accounts, in UK Treasury bills and in securities with less than 12 months to run. The remainder, termed the hard core, could be placed in longer term securities with maturities of over one year, but only if the Agents were satisfied that the Fund was in a 'thoroughly liquid position'. Colonial advances could continue to be made, though restrictions were imposed, and they were to be classed as liquid or hard core depending on the repayment period.[49]

The resulting harmony between the Agents and the Treasury and the Bank lasted less than four years. Suspicious of their investment activities, the Treasury in December 1936 asked the Colonial Office for a copy of the annual JCF statement. The Agents refused point blank to provide it.[50] Two years later, the Treasury again asked for details of investments, unable to understand how a largely liquid Fund managed to pay a relatively high dividend of 2 per cent.[51] The CAs again refused, claiming that the Treasury 'and more especially the Bank of England, who have been behind ... these matters' would use the information to gain control of the Agency and force the adoption of an investment strategy even less in the interests of the colonies than the one presently followed.[52] The Treasury, however, was not to be rebuffed a second time and insisted on the provision of the information. Placed under pressure by the Colonial Office, which warned 'that it would be unwise to get into conflict with the Treasury', the Agents relented and agreed to send the Bank and the Treasury the JCF's quarterly and annual statements.[53]

On receiving this information, the Treasury discovered why the Agents had

46 T 233/959, memo, Granger-Taylor, 21 April 1951.
47 CAOG 9/230, meeting, 23 Feb. 1932.
48 CAOG 9/252, note, approx. early 1932.
49 CAOG 9/230, meeting, 23 Feb. 1932.
50 CAOG 9/252, CO to CAs, 24 May 1938.
51 T 233/959, memo, Granger-Taylor, 21 April 1951.
52 CAOG 9/252, Flood to CO, 30 May 1938.
53 *Ibid.*, CO to CAs, 24 May 1938; T 233/959, memo, Granger-Taylor, 21 April 1951.

stubbornly resisted what had appeared such a minor request. The Fund could pay a high rate of interest because the Agency had failed to follow the 1932 agreement. The liquid portion of the Fund had shrunk to less than 50 per cent of the whole and included securities with maturities of up to two years, rather than of up to 12 months, and type 'b' mortgage loans to Local Authorities. Although theoretically these loans could be recalled at six months notice, in reality, such repayment would only be made in extraordinary circumstances. The hardcore, meanwhile, had expanded, largely through the provision of Local Authority mortgage loans that were not recallable by notice, and included securities with maturities of more than two years rather than over one year as agreed.[54] Fearful that if there was a financial crisis the Fund would again be insufficiently liquid to meet the demand for advances, the Treasury demanded that the Agents follow the agreed investment policy and also halt the provision of mortgage loans, which were the preserve of authorized banks.[55]

The Agents, unembarrassed that their subterfuge had been discovered, strongly defended their actions and refused to revert to their former investment strategy. They argued that the size of the liquid portion had been reduced as there was little likelihood of a simultaneous run on the Fund, and the maturity definitions of securities had been changed because, from 1933, it had been difficult to find investments with lives of less than one year at suitable prices, due to the fall in deposit rates, which had increased the demand for such securities.[56] The shortage of appropriate investments and the low return from bank deposits was also the reason for their provision of Local Authority mortgage loans. There was no legal reason why they could not make these loans, the fact that type 'b' advances could be recalled at notice made them perfectly suitable for the liquid portion of the Fund, and such loans paid a high average return of 3.25 per cent.[57]

Faced with the Agents' intransigence, the Treasury modified its demands and it was eventually agreed that the liquid portion of the Fund should be fixed at 60 per cent and include bank deposits, UK Treasury bills, Local Authority mortgage loans that were recallable with just one months notice, and, as per the previous agreement, securities with a life of less than 12 months. The hardcore, meanwhile, would make up 40 per cent of the Fund and comprise Local Authority mortgages, including type 'b' loans, and, as in 1932, securities with over one year to run.[58] In the event, the Agents halted the provision of type 'b' mortgage loans until 1952, when they restricted lending to 5 per cent of the Fund.[59]

Ironically, the new investment policy could not be immediately implemented. A few months after receiving permission to reduce the liquidity of the Fund, there was a significant fall in gilt prices caused by the Conservative Party's unexpectedly small election majority, a rise in the Bank rate, and the government's

54 CAOG 9/252, Treasury to CO, 8 Dec. 1938; *ibid.*, Treasury to CO, 16 May 1939. In 1938, almost 25 per cent of the Fund was lent to Local Authorities (CAOG 1/1, JCF annual report, 1936).

55 T 233/959, memo, Granger-Taylor, 21 April 1951.

56 CAOG 9/252, Treasury to CO, 16 May 1939; CAOG 1/1, JCF annual reports, 1934–1937.

57 CAOG 1/1, JCF annual report, 1936; CO 323/1422/3, Ezechiel to CO, 21 Oct. 1937.

58 CAOG 9/252, CAs to CO, 15 Nov. 1945.

59 *Ibid.*, note, 31 Feb. 1956.

conversion of £1,000m of Treasury bills.[60] Inevitably, the price collapse affected the value of the JCF's long-term stock holdings - to such an extent that its £1m reserve had disappeared by the end of the year.[61] At the same time, the rise in the Bank rate caused deposit and Treasury bill rates to appreciate above that paid by the JCF and there was a real danger that depositors would begin to withdraw their balances, leaving the Fund 'in a mess'.[62]

Fearing that gilt prices would fall further and wishing to take advantage of the higher bank deposit and Treasury bill rates, the Agents sold a large proportion of their long-term investments at a loss, using the proceeds to increase the liquid portion of the Fund and to buy more UK government securities, which could be easily realized if the crisis worsened.[63] They also kept all new deposits liquid, and, to allow a new reserve to be built up and to finance the losses suffered, reduced the Fund's dividend to 1¹/₈ per cent.[64] Their actions and the recovery of gilt prices in 1953 ensured that a disaster on the scale of 1931 was averted. The episode, however, forced them to accept the dangers of illiquidity and their twenty year campaign for a wider JCF investment policy ceased.

Their new found belief in liquidity was further strengthened by the fall in the Fund's assets during the late 1950s. From 1954 to 1958, JCF deposits fell from £133m to £77m and there were large calls on the Fund. Those newly independent countries that dispensed with the Agents' services withdrew their money, Ghana for example took out £5.5m, and the clients that remained reduced their holdings.[65] The change in the terms of trade had depressed raw material prices and government revenues, territories followed the Treasury's advice and increasingly financed development from their own resources, and the newly formed and more financially astute central banks kept smaller balances in the Fund, bought local treasury bills and, when profitable to do so, redirected money to other UK investments, such as UK Treasury bills, bank deposits and Local Authority loans.[66] The Fund, consequently, had to be managed far more closely and an extremely high level of liquidity maintained.

The Joint Miscellaneous Fund

In addition to colonial government balances, the Agents held balances for non-governmental institutions, such as colonial town councils, harbour boards and universities. These could not be placed in the Joint Colonial Fund, as, unlike their government counterparts, the holding organisations were liable to UK taxation. Their presence in the Fund would thus have forced the Agents to restrict its investments to those securities that paid dividends free of tax and

60 CAOG 1/1, JCF annual report, 1951.
61 CAOG 9/226, circular, 21 April 1952.
62 CAOG 9/225, memo, 13 Dec. 1951.
63 *Ibid.*; CAOG 9/226, CAs to N Rhodesia, 2 Aug. 1955.
64 CAOG 1/1, JCF annual report, 1951; CAOG 9/226, circular, 21 April 1952.
65 T 233/1425, memo, April 1958.
66 *Ibid.*; CAOG 23/5, circular, 8 July 1960; L 18/11, p. 30; CAOG 9/227, memo, 4 June 1956; CAOG 9/228, CAs to Nyasaland, 13 Sept. 1961.

that carried a relatively low rate of interest. The monies were therefore largely deposited at banks, where they earned a measly ½ per cent interest in 1950, though, unbeknown to the Inland Revenue, some were indeed kept in the JCF.[67] Colonial governments surreptitiously added them to their JCF deposits, a practice to which the CAs turned 'a blind eye', and the Agents put money belonging to trading concerns, such as railways and harbours, in the Fund, failing to inform the UK tax authorities of their presence.[68]

By the late 1940s, a large expansion in these balances caused the CAs to propose the setting up of a new Fund, to be named the Joint Miscellaneous Fund, the contents of which would be exclusively invested in securities whose dividends were not applicable to UK tax or would be advanced to depositors. Inevitably, the Bank of England opposed the scheme. It was argued that it would reduce the liquidity of the monies, and, by increasing the rate of interest they earned, augment the amount of money flowing away from Britain, and that the Agents' motives in setting it up were highly suspect - a hope that the Gold Coast and Nigerian Marketing Boards would transfer the management of their vast fortunes to the Agency.[69] Nonetheless, the Treasury decided to give the Agents the benefit of the doubt, and, in 1950, allowed the project to go ahead, though it required a quarter of the Fund to be held in cash and the remainder in short-term securities.[70] As ever, the Agents enthusiastically agreed to the terms, which they then promptly ignored until the Bank of England revealed their duplicity to the Treasury.[71] Astonished that their 'cash holding [was] down to nothing', Treasury officials demanded that they stick to their agreement, and, not wanting to 'squabble over' what they claimed was 'a relatively minor point', the CAs concurred.[72]

From 1950 to 1969, the size of the Fund rose from £1m to £10m and the dividend paid averaged 3.6 per cent.[73] To encourage the success of the scheme, the CAs lent the Fund £25,000, interest-free, from their Office Fund, which was used to establish a reserve against the depreciation of investments. In the event, the reserve proved inadequate. In 1955, gilt prices again fell and a further interest free loan of £25,000 had to be arranged.[74] The Agents also initially made no charge for administering the investments, and restricted the amount of money that could be kept in the Fund to £150,000 per depositor.[75]

67 OV 44/70, no. 38, Bourdillon to Treasury, 24 Feb. 1950.

68 CAOG 17/137, memo, 18 Jan. 1957; CAOG 9/229, memo, 11 Oct. 1930; *ibid.*, memo, 17 Oct. 1930.

69 OV 44/70, no. 38a, memo, 28 Feb. 1950; *ibid.*, no. 38d, memo, 7 March 1950. See also *ibid.*, no. 38, memo, 13 March 1950; *ibid.*, no. 38, Powell to Clough, 14 March 1950. It seems likely that the Bank also coveted the Boards' funds.

70 T 233/959, memo, Beighton, 9 May 1951.

71 OV 44/70, no. 140, memo, 29 March 1951.

72 T 233/959, memo, Beighton, 9 May 1951; CAOG 9/225, CAs to CO, 9 July 1951.

73 CAOG 1/2.

74 CAOG 1/2, JMF annual report, 1951; *ibid.*, JMF annual report, 1955.

75 WN 13, A1988; CA (m) 25, p. 5.

Progress of the JCF and the JMF in the 1960s

The Agents' response to the fall in JCF and later JMF deposits was to further increase the liquidity of both Funds, now termed the Joint Funds, and, as discussed in chapter two, to provide fewer advances to colonies.[76] In the 1960s, to maintain and, if possible, to increase deposits, they also made other changes to the Funds - altering the manner in which the dividends were calculated, accepting fixed and foreign currency deposits, and widening the range of investments in which their contents were placed.

The dividend changes occurred in 1962 and were made because payment in arrears was believed to discourage use of the Funds. Depositors preferred to know the return that they would receive on their money before it was deposited, and the payment of an average rate of interest over each quarter disadvantaged those clients that had large amounts of money in the Funds when the rate earned was high and small amounts when it was low. The retrospective dividend was replaced by a current interest rate, which varied as the financial environment changed.[77] It was also decided that, if the Funds earned more money than they paid out at the agreed rate, the surplus, rather than being returned to the JCF or JMF, would be placed in the Agents' own Office Fund, which would meet any net deficits. This was normal banking practice and its adoption transformed the CAs from agents to pseudo bankers.[78] However, unlike banks, they continued to charge a fee for managing the Funds, $^1/_5$ per cent of deposits, even though their costs were more than covered by the investment surpluses. Moreover, they failed to inform either their clients or the Bank of England of the continued existence of the commission, which, levied on the Funds and not directly on clients, did not appear on their published scale of charges and was effectively hidden.[79]

The CA's motive for the scam was largely self-interest. The extra money earned ensured the survival of the Office and the 'façade' of agency was essential if the Funds were to accept foreign currency deposits from clients, the investment of which encouraged depositors to use the JCF/JMF by increasing their dividends. Only banks and agents could invest foreign currencies overseas, and, as the Agency was not a bank, if the Bank of England had suspected that it was not acting as an agent its whole foreign currency business would have had to have been closed down.[80] Indirectly, the policy also helped the CA's clients. The extra income earned from the management fee subsidised the provision of other services, for which a relatively low commission was charged, and all the JCF/JMF depositors benefited from the higher dividend paid.

The Agents accepted two new types of deposit for the Funds – fixed deposits and foreign currency deposits. Territories were allowed to lodge monies in the Funds for fixed periods from 1965 to 1968. Money was accepted for terms of

76 ADM 14/50, no. 30, memo, 16 Jan. 1958.
77 CAOG 9/228, memo, 17 Dec. 1962.
78 L 228, memo, Hewins, 14 May 1975; PP 1981–2, 364, p. 27.
79 L 228, memo, Hewins, 14 May 1975.
80 *Ibid.*

3 months, 6 months, 12 months, and, after June 1967 and changes in the Inland Revenues' procedures, for over one year, and the interest rate paid increased the longer the money was held.[81] The CAs were aware that if they failed to provide this service, clients would turn to other financial institutions, and, in particular, to the Bank of England. The knowledge that deposits would be available for a given amount of time also allowed them to increase the Funds' long-term investments, which paid relatively high interest rates.[82] Such was the success of the business, that, by the end of 1966, the Funds held £102m of fixed deposits, which accounted for 53.4 per cent of their total holdings.[83] From 1968, however, the deposits were fed into Finvest, the Agency's secondary banking Fund, where they helped to finance the new enterprise, and, invested more widely, earned higher returns. Over the years 1969 to 1974, Finvest held a monthly average of £107.7m of these deposits, and, in December 1974, £186.3m.

Foreign currency deposits began to be accepted into the Joint Funds in 1968. As with fixed deposits, there was a great demand from colonies for the new service, especially as the Bank of England was not permitted to take non-sterling monies.[84] Independent territories were increasingly trading with non-sterling countries and earning large amounts of foreign currency, the Agents were purchasing more goods overseas, which had to be paid for in the local medium of exchange, and loans provided by the International Bank of Reconstruction and Development and kept in the Funds until spent were largely in the form of US dollars.[85] The Agents' eagerness to take on the new role was related to the investment of the deposits overseas, which increased returns and allowed the Finance Department to gain experience of foreign bond and equity markets that would prove useful when the flight from sterling accelerated and clients began to demand that their Investment Funds be placed outside the UK.[86]

The amount of foreign currency in the Funds rose from £3.7m at the start of 1969 to £59m in December 1970 and £220m at the end of 1974, £108m of which belonged to Abu Dhabi.[87] The deposits were lodged for fixed periods at a set rate of interest that rose with the length of time the money was to be held. They were invested overseas in bank deposits and bonds and equities and lent on the inter-bank market.[88] Cardinal rules of investment were that the currencies were kept separate and placed in assets valued in the same currency, and that a portion of each medium of exchange was held in relatively liquid form in order to allow withdrawals to be met.[89]

As the Agents themselves admitted, the deposits were 'quite unsuited' to

81 PP 1981–2, 364, p. 27; JCF annual report, 1966, 1967.

82 SA, Tribunal, vol. 2, papers from Jan. 1979, 22 May 1979, p. 49.

83 JCF annual reports, 1966.

84 *Ibid.*, 1968 ; L 121, 1976, Vol. 5, 73/76, deposit taking.

85 L 121, 1976, Vol. 5, 73/76, deposit taking; L 35, 1968, no. 38; L 227, CAs to B of E, 27 March 1972.

86 JCF annual reports, 1968; CAOG 21/377, memo, Shuter, 20 Feb. 1974.

87 JCF annual reports, 1969; L 188, file 1, Finance directorate contribution to 1971 annual report; *ibid.*, file 2, meeting, 29 May 1975.

88 L 4, Finance Dept., Nov. 1968; L 35, 1968, no. 38; L 38, no. 44.

89 L 227, statement, Hewins; L 188, file 1, field of investment for JCF, approx. may 1971; JCF annual report, 1968.

the Joint Funds, and were 'forced into [their] framework' in order to by-pass exchange control regulations.[90] The Agency could invest currencies overseas only if it acted as an agent to others, which appeared to be the case as regards the JCF/JMF. Because their true relationship with the Funds was one of pseudo banker, the CAs, not wishing to attract attention to their activities, did not apply for authority from the Bank of England to deal in foreign currencies, and, when the Bank requested an application to be made in 1971, the letter, though apparently written, was never sent.[91] Some time later, however, it appears that Bank officials became aware of the Agents' actual status, but chose to 'shelter behind the façade of agency' and to rule that they were not in contravention of exchange regulations.[92] The reason for this untypical act of charity remains obscure, but may be related to a wish not to upset the depositors of these currencies, in particular Abu Dhabi, which had large holdings in the London market.

The Finance Directorate widened the range of investments in which Joint Funds could be placed in 1966, when the CA Board decreed that they could additionally be lent on a secured and on an unsecured basis to Finance Houses, the London branches of US banks, the Commonwealth Development Corporation, and UK water companies.[93] It was believed that 'in view of the degree of independence reached by the Office, it was appropriate that [it] should have complete discretion in the selection of investments' and that a move into other areas would increase returns and protect the Fund from the depreciation suffered by gilts and Treasury bills.[94]

Having shrugged off their former restrictions, over the following few years the Agents became even more adventurous in their use of the Funds. Money began to be placed in trade bills, invested in overseas equities, and, deposited or lent to fringe banks and companies, including those institutions in which the Agents' secondary banking arm had interests.[95] From the late 1960s, the Funds also began to borrow sums from the London money market, which were re-lent at a slightly higher interest rate to other financial institutions, and started to obtain loans from overseas banks, the proceeds of which were re-invested in foreign equities.[96] By December 1970, total borrowings on the London market amounted to £38.63m, and, in March 1972, foreign banks had lent the Funds the equivalent of £6.7m.[97]

Inevitably, the Bank of England expressed concern at the Agents' new policy. In October 1972, it concluded that the Fund's overseas borrowings were contrary

90 L 228, memo, Hewins, 14 May 1975.

91 L 118, p. 77; L 227, statement, Shuter.

92 L 228, memo, Hewins, 14 May 1975.

93 L 188, file 1, unsecured lending, approx. May 1971; L 35, 1966, no. 13. The Finance Houses had to be owned by or associated with clearing banks and the US banks had to be members of the American Reserve Bank system (L 35, 1966, no. 13).

94 L 36, 1965/6, meeting, 22 March 1966; L 188, file 1, unsecured lending, approx. May 1971.

95 PP 1977–8, 8, p. 19. In December 1970, the JCF had £250,000 and $756,301 in current accounts at E. D. Sassoons, had lent £100,000 to International Hotels Kenya Ltd, and held £1.5m of shares in the Provident Clothing Co. (CAOG 21/68). In September 1971, it lent £3m to FNFC (CAOG 21/186, note, 15 Sept. 1971).

96 L 228, memo, Hewins, 18 June 1975; L 185, memo, Dec. 1973.

97 L 6, Banking Dept., Dec. 1970; L 227, CAs to B of E, 27 March 1972.

to regulations and should be halted. Alan Challis, the Head of the Agents' Finance Department, however, appealed to the higher echelons of the Bank and the Agents appear to have unilaterally decided that borrowings should continue, albeit on a smaller scale, until a final decision had been reached, which appears never to have occurred.[98] During the early 1970s, the Bank also conducted a running battle with the Agents over their purchase of Treasury bills for both the Joint Funds and colonial Investment Funds. When the CAs had excess money at the end of the day, they were in the habit of buying from the Bank Treasury bills that matured in 91 days, which they later sold to discount houses. The Bank objected to the practice because the purchases made the management of the market more difficult and the bills were sold to just three institutions, which were thus placed in a favoured position. There were also concerns that the Agents made a loss when they sold the bills, which were rarely held for the full 91 days.[99] Bernard Wheately, the CA's Sterling Money Market Manager, was therefore asked in June 1970 to deposit all such surplus cash in the discount market.[100]

At first, the CAs followed the Bank's advice, but in December 1970 requested permission to buy bills on those few occasions when the discount market was reluctant to take their funds. The Bank reluctantly agreed, though strongly suggested that short-dated bills be purchased ie those that matured in less than 91 days.[101] But, for some reason, Wheately continued to buy 91 day bills. The Bank on a number of occasions reminded him that this was costly, but 'the point seems not to have struck home!' and the purchases continued.[102] Moreover, the Agents gradually increased the number of bills they bought, and, when they missed the deadline for the purchase of bills, placed the uninvested sums in their current account at the Bank, which paid no interest. Eventually in 1973, the Bank broke its own regulations and gave the CAs an interest bearing account, usually reserved for banking customers, into which all spare liquid funds could be deposited.[103] This appears to have largely solved the problem, though 91 day bills continued to be occasionally bought.

The new investment policy was far from a success. By the end of December 1970, the JCF had a deficit of £1.64m, largely due to falls in foreign equity prices and 'a substantial unwise investment in the American market'.[104] For the Agents, the loss was nothing short of a 'disaster'.[105] Knowledge of the deficit would discourage depositors placing money in the Fund and could even lead to large withdrawals and would damage the Agency's reputation in the City, reducing the ability of its secondary banking arm to attract funds. Fearing for his own position and confidant that foreign equity prices would rise, Challis thus disguised the loss through a complex rearrangement of the CAs' accounts. The property assets of their Office Fund, which largely comprised their London headquarters,

98 L 188, file 2, memo, Shuter, 28 Dec. 1973.
99 HO 268/337, memo, B of E, 21 May 1970.
100 *Ibid.*, memo, B of E, 29 June 1970.
101 *Ibid.*, memo, B of E, 4 Dec. 1970.
102 *Ibid.*, memo, B of E, 6 Dec. 1971.
103 *Ibid.*, memo, B of E, 1 March 1973.
104 PP 1977–8, 8, p. 49; L 118/5, p. 150.
105 PP 1977–8, 8, p. 50.

were written up by £1.64m and this amount then transferred to the JCF. To hide the transfer, the Agency published a set of consolidated accounts, which allowed the £1.64m to be described as 'due from Office Fund' in the JCF balance sheet and as 'amounts due to Funds managed by the Crown Agents' in the Office Fund sheet.[106]

To the Agents' accountant, P. W. Nowers, this amounted to a 'rigging of the books', and, in the Fay enquiry, he claimed that he remonstrated with Challis, only to be told to 'keep out – this is nothing to do with you'. 'Shaken' by the confrontation, he considered taking the matter higher, but eventually decided to take no further action, fearful that 'Challis would have stabbed me in the back', and that he would destroy the Agency.[107] Strangely, Nowers failed to repeat these accusations when giving evidence to the later Croom-Johnson enquiry and they were not supported by other witnesses.[108] Challis categorically denied that the meeting took place, and, furthermore, vehemently rejected the suggestion that the rearrangement of the accounts amounted to a cover-up. He insisted that the deficit was an 'unimportant transient phenomenon' and there was 'no risk in publication', the writing up of the Office Funds property assets was long overdue, and the Agency had been pressured into the use of consolidated accounts by the Exchequer & Audit Department. Rather than concealing the loss, he had merely sought to 'camouflage it', and, in doing this, he had done nothing improper, nor, in the context of company accounts, unusual.[109]

Much to Challis's relief, equity prices recovered. The Agents, however, continued to invest in overseas equities and did nothing to reduce their US portfolio. When, in 1973, there was a further fall in prices, the JCF was therefore again plunged into deficit. The situation was made even worse by the fall in the dollar exchange rate, which further reduced the value of the investments, and the fact that much of the money used to buy the shares was borrowed.[110] These loans would eventually have to be repaid, and, in the meantime, interest payments had skyrocketed. By July 1973, the CAs' US portfolio, which had been financed by \$11.5m of loans, was worth just \$5m and the loan service costs amounted to 23 per cent.[111]

To prevent complete meltdown, John Shuter, the Head of Investment, and G. R. Towse, Controller of Financial Services, recommended that the JCF should be given a £2.5m loan from the Office Fund, which would be used to pay off the bulk of the overseas borrowings and permit the liquidation of portfolios. Challis rejected the proposal, arguing that a subvention would cause the losses to become public knowledge, that the money could be used more profitably elsewhere, and that markets would eventually recover.[112] In fact, prices fell further, losses mounted, and, early in 1974, Shuter and Towse received their subvention.

106 L 185, meeting, 15 Dec. 1970; *ibid.*, note, 15 Dec. 1970.

107 L 118/5, p. 169; PP 1977–8, 8, pp. 49–50. After making the accusations to the Fay enquiry, Nowers collapsed in the witness box.

108 L 118/5, p. 151, 169.

109 *Ibid.*, pp. 152–3, 158.

110 L 188, file 2, memo, Shuter, 28 Dec. 1973; *ibid.*, notes, Shuter, no date.

111 *Ibid.*, notes, Shuter, no date.

112 *Ibid.*; *ibid.*, memo, 28 Dec. 1973.

By the middle of that year, the Fund had pulled out of the Belgium and French markets, reduced its Dutch, German, and North American holdings and had borrowings of £3.8m down from £13m in November 1973.[113] Having limited future equity losses, however, they were then faced with the consequences of the secondary banking collapse, described in detail in chapter nine. Like the Agents' secondary banking arm, the Fund had lent large sums to a number of fringe banks. As the banking crisis worsened, these found it difficult to make repayments or succumbed to bankruptcy and the Fund was forced to write off even more debts.[114] By December 1974, the JCF thus had an overall deficit of £2.5m, and was only kept afloat by a further subvention from the Office Fund in April the following year.[115]

Conclusion

The main aim of the Agents in their management of the JCF and the JMF was to maximise depositors' returns, and, to make sure that this goal was fulfilled, they sought to invest as large a portion of the Funds'contents as possible in long-term securities, which paid relatively high interest rates. The Treasury and the Bank of England, on the other hand, wished the Funds to be highly liquid, in order to ensure that large sums were invested in UK government securities, to reduce the outflow of monies from the UK, and to avoid a JCF/JMF collapse, which could damage the stock market and prompt the CAs' clients to sell their other sterling investments.

In the case of colonial Investment Funds, the Agents' return maximisation strategy was acceptable. Principals made few and generally predictable demands on the Funds to which they remitted given amounts each year. With the Joint Funds, however, this was not the case. The Funds were in a constant state of flux and the amount of money deposited and withdrawn was dependent on a range of factors and could change rapidly. The Agents, overconfident and lacking a great understanding of the wider world, seem never to have fully understood the unique nature of the JCF/JMF, and, as a result, kept liquidity excessively low and in 1931, 1951, 1971 and 1974 faced financial crises. Through their technical abilities, and, in the early 1930s, sheer luck, they managed to prevent the Funds collapsing. However, their liking for risk and the regular crises diminished the Treasury's and the Bank's faith in their financial abilities, which prompted both organisations to demand an excessively cautious investment policy for the colonies' Investment Funds, and, in 1974 to lay most of the blame for the bankcruptcy of the Agency on the CAs themselves.

To meet their primary objective, the Agents were also prepared to resort to behaviour that, though commonplace in the City, was regarded as unethical in government circles, where the moral norms of the Civil Service predominated.

113 *Ibid.*, meeting, 21 Aug. 1974; L 10, Investment Dept., July 1974; *ibid.* March 1974.

114 Loans to the Burston group, the Israel-British Bank, SIS, and the Stern Group failed to be repaid (*ibid.*, meeting, 21 Aug. 1974; *ibid.*, meeting, 27 Feb. 1975).

115 *Ibid.*, meeting, 27 Feb. 1975; *ibid.*, meeting, 21 April 1975.

The CAs flouted their 1932 JCF and 1950 JCM liquidity agreements with the Treasury, defrauded the Inland Revenue in their management of non-colonial floating balances, circumvented foreign currency regulations in the late 1960s, and, in 1971, issued a disingenuous set of accounts. These actions again damaged relations with the Treasury and the Bank of England, both of which regarded the Agency as untrustworthy and undeserving of respect.

On a number of occasions, the CAs also acted in the pursuit of their own interests. From 1925 to 1947, underwriting commission was placed in the Office Fund rather than in the JCF, in 1932 they sold the contents of Sinking Funds at a loss in order to save the JCF, and, from 1962 to 1975, they charged a fee for managing the Joint Funds, even though their costs were covered by interest rate surpluses. All these actions were undertaken to ensure the success of the Agency and the continued employment of its staff. It seems doubtful that the Office would have survived the collapse of the JCF, underwriting commissions prevented fee increases for other services, which could have led to the loss of clients, and, without the greater returns earned by foreign currency deposits, fewer depositors would have been willing to make use of the Joint Funds. Whether these actions were also against the interests of their principals, however, is debatable. The collapse of the JCF would have equally harmed colonial finances, and clients undoubtedly benefited from the subsidisation of the Agency's other services and from the higher JCF returns.

5

The Cost of Supplies

From 1920 to 1974, the Agents purchased £2,064m of supplies (Figure 5.1). At the start of the period, colonial clients were required to buy of all of their stores that were not manufactured or produced within their own colonies or in adjacent countries from the Agency. Over time, however, this requirement lapsed, and, by 1959, they were free to buy supplies themselves either direct from overseas manufacturers or from local merchants. The articles purchased by the Agents largely went to Africa, the Far East and the West Indies and Caribbean in 1936 and to Africa and the Far East in 1964 (Table 5.1, Appendix 4), and comprised engineering equipment, which in 1963 accounted for 48 per cent of orders, and a wide range of other goods, including cement, clothing and textiles, medical supplies, stamps and stationery.[1] Clients ordered merchandise via indents, which varied in value from trifling sums to thousands of pounds and could contain a request for a single item or for many hundreds of articles. Depending on their contents, the indents were passed to either an Engineering Purchasing Department or a General Purchasing Department, where they were split into orders and sent, directly or after competitive tender, to manufacturers. To ensure that only quality products were dispatched, a large proportion of the orders were inspected after, and, in some cases, during production, and, to make sure that they arrived at their destination in good condition, some were also packed in the Agency's packing store. The CAs then arranged their shipment, and, if requested, provided freight insurance through their Marine Insurance Fund.

Throughout the period, the Agency's procurement activities were the subject of much complaint from both colonial governments and merchants, who claimed that the cost of the stores delivered was excessively high, that cheaper goods could be bought from the local merchant community, and that supplies were subject to long delivery delays. There was also much internal concern about the efficiency of the buying procedures adopted. From 1943 to 1973, there were nine investigations of the work of the purchasing departments, one of which was required by the Parliamentary Select Committee on Estimates, working parties were set up in 1968 and 1969 to investigate the inspection and packing of goods, and there

1 L 1, Electrical Engineering Dept. report, 1963; *ibid.*, Mechanical Engineering Department report, 1963. From 1920 to 1954, the average annual value of orders for clothing, textiles, paint and oil was £2.29m, of cement £425,690, of stationery £610,473, of medical supplies £1.196m, and of stamps £144,205 (CAOG 12/40, annual returns, CAOG 12/41, annual returns).

Figure 5.1. Supplies purchased, inspected and insured, 1920–74

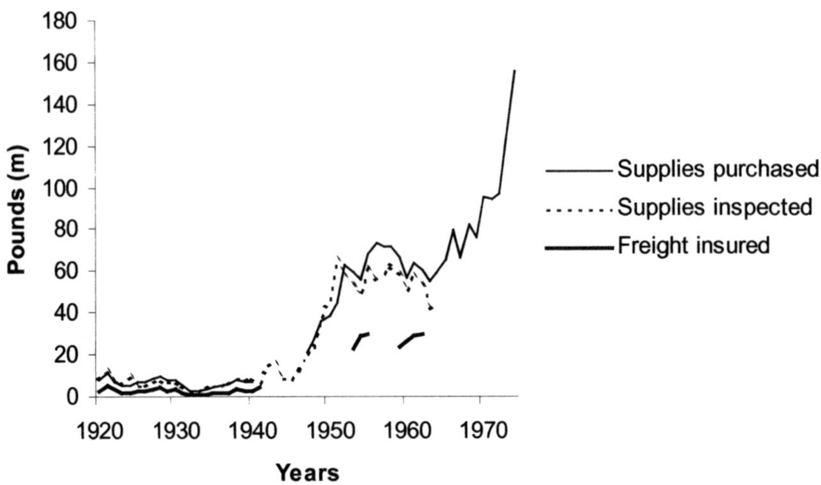

Source. Supplies purchased: 1920–61 - SA, CA annual accounts; SA, notes for office history, 1958–65, p. 22. 1966–74 - L 1, Contracts Dept. reports, 1963–65. Supplies inspected: SA, CA Engineering Inspection Dept. annual reports. Freight insured: L 245, memo, 16 Nov. 1965.

Notes. No purchasing figures found for 1941–46. No inspection statistics for 1964–74. No insurance figures for 1942–52, 1956–58, and 1963–74.

were two reviews of all the tasks undertaken by Agency, which included studies of procurement. In addition, purchasing staff, through the Society of Civil Servants and the Whiteley Council, criticised the effectiveness of their departments in 1951 and 1956, and, in 1973, Executive Officers in the General Purchasing Department submitted a paper detailing more defects.[2]

This chapter and the one that follows seek to evaluate these criticisms. The present chapter examines the cost of the goods supplied by the Agents. Part one investigates the prices paid for merchandise by considering, in turn, the various factors that had an impact on price. The section thus explores how goods were bought, the adequacy of the knowledge of market prices possessed by CA buyers and the possibility that they were influenced in their choice of supplier by bribes or other inducements, the competitiveness of the purchasing contracts negotiated, and the type of manufacturer that received orders. Part two discusses the non-price costs of the goods bought, specifically the Agents' purchasing commission, the fees paid for inspection and packing, and the freight and insurance charges. The chapter concludes with an examination of the regulations that required colonial governments to use the CAs and of the allegation that clients could have purchased cheaper goods from local merchants.

2 See later references.

Table 5.1. Stores purchased and shipped by territory, 1936 and 1964

	1936		1964	
	Amount (£m)	**Percentage**	**Amount (£m)**	**Percentage**
E Africa	6.8	16.3	11.4	19.8
Central Africa	1.4	3.4	1.4	2.5
West Africa	9.4	22.5	12.8	22.2
W Indies and Caribbean	6	14.4	3.9	6.8
Far East	6.6	15.8	20.8	36.1
Middle East and Mediterranean	4.6	11	4.8	8.4
Pacific area	4.2	10.2	1.8	3.2
Atlantic area	0.3	0.8	0.48	0.8
United Nations			0.08	0.1

Source. CAOG 12/40, memo, 1936; L 13, minutes of meetings 1965–6, draft for 1964 annual report.

Price

Methods of purchase

The Agents purchased supplies via competition, simultaneous tender, check tendering, direct purchase and running contract. It was their proud boast that the majority of goods were bought by competitive tender.[3] In reality, competition was limited both as regards the number of orders that went out to tender and the firms that were asked to compete. Not all orders were subject to full competition, defined as the issue of more than two tender forms. Up to 1929, tenders were sent out when orders exceeded £100. It was then decided that only orders worth over £150 should be tendered, as competition 'very often makes for considerable delay and saves little money'.[4] During the war, the lack of staff forced competition to be even more limited, and, in 1953, the order value above which tendering occurred was increased to £500.[5]

Relatively few firms were asked to tender - up to eight from 1929, and, in 1947/8, generally four or five - and of these few replied.[6] In 1947/8, for example, of the eight firms that were requested to compete for the supply of books for Northern Rhodesia, only two made offers, one of which was unable to make a delivery by the required date.[7] Moreover, tender forms were only sent to firms on the Agents' lists of suppliers, to which it was difficult to gain access. Manufacturers had to furnish details of their companies' operations, a banker's reference, and the names of government departments, public bodies or important

3 CA (m) 25, '*The Crown Agents, London. Their Organization and Functions*, London 1955.

4 CAOG 12/56, Warde, 15 May 1929; CAOG 12/73, memo, 27 Nov. 1944.

5 CAOG 12/73, memo, 27 Nov. 1944; L 18/5, guide to the organisation and method of working of the Stores Dept., May 1953, p. 11.

6 CAOG 12/56, Warde, 15 May 1929; PP 1947/8, vii, q. 5465.

7 CA (m) 29, report on buying methods, 27 May 1949, p. 56.

customers that they had supplied in the past. These clients were then approached for references, and, if these were satisfactory, the firm's works were inspected by a CA inspector on whose report a final decision as to inclusion was made.[8] Because of the rigorousness of the selection process, the lists contained a relatively small number of firms. An analysis of successful tenders for large orders that were published in the *Ministry of Labour Gazette* in 1937 found that the Agents placed orders with only 530 companies, and an internal investigation discovered that in 1980 they used just 5,602 contractors.[9] The lists, at least in 1949, were rarely updated and excluded a number of leading firms, which had failed to apply for inclusion or had been rejected because they completed little public sector work.[10]

The companies chosen to tender were given just five days in 1958, and, thereafter, five working days to return their tender forms, a wholly inadequate amount of time, and the winner of the competition was not always the company that offered the lowest price.[11] In 1953, the Agents, when deciding which bid to accept, took into account price, but also delivery date, which, as discussed below, was of particular importance in the 1950s, the quality of the articles supplied, and 'any other relevant factor'.[12]

Increasingly, client governments required tenders to be held simultaneously in the UK and in their own countries, the CAs tendering UK firms and the government approaching local merchants. The process, again, often led to higher prices. Many clients had no intention of giving the Agents the work, whatever the price quoted, merely wishing to receive their tenders for budgetary purposes, to check that colonial suppliers were not wildly overcharging them, and to 'beat down' local prices, threatening to use the CAs if they were not reduced.[13] Others genuinely compared tenders, but gave the local suppliers preference, awarding them orders if their prices were not more than 5 per cent, and, in the case of Ceylon and Malaya in the mid-1960s, 10 per cent greater than those quoted by the Agents.[14] In order to discourage the adoption of such tenders, the CAs from 1927 charged clients their 1 per cent commission even if goods were purchased locally. It was argued that the tendering process involved much work for which they would otherwise receive no remuneration and discouraged firms on their supplier lists from taking part in competitions.[15] The charge, however, caused many colonies to abandon their use of the Agency altogether and led to a large number of complaints, and, in 1933, it was abolished.[16]

Check tendering involved the Agents, after having chosen a contractor from

8 CAOG 10/170, memo, 5 July 1954.

9 *Ministry of Labour Gazette*, Feb. 1937 to Jan. 1938; L 145, buying intelligence report, Feb. 1981.

10 CA (m) 29, report ..., p. 60.

11 CAOG 12/73, Export Group to CAs, 26 March 1958; *ibid.*, CAs to Export Group, 3 April 1958.

12 L 18/5, p. 5.

13 L 1, General Dept. report 1965; CS 6852, memo, 7 July 1956.

14 CAOG 14/14, Buckley, 30 June 1965; *ibid.*, Buckley, 7 June 1966. See, for example, WN 17, O Kenya 1 and L 178, Abbot, no date.

15 CO 323/985/19, CAs to CO, 8 July 1927.

16 L 12, meeting, 12 June 1963, circular, 15 March 1933.

their lists of suppliers, sending a tender to another firm to check that the price quoted was competitive. From 1929, check tenders were used, at the discretion of buyers, for all orders over £25 but under £150, and, from 1953, for all orders under £500.[17] The tenders ensured relatively low prices, as it was assumed that recipients would be unaware that an order had not been subjected to full competition, and reduced the Agents' costs and the time it took to process a request for goods. During the Second World War, the vast majority of orders put up to competition were sent to just two firms, and, in 1947/8, 70 per cent of such orders.[18]

Orders were sent direct to manufacturers without any form of competition in a number of circumstances. Most commonly when a colonial government named a manufacturer or a proprietary brand on its indent. Under colonial regulation number 52, when this occurred, the CAs were required to follow the wishes of the colony unless they believed the employment of the named supplier was not in its best interests.[19] Privately, the Agents abhorred the regulation. They believed that the use of named manufacturers damaged their relations with those on supplier lists and that local agents put pressure on or bribed local purchasing officers to name their employing companies and that this led to the purchase of high priced poor quality goods.[20] Nonetheless, they rarely queried a colony's choice of supplier or refused to carry out a request, even when a high price was quoted.[21] Correspondence with a client government and the discovery of another supplier was time-consuming and increased costs, suggestions that the goods should be obtained elsewhere would be 'ignored' or 'resented' by the indenting officer, and it was feared that a refusal to use a named manufacturer could prompt the indenter and the company concerned to complain to the Colonial Office and the Board of Trade, damaging the Agents' relations with these departments.[22]

The CAs sent orders direct to manufacturers on their own volition when their contents were needed urgently; they were for books, periodicals, stationery, and, until 1952, for drugs; they were to be obtained abroad; their description on the indent was vague; and if the value of the order was under £25.[23] The decision to abandon competition was made by the buyer, who also chose which firm on the supplier lists would receive the order.[24] The extent to which direct ordering was used varied over time. By the early 1950s, staff shortages had caused this method of purchase to 'increase considerably'.[25] Around half of engineering orders were being placed without tender and there was a fear that the Agents were paying relatively high prices for goods. At the same time, it was discovered that there

17 CAOG 12/73, memo, 27 Nov. 1944; L 18/5, p. 11.
18 CAOG 12/73, memo 27 Nov. 1944; CA (m) 29, report …, pp. 12, 63.
19 CO 323/1073/12, memo, no date; *ibid.*, CAs to CO, 14 Jan. 1930.
20 CO 323/995/5, Lambert to CO, 11 Jan. 1928.
21 CA (m) 29, report …, p. 58.
22 *Ibid.*, p. 17; L 18/8, Hicks' interim report, 18 March 1957, p. 1. See, for example, CAOG 17/77, B of T to CAs, 24 May 1950.
23 CAOG 12/74, memo, 29 June 1951; L 18/5, p. 12; CAOG 12/56, memo, 5 Dec. 1929.
24 PP 1947/8, vii, q. 5466.
25 CAOG 12/74, memo, 20 April 1951.

were problems in the operation of the system. In theory, before approaching a supplier, the buyer placed the estimated price of the good required on the order, which was sent to the chosen firm. The company then told the buyer the price it would charge, and, if this was close to the estimate, it was allowed to commence work. In reality, in the Engineering Purchasing Department buyers failed to place an estimated price on orders, which allowed suppliers to 'charge more or less what they like'.[26] In the General Purchasing Department, an estimated price was given, but it was the price supplied by the indenting colony. Such prices were 'often very wide of the mark', and, if excessive, there was a danger that 'unscrupulous suppliers' would charge the estimated price rather than the actual price.[27] It was also found that many contractors only informed the buyers of the price to be charged after a good had been manufactured, and that there was great inconsistency in the use of direct ordering – whereas some buyers went direct to manufacturers 'very frequently', others almost always called for tenders.[28]

In 1952, therefore, it was decided that direct ordering should be overhauled. All requests for drugs had to be put out to competition, check tenders had to be issued for orders between £25 and £150, and, for all other items, direct orders had to be used sparingly.[29] As regards prices, only the known price was to be placed on orders, and no contract was to be given until the suppler had informed the purchasing department of the eventual cost.[30] The result of these changes was that the time taken to place orders lengthened to 20 to 30 days, colonial complaints of delay mounted, and the Agency' s costs soared. Fearful that colonies would abandon them on independence, the CAs thus gradually began to reverse the new policy.[31] In 1955, the Engineering Purchasing Department allowed direct orders to be made for small value goods for which the current price was available, and, in the following year, drugs began to be bought direct.[32] Finally, in 1959 all purchasing departments were required to abandon check tenders and competition for all orders under £50, and, in the case of orders worth between £50 and £500, to use check tenders only when the current price was not known or 'a great advantage would accrue'.[33]

A form of direct purchase was the running contract, orders financed from the Joint Colonial Fund that were placed with suppliers before indents for the goods concerned had been received. Because of the size of the orders, the Agents could negotiate favourable prices with manufacturers, and, as the goods were immediately available, there were no delivery delays.[34] Unfortunately, the Colonies' insistence on non-standardised supplies reduced the amount of merchandise that could be bought in this way, and the contracts involved a degree of

26 *Ibid.*, memo, 10 April 1951.
27 *Ibid.*, memo 11/1/52; CA (m) 29, report …, p. 18.
28 CAOG 12/74, Memo 29/6/51; L 18/3, Curtis's report on G procedure and method, 13 Oct. 1950.
29 CAOG 12/74, memo, 29 June 1951.
30 *Ibid.*; *ibid.*, memo, 21 May 1951.
31 *Ibid.*, memo 1 March 1955; *ibid.*, memo, 15 June 1959; L 18/9, p. 7.
32 CAOG 12/74, memo, 1 March 1955; *ibid.*, CAs to Singapore, 10 July 1956.
33 *Ibid.*, memo, 15 June 1959.
34 L 18/5, p. 14.

risk and the Colonial Office therefore opposed their adoption. It was difficult to determine future colonial demand, and, if the Agents over-ordered, any loss on sales in the open market could have to be borne by the Office Fund. Manufacturers, in the immediate post-war years, were also reluctant to take on long-term commitments, and any price saving was partially offset by the cost of storage, double-handling and the loss of the interest on the money tied up in the goods.[35] The use of such contracts was therefore limited, and, in 1947/8, the Agents bought in advance only cement, galvanized sheets, military and police clothing and steel bars.[36] After independence, numerous clients called for the greater use of the contracts, and, in 1966, purchasing departments were allowed to buy in advance up to £150,000 of goods at any one time, and, if necessary, to finance such orders from the Office Fund, adding the interest loss to the price charged.[37] Clients, however, when actually given the option of advance bulk purchase were unwilling to put up the money or to pay the extra cost if the goods had been financed by the Office Fund, and, in 1975, the accountants Coopers & Lybrand in their review of the Agency's activities reported that a disappointing number of running contracts were in operation.[38]

Determination of prices

The competitiveness of the prices accepted by buyers after a tender had been held and when purchasing goods direct was dependent on their knowledge of ruling market prices. Unfortunately, a number of internal investigations concluded that purchasing department employees had difficulty determining whether the prices quoted by suppliers were excessively high, partly because of the way the divisions were staffed and partly because of the purchasing procedures adopted.[39] Staffing problems comprised the employment of too few buyers, many of whom had little experience of buying. From 1940 onwards, the purchasing departments were understaffed. During the war, a large number of clerks joined the armed forces or were seconded to other government departments, and, at the end of hostilities, the seconded employees, who had often achieved promotion in their new departments, were unwilling to return to their pre-war lower grade positions, and the employment of replacements was made difficult by the tight labour conditions.[40] As time passed, there was also a marked reluctance to employ more buyers. A larger establishment could only be financed by an increase in the purchasing commission, which would lead to the loss of customers, and there was the fear that the Agency would be left with a huge redundancy bill if demand for its services plummeted after independence.[41]

The situation was not helped by the constant movement of staff. The purchasing division was regarded as a training ground for new entrants, who,

35 PP 1947/8, vii, q. 5408, 5469, 5471; CAOG 17/21, Parliamentary question, 25 May 1925.

36 PP 1947/8, vii, q. 5468–9.

37 L 36, meeting, 23 Aug 1966; *ibid.*, meeting, 26 Aug. 1966.

38 L 9, General Dept. reports, Oct. 1973; L 18/25, Coopers and Lybrand report, 16 May 1975, p. 12.

39 See, for example, CA (m) 29, report …, p. 13; L 18/8, p. 7.

40 PP 1947/8, vii, q. 5405; Abbott, *A Short*, p. 55.

41 L 18/8, meeting with Whitley Council, 1 May 1956.

after initial instruction, were transferred to other departments.[42] Few buyers thus had much experience of buying and the training received was regarded by many to be inadequate.[43] In 1947/8, newcomers 'learnt the job by working alongside a more experienced individual for a comparatively short period', and were then left to 'sink or swim'.[44] Those lower grade staff and Executive Officers who were permanently employed in the department, similarly, stayed a relatively short time and were generally the less able employees. Purchasing was regarded as a dull backwater and staff with initiative who wanted to advance in the Agency sought to leave the division as quickly as possible.[45] As already discussed, it was also the policy of the Agents to move Executive Officers every few years to new departments.

The purchasing procedures adopted made the determination of prices difficult in a number of ways. In 1949, the Salmon enquiry criticized the failure of buyers in the General Purchasing Department to specialize in the acquisition of particular commodities, which would have allowed them to gain the technical knowledge necessary to judge prices, and disparaged their poor relations with suppliers. They rarely, if ever, visited manufacturers or met their representatives and were even discouraged from phoning them, the telephone only being used 'in specially urgent or exceptional cases'.[46] The enquiry also complained that there was no 'regular provision for obtaining and holding copies of catalogues, current price lists or suppliers stock lists'.[47] A criticism taken up in 1957 by the Hicks enquiry, which further noted that the filing of tenders and orders by purchasing colony made it difficult for buyers to discover the most recent price quoted by a manufacturer.[48]

Corruption

Throughout the period, the Agents were subject to claims that they favoured certain firms that supplied expensive or poor quality goods in return for bribes or other inducements. Until the 1960s, there is no evidence of corruption. Thereafter, with one exception, the unethical behaviour that occurred was low grade and relatively unimportant. Members of the purchasing departments accepted low value gifts from contractors at Christmas, a common practice in the private sector, and the Crown Agent, Sir Claude Hayes, used his office 'to his own personal advantage'.[49] When he moved house, he used the purchasing departments to buy new furnishings at a discount, and he was constantly, unsuccessfully, urging officials to give work to companies managed by his friends.[50] In

42 L 18/16, paper submitted by G Dept. Executive Officers, approx. 1973.
43 L 18/8, p. 7.
44 CA (m) 29, report..., p. 18.
45 L 18/16.
46 CA (m) 29, report ..., pp. 12, 16. The Agents feared corruption (L 18/5, p. 13).
47 CA (m) 29, report ..., p. 12.
48 L 18/8, p. 7.
49 Philip Knights' Papers, Les to Knights, 2 Jan. 1969; Pen Portraits, Hayes, Morris to Knights, 2 May 1990.
50 Pen Portraits, Hayes, Morris to Knights, 2 May 1990; anonymous. In his *Who's Who* entry, Hayes listed 'getting value for money in shops' as one of his recreations (*Daily Telegraph*, 3 Dec. 1977, p. 12).

1969, for example, he suggested that the Agency use a firm that employed an old work colleague, and, in 1970, that they 'should get on better terms' with Sir Robert Taylor, Chairman of Costains, who was 'an old friend from Rhodesia days'.[51]

A more important ethical breach involved the firm operated by the Conservative MP John Cordle, E. W. Cordle & Son Ltd, which produced linen and cotton textiles and did a great deal of work for the Agency, completing in 1974 £500,000 of orders, mostly for West Africa.[52] The company appears to have obtained preferential treatment from the CAs. Although it lied in its application to join their list of textile suppliers, falsely claiming that it had completed 'a dozen or more' orders for the Ministry of Supply, and an inspector suspected that it did not manufacture all of its goods itself, in 1957 its name was added to the list.[53] Almost immediately, however, there was disquiet regarding its activities. Cordle made repeated trips to West Africa, where he encouraged governments to place orders with his own company and perhaps other firms, giving them 'the impression … that he represented the CAs and was a drinking partner of Mr Strachan [a CA official]', 'entertaining' senior officials, 'bullying' local storekeepers, making inappropriate use of his status as an MP, and 'leaning' on High Commissioners to recommend his firm to local Ministers.[54] There was also criticism of the goods supplied, which appeared over-priced and were often delivered late.[55]

Despite its poor performance, the firm continued to be used by the Agents, largely because Cordle had the support of Edward Morris, the Assistant Crown Agent. When, in 1968, the Head of the General Purchasing Department, disgusted by Cordle's behaviour, decided to ask for tenders for all indents that named his company, his decision was over-ruled by Morris. After being berated over the phone by Cordle for 'causing trouble', the official was advised to 'get the matter into better focus' and to view Cordle's actions as an example of the 'modern business methods' that had to be employed 'to achieve success'.[56] He was then directed to send all indents that named E. W. Cordle & Son Ltd to the company, to always ask the firm to provide a tender when it was not named, and to pass all phone calls from Cordle to the Agency onto Morris or one of his lieutenants.[57]

51 CAOG 22/28, Hayes, 10 Nov. 1970; *ibid.*, Hayes, 12 Jan. 1973. See also *ibid.*, Hayes, 6 Nov. 1069; *ibid.*, Hayes, 7 Jan. 1969.

52 Michael Gillard and Martin Tomkinson, *Nothing to Declare. The Political Corruptions of John Poulson*, London 1980, p. 131; CAOG 12/128, Clark, 24 May 1974.

53 CAOG 12/128, Cordle to CAs, 14 Dec. 1950; *ibid.*, Ministry of Supply to CAs, 6 Jan. 1951; *ibid.*, Inspector's report, 7 March 1957.

54 Author's interview with John Shuter, 20 October 2004; CAOG 12/128, memo, 22 July 1963; *ibid.*, memo, 25 April 1968; L 168, Goodchild, 19 May 1975. Cordle also 'represented', in West Africa and Libya, Construction Promotions Ltd, a company owned by John Poulson (Alan Doig, *Corruption and Misconduct in Contemporary British Politics*, London 1984, p. 151). The CAs' connections with Poulson are discussed in Chapter nine.

55 See, for example, CAOG 12/128, Principal Pharmacist, Nigeria, 18 July 1963; *ibid.*, memo, 25 April 1968; *ibid.*, CAs to Cordle, 19 June 1959; *ibid.*, memo, 3 Dec. 1964; L 168, Goodchild, 19 May 1975.

56 CAOG 12/128, memo, 25 April 1968; *ibid.*, Dent, 3 May 1968.

57 *Ibid.*, memo, 9 May 1968; *ibid.*, 3 May 1968.

In addition to protecting him from internal criticism, Morris also performed personal favours for Cordle. In 1967, he asked a Senior Executive Officer to allow E. W. Cordle & Sons' orders' to be financed by a recent Ghana loan. The official believed such an action would be 'highly irregular' and asked for a written request, which was not forthcoming.[58] Later that year, Morris insisted that the company be paid £6,599 from the Eastern Nigerian account, even though it was frozen for the duration of the Biafran War, and, since the linen could not be delivered and was eventually rejected by Eastern Nigeria, bizarrely required that it to be stored in the Millbank basement from where it was sold over the following decade.[59] In 1971, meanwhile, he provided Cordle with confidential information regarding a Nigerian broadcasting project, and, later, considered giving part of the scheme to an individual, regarded by the British Embassy in Kuwait as 'the smoothest crook in the Middle East', who had been strongly recommended by the MP as 'a very worthwhile and honest person'.[60]

The reason for Morris's favourable treatment of Cordle is something of a mystery. The CAs dismissed the possibility of bribery, and, if financial inducements were given, they were either very small or not placed in Morris's bank accounts, the contents of which were revealed by the ODA's later analysis of his tax records.[61] Other explanations for his behaviour are blackmail, some at the Crown Agents believed that he was influenced by the 'stick rather than the carrot', or simply friendship.[62] Cordle declared that he was a 'personal friend of Mr Morris', and, in 1971, recommended to an ODA official that Morris be given a knighthood on retirement, and, later that year, intervened on his behalf when, after a share scandal, the ODA insisted that he retire earlier than he had intended.[63] There is also a possibility that Morris may have wished to reward Cordle for generating work for the Agents or for protecting them from Parliamentary criticism. When 'persuading' West African officials to give work to his own and perhaps other companies, Cordle always insisted that the orders be placed through the Crown Agents, and, in 1974, when attempting to persuade a CA official to pay him in advance of delivery, he pointed out that he drummed up indents worth 'hundreds of thousands of pounds' for the Agency.[64] Whether he used his influence to encourage his fellow MPs to defend the Agents from the Parliamentary criticism to which they were being increasingly subjected in the late 1960s and early 1970s is not known. He did, however, perform a similar role for the disgraced architect John Poulson, and, in 1977, was forced to give up his seat in Parliament when it was discovered that he had received a fee for this representation.[65]

58 L 168, Lousley, 26 Oct. 1976.

59 *Ibid.*, Alexander, 20 May 1975; CAOG 12/128, memo, 3 Feb. 1976. In 1976, the basement still held linen worth £1,400 (L 168, Lousley, 26 Oct. 1976).

60 L 168, Morris to Cordle, 10 March 1971; CAOG 10/129, Curtis to Morris, 12 May 1971; L 168, Morris, 18 March 1971.

61 See chapter eight.

62 L 168, memo, 21 Oct. 1976.

63 OD 20/503, Deare, 20 Sept. 1971. The share scandal is discussed in chapter eight.

64 CAOG 12/128, Clark, 24 May 1974.

65 *The Times*, 23 July 1977, p. 1.

Purchasing agreements

The prices paid for the goods bought were dependent on the degree to which indents were split into orders, the discounts offered by suppliers, and the existence in purchasing contracts of price variation clauses. Generally speaking, splitting indents, which often contained requests for many different goods, into a large number of orders increased the Agents' costs and led to delay, but reduced prices, as each article or group of goods was bought from a specialist producer rather than combined with non-related items and sent to a general manufacturer or wholesaler.[66] Over the period, the average number of orders per indent issued by the General Purchasing Department rose from 2.43 in 1914 to 5.13 in 1942, suggesting that competitive prices were obtained, but fell to 2.73 in 1954 to 2.15 in 1963 as independence approached and delay and costs became important determinants in the Agents' survival.[67]

Price discounts comprised trade rebates given to all customers who purchased goods in bulk and concessions for prompt payment. As the Agents placed large orders and paid for them immediately an invoice was received, they obtained both of these rebates.[68] In addition, they received special discounts applicable only to themselves, which were generally kept secret, as suppliers feared that colonial merchants would demand similar price reductions if their existence was made public.[69] These were provided because the CAs gave manufacturers unusually large orders on a regular basis and continued to do so even during trade depressions, albeit at a lower level.[70] Contractors also acquired work without incurring the expense of overseas representation, were freed from the cost and inconvenience of arranging the shipment of the goods supplied, and, after independence, could be assured that full payment would be made and that it would be in sterling rather than in a local currency.[71]

By 1931, the Agents obtained discounts from 181 companies, which averaged 10.9 per cent of the catalogue price and ranged from 1.25 per cent to 70.5 per cent.[72] In that year, however, they became concerned that they were not receiving all the concessions to which they were entitled. Colonial governments constantly informed them that local merchants quoted lower prices for articles sourced from the same suppliers, and, in 1929, it was discovered that whereas A. Gallenkamp & Co. gave the Admiralty and the India Office a 20 per cent discount for its goods, it charged the Agents the full price.[73] Investigation found that discounts failed to be furnished because manufacturers exploited the CAs' laissez faire attitude towards rebates. Buyers only checked that prices were close to the estimate given, many manufacturers did not list price reductions on tender

66 CAOG 12/73, memo, 27 Nov. 1944; L 18/9, p. 24.

67 CAOG 12/40, annual returns; CAOG 12/41, annual returns; L 1, General Dept. report. 1964.

68 CAOG 12/56, memo, 31 Dec. 1931; L 35, 1969, no. 8.

69 CAOG 12/76, CAs to CO, 29 Dec. 1920; L 36, meeting, 5 Jan. 1965.

70 CA (m) 104, Sir John Calder, *Buying and Selling Agents*, London 1947.

71 *Ibid.*; L 76, Frood to Dept. of Trade, 12 Nov. 1981; L 18/22, review of G. Dept. Procurement, Aug. 1973, vol. 3, p. 21.

72 CAOG 12/56, memo, 31 Dec. 1931.

73 *Ibid.*, memo, 27 Oct. 1931; *ibid.*, memo, 3 Dec. 1929.

and direct purchase forms as required, and the purchasing departments had no records detailing contractor rebates.[74]

To rectify the situation, the Agents made substantial changes to their procurement procedures. Instructions were issued that buyers should return to suppliers all completed tender and direct purchasing forms that failed to list concessions, question contractors who did not provide a discount, and 'closely scrutinise' any rebates granted, and, if necessary, demand further concessions.[75] In addition, a new direct order form was designed that emphasized the need to list discounts, suppliers were sent circulars reminding them that their terms should be, at least, as favourable as those offered to other customers, and the purchasing departments were required to obtain details and keep a record of all discounts granted.[76] The result of these reforms was that in the four years from 1932 to 1935 an additional 376 discounts were obtained.[77]

The number of rebates received again fell in the immediate post-war period, largely because manufacturers, faced with a 'sellers' market', had little need to offer incentives to customers, and in the early 1960s, when independence reduced the Agents' turnover and the size of their orders.[78] To encourage the provision of rebates, senior members of staff began to contact the owners and directors of companies on supplier lists, who were informed that their failure to give concessions ultimately damaged the UK economy, as it encouraged client governments to abandon the Agency and instead to purchase goods from foreign suppliers. They were also told that their names could be removed from the lists or orders placed abroad if rebates were not forthcoming.[79]

Contract price variation clauses stated that the final price charged for a good could be different from the agreed price. They were first used by the locomotive industry in the late 1930s, as many manufacturers had made substantial losses during the depression and could not afford to absorb any cost increases that occurred during the completion of orders.[80] After the war, they were more widely adopted. Post-war reconstruction and the increased demand for goods led to labour and raw material shortages and rapid rises in wages and prices and caused long delays to occur between the placing of an order, the purchase of the materials and components needed for its fulfilment, and the manufacture of the article required.[81] Final production costs could therefore be far higher than anticipated, and, to avoid losses, suppliers increasingly began to insist that price variation clauses be included in their contracts. Although most industries used the clauses, they were particularly popular in trades that were organized into an

74 *Ibid.*, memo, 27 Oct. 1931.
75 *Ibid.*; *ibid.*, memo, 14 Dec. 1931.
76 *Ibid.*, memo, 14 Dec. 1931; *ibid.*, circular letter, 8 March 1932; *ibid.*, memo, 31 Dec. 1931.
77 *Ibid.*, six monthly lists of new discounts.
78 CAOG 16/64, Curtis, 26 Oct. 1946; L 18/10, memo, 24 May 1961.
79 L 18/9, p. 26; *ibid.*, Head of X Dept., 14 April 1960.
80 CAOG 10/133, memo, 16 June 1939.
81 CAOG 10/134, memo, 9 July 1954; CAOG 10/136, CAs to EARH, April 1953; *ibid.*, CAs to EARH, 19 Jan. 1956.

association or a cartel or that had little foreign competition or long production processes.[82]

The effect of the clauses on the colonies was extremely damaging. Their existence greatly increased prices. As accurate price comparison was impossible, they made the tender system unworkable, contractors had little incentive to control costs, and some acted fraudulently, claiming for fictitious excess expenditure or delaying delivery after production in order to enhance prices.[83] They also created much inconvenience. The final price of goods often exceeded the amount budgeted and was submitted to the colony years after shipment, forcing funds to be tied up for long periods.[84] After receiving what they assumed to be the final bill, moreover, colonies could receive further demands for money, for which they had to seek additional financial authority.[85]

To reduce the impact of the clauses, the Agents in 1948 persuaded most of their suppliers to agree to pay half of any excess cost accumulated after the agreed shipment date themselves, and, in 1953, added a clause to all contracts that disallowed all claims for extra expenditure after delivery; initiatives that prompted many contractors to quote longer delivery dates.[86] They also required all claims to be accompanied by auditors' certificates in an attempt to halt fraud, and, before a contract was signed, began to ask suppliers to give them some indication of likely price increases, and, from 1958, to provide an undertaking that claims would be lodged as soon as possible and not later than 12 months after shipment. Despite these changes, however, clauses continued to damage colonial economies.[87] In 1956, for example, the East African Railways and Harbours Board faced extra costs on its orders of £1.14m, an average increase of 7.2 per cent or £12,320 per order.[88]

Suppliers

Since contractors set prices, the cost of goods was inevitably influenced by the Agents' choice of supplier. Broadly speaking, prices were raised by their tendency to use a restricted number of small sized firms and by their preference for British companies, but were reduced by their patronage of manufacturers, as opposed to merchants, and the way in which they dealt with cartels. Analysis of orders suggests that they obtained supplies from a restricted number of companies that tended to be located in particular geographical regions, which may have restricted the range of prices obtained. Thirty one per cent of the large orders listed in the 1937 *Ministry of Labour Gazette* went to just 5.5 per cent (29 companies) of all the

82 CAOG 10/134, memo, 19 Aug. 1954; CAOG 14/14, CAs to High Commissioner, 21 Dec. 1955.
83 CAOG 14/14, Ceylon Treasury to CAs, 29 Nov. 1955; CAOG 10/133, memo, 12 June 1939; CAOG 10/136, CAs to EARH, 29 June 1953; CAOG 10/134, extract from report of the UK trade mission to Iraq, 1953.
84 CAOG 10/133, memo, 12 June 1939; CAOG 10/136, EARH to CAs, 15 Feb. 1956.
85 CAOG 10/136, EARH to CAs, 15 Feb. 1956.
86 *Ibid.*, memo, 25 April 1948; CAOG 10/170, CAs to Commission, 20 Nov. 1953.
87 CAOG 10/136, CAs to EARH, 29 June 1953; *ibid.*, CAs to EARH, April 1953; *ibid.*, note, 26 March 1958.
88 *Ibid.*, statement, 30 July 1956.

Table 5.2. Geographical location of contractors, 1937

	Percentage of total contractors located in the region	**Percentage of total orders completed in the region**
SE England	2.84	2.1
London	42.7	45.9
North	23.8	20
E. England	5.1	4.9
Midlands	14.4	13.1
West Country	1.9	1.3
Scotland, Wales, Ireland	9.3	12.7

Source. *Ministry of Labour Gazette*, Feb. 1937 to Jan. 1938.

businesses used, and 43 per cent of the firms that won orders were based in the South East (Table 5.2).[89] In 1980, meanwhile, an internal investigation revealed that 5 per cent of all suppliers (280 contractors) received 83 per cent of total orders, and a study of the companies that received aid orders over £20,000 from 1974 to 1978 by R. S. May and N. C. Dobson indicates that 24.6 per cent of orders were undertaken in Scotland.[90] The Agents, similarly, appear to have had a preference for smaller sized suppliers with fewer economies of scale than their larger brethren. May and Dobson found that 20.6 per cent of the companies used employed fewer than 100 staff and 45 per cent less than 500, though this may partly be because many of the goods purchased were naturally produced by small companies.[91]

Prices were further raised by the CAs' preference for UK firms. In the inter-war years, they were under great pressure to buy British goods and to ensure that these contained only UK or dominion raw materials and parts. When purchasing goods financed by UK aid they were required to buy articles manufactured in the UK, and, although they were not officially covered by the principle of imperial preference laid down in the Colonial Conferences of 1902 and 1923, they would have received much criticism if they had significantly diverged from the policy when buying non-aid merchandise.[92] There were numerous questions in Parliament enquiring where their orders were placed, many colonial Governors insisted that they supported the mother country, and UK trade associations almost always complained if goods were bought overseas or their manufacture

89 *Ministry of Labour Gazette*, Feb. 1937 to Jan. 1938.

90 L 145, buying intelligence report, Feb 1981; R. S. May and N. C. Dobson, 'The impact of the UK's bilateral aid programme on British industry', *ODI Review*, 2 (1979), p. 18. The 1937 geographical bias may be false, caused by the tendency of suppliers to list headquarter addresses rather than plant addresses. The 1974/8 bias may be related to the large number of engineering firms found in Scotland.

91 May and Dobson, 'The impact', pp. 5, 6.

92 T 161/980/s34783; CO 323/1035/6027; CO 323/1341/4, Colonial paper 60279/29.

was sub-contracted abroad.[93] From 1940 to the early 1950s, they were also subject to currency controls. During the war, Treasury approval was required before orders were placed in hard currency countries, and, from 1948, the consent of the Treasury had to be sought for the purchase of foreign goods using sterling and that of the indenting colony for the acquisition of overseas supplies priced in dollars.[94]

Despite the pressure to buy British, however, the Agents did little to ensure that UK sourced goods contained only British or dominion parts and raw materials, fearful that monitoring would raise their costs, and, in certain circumstances, they were more than prepared to use overseas manufacturers.[95] In 1938/9, £32,000 of orders were placed abroad, and, in 1956, £1.7m.[96] Articles were largely purchased in Europe, mainly France, Germany and Italy, and, to a lesser extent, in the USA and Scandinavia, but rarely in Commonwealth countries, apart from natural products such as Australian jarrah, Canadian fir wood and South African coal.[97] The distance of the Commonwealth from Britain made the inspection of manufacturing works and outputs difficult, the Australian Trade Commissioner insisted that tenders be sent to all the firms producing the requested article, and it was believed that Indian companies produced relatively poor quality goods.[98]

Foreign suppliers were used when they offered prices at least ten per cent less than those quoted by UK companies, though each case was determined on its own merits, and when British prices were kept artificially high by a monopoly and it was believed that the abandonment of the cartel would force it to reduce its rates.[99] In 1955, for example, the Agents bought Italian drugs in a successful attempt to force domestic pharmaceutical rings to lower their prices, which were up to 64 per cent higher than those quoted on the Continent, and, in 1957, expanded metal and mosquito gauze was bought from Germany and Holland for the same reason.[100] Overseas purchase was also adopted to avoid price variation clauses, many foreign manufacturers quoting firm prices, and when colonial governments required the Agents to order from a particular foreign firm, goods were needed urgently and UK companies could not guarantee early delivery, and there were problems in obtaining the articles ordered in Britain.[101] Continental firms were thus approached in industrial disputes, during supply shortages, such

93 See, for example, CAOG 9/114, meeting, 29 Aug. 1957; CAOG 17/21, Parliamentary question, 2 Aug. 1922; *ibid.*, Parliamentary question, 20 Nov. 1929; *ibid.*, Parliamentary question, 4 May 1932; CAOG 12/97, memo, approx. 1928.

94 T 236/3354, Dunn, 7 Nov. 1953; *ibid.*, Treasury to CO, 29 Oct. 1948.

95 Although engineering and merchant tender forms asked tenderers to state the place of origin of equipment and components, General Purchasing Department tender forms and direct order forms contained no such requirement (CAOG 12/97, memo, 11 March 1926; CO 323/1073/12, CAs to CO, 14 Jan. 1930).

96 CAOG 12/97, CAs to CO, 27 Sept. 1939.

97 *Ibid.*, memo, 6 Oct. 1933; CAOG 12/43, memo, 5 Jan. 1939.

98 WN 10, CS 6501.

99 CAOG 12/97, memo, 1 Feb. 1930; *ibid.*, memo, 13 Jan. 1933.

100 CAOG 12/98, memo, 30 Nov. 1955; CAOG 10/13, memo, 6 Sept. 1957; *ibid.*, meeting, 29 Aug. 1957.

101 CAOG 10/134, memo, 19 Aug. 1954; CAOG 12/97, memo, 13 Jan. 1933; CAOG 10/13, memo, 6 Sept. 1957.

as those for paper and steel in the 1950s, and when the goods indented were only manufactured overseas or UK firms refused to meet the specification laid down.[102]

Purchases from overseas increased from the late 1950s, largely because the Agents were forced to buy the lowest priced goods, whatever their origin, in order to retain politically independent clients, and the World Bank and other development agencies, which increasingly financed purchases, demanded the use of world-wide tenders.[103] By 1962, 11 per cent of total orders by value were placed abroad, and, in 1964, this figure had risen to 15 per cent, and, in 1972, to 28 per cent.[104] Goods were also sourced from a larger array of countries, helped by the establishment of purchasing offices in Australia, Japan, and the USA. In 1966, 54 per cent of orders fulfilled overseas by value went to Europe, 14 per cent to the USA, 12.6 per cent to Commonwealth countries and 9.2 per cent to Japan.[105]

Given the state of British industry in the 1960s, however, domestic purchase remained remarkably high, and it seems likely that lower prices could have been obtained if even more articles had been sourced abroad. Large amounts of UK goods continued to be bought because more orders were financed by UK government aid, which could only be spent in Britain, many colonial clients continued to request the use of British firms, and the Agents possessed a natural and self-confessed bias towards home purchase.[106] They were located in Britain, employed British born staff, their engineers tended to think in terms of British specifications and standards, their payment arrangements were orientated towards sterling, and business with UK suppliers reduced their costs and permitted the relatively rapid processing of indents.[107] They were also aware that there existed a government preference for them to use UK manufacturers, though they received no specific directive to do so.[108]

The Agents reduced prices through their almost exclusive use of manufacturers and their relationships with cartels. The CAs used merchants in the early 1920s to buy goods produced in Birmingham, and, until 1964, placed some orders for articles manufactured overseas with the London agents of Continental firms.[109] Many foreign manufacturers would only sell through such agents, most of whom did not charge a commission, and their use reduced the CAs' costs and minimized the language difficulties that could lead to the acquisition of the

102 CAOG 12/97, memo, 13 Jan. 1933; CAOG 10/13, memo, 6 Sept. 1957; CAOG 12/36, CAs to Iran, 25 Feb. 1955; CO 323/1064/2, Lambert to Vernon, 12 Jan. 1928; WN 34, W.Gen. 1028.

103 CAOG 10/13, memo, 12 Sept. 1957; L1, Contracts Dept. report 1965.

104 L 1, Contracts Dept. reports 1963–5; L 145, memo, 20 Jan. 1976.

105 *Trade and Industry*, 11 May 1972, p. 226; L 2, Contracts Dept. reports 13 Oct. to 12 Nov. 1966. Of the orders completed in Europe, 65 per cent went to Belgium, Germany and Italy (L 2, Contracts Dept. reports 13 Oct. to 12 Nov. 1966).

106 L 76, overseas trade memo no. 28/69.

107 *Ibid.*, Frood to Ford, 12 Nov. 1981.

108 A suggestion by the Chancellor of the Exchequer in 1966 for the Board of Trade to persuade them to make more domestic purchases was rejected by the Board, which pointed out that such government interference would compromise the CAs' independence and discourage clients from using them (T 312/1723, Armstrong, 22 Dec. 1966; *ibid.*, memo, 15 May 1967).

109 CAOG 12/127, memo, 13 April 1920.

wrong product.[110] On all other occasions, they bought direct from manufacturers, in the inter-war years even when a colony specifically named a wholesaler as the preferred supplier on the indent form.[111] Although, as pointed out by merchant associations, this may have hurt UK exports by damaging the viability of wholesalers and reducing their ability to employ overseas travellers and distribute catalogues in the colonies, it greatly reduced the price of goods bought, which did not include a wholesalers' commission.[112]

Cartels set high prices for goods and either refused to take part in competitions or fixed the result. If the latter occurred, to ensure that all members benefited, each company would be allowed to make a successful bid in rotation or the profits of the winning offer would be distributed among the unsuccessful bidders, as happened in the electrical generating equipment cartel, or a member would pay its counterparts a fixed sum each year to submit low tenders.[113] In 1923, for example, it emerged that the stamp manufacturer De La Rue gave its competitors £5000 per annum in return for an agreement not to put in excessive bids for the UK government's and Agents' stamp contracts.[114] The nature of the price regime adopted varied between rings. The track fittings cartel in the inter-war period, for instance, had a sliding scale of prices. The Agents were charged the very highest price of all of its customers and the profits were placed in a pool and used to subsidise members' low priced bids in non-colonial tenders in which there was likely to be overseas competition.[115] Alternatively the Cement Marketing Co. Ltd, which had a monopoly of colonial supply from the UK, assigned a different price in each colony, which was determined by the presence of foreign competition. Where foreign companies were active, it charged low, and, in some cases, below cost prices, and, where there was no competition, it set excessively high prices, which subsidized supplies to low price territories.[116] Furthermore, in all colonies it sold cement to local merchants at a lower cost price than to the Agents, arguing that the merchants charged a higher commission than the CAs and that their retail price (cost price plus commission) would breach the cartel's fixed price if equal cost prices were set.[117]

The Agents fought cartels in a number of ways. The most common method adopted was to favour firms that operated outside a ring, a strategy used in the inter-war period with regard to the cement cartel, and, in the 1950s, to weaken the pricing power of the transformer and iron and steel rings.[118] In the case of the Cement Marketing Co. Ltd (CMC), the Agents gave orders to Beynon

110 CS 6852, memo, 31 Aug. 1960; *ibid.*, CAs to Kenya, 24 Sept. 1964; *ibid.*, memo, 5 Nov. 1964.

111 CO 323/1014/1, CO to London Chamber of Commerce (LCC), June 1928.

112 *Ibid.*, LCC to CO, 22 Aug. 1928.

113 CAOG 10/170, CAs to Commission, 20 Nov. 1953.

114 NA, IR 79/34, cutting, *The Times*, 27 June 1924; Lorne Houseman, *The House that Thomas Built. The Story of De La Rue*, London 1968, pp. 155–6.

115 J. F. Hargrave, 'Competition and collusion in the British railway track fittings industry. The case of the Anderston foundry, 1800–1960', University of Durham, PhD thesis, 1991, pp. 238–9.

116 CAOG 12/125, memo, 31 Oct. 1924.

117 CO 323/1341/5, Eastwood, 29 June 1935. In Jamaica, the merchant cost price was 6d per 400lb cask less than the CAs' cost price (*ibid.*).

118 CAOG 10/170, CAs to Commission, 20 Nov. 1953; CAOG 10/129, memo, 1 April 1958.

Ltd, which operated independently of the ring. Unfortunately, whereas CMC's members were largely located in SE England and its cement was shipped from London, Beynon's works were in South Wales and its output was transported from Bristol, which reduced the firm's competitiveness. Cement carried from Bristol was charged a higher freight rate than that conveyed from London, ships called relatively less regularly at the port, and the conference steamers sailing to Jamaica did not stop there at all. To overcome these drawbacks, the Agents encouraged colonies not to demand early deliveries of cement, which could only be met from Thames ports; put 'pressure' on the shipping line Elder Dempster to ship cement from Cardiff once every two months at 'considerable inconvenience'; and persuaded the lines operating from Western ports to reduce their freight rates to below the rates of those working on the East coast, but failed to give the East coast companies the opportunity to match the cuts.[119] They also induced non-conference lines to call at Cardiff; tried, but failed to persuade the Elders & Fyffes to transport cement from Bristol; when CMC offered to supply cement in metal drums, helped Beynon to purchase similar containers; and, to prevent the company paying the higher fee charged by their inspector for inspecting cement in Wales, allowed them to check their own output.[120]

Not surprisingly, CMC believed the Agents' actions to be 'unfair' and 'a violation of the sanctity of tenders'.[121] To persuade them to treat it fairly, it threatened to arrange for the matter to be raised in Parliament, and, in 1927, offered them merchant prices provided that they pressured Beynon into joining the cartel.[122] When these ruses failed, it turned its attention to Beynon, and, in 1930, finally persuaded the company to become a member of the ring.[123] In response, the Agents began to favour another non-cartel member, Casebourne & Co, to which in 1931 it gave a three-month contract without first holding a tender. Enraged, CMC threatened to inform the colonies that it would have quoted a lower price than Casebourne had it been allowed to bid for the contract, and, in 'an attempt to undermine the Crown Agents', instructed its merchants to offer to supply colonial governments with cement at prices far below cost.[124] Perturbed, the Agents again began to buy from CMC, but kept the company on its toes by occasionally purchasing cement from Casebourne, even when it tendered relatively high prices.[125]

Another way of tackling rings was to put pressure on weak cartel members. In the 1930s, for example, the Agents threatened to remove from their supplier lists those members of the track fittings ring that depended on the Agency's orders for their continued existence.[126] They also bought or threatened to buy goods over-

119 CAOG 12/118, CAs to Tanganyika railways, 31 July 1927; *ibid.*, Elder Dempster to CAs 17 May 1928; CAOG 12/125, memo, 23 April 1926.

120 CAOG 12/118, CAs to CO, 6 June 1928; *ibid.*, CAs to Jamiaca, 15 Nov. 1927; *ibid.*, CAs to Tanganyika railways, 31 July 1927; *ibid.*, memo, 4 Aug. 1927.

121 CAOG 12/125, memo, 26 April 1926.

122 *Ibid.*; *ibid.*, memo, 27 April 1926.

123 *Ibid.*, CMC to CAs, 1 Dec. 1930.

124 *Ibid.*, memo, 5 June 1931; *ibid.*, memo, 22 July 1931.

125 *Ibid.*, memo, 6 May 1933.

126 Hargrave, 'Competition', p. 335.

seas, and asked Colonial Office and Board of Trade officials to intervene.[127] In many cases, the cartels acquiesced and gave the Agents special prices. Agreements were signed in the 1950s with the Metal Windows Association, the Meter Manufacturers Association and the Telephone Cable Manufacturers Association, and, in 1935, after Casebourne joined the cement cartel, the CAs 'in essence' gave the CMC a monopoly of its business in return for merchant prices, an arrangement that lasted until 1964.[128] Other rings, however, proved resistant to their threats and blandishments. In the 1950s, for example, the tyre cartel resolutely refused to charge the colonies special rates, despite numerous requests to do so.[129]

Other costs

The non-price cost of goods ordered by the Agents comprised their purchasing commission, the fees paid for inspection, packing and insurance, and the cost of shipment. Until 1925, the CAs charged a purchasing commission of 1 per cent of the value of all goods bought. This was then increased to 1.33 per cent, and, in 1961/2, a sliding scale commission was introduced, which ranged from 0.75 per cent for orders of less than £50,000 to 4 per cent for indents worth over £250,000.[130] The actual commission paid by clients, however, was far lower than that advertised. Principals earned interest on the money kept in the JCF and JMF to meet purchases, and, from 1930 to 1960, colonies received refunds when the Agents' income exceeded agreed levels.[131] The commission also covered the cost of a range of other services for which no remuneration was received, such as the negotiation of mineral concessions and the repatriation of distressed natives.[132]

Although far lower than that charged by local merchants, the commission was still subject to criticism that it was excessive, and there does, indeed, seem to be evidence that the Agency's expenses were unnecessarily high.[133] Costs were increased by the inexperience of buyers, the labyrinthine office politics, which acted against innovation, excessive bureaucracy, and the obsessive checking of work.[134] The Curtis enquiry in 1950 found that an order went through the hands of sixteen members of staff before it was posted to the contractor, and the 1957

127 See, for instance, CO 323/1341/5, Clauson, 4 July 1935.
128 CAOG 10/170, memo, 12 Nov. 1956; CS 6852, memo, 15 March 1956; CAOG 12/52, memo, 17 Jan. 1964.
129 CAOG 10/130, CAs to Hong Kong, 1 Oct. 1958.
130 L 12, meeting, 13 Oct. 1964.
131 CAOG 14/14, CAs to High Commissioner, 21 Dec. 1955.
132 CAOG 17/28, memo, approx. 1937.
133 For example, CAOG 14/14, cutting, *Sunday Times of Ceylon*, 30 June 1957; CA (m) 25, Seel to Blackburne, 22 Dec. 1952.
134 Office politics often descended into open warfare. Frank Blomfield, Head of the General Purchasing Department in the late 1950s, for example, was subjected to regular verbal attacks by his deputy Walter Curtis, who had been promised the job by Blomfield's predecessor (Pen Portraits, Blomfield, Morris to Knights, Jan. 1991). There was similar 'venom' between Curtis and Edward Morris, when the latter was Head of O & M (Pen Portraits, Curtis, Morris to Knights, June 1991).

Hicks enquiry discovered that Executive Officers spent most of their days monitoring the work of junior employees.[135]

A more important factor was the existence of two purchasing departments – one to buy engineering goods, which employed highly paid buyers with engineering experience, and the other to purchase general supplies, staffed by ordinary buyers who earned relatively low salaries. In 1943, various high ranking officials proposed that these be amalgamated into one department employing non-technical buyers, arguing that little specialist knowledge was required for the purchase of most of the engineering equipment bought, and that the existence of two divisions led to the duplication of work, with officers in both departments often dealing with the same firm for similar commodities.[136] The proposal, however, was strongly opposed by senior staff in the Engineering Purchasing Department, who feared that reorganization would lead to redundancies and reduce their status, and insisted that the purchase of engineering goods required technical knowledge.[137] Unwilling to damage the morale of their engineers, the Agents compromised, and, in 1949, formed a third department, which bought non-technical engineering goods and employed ordinary buyers assisted by engineers and later Executive Officers.[138] Although the compromise partially solved the problem, the 1960 Taylor enquiry confirmed that there were large amounts of goods bought by the Engineering Purchasing Department that could easily be purchased by ordinary buyers, and an investigation of the work of the Admiralty and other public organizations that bought engineering goods found that few employed engineers to perform the work.[139]

From 1919 to 1948, £58m of goods were inspected – most of the equipment bought by the Engineering Purchasing Department, and, in 1949, 35 per cent of orders processed by the General Purchasing Division, largely chemicals, clothing, drugs, paper, and textiles, plus a variety of miscellaneous articles (Figure 5.1).[140] Clothing, stationery, textiles and sundry other items were examined in the Agents' inspection branch, which included a laboratory in which chemical tests were carried out. Other articles, such as brush ware, cement and paints, were sent to external inspectors, all of whom were specialists in their respective fields and received a fee for their work.[141] Engineering equipment, meanwhile, was checked by factory inspectors, who were directly employed by the CAs, located around the country, and inspected orders and major components, both during and after production. By 1957, 120 such inspectors were employed in the UK, and, from the mid-1950s, five inspectors operated on the Continent.[142] To cover their costs, which were not always fully compensated by the fee charged, the Agents also inspected goods not purchased by themselves, earning £41,646

135 L 18/3; L 18/8, p. 2.
136 L 18/1, Nattriss's report, May 1943; L 18/ 2.
137 'Notes for Office history, 1958–65', p. 40; L 18/1, Thornton, approx. 1943.
138 CAOG 10/166, memo, 5 Dec. 1949; L 18/9, p. 11.
139 L 18/9, p. 8; *ibid.*, memo. 22 April 1960.
140 CA (m) 29, report ..., p. 18; Anon., *The Crown Agents for the Colonies. Centenary*, London 1933.
141 L 18/5, p. 17.
142 CO 323/1014/1, CO to LCC, June 1928; *FBI Review*, June 1957, no. 8, p. 43; CAOG 16/75, memo, 7 Nov. 1957.

in 1958.[143] Clients included local authorities, private organizations, the World Bank, other UK government departments, and foreign governments, including Australia, Canada, Egypt, India, New Zealand, Russia and South Africa.[144]

The CAs believed that the inspection of orders was essential, as it prevented manufacturers supplying the colonies with poor quality goods, the shipment of which could prove extremely costly. The goods supplied were often used in areas with few tools for repairs and situated a considerable distance from the nearest repair depot, which often kept small stocks of spare parts, and, if an article could not be mended, an order for a replacement would have to be made. The provision of faulty articles, therefore, could involve the loss of the use of equipment for a considerable period of time.[145] In addition, factory inspectors monitored the progress of orders, reducing delays; in the inter-war period, ensured that goods were wholly of British manufacture; and formed close trust relationships with suppliers that could pay dividends if articles needed to be produced quickly or to an unusual specification.[146]

Many colonies and increasingly some of the Agents' senior staff, however, disagreed with these sentiments, arguing that inspection was unnecessary, a waste of money, and led to delivery delays. Most reputable manufacturers sold only good quality articles, conscious that criticism would damage their 'good name' and future sales, and were willing to provide test certificates and/or written guarantees.[147] Quality was also assured by the use of patterns, specifications and standards, and, even if faulty goods were delivered, most colonies possessed the tools, skills and spare parts necessary to undertake repairs.[148] Over time, therefore, more and more clients rejected inspection, and the Agents themselves decided that the examination of certain goods should cease. The inspection of cement was abandoned in 1940, largely because not one batch had ever been rejected and the manufacturers were willing to provide certificates that their products complied with British Safety Standards.[149] Drugs, whether sourced from the UK or the Continent, were no longer tested from 1956, and, in 1960, it was decided that small orders should only be checked if it was thought 'really advisable'.[150]

Other non-price costs arose from the packing, shipment and insurance of the goods bought. By 1953, the Agents packed in their own store around 7,500 orders, largely soft merchandise, such as clothing and textiles, whose manufacturers lacked the necessary parceling experience and facilities. They also checked that the packing undertaken by suppliers who parcelled their own goods was of

143 CAOG 17/35, memo, 1 July 1937; L 18/9, p. 19; CAOG 22/23.

144 Local authorities included Westminster City Council and the boroughs of Lambeth and St Marylebone (WN 10, CA 91). UK government departments included the Atomic Energy Authority and the Ministry of Supply (WN 10, CA 91; L 18/11, p. 22).

145 CS Bahamas 4, CAs to CO, 9 Oct. 1935; *FBI Review*, June 1957, no. 8, p. 43; *Crown Colonist*, 3 (1933), p. 350.

146 CO 323/1014/1, CAs to LCC, 9 March 1928; L 18/1, Thornton, approx. 1943.

147 CAOG 16/64, Curtis, 26 Oct. 1946; CO 323/1159/8, Johore to CO, 27 Aug. 1931; L 35, 1969, no. 25.

148 CA (m) 25, Calder to Seel, 4 Nov. 1952.

149 CAOG 12/69, memo, 10 July 1940; *ibid.*, memo, 13 May 1936.

150 CAOG 12/98, meeting, 4 July 1956; L 18/9, p. 19; *ibid.*, meeting, 8 July 1960.

the correct standard.[151] As with inspection, however, the necessity of the service was questioned, as time passed demand fell, and, in 1968, an internal investigation criticized the efficiency of the Packing Store.[152] Later that year, therefore, the Store was closed and the remaining packing work transferred to a Messrs Evan Cook Ltd.[153]

Generally, the transportation of goods from England was organized by the Agents rather than manufacturers. It was argued that shipment by suppliers would further lengthen delays, as most exported only a small proportion of their output and would therefore be unable to obtain the special priorities given to the Agents when shipping was scarce; that their unique documentation would create confusion in the colonies, slowing transhipment; and that many had little experience of arranging shipment.[154] The CAs, on the other hand, possessed a highly experienced Shipping Department, had a branch office close to the London docks, and employed representatives at all the major ports to supervise loading.[155] It was also claimed that supplier shipment would lead to the use of non-British carriers, which the Agents only resorted to if no UK service was available, and would increase the final costs of the goods purchased.[156] Many manufacturers added a premium to their shipping charges to cover the risk of loss at sea, those with no experience would use commercial agents, whose fees were relatively high, and neither suppliers nor commercial agents could obtain freight rates as favourable as those negotiated by the Agents.[157]

The CAs' freight rates were low because of their large and regular cargoes and because they signed exclusive contracts with the shipping conferences (cartels) that controlled each route, agreeing to use only conference ships in return for large rebates. Over time, however, the size of the concessions negotiated fell. The Agents' proportion of total cargoes carried on each route declined, and the conferences were increasingly subjected to criticism from other customers, who paid higher rates.[158] In the case of the West African route, for example, Elder Dempster, which first signed an exclusivity agreement with the Agents in 1934, was subjected to much pressure to cut their rebates from both local merchants and the foreign members of the conference.[159] The merchants argued that the CAs' rates constituted unfair competition, and, from 1956 and the passage of the Restrictive Trade Practices Act, were probably illegal; whilst the foreign cartel members complained that they received little benefit from the agreement, as the Agents largely bought British goods, shipped from UK ports and therefore primarily used Elder Dempster, the only British member of the conference.[160]

151 L 18/5, p. 18; CAOG 16/91, memo, 23 April 1965; *New Commonwealth*, 31 (1956), p. 331.
152 L 35, 1968, no. 44.
153 L 5, General Purchasing Dept., July 1969.
154 L 18/9, p. 25; L 35, 1971, no. 2.
155 CO 323/1099/15, memo, Jan. 1930; CA (m) 25, 'Handbook for colonial municipalities…, 1946, p. 4.
156 WN 15, O Sec Bahamas 10.
157 L 35, 1971, no. 2; L 18/9, p. 25.
158 CAOG 11/70, CAs to Nigeria, 31 March 1953.
159 CAOG 11/71, memo, 19 July 1962.
160 *Ibid.*, memo, 8 May 1962; CAOG 11/70, memo, 19 Dec. 1956; *ibid.*, memo, 18 Jan. 1957.

From the early 1950s, the Agents also had difficulty gaining favourable air rates. The large airlines were members of the International Air Transport Association, which only allowed rebates to be given to commercial shipping agents, and the CAs rarely had sufficient freight that needed to be transported by air to justify the charter of independent lines.[161] They were thus forced to pay rates that were relatively higher than those obtained by merchants and exporting manufacturers.

The majority of the freight transported by the Agents was insured by their own Marine Insurance Fund, which provided cover for £1,116m of cargo from 1914 to 1964, and, non-profit making, charged low rates and provided prompt settlements of claims (Figure 5.1).[162] Goods not insured by the Fund included those bought by clients (such as Ceylon) who refused to pay for cover, and currency, food, livestock and timber, which were insured on the open market, as the calculation of rates required specialist knowledge.[163] To spread risks and thus ensure the survival of the Fund, large cargoes were reinsured by the London Assurance Co., which charged rates that some at the Agents believed to be excessively high.[164] Despite this precaution, however, in 1974 the Fund was in 'serious' financial difficulties, partly because of the 1968 decision by the Malaysian government to obtain insurance elsewhere, but largely due to claims from Nigerian clients whose goods had been stolen from the port of Apapa.[165] Assured by the Lagos Ports Operating Committee that the supplies had been misplaced or were in storage, the Agents, unlike commercial insurers, continued to cover cargo beyond discharge at the port and refused to reject claims on technicalities or increase premiums.[166] Low rates, indeed, continued to be set even after it was discovered that the goods were being stolen, as the Federal Ministry of Transport put pressure on the Agents to restrict increases and then refused to pay the new slightly higher premiums.[167] The result of these mistakes was that, in August 1974, the Fund faced claims from Nigeria of £712,268 and had a deficit of £100,000.[168]

The CAs' embarrassment was magnified by the fact that six years previously they had transferred £100,000 of the Fund's reserves to their own Office Fund, and, from there, to their Finvest account, where it financed their secondary banking activities. To say the least, their raid on the Fund was controversial. Some at the Agents argued that the reserves should not be touched, and, if they were reduced, the money should be returned to the clients who had financed and therefore owned the Fund. Their misgivings, however, were ignored. An insurance expert concluded that the reserves were excessive having regard to risk and inflationary trends, and the Agents solicitors claimed that the Colonial Office

Elder Dempster reduced its rebates to the Agents in 1963 (CAOG 11/71, Elder Dempster to CAs, 19 March 1963).

161 CAOG 11/141, BOAC to CAs, 16 Feb. 1950; *ibid.*, CAs to Ceylon, 6 June 1955.

162 L 245, memo, 16 Nov. 1965; *FBI Review*, June 1957, no. 8, p. 43.

163 CAOG 14/14, CAs to High Commissioner, 21 Dec. 1955; L 245, memo, 16 Nov. 1965.

164 L 265, memo, 26 July 1928; L 246, Eaton, 11 July 1973.

165 L 246, Batchelor, 17 Oct. 1974; L 36, meeting, 21 May 1968.

166 L 246, Ferne, 5 Sept. 1974.

167 *Ibid.*, Batchelor, 17 Oct. 1974; *ibid.*, Federal Ministry of Transport, Nigeria to CAs, 3 Dec. 1974.

168 *Ibid.*, Jefferies, 23 Aug. 1974; *ibid.*, Batchelor, 17 Oct. 1974.

circular that had announced the setting up of the Fund was 'too vague in its wording' to create a legal trust and that the reserves could be used in any manner 'provided it is for the direct or indirect benefit of all or some of [the] principals'.[169] It was also argued that the Fund's clients had already received large benefits from its existence, as its premiums 'had always been below the commercial level', and that a refund would be difficult to organize – some current insurers had only recently become customers and a number of early clients insured elsewhere.[170]

Colonial regulations and merchant prices

The colonial regulations covering the purchase of government supplies changed over time. Prior to 1928, administrations theoretically could only buy supplies that had been manufactured or produced in their own colonies or in adjacent countries. All other goods had to be ordered through the Crown Agents. In reality, many colonies simply ignored the regulations and bought a proportion of imported goods from local retailers, and the Colonial Office specifically permitted some of the more advanced territories to flout the rules.[171] The Gold Coast, for example was permitted to obtain supplies required urgently or that were difficult to store from local merchants, and Kenya was allowed to buy locally if the articles required were made in Britain and were not more expensive than or inferior to the goods that would otherwise have been ordered through the Agents.[172]

In 1928, the World trade depression prompted the Colonial Office to apply the regulations more rigorously. Requiring colonies to purchase from the Agents ensured that goods were bought in the UK and shipped in British ships and thus helped to relieve domestic unemployment, made sure that the Agency would survive the downturn in its business caused by falling colonial revenues, and prevented administrations cutting expenditure by purchasing cheap poor quality goods, which would prove costly in the long run.[173] The Colonial Office thus informed all administrations, including those that it had treated leniently, that they would have to comply with the regulations in the future, and, to encourage compliance, slightly relaxed the rule that restricted local purchase. In addition to products manufactured or produced in the colony, administrations were permitted to buy from local retailers goods required urgently, proprietary articles, though only where the manufacturers gave their local agents larger price discounts than the CAs, and goods such as explosives, which could not be easily stored and were purchased in large quantities by merchants for sale to the private sector.[174]

169 L 245, Radcliffes and Co. to CAs, 22 July 1966.
170 *Ibid.*, Farquharson, approx. 1965; L 35, 1965, no. 26.
171 Abbott, *A Short*, p. 87, 88; WN 20, O Sec. 231.
172 CO 323/1021/11, Lambert to Grindle, 9 Nov. 1928; CO 323/1051/6, Kenya to CO, 20 July 1929.
173 CO 323/1037/21, CO to British Guiana, 27 Dec. 1929; CO 323/1159/8, CAs to CO, 18 Aug. 1931; *ibid.*, Trinidad Chamber of Commerce to Governor, 8 Aug. 1931; CAOG 17/35, CAs to CO, 4 June 1934.
174 CO 323/1037/21, CO to British Guiana, 27 Dec. 1929.

Not unexpectedly, the changes prompted much criticism from both colonial governments and merchant communities, and the Colonial Office was again forced to allow certain territories to depart from the rules.[175] Kenya, for example, was permitted to reduce their local purchases gradually, and British Guiana and Jamaica were given authority to continue to buy supplies from Canada, even though it was not an 'adjacent' country.[176] Over time, this leniency spread to other countries. In the early 1950s, the regulations deprived the UK economy of the some of the output of British industry, and, as the decade advanced, both the CO and the CAs realised that their implementation would damage relations with colonies and increase the likelihood that they would abandon the Agency on independence.[177] In the mid-1950s, therefore, administrations were allowed to purchase goods locally, provided they could do so on terms 'as favourable as those of the CAs', and, by 1959, the regulations were 'to all intent and purpose a dead letter which would never in the present circumstances be invoked'.[178]

The main arguments used by colonial governments and merchants for the abandonment of the regulations were that it would result in the purchase of less expensive goods, and benefit local economies. In response, the Agents claimed that merchants would sell governments higher priced stores, ensuring their purchase by bribing local purchasing officials, and that on 'a flat playing field' their own supplies were far cheaper.[179] Although, as already discussed, the CAs could probably have obtained lower prices for their purchases and reduced the additional costs of supplies, it is does, indeed, seem doubtful that local merchants could have done any better; a conclusion supported by an investigation of prices and costs conducted by Ceylon in 1939, and the tendency for clients, such as Ceylon, Iraq and Jordan, to continue to use the Agency after independence.[180] As regards prices, merchants bought goods without competitive tender, from a relatively small number of firms and often from wholesalers, who charged a high commission. [181] Given their relatively low turnovers, they also probably received lower price discounts than the Agents, though this was not always the case when they acted as local agents of large manufacturers, and many failed to pass these concessions onto their customers.[182] On those occasions when they undercut the CAs, the prices quoted were often false. Some merchants took no profit for the first few government orders they obtained, but then slowly raised prices when they had secured the business, quoted the price of standardized goods rather

175 CAOG 14/36, CAs to CO, 5 Oact. 1932; Abbott, *A Short*, p. 88.

176 CO 323/1051/6, CO to Kenya, Nov. 1929; CO 323/1037/21, CO to British Guiana, 27 Dec. 1929; *ibid.*, Darnley, 10 Jan. 1929. It was accepted that Canadian goods were far cheaper than those bought by the Agents and halting the purchases would have damaged the UK's relationship with the dominion and the rest of the Commonwealth (*ibid.*).

177 CO 323/1886/3, memo, 25 July 1949; *ibid.*, Trafford-Smith, 6 May 1949.

178 L 178, Abbot, no date; Abbott, *A Short*, p. 87.

179 CAOG 14/36, CAs to Gold Coast, 7 April 1953. There are a number of examples of corruption. See, for instance, CO 323/995/5, Lambert to CO, 11 Jan. 1928.

180 CAOG 14/36, report of committee of the Ceylon State Council, Dec. 1939; *West Africa*, 19 Sept. 1953, p. 865.

181 CA (m) 25, 'The Crown Agents', 1955.

182 CAOG 22/28, Hayes, 19 March 1969.

than the unique items required, or, when they were overstocked cut prices to release capital.[183]

The competitiveness of merchants as regards additional costs is more difficult to determine. They undoubtedly paid higher freight rates than the Agents and charged higher commissions, which included a profit margin, and (bereft of the CAs' economies of scale) relatively high order processing costs, though some merchants were willing to take little or no profit on government contracts, as the prestige of supplying the local administration helped to attract other customers.[184] On the other hand, the goods supplied did not carry an inspection, packing or freight insurance charge, though the Agents argued that these were false economies in the long run, and governments were not forced to shoulder additional assembly, service and storage costs. Unlike merchants, the Agents could not assemble or service the equipment supplied, forcing purchasers to employ local workmen to undertake these tasks, and were unable to deliver the goods immediately. Governments therefore had to wait weeks or months for their indents to be fulfilled and had to keep large stocks, which tied up funds on which interest was lost, necessitated the construction of storehouses and the employment of staff to run them, and could involve capital losses if the goods stored deteriorated.[185] However, only a small amount of equipment needed assembly and maintenance, most governments were perfectly able and preferred to undertake this work themselves, and many merchants added a premium to the price of equipment that they guaranteed to assemble and maintain and performed both tasks poorly.[186] Likewise, not all merchants were able to deliver purchases immediately, and, where this was the case, the goods had been stored by the retailer and the associated cost was added to their commissions or prices.[187]

Colonial administrations were probably on firmer ground when they argued that purchase through the Agents damaged local economies. Although it seems unlikely that use of the CAs increased colonial expenditures and therefore slowed development, it did weaken the economic viability of local merchants and their chances of survival, particularly during trade downturns, and damaged the service they provided to the private sector.[188] Government contracts would have enabled them to purchase goods in bulk and at lower prices; keep a better stock of materials, ensuring prompt delivery; and reap economies of scale, allowing them to reduce their commissions.[189] Purchase of goods in the UK also reduced local employment and the circulation of money, discouraged the development of local industry, as merchants would have bought many of the goods from local manufacturers, and reduced local government tax receipts.[190]

183 CS 6852, memo, 31 Aug. 1960; *ibid.*, memo, 1 Nov. 1956; *ibid.*, Abbot to Kenya, 21 Feb. 1957; CO 323/1006/17.

184 *West Africa*, 21 July 1939.

185 CAOG 14/49, LCC to CO, 26 March 1952; CO 323/1159/8, Trinidad Chamber of Commerce to Governor, 8 Aug. 1931.

186 CS Bahamas 4, memo, approx. Oct. 1952.

187 CS Kenya 4, McClure, 17 April 1959.

188 *West Africa*, 21 July 1939.

189 CO 323/1051/6, CO to Kenya, Nov. 1929; CO 323/1198/9, CO to Elibank, Feb. 1932.

190 CAOG 14/49, LCC to CO, 26 March 1952; CO 323/1051/6, CO to Kenya, Nov. 1929; *West*

Conclusion

In 1927, an anonymous colonial official congratulated the Agents on their purchasing role, which he believed acted as a 'bulwark and a last line of defense' against 'the leeches and vultures from across the North Sea', which, in their absence, would 'gorge and distend themselves with the remnants of our fast disappearing iron, steel and other manufacturing trades'.[191] Although an exaggeration, this view is essentially correct. The Agency, backed by the colonial purchasing regulations, ensured that British goods made of British or Commonwealth components and raw materials were bought by the colonies and were delivered by British-owned shipping lines. If it had not existed, colonial governments would have bought a proportion of their supplies direct from foreign companies or turned to local merchants, some of whom were agents of foreign manufacturers, or obtained much of their merchandise from non-British sources, and used non-UK shipping fleets.

Whether the existence of the Agents was wholly beneficial for British industry, however, is debatable. It can be argued that their presence gave manufacturers little incentive to employ overseas representatives and that their orders propped up declining and uncompetitive industries, delaying economic reorganisation.[192] R. S. May found that those industrial sectors that received orders financed by UK aid and handled by the CAs during the period 1978 to 1984 on average had 32 per cent less output growth and experienced 25.3 per cent more unemployment than all manufacturing over the same period.[193] It was also claimed that they made it more difficult for colonial merchants who sold British goods to meet foreign competition and thus damaged British exports to the colonies. Local government indents would have allowed these retailers to obtain greater economies of scale and to carry a wider range of products, and they could have charged administrations relatively high prices, using the profits to subsidise bids for foreign orders.[194]

As regards the impact of the Agents' purchasing activities on colonial expenditure, the CAs' protected local administrations both from themselves and from rapacious suppliers. There was a constant danger that colonial government staff would act dishonestly, and, more importantly, that local governments would operate in the interests of domestic business elites rather than the colonies they governed. The existence of the Agents, along with the requirement that most government goods had to be purchased through them, stopped local administrators accepting bribes from suppliers offering overpriced goods and prevented administrations buying expensive and poor quality materials from

Africa, 15 July 1939, p. 1; *West Africa*, 22 July 1939, pp. 979–80. The Agents argued that the tax lost through lower merchant incomes was offset by the higher prices that would otherwise have been paid for supplies (CAOG 14/36, CAs to Gold Coast, 7 April 1953).

191 CO 323/1021/11, Anonymous to CAs, 25 Oct. 1927.

192 *West Africa*, 21 July 1939.

193 R. S. May, Dieter Schumacher, Mohammed H. Malek, *Overseas Aid. The impact on Britain and Germany*, London 1989, p. 110.

194 CAOG 14/49, Commercial Secretariat, Baghdad, 19 June 1952.

local merchants. The CAs, furthermore, ensured that suppliers did not defraud the colonies. Goods were bought from only a small number of trusted firms, which were thoroughly investigated before a business relationship commenced, and immediate action was taken if it was believed that they were exploiting their customers. To avoid paying the extortionate prices demanded by cartels, for example, the CAs bought goods outside the ring or from foreign companies.

However, although their goods were probably cheaper than those that would otherwise have been supplied by local merchants or bought direct by colonial administrations, it seems likely that the Agents could have supplied less expensive goods. Some of the excess expenditure can be blamed on their bias towards British manufactures and the environment in which they operated. For example, they could do little to eliminate price variation clauses or prevent colonial administrations demanding the purchase of non-standardised articles. A more important factor, however, is that the CAs often performed their duties in ways that benefited their own interests rather than those of their clients. In order for the Agency's purchasing role to survive and prosper, it was crucial that they charged relatively low fees and minimised colonial complaints to the Colonial Office regarding the supply of defective goods, about which the colonies were extremely vocal. They thus cut their costs to the bone and gave priority to the provision of quality materials. To cut costs, little use was made of open competition, low priority was given to the checking of prices, indents were split into relatively few orders, and the colonial choice of supplier was rarely queried. While, to ensure the purchase of quality articles, orders were sent to a small number of trusted and high status firms and to manufacturers rather than wholesalers, and went through a slow and costly inspection process. The result was that, although the CAs' fees remained low and there were few complaints regarding quality, the goods purchased were expensive and orders were often delivered late.

6

Procurement from the Early 1960s and Delivery Delays

In 1959, the Agents' purchasing departments made a loss of £134,455, which by 1962 had increased to £300,311.[1] The deficits arose from a fall in indents and a rise in costs. The more important of these two factors was the decline in the demand for the CAs' services, which was related to colonial independence, environmental change, and greater competition from the private sector.[2] On independence, some client governments left the CAs and many used them less because they wished to demonstrate to their own supporters and to other independent countries their freedom from the old Imperial power, found it expedient to give work to politically powerful merchant communities, or wanted to gain the freedom to pay for goods late or not at all and to demand bribes for the provision of orders.[3] Others lacked the money or the foreign currency to buy Western goods or had formed bilateral trade and barter agreements with other governments, which precluded the use of the CAs.[4] A number were also unwilling or unable to employ expatriate administrative staff, who had favoured the Agents, and ran down their Public Works Departments, preferring to appoint foreign consultants, who were biased towards the products of their own countries, and to allow capital projects to be built by contractors, who generally supplied their own construction materials.[5]

Environmental change included the development of indigenous industry and the continued growth of merchant communities; the transference of the management of utilities to public corporations, the Boards of which often comprised local merchants and thus bought goods locally; the finance of orders by development agencies, whose aid was often tied; and the increasingly technical nature of the goods purchased, which required on-the-spot service and advice.[6] Competition from the private sector, meanwhile, came from both

1 L 18/9, p. 2; L 18/11, p. 5

2 The annual value of orders placed fell from £54m in 1959 to £45m in 1962 (OD 20/410, Luke, Nov. 1964; L 141, Luke to Cohen, 25 Jan. 1966).

3 OD 20/410, Luke, Nov. 1964; Bangura, *Britain*, p. 213; T 213/1114, Dept. of Technical Co-operation (DTC) to Treasury, 17 Jan. 1962. In addition, Ministers and indigenous purchasing staff had relatively few connections with the CAs or London, and, subject to frequent departmental moves, were unable to gain experience of the comparative abilities of the CAs and commercial suppliers (CAOG 13/161, Luke, 9 Jan. 1961).

4 L 193, 18th batch of summaries, weeding note no. 23; Bangura, *Britain*, p. 213; L 18/11, p. 6.

5 CAOG 14/14, Buckley, 7 June 1966; 'Notes for', p. 10; L 18/11, p. 6.

6 OD 20/410, Luke, Nov. 1964; L 18/11, p. 6; L 18/22, p. 21; WN 10, O Sec. 338; WN 15, R Cyprus.

UK and foreign companies. These firms gained work because they could offer governments finance or deferred payment terms and were more than willing to act unethically.[7] Companies such as Renault and Peugeot simply refused to accept orders from client governments except through their local representatives, and others bribed officials, either to obtain orders or to acquire information regarding the Agents' prices.[8] UK companies, additionally, gained much help from the Board of Trade. In 1955, for example, the Kenyan Trade Commissioner actively encouraged local merchants to apply for government contracts by making them aware that the local purchasing board operated a 5 per cent price bias against the Agency.[9]

Attempts to increase demand

In order to increase demand for their services, the Agents sought help from the Treasury and the Department of Technical Co-operation (DTC), their controlling department, and, when the assistance given proved inadequate, directed their own energies to increasing business. Both the Treasury and the DTC were receptive to their calls for support. It was believed that they offered 'a remarkably comprehensive range of … services' for undeveloped nations, which these countries could not supply themselves, and, more importantly, contributed a great deal to the UK. Not only did they provide 'machinery through which … aid [could] … be channelled', but they constituted a 'non-political link between [Britain] and many overseas governments and institutions' and helped to keep the Balance of Payments healthy by purchasing 2 per cent of UK exports.[10]

The two departments therefore did their utmost to ensure that the Agency continued to trade. Among the survival strategies proposed were that the CAs should undertake work for other UK government departments or the private sector and provide a new advisory service to clients. None of these proposals, however, were actually implemented. A Treasury letter sent to the Admiralty, the Board of Trade, the Ministries of Aviation and Health and the War Office offering the Agents' services produced a generally non-committal response, as did further direct approaches to the Atomic Energy Authority, the Ministry of Works, the Post Office, and the Stationery Office.[11] The possibility that they could help small traders to export by offering advice and arranging the insurance and shipment of goods was vetoed by the Board of Trade.[12] The Board argued that they lacked the necessary expertise and experience for this role, that their entry into the field would damage the business of banks, export houses, shipping and forwarding agents, and that 'to introduce a new competitor sponsored by the government and operated on a … non-profit making basis would provoke

7 L 18/11, p. 6.
8 L 4, General Purchasing Dept., Oct. 1968; 'Notes for', p. 10; RANS report, p. 16.
9 CAOG 17/77, CAs to B of T, 13 Dec. 1955.
10 T 213/1114, DTC to Treasury, 17 Jan. 1962.
11 *Ibid.*, Clark, 22 May 1962; OD 20/119, brief for Director General's meeting with Luke, 23 April 1963; T 213/1114, Collier, 28 Sept. 1962.
12 OD 20/119, brief for Director General's meeing with Luke, 23 April 1963.

great controversy'.[13] Board officials, similarly, opposed the provision of advice and inspection services to existing and new clients, again pointing out that this work was already undertaken by the private sector.[14]

Aware that little help would be forthcoming from the UK government, the Agents sought to increase business themselves by trying to capture new clients and to retain existing customers through improvements in the service offered and the adoption of less ethical business practices. The Agency had first begun to buy goods for non-colonial and non-governmental clients in the inter-war period when they variously acted for Iraq after its mandate had terminated in 1932, the High Commission territories of Basutoland, Bechuanaland and Swaziland, the Singapore Harbour Board and the Foreign Office, for whom they purchased and arranged the transportation of foodstuffs to Spain after the Spanish Civil War.[15] It was only after 1945, however, that they actively began to seek out new customers, motivated by the realization that independence could result in them losing many of their traditional clients and the belief that a larger client base would allow them to reap economies of scale and thus increase their competitiveness, and that, if they failed to plan for the future, many of their experienced staff would seek employment elsewhere, reducing the efficiency of the Agency.[16]

Initially, the Colonial Office was reluctant to allow them to expand their business. Officials feared that politically independent clients would fail to pay for their supplies, damaging the CAs' relations with suppliers and their ability to gain price discounts; and that they would be tempted to advance new customers colonial funds from the JCF, which, much to CO's chagrin, had occurred in 1948/9 when Iraq had found itself in difficulties. Some even predicted that nonpayment could bankrupt the Agency, and, in the worst scenario, that the UK Treasury would be forced to meet its independent customers' debts.[17] Attempts were therefore made to dissuade the CAs from expanding their client base, and, when these were unsuccessful, it was decided that they should be permitted to go ahead only on three conditions. They had to obtain the Secretary of State's approval before accepting fresh customers; no colonial funds were to be involved in the new relationships; and, 'if the worst happens' and orders went unpaid, in no circumstances would they be allowed 'to come to HMG for help'.[18]

Having obtained the Colonial Office's permission, the Agents from 1950 to 1956 recruited an additional twenty customers, including the former Italian colonies of Cyrenaica, Eritrea, Somalia and Tripolitania, Jordan, Libya, and, after independence, Ceylon.[19] To avoid legal liability for unpaid bills, they made

13 T 213/1114, B of T to DTC, 9 May 1962.

14 L 13, minutes of meetings 1965–6, SEVL to Morris, Sept. 1964; T 213/1114, B of T to Treasury, 23 July 1962. The CAs also had little enthusiasm for these initiatives, fearing that they would prompt hostility among consulting engineers and that there was little demand for such services (L 13, minutes of meetings 1965–6, SEVL to Morris, Sept. 1964; OD 20/119, brief for Director General's meeting with Luke, 23 April 1963).

15 Abbott, *A Short*, p. 62.

16 CA (m) 118, O/Conf. 232, CAs to CO, 20 March 1951.

17 CAOG 14/49, CO to CAs, 25 June 1952; SA, File no. 54, Abbot, 1966.

18 CAOG 14/49, CO to CAs, 25 June 1952.

19 Abbott, *A Short*, p. 62; Avery, 'The Crown', p. 329; CO 323/1886/3, CAs to CO, 18 May 1949.

it clear to all suppliers that they acted as agents and not as principals, and, to reduce the likelihood of nonpayment, where possible, they required independent clients to provide 100 per cent cover for purchases, that is to hold sufficient funds in the JMF to pay for the goods indented before the orders were placed.[20] Where this was not practicable, they accepted smaller covers, in the case of the Iraq Ports Administration 25 per cent, or allowed others to ensure payment.[21] For example, the cover for Arab Legion indents was provided by the Foreign Office out of its annual subsidy to the Legion, and that for Libyan orders from the country's UK grant-in-aid.[22]

From the early 1960s, new clients were largely sought in the Middle East, where British influence was strong, national incomes were high, and local purchasing departments were commonly managed by expatriates, many of whom had served in the colonies and had previously used the Agency. To gain a foothold, the Agents undertook small tasks for no remuneration, which demonstrated their effectiveness and generated trust, and began to publicise their services.[23] Booklets and circulars were published; two short films produced; from 1971, press notices were issued; and, in 1972, pressure was exerted on the ODA to give them their due share of publicity in various UK government publications.[24] Attempts were also made to cut all business relations with Israel. The Arab League operated an economic boycott of Israel, and, in 1957, its members had temporarily blacklisted the Agents merely because a supplier had provided the Iraqi State Railways with wagons that had originally been destined for that country.[25] The Senior Agent, Sir Stephen Luke, who some believed to be anti-Zionist, thus instructed that little use should be made of Jewish suppliers or service companies owned by Jews.[26] Any orders for goods made in Israel had to be referred to the Head of the relevant purchasing department and thence to the Secretariat, and, if purchases were made, every attempt was made to keep them secret.[27] Similarly, two requests by the Israeli government for the Agents to act as its UK inspectors were rejected; Jewish organizations that wished to become clients were turned away; and, in 1964, a Board of Trade invitation to supply arms to Israel was declined.[28]

20 CA (m) 118, O/Conf. 232, Abbot, 7 April 1954; CAOG 14/52, CAs to Foreign Office (FO), 2 Dec. 1946.

21 S 6, A1573.

22 CAOG 14/52, memo, 5 March 1956; WN 17, O Libya 1a and 1b.

23 CAOG 14/161, Jarvis, 29 June 1967.

24 L 1, General Stores report 1964; L 35, 1971, no. 16; *ibid.*, 1972, meeting, 25 Jan. 1972.

25 SA, RC 2063, Jones, 19 Nov. 1976.

26 In 1941, whilst Assistant Secretary at the CO, Luke overruled the British Ambassador in Istanbul, who urged that the refugee ship, the Struma, refused docking facilities by the Turkish authorities, be permitted to proceed to the Dardanelles from the Black Sea. Luke minuted 'this is the first occasion on which…the Turkish government has shown any signs of being ready to help in frustrating these illegal immigrant ships and the Ambassador then goes and spoils the whole effect on absurdly misjudged humanitarian grounds'. The ship was eventually towed back to the Black Sea, where it sank with the loss of all but one of the 769 Jewish immigrants on board (Bernard Wasserstein, *Britain and the Jews of Europe, 1939–45*, London 1979, p. 130).

27 CAOG 11/47, memo, 8 Jan. 1960; *ibid.*, memo, 3 April 1964.

28 RC 2326, VAS to Calder, 27 March 1968; *ibid.*, Board meeting, 28 Oct. 1964; *ibid.*, memo, 22 Oct. 1964.

Despite these efforts, the CAs found it difficult to attract new clients. There were language and currency obstacles, Kuwait and Saudi law dictated that government contracts could only be given to those born in these countries, Iraqi tendering conditions were severe, and Oman was reluctant to abandon its close relationship with the British trading company Charles Hendall & Partners.[29] Within the Middle East and elsewhere, the Agents also received little help and some hindrance from UK government departments and from British manufacturers. The British Embassies in Saudi Arabia and Abu Dhabi both kept them at arms length.[30] Abu Dhabi Embassy staff believed that they had taken the local government 'for a ride in the worst tradition of commercial sharks' when setting up the local television station and that any association with them would damage their own local reputation and effectiveness.[31] The Board of Trade and the UK business community, meanwhile, strongly opposed their attempts to move into territories where British merchants were already established. The London Chamber of Commerce in 1957 criticised their operations in Iraq, the Board of Trade in the same year insisted that they should not be allowed to operate in Bahrain, and, in 1960, the National General Export Merchant Group complained about their presence in Addis Ababa.[32] In response, the Agents argued that neither the Board of Trade nor manufacturers had any right to dictate the purchasing policies of foreign governments, and claimed that the only trade they captured was that which would otherwise go to non-UK businesses.[33]

A number of new services were provided. The Agents began to prepare tender documents and pay for and arrange the shipment of goods not ordered through them, and set up an advisory service, which provided specialist advice on stock control and the management and organisation of stores.[34] More importantly, they entered the arms business and also began to buy goods for aid organizations. The purchase of armaments, which in 1975 accounted for 10 per cent of total procurement, was partly stimulated by independence.[35] On the withdrawal of British forces, newly independent countries were forced to establish their own air forces, armies, and navies, the existence of which added to their prestige and discouraged adjacent states from encroaching on their territories. At the same time, Middle Eastern countries, such as Iran, Jordan and Yemen also began to purchase weaponry, largely to counter the military threat posed by Israel.[36]

Although lucrative, the new role presented a veritable 'jungle of minefields' through which the Agents had to 'delicately pick their way'.[37] When they 'put a foot wrong', the offence was inevitably taken up by 'spiteful' journalists, Parlia-

29 L 13, minutes of meetings 1965–6, SEVL to Morris, Sept. 1964; SA, TS 1310, brief on Kuwait, Oct. 1976; WN 10, O Sec. 381/39; CAOG 14/161, Jarvis, 29 June 1967; L 146, Middle East, 1978, brief.

30 Shuter to author, 4 Nov. 2004.

31 *Ibid.*, enclosure, Shuter, 20/2/75. The CAs denied the accusation (*ibid.*)

32 CAOG 14/49, LCC to CO, 26 March 1952; WN 15, R Bahrain 1; WN 10, O Sec. 381/8.

33 CAOG 14/49, CO to LCC, 28 May 1952; CAOG 14/49, CAs to CO, 16 May 1952.

34 CAOG 16/101, Goodchild, 8 Oct. 1964; *Trade and Industry*, 11 May 1972, p. 227.

35 L 11, Director of supplies' report, Jan. 1975.

36 'Notes for', p. 7.

37 CAOG 14/161, weeding note.

ment, and their private sector competitors and used to 'damage' them.[38] In 1967, the *Guardian* claimed that rifles they had supplied to Southern Arabia were being sold on to terrorists in Aden, where they were used against British troops, and, from 1967 to 1968 they were severely criticised in Parliament and the press for arming both sides in the Biafran war.[39] The purchases also complicated their relationship with the UK government. The CAs were well aware that, if they were to retain customers, transactions had to be in the strictest confidence and free from outside interference.[40] On the other hand, the British government believed that it was essential that it was informed of all orders and that it had the power to veto supply, as otherwise purchases could lead to political embarrassment.[41] At first, the Agents stayed 'silently on the tightrope', declining to inform the government of requests for arms.[42] After negative publicity over the supply of bombs for the Congo, however, they agreed to submit all orders for approval to the Foreign Office and Commonwealth Relations Office, which, in return, guaranteed that UK government involvement in supply would never 'be revealed, even in confidence'.[43]

Generally, the agreement worked well. If the Agents believed that government permission would not be forthcoming, as for example in the case of weapons for the Cyprus Defence Force in 1969, they declined to take the order.[44] When the government refused to allow supply, they simply informed clients that their request for an export license had been turned down, and, when it took several years for officials to come to a decision about the purchase of defence equipment for Yemen, they conjured up 'a thoroughly bad cover story ... that the items could not be spared from UK production'.[45] Occasionally, however, there was intense disagreement regarding supply. The Agents only accepted the loss of a Yemeni order when the Foreign Office agreed to do 'everything practicably (as a quid pro quo) to encourage the British Defence Secretary in Oman to place arms orders' through the CAs rather than direct to suppliers.[46] In the case of the supply of ammunition and a patrol boat, respectively, to the Cypriot prison service in 1969 and the Cypriot police in 1971, they simply refused to accept the government's decision. The resultant stand-off was eventually broken by the Foreign Office agreeing to permit the goods to be bought overseas, which would allow the purchases to be kept secret as no export licenses were required and the

38 L 166, Hayes, 22 April 1971.

39 CAOG 14/161, weeding note; *ibid.*, Firearms Co. Ltd to Press Council, 16 Aug. 1967; CA (m) 106, House of Lords (H of L), 29 April 1968, 948–72; *ibid.*, H of L, 6 May 1968, 1261–64; *ibid.*, House of Commons (H of C), 17 May 1968, 291–2; *ibid.*, H of C, 2 July 1968, 1277–80; *ibid.*, cutting, *Sunday Times*, 20 Aug. 1967.

40 OD 20/161, Luke to Commonwealth Relations Office (CRO), 1 March 1962; L 166, CAs to and Commonwealth Office (FCO), 8 May 1969.

41 OD 20/161, FO to CAs, 14 Feb. 1962.

42 L 166, Hayes, 22 April 1971.

43 OD 20/161, FO to CRO, 16 Feb. 1962; SA, Folder 117, Luke to CO, 24 Jan. 1964; FCO 46/447, Knights to Crosthwait, 8 May 1969.

44 L 166, memo, 29 Sept. 1969.

45 *Ibid.*, Hayes, 22 April 1971; *ibid.*, Osgodby, 29 April 1971.

46 *Ibid.*, Osgodby, 22 June 1971.

Agents could excise any reference to themselves from both the shipping documentation and freight marks.[47]

The Agents bought goods with both UK government aid funds and those provided by international development organizations. The purchases kept them in the public eye, encouraged aid recipients to use them for their normal procurement work, and were relatively profitable. Many aid organizations employed overworked poorly trained staff, who were unconcerned about cost, and, in order to ensure that their prestigious projects were a success, placed a high value on quality. The CAs were therefore able to purchase expensive high quality goods on which they earned a high commission.[48] During the colonial era, UK aid funds had always been expended by the Agents, but, after independence, beneficiaries could spend the money themselves or use a local agency. Generally, the Overseas Development Ministry (ODM) encouraged recipients to use the Agents by bringing the existence of the Agency to their notice and permitting the Export Credits Guarantee Department to inform the CAs of loans proposed or in negotiation, which allowed them to lobby for work.[49] The Agents were familiar with the ODM's procedures, which reduced its costs, could be relied upon to ensure that only British goods and services were used, and prevented the misuse of monies through 'bad planning, inefficiency or corruption'.[50]

Not all recipients of Government aid, however, were willing to use the Agents. Many had their own well-established purchasing arrangements and a large and active local business community, which could supply all the goods needed.[51] Others were discouraged by a belief that UK manufacturers charged exorbitant prices for merchandise financed by aid, and by the CAs' high purchasing commission and their failure to meet delivery deadlines.[52] As already discussed, the Agency was renowned for the slowness of its operations, which, in the case of goods purchased with aid, was exacerbated by poor co-ordination with the ODM, the multiple nature of the orders, and the difficulty of finding articles with no foreign components.[53]

Such was the reluctance to use the Agents that in 1970 only half of UK government aid went through the Agency and in 1971 just 36 per cent.[54] To encourage their use, the CAs sought to limit delays by setting up a special purchasing branch, which concentrated on the acquisition of aid goods, improving co-ordination with the ODM, and encouraging loan recipients to prepare indents in anticipation of the completion of a loan agreement, thus allowing purchasing to

47 *Ibid.*, Crosthwait, 7 Aug. 1969; *ibid.*, FCO meeting, 29 Aug. 1969; *ibid.*, FCO meeting, 7 April 1971.

48 Notes for Office history 1966, p. 2; L 38, 1975, no. 48; L 18/14, Dent, 20 Nov. 1970.

49 OD 20/410, memo, 2 Feb. 1966; L 13, minutes of meetings 1965–6, SEVL to Morris, Sept. 1964.

50 OD 39/16, Overseas Development Administration (ODA) to Malaysian-Singapore Commercial Association, 21 Oct. 1968; T 213/1114, Pliatzky, 17 April 1962.

51 T 213/1114, Pliatzky, 17 April 1962.

52 OD 39/16, Browning to CAs, 10 July 1968; CAOG 17/30, CAs to Ministry of Overseas Development (MOD), 2 Oct. 1967; *ibid.*, British High Commission, Ceylon to CAs, 25 Feb. 1968.

53 L 18/14, Watts, 28 May 1970; *ibid.*, memo, Aug. 1970; L5, Contracts Dept. report, Dec. 1969.

54 L5, Contract Services Dept. monthly reports; L6, Contract Services Dept. monthly reports.

begin immediately after funds had been granted.[55] They also tried to persuade the ODM to make their employment obligatory, a suggestion that was strongly opposed by Treasury officials, who believed that attaching conditions to bilateral aid would have political ramifications.[56]

The foreign aid funds spent by the Agents came from the World Bank, the US Agency for International Development, the African Development Bank and the United Nations. Purchasing goods financed by World Bank loans was unremunerative, largely because the Bank required the issue of costly Worldwide tenders.[57] Nevertheless, the Agents were keen to undertake the work, as it was prestigious and introduced them to new clients. Like the ODM, the World Bank regarded the Agents positively. The CAs possessed integrity and had developed and extended their purchasing procedures along lines acceptable to the Bank, their Washington representative kept in close contact with Bank officials, and Sir Stephen Luke was on good terms with Geoffrey Wilson, a high ranking official, who was an 'old personal friend'.[58] The Bank therefore gave the Agents a great deal of help in gaining commissions. Although it could not favour one institution or recommend an organisation to borrowers, it 'mentioned the CAs' if consulted on technical matters, gave them advice on the contents and the distribution of a pamphlet they had produced detailing the services they offered loan recipients, and, from 1967, passed a copy of its confidential monthly operational summary to the Agents' Washington Office, which gave them 'an early view of … projects coming under consideration' and enabled them to be the first agency to lobby applicants.[59] As a result of this assistance, the Agents had 'a fair measure of success' in persuading borrowers to employ them. By 1971, purchases financed by the Bank amounted to £5m, and, in 1974, to $24.5m, and, among others, the Agents acted for the East African Harbour Board, the Nigerian and Singapore Ports Authorities, the Sarawak Electricity Supply Corporation and Swaziland.[60]

The CAs were less successful in gaining work financed by the other aid organisations. The US Agency for International Development (AID) required goods and services financed by its loans and grants to be spent in the USA. Unfortunately, the CAs had less experience of the American market than US companies, and, as they were classed as a service organisation, their fee had to be met from a recipient's own funds rather than from the loan or grant.[61] AID and American embassies also appear to have encouraged beneficiaries to use US purchasing agencies, and, from 1965, the Afro-American Purchasing Centre, a buying organisation established by Aid for the acquisition of goods for Africa.[62] The Agents, conse-

55 L 18/25, p. 13; OD 39/16, Finance Dept. circular no. 81, 19 May 1969.

56 OD 20/119, brief for Director General's meeting with Luke, 23 April 1963; T 213/1114, Pliatzky, 17 April 1962.

57 L 3, General Purchasing Dept. report, Dec. 1967.

58 L 38, 1975, no. 48; CAOG 17/145, Luke, 30 Jan. 1962.

59 CAOG 17/145, Luke, 20 Feb. 1962; *ibid.*, meeting, 25 June 1962; CAOG 17/146, Roe to Leavens 1 Jan. 1967; L 38, 1975, no. 48.

60 CAOG 17/146, Roe to Leavens, 1 Jan. 1967; *Trade and Industry*, 11 May 1972, p. 226; L 38, 1975, no. 48.

61 L1, Contract Services Dept. report, 1963; L 13, minutes of meetings 1965–6, SEVL to Morris, Sept. 1964.

62 L1, Contract Services Dept. report, 1963; L 35, 1966, no. 30.

quently, obtained relatively little business from this source. Likewise, only a small amount of work was forthcoming from the African Development Bank and from the various United Nations organizations, which often had their own service centres and were under political pressure to ensure that purchasing was equally distributed among UN members.[63]

To retain existing customers, the Agents from the early 1950s improved the service offered and adopted less ethical business practices. Service improvements included greater overseas purchase, the introduction of new methods of payment, and the creation of better relations with clients. Until the 1950s, goods were largely paid for with money kept in the Joint Colonial Fund or Joint Miscellaneous Fund. As colonies attained independence, however, there were calls for credit, some clients were reluctant to keep money in the JCF or JMF, fearing that it would be siphoned off by the Agents, and public corporations were sometimes prevented by local exchange control regulations from depositing funds overseas. As discussed in chapter two, the Agents therefore began to allow client governments to obtain credit from suppliers and banks and eventually provided temporary finance themselves through the merchant bank, Sassoons, MTS and later the Finvest Fund. They additionally permitted public corporations to have access to money in an associated central government's JCF/JMF account, allowed the ODM to pay for supplies financed by UK aid in arrears, and let client governments place funds in special local bank accounts, from which payment was taken via the London branches of these banks. On at least one occasion, the CAs' also accepted promissory notes in lieu of payment.[64]

For those clients that continued to meet their debts from funds kept in the JCF or JMF, the Agents in 1970 created a new suspense account into which the sums that would be used to pay for purchases were placed. To prevent delays in the delivery of orders owing to lack of money, it was also decided that any temporary deficit in the account would be met from the CAs' own Office Fund, which, in recompense, would receive the interest earned by the account's contents when it was in credit.[65] The new arrangement was much criticized by the Croom-Johnson tribunal, which claimed that the account had not been sufficiently explained to principals and was merely a way of earning extra money for the secondary banking adventure.[66] The Agents rejected both claims, denying that that they had sought to conceal the account, though in 1978 they sent principals a more detailed explanation of its operation, and arguing that the interest earned partly subsidized the Agency's low purchasing commission.[67]

Customer relations were improved through greater contact with principals both in Britain and in client countries. Visits to the Agents headquarters at Millbank by colonial government officials on leave in England began in the late nineteenth century. By the 1960s, client representatives regularly visited Millbank during official or personal trips to London and everything was done to build

63 L 10, Contracts Dept. report, April 1974; L 38, 1975, no. 48.

64 CAOG 17/136, Overseas Representatives conference, Aug. 1970, session 17.

65 L 118/1, para. 84, 88.

66 SA, Croom-Johnson Tribunal. Papers from Jan. 1979, vol. 2, Lousely, 16 March 1979.

67 *Ibid.*, Lousley, 3 Sept. 1979; L 118/1, para. 84.

trust relationships with them – they were allowed to stay at flats owned by the Agency free of charge, provided with night time entertainment, including visits to Crockfords, the private casino, and were helped in various other ways.[68] At the same time, as discussed in the following chapter, a range of training courses were established for overseas officials, and, in the early 1970s, vacation jobs were occasionally given to students from client countries, some of whom on their return home attained positions of responsibility.[69]

Visits to client countries began in earnest in the early 1950s and became a regular feature in the later years of that decade. Many new leaders and their staffs were unfamiliar with the nature and advantages of the Agents' services, but were reluctant to visit London, lacking the necessary funds or fearing that their positions would be usurped or irregularities discovered while they were away.[70] Middle Eastern clients, with their culture of personalized business relations, also expected to meet CA officials before placing orders, and it was believed that visits allowed staff to gain valuable knowledge of local conditions and were 'the best way to clear up misunderstandings' that could otherwise escalate into major disputes.[71] Visits were supplemented by a number of secondments of CA staff in the mid-1950s, and, from 1965, by the employment in the more important overseas territories of permanent representatives, who dealt with supply problems, identified new business opportunities, and monitored political and economic developments that could influence the level and type of indents received.[72] Relations were also improved by the employment of liaison officers and ethnic staff, 30 per cent of all the Agency's Clerical Officers in 1972 being of overseas origin, and by the adoption of a more personal and politically correct style of correspondence, which, for example, no longer referred to independent countries as 'territories'.[73]

Compared to the private sector, the Agents' methods of doing business were highly ethical. In the Middle East, the provision of bribes was 'the normal way of life' and they lost a great deal of business as a result of their refusal to participate in this practice.[74] There is some evidence, however, that occasionally they lowered their moral standards. In the mid-1950s, for example, CA staff deliberately informed clients of the failings of local manufacturers in order to gain orders, and, in 1975, a CA official falsely presented himself as an accredited agent of the ODM in order to persuade a Caribbean planning division to purchase goods from the Agency. [75] Likewise, a 1954 Gold Coast report on the Agents' purchasing

68 SA, 'Winding up', no. 57; L 193, 18th batch of summaries, weeding note no. 7.

69 CAOG 16/92, memo, 3 Jan. 1972.

70 Abbott, *A Short*, p. 79.

71 CAOG 14/161, Jarvis, 29 June 1967; L 35, meeting, 24 Nov. 1970.

72 L 35, 1969, no. 4. For examples of secondments see CAOG 14/38, Abbott to Curtis, 11 March 1954; L 193, 18th batch of summaries, weeding note nos. 10, 26

73 WN 10, CA 90; CAOG 16/92, memo, 3 Jan. 1972; L 198, Goodchild, 18 Feb. 1976. The CAs also considered setting up a Board or committee of client representatives to direct the work of the Agency, building closer relationships with High Commissioners and Agents General based in London, and encouraging principals to post liaison officers to the Office (CAOG 13/161, Luke, 9 Jan. 1961; *ibid.*, 4 April 1962).

74 CAOG 14/161, Jarvis, 29 June 1967; CAOG 14/49, memo, 5 June 1953.

75 CS 6852, memo, 7 July 1956; Shuter to author, 4 Nov. 2004, enclosure, memo, 7 April 1975. See also Philip Knights' Papers, Goodchild to Knights, 18 March 1970.

activities, which was circulated to the Colonial Office, other clients, and the press, was not as impartial as it first appeared.[76] The report, which concluded that the CAs provided an 'excellent service at a very low cost' and strongly recommended their continued employment after the country became independent, was supposedly written by the Chairman of the Public Accounts Committee of the Legislative Assembly, a Mr Ofori-Arra.[77] In fact, Ofori-Arra allowed it to be compiled by an expatriate official in the Gold Coast Finance Ministry from material wholly supplied by the Agents.[78] In return, the CAs picked up the 'bill' for his trip to London to investigate their buying procedures, which amounted to an impressive £5,000; gave a job to 'a promising lad' he recommended for employment, even though they were 'not, at the moment, recruiting staff'; and helped him in relation to 'a few personal matters', the nature of which are not divulged, but may have related to his business dealings.[79]

Rise in costs

The rise in costs was caused by heavy retrospective Civil Service pay awards, which caused wage and pension expenses to double from 1954 to 1962, and an increase in the work involved in the processing of indents, largely the result of independence.[80] Newly independent governments generally replaced their expatriate staff with unskilled local officials, who often lacked knowledge of basic stock control methods. There was therefore a collapse in the standard of indent presentation, necessitating greater correspondence, and an increase in the number of urgent indents, which took a relatively long time to process.[81] Independent countries also increasingly financed purchases with money provided by aid organizations, which required world-wide tenders and voluminous record keeping, and, along with new clients, demanded credit, the right to pay for goods via local bank accounts, highly competitive prices, greater involvement in the adjudication of tenders, simultaneous tenders, and prompt delivery – all of which increased the amount of work that had to be completed by the Agency. Many clients, furthermore, began to buy high value and basic goods themselves and to send the Agents only low value and highly technical indents, which were

76 SA, CAOG 14/38, weeding note. See *Journal of West Africa*, 22 May 1954, p. 459.

77 CAOG 14/38, weeding note.

78 *Ibid.*, Curtis to Abbot, 9 Feb. 1954.

79 *Ibid.*, Curtis to Abbott, 15 Feb. 1954; *ibid.*, Ofori-Arra to Abbot, 30 Nov. 1953; *ibid.*, Abbot to Ofori-Arra, 22 Dec. 1953; *ibid.*, Ofori-Arra to Abbot, 20 April 1954; *Whitakers Almanac, 2004*, p. 563. A few months after the report was published, Ofori-Arra, who had lost his seat in the Gold Coast Assembly, asked the Agents to help him set up a transport business (CAOG 14/38, Ofori-Arra to Abbot, 24 Aug. 1954). No assistance was provided (CAOG 14/38, Abbot to Ofori-Arra, 17 Sept. 1954).

80 T 213/1114, DTC, 17 Jan 1962. The number of orders handled by each member of staff in the General Purchasing Department rose from 339.2 in 1914 to 675 in 1938, but then fell to 560 in 1959 and 450 in 1964 (CAOG 12/40, annual returns; CAOG 12/41, annual returns; L 18/9). If allowance is made for the longer working week, 42 hours in 1959 as opposed to 38 hours in 1938, the fall is even greater.

81 L 18/9, p. 11; RANS report, p. 2.

relatively costly to process.[82] From 1950 to 1963, the average value of orders handled by the General Purchasing Department fell from £217 to £51, and, in 1963, 91 per cent of its orders were worth less than £500, though this figure subsequently fell to 88 per cent in 1967 and 85 per cent in 1969.[83]

The Agents sought to solve the problem of rising costs by increasing revenues and cutting expenses. Revenue was raised through the attraction of new clients, higher purchasing commissions, and delayed invoice payment. Pressure for the CAs to raise their fees came from the Treasury, which argued that their low commissions weakened the Balance of Payments account, gave them an unfair advantage over the private sector, benefited wealthy foreign countries, such as the 'oil rich states', which had no need for subsidized services, and would increase the cost of government support if the Agency went bankrupt.[84] The CAs, however, were unconvinced by these arguments, fearing that higher rates would drive away existing customers and discourage new clients from joining them.[85] Nonetheless, in 1961/2, they introduced a new sliding scale of commissions, which incorporated relatively high fees for small value orders, so as to take account of the related higher processing costs, and, in 1973 and 1974, increased charges still further.[86]

More income was raised by delaying the payment of invoices issued by those manufacturers that did not provide prompt payment discounts. In such cases, instead of paying for goods immediately after they were delivered, the Agents placed the purchaser's payment in their own account and paid the invoice 30 days later, thus earning 30 days interest on the money.[87] They also seriously considered accepting secret payments from suppliers in return for orders. A 1963 offer from Griffin & George Ltd of a 2.5 per cent 'commission' if the business they received increased by 25 per cent was turned down only because it was believed that 'the secret will out eventually and sully our image in the eyes of our principals'.[88] In the following year, after much discussion, they were on the point of agreeing to accept a discount from the international paper cartel on the supply of paper to Ceylon, when the deal collapsed, and, in 1971, the subject of secret commissions was again discussed, before eventually being dismissed as unacceptable.[89]

To reduce expenses, the Agents made two hundred staff redundant from 1960 to 1963, 18 per cent of the workforce, most of whom moved to equivalent posts in the Civil Service.[90] They additionally relocated some departments to new offices in Sutton, Surrey, where staff could be more easily and cheaply recruited, closed the packing store, reduced the number of factory inspectors, created a Risk Assessment Panel to guard against the acceptance of orders from

82 L 35, 1967, no. 8; L 18/25, p. 6.
83 CAOG 12/41, annual returns; L 18/11, p. 4, 17; L 35, 1970, no. 6.
84 T 317/1498, Couzens, 24 Nov. 1970; *ibid.*, meeting, 4 Dec. 1970; CA (m) 61, p. 26.
85 L 18/9, p. 3.
86 L 18/11, p. 17; L 18/25, p. 10.
87 RANS report, p. 15; L 168, memo, 18 Nov. 1976. There is a possibility that some companies will have raised their prices to compensate for the loss of interest.
88 CAOG 12/56, memo, 17 Dec. 1963; *ibid.*, Smith, 19 Dec. 1963.
89 *Ibid.*, memo, 17 Dec. 1964; *ibid.*, memo, 22 Jan. 1965; CAOG 22/28, Hayes, 1 Sept. 1971.
90 PP 1977–8, 8, p. 3; OD 20/410, Luke, Nov. 1964.

clients unlikely to pay for them, and made a number of minor economies.[91] For example, staff were no longer provided with free morning coffee and the £6,000 pa subscribed to the British Standards Institution was halved.[92] To cut costs via improved efficiency, they also bought a large mainframe computer and established an Ideas Committee to study the feasibility of staff suggestions for improving productivity, and an Organisation and Methods Division, which investigated each department in turn.[93]

Delay

There were complaints about delays in the delivery of the Agents' goods throughout the period. Many of the criticisms were exaggerated, 'one bad case ... [being] better remembered than a large number of punctual deliveries', and some of the critics had ulterior motives for their complaints, wishing to find an excuse to buy from local merchants or using the CAs 'as a convenient whipping boy ... for [their own] incompetence'.[94] It cannot be denied, however, that many supplies took months, and, occasionally, years to arrive. In October 1949, for example, there were 64 outstanding indents that were over 4 years old, in 1954 70 orders had been 'ongoing' for over three years, and, in 1957, 45 indents were more than two and a half years old.[95] The delays slowed development and increased colonial costs.[96] Governments had to carry large and expensive stockpiles of spare parts and items in general use; if late delivery prevented public works being completed during the year for which the necessary funds had been made available, the local legislature had to pass fresh legislation; and, if goods were to be financed by UK aid granted for a particular year, the territory lost these funds if payment did not occur within these twelve months.[97] Delays, additionally, damaged colonial governments' perception of the efficiency of British industry, reducing the demand for UK goods after independence, and undermined the morale and productivity of the Agents' own staff.[98]

Some late deliveries were outside the Agents' control and the result of environmental factors or colonial inefficiency. Changes in the environment had their greatest impact on delivery times during and after the Second World War. Wartime delays were caused by government restrictions on the export of materials such as steel, textiles and tyres, which prevented the CAs immediately fulfilling orders, and the scarcity of shipping, the result of government controls and enemy action.[99] The Agents also had a much-enlarged workload, owing to

91 'Notes for', p. 43; L 35, 1969, no. 25; *ibid.*, 1968, no. 33.
92 L 18/9, p. 6; *ibid.*, meeting, 29 June 1960.
93 L 35, 1967, no. 46; *ibid.*, 1966, no. 31; L 18/9, meeting, 8 July 1960.
94 CAOG 10/13, meeting, 9 Sept. 1960; SA, Summaries of o/sec. files, o/sec. 359; L 18/22, p. 18.
95 CAOG 10/13, meeting, 9 Sept. 1960.
96 CAOG 10/133, CAs to File Trade Association, 15 Sept. 1948.
97 *Crown Colonist*, 3 (1933), p. 357; CO 323/1341/4, Howell, 15 Oct. 1935; L 35, 1969, no. 18.
98 *FBI Review*, June 1957, no. 87, p. 43; CAOG 16/64, Curtis, 26 Oct. 1946.
99 Abbott, *A Short*, pp. 51, 53.

the bureaucracy generated by government restrictions and the completion of work for the Ministry of Supply, but, as already discussed, relatively few experienced employees.[100]

Conditions failed to improve after the war. British industry was unable to cope with the large increase in colonial orders that resulted from the completion of six years of postponed maintenance, the repair of war damage, and the start of new development projects. UK demand had risen in a similar manner and there were shortages of both raw materials and labour. Manufacturers therefore had little option but to quote long delivery dates and unpunctuality was rife.[101] At the same time, the causes of the wartime delays remained in force. In order to ensure that essential commodities were available for post-war reconstruction and export to hard currency countries, even more government restrictions were introduced, which made it difficult for the Agents to fulfil orders, and, again, increased their workload. Problems were particularly encountered in the acquisition of iron and steel, largely because the CAs had no separate allocation, and in the supply of railway materials for which the colonies had low priority due to the small size and non-standardised nature of their orders.[102]

The Agents also continued to lack experienced staff. Particularly damaging was the shortage of copy and shorthand typists, which continued throughout the 1950s. Because the Agency was not a public department, it was not included in the government's freezing order that prevented typists in the public sector leaving their posts. The CAs thus lost a large proportion of their typing staff to high paid posts in the City, and, owing to low pay, poor conditions, lack of pensions and the routine nature of the work, had problems finding substitutes. As typists were needed to type order forms, the shortages inevitably led to delays, though the impact was lessened by the use of secretarial agencies and later the purchase of dictating machines.[103]

In the case of many late deliveries, blame lay with colonial governments. Colonies often sent all their indents at the start of the financial year, leading to bottlenecks in the Agents' purchasing department, and the orders were sometimes compiled in the Governor's office, which obtained the necessary information from requisitioning department heads, a process that could involve much time consuming correspondence.[104] Some of the indents produced failed to include adequate descriptions of the goods required, causing the Agents to correspond with the colony or to become involved in negotiations with the manufacturer to determine an agreed specification. Others demanded non-standardised goods that took a relatively long time to manufacture, or included an inaccurate price estimate, again forcing the Agents to refer back to the colony if the tender price exceeded the estimate by a given percentage amount.[105]

Even after the indent had been written, dispatch to London was not imme-

100 WN 38, O 353.

101 Abbott, *A Short*, pp. 55, 57.

102 PP 1947/8, vii, q. 5367, 5407. Colonial iron and steel came from the Board of Trade allocation.

103 *Ibid.*, q. 5427; Abbott, *A Short*, p. 55; L 18/8, p. 2.

104 L 18/8, p. 2; CAOG 17/35, memo, 4 June 1934.

105 PP 1947/8, vii, Evidence, q. 5404, 5430; WN 9, CS 5303b.

diate. It could sit in an in-tray for days awaiting confirmation from the local financial authority, which, after independence, could be a long time coming, as many clients suffered foreign currency shortages.[106] It was then often sent by surface mail as opposed to the far more rapid telegraph.[107] Further delays occurred when the colony received the tenders. Some administrations took weeks or even months to decide which offer to accept, during which time the price often rose, particularly in the 1950s, forcing the Agents to renegotiate with the successful tenderer or require the colony to sanction the new higher price.[108] Finally, when the goods were eventually delivered, clearance from the port of destination could take days or weeks, and the supplies could then sit in a central store for a considerable period of time before being transported to the indenting department.[109]

The Agents, however, cannot totally escape censure for the late deliveries. As already discussed, delay arose from the employment of too few and inexperienced buyers, excessive bureaucracy, the obsessive checking of work, competitive tendering, the exclusive use of manufacturers, and inspection. Orders would also have been fulfilled more rapidly if indents with named suppliers had been referred back to colonies when the manufacturer quoted an unacceptable delivery date; if order forms had contained less information, many in 1969 containing 'utter tripe'; and if better working conditions had been provided.[110] In the 1950s, buyers were distributed in a number of rooms, which restricted the flow of papers, worked 'in cramped conditions with files piled high on and around their desks', and had difficulty accessing information, the Curtis enquiry noting in 1950 that 'the filing particularly of contract files [was] very untidy and often not in date order'.[111]

The monitoring of the progress of orders and deliveries and the use of sanctions was also inadequate. It was believed that periodic enquiries about the progress of work would increase the Agents' costs and damage their relations with suppliers. The tracking of orders was therefore left to factory inspectors, who made informal enquiries about the goods being manufactured and reported any problems to the Chief Inspector.[112] The monitoring of deliveries was undertaken by the Shipping Department, but was again generally slip-shod. The department was understaffed, containing in 1949 only 19 clerks, and the supervision of delivery was not its main responsibility. Inadequate records made it difficult to determine whether an order was late, the form letters sent to recalcitrant manufacturers would have been more effective had they been typed and personalized, and the geographic organisation of the department, which involved clerks dealing with groups of colonies, prevented the recognition of serial late deliverers and, even when these were identified, the information failed to be

106 Abbott, *A Short*, p. 93; SA, RANS report, p. 3.
107 Abbott, *A Short*, p. 93.
108 CAOG 14/14, CAs to High Commissioner, 21 Dec. 1955.
109 RANS report, p. 3.
110 CA (m) 29, report …, p. 58; Philip Knights' Papers, Joe to Knights, 16 April 1969.
111 CA (m) 29, report …, pp. 11, 12; L 18/3.
112 PP 1947/8, vii, q. 5449, 5450.

passed onto buyers.[113] Over time, the system improved, and, in 1971, the Agents' new computer automatically kept track of work. However, there continued to be criticisms of its adequacy and the introduction of the computer itself led to delays.[114]

Finally, manufacturers would perhaps have thought twice about giving the Agents' low priority in their production schedules had they been punished for delays, but this failed to occur. Contracts included clauses that allowed late deliverers to be fined, but these were rarely used. There were doubts about their legality and it was believed that their enforcement would damage the Agency's relations with their suppliers and lead to higher prices.[115] Likewise, few late orders were cancelled and slow deliverers were rarely removed from the supplier lists. It was claimed that the cancellation of orders would discourage manufacturers taking on work, lead to legal action, and would merely lengthen the delay still further, as the purchasing process would have to start again from scratch.[116] The removal of dilatory companies from supplier lists, meanwhile, would again restrict competition and the Agents would still have to use the firms if they were named by colonies in their indents.[117]

Conclusion

Those colonies that, on independence, left or reduced their use of the Agents often suffered as a result of their hasty decisions. Not only did they have to pay relatively high prices for poor quality goods, but they had to maintain buying organizations in the UK, and/or support expensive, and, in some cases, inefficient and corrupt procurement departments at home, which often employed staff that could be used more productively elsewhere.[118] Not all newly independent countries, however, abandoned the Agency. Many continued to be customers out of habit, loyalty or because they had relatively few needs, which private sector agencies were reluctant to meet.[119] Having experienced the harsh realities of the commercial world, many of those countries that had turned their back on the Agency in the first flush of independence also eventually returned to the fold, encouraged to do so by improvements in the service offered.

Aware that they had to compete to survive, the Agents began to buy a larger proportion of merchandise from foreign suppliers, introduced new purchasing methods, and sought to build closer trust relationships with their clients. At the same time, they sought to cut costs and raise receipts. Expenses were reduced via redundancies and greater efficiencies, and, to increase turnovers, new services were introduced, in particular, the purchase of armaments and goods for aid organizations, purchasing commissions were increased, invoice payments

113 CA (m) 29, report …, p. 14; L 18/8, pp. 4, 6.

114 RANs report, pp. 13, 14.

115 CAOG 10/13, meeting, 9 Sept. 1960; OD 20/410, meeting, 1 April 1965.

116 CAOG 14/14, CAs to High Commissioner, 21 Dec. 1955.

117 CAOG 10/13, meeting, 9 Sept. 1960.

118 L 4, General Purchasing Dept. report, Feb. 1968; L 7, General Purchasing Dept. report, March 1971; L 18/22, p. 20.

119 'Notes for Office history, 1958–65', p. 24; RANS report, p. 10.

delayed, and, on one or two occasions, clients defrauded. In 1968, for example, the Agents transferred £100,000 of the Marine Insurance Fund, which strictly belonged to the colonies, to their own coffers, and, from 1970, kept the interest earned on the new suspense account. Unfortunately, in their attempts to expand their business interests, they received little help and were sometimes obstructed by UK government departments. Seeking to protect the private sector, the Board of Trade opposed moves into territories where British merchants were already established and rejected a proposal to provide insurance and shipping advice to small UK companies. The Foreign Office halted a number of defence contracts that had the potential to embarrass the government, and, fearing that any connection with the Agents could damage their own reputation, British embassies in the Middle East were often reluctant to help them make local contacts.

In its attempt survive, the Agents' Purchasing Division was also assisted by changes in the external environment, which were themselves related to independence, and developments elsewhere in the Agency. The increased incidence of armed conflict in former colonies, in particular in Nigeria and Malaysia, greatly increased the demand for weaponry and medical supplies, and the reluctance of the private sector to invest in the developing world and a wish to halt the march of Communism led most Western countries to increase the proportion of their GDP's they devoted to aid.[120] As will be discussed in chapters eight and nine, the Agents' movement into secondary banking, meanwhile, initially generated large sums of money, a portion of which was used to subsidise their loss making procurement activities.[121]

120 L 35, 1970, no. 6.
121 L 36, meeting, 23 April 1968.

7

Miscellaneous Roles

The chapter examines a host of miscellaneous roles performed by the Agency, including the completion of a variety of personnel duties, the provision of various engineering services, and the discharge of a number of less important tasks, such as the sale of stamps, the granting of concessions, the purchase and rental of London properties, and the employment of solicitors.

Personnel duties

The Agents' personnel duties included the recruitment of expatriate officers, the arrangement of their journeys to and from the country of employment, the payment of their pensions and some salaries, and, from the mid-1960s, the provision of training courses. As well as recruiting expatriate staff, the CAs drew up employment agreements and arranged medical inspections for re-engaged officers and those who had been selected by the Colonial Office and by certain colonial public institutions.[1] Their recruitment duties involved advertising vacancies, and, if appropriate, sending details to University Appointment Boards, professional associations or consulting engineers; dispatching application forms to those who expressed an interest; choosing the candidates to be interviewed, in the case of engineering posts with the help of a consulting engineer; taking up their references; and conducting the interviews, generally with a professional adviser and someone from the employing government or a retired expatriate officer. They then recommended the most suitable candidate to the colony concerned, and, if their advice was accepted, arranged a medical inspection.[2] In return for this work, they charged commissions, which in 1960 were between 14 per cent and 39 per cent less that those set by commercial employment agencies.[3] These never covered the costs of making appointments, but were kept low, as it was feared that higher fees would prompt principals to find staff elsewhere, and, in the long term, damage the Agency. It was believed that recruitment created much goodwill among the officers engaged and drew their attention to the work of the

1 In 1958, they drafted 994 re-engagement agreements and 808 and 113 contracts for people hired by the Colonial Office and colonial institutions respectively (CAOG 13/151, memo, no date; *ibid.*, memo, 5 Jan. 1959).

2 OD 20/410, meeting, 7 April 1965; *Crown Colonist*, 3 (1933), p. 345; CAOG 13/118, memo, 17 June 1957; CAOG 13/120, memo, 11 May 1961.

3 L 18/9, p. 17.

Figure 7.1. Appointments, passages and pension and salary payments, 1920–67 (000s)

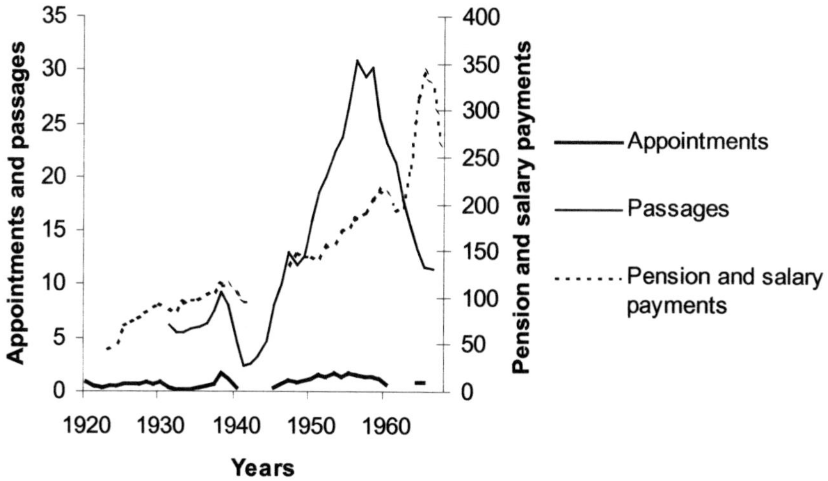

Source. Appointments: L 1, M Dept. report 1965; CAOG 13/3, memo, 9 June 1961; CAOG 13/148, memo, 16 Dec. 1948; ibid., memo, 19 Feb. 1958; CAOG 13/338; CAOG 13/339. Passages: CAOG 13/276; CAOG 13/338. Pension and salary payments: CAOG 15/41.

Agency and thus encouraged them to make use of its services and reduced the likelihood that they would criticize its activities.[4]

From 1920 to 1960, the Agents recruited an average of 848 men and women per year, appointments reaching a peak immediately before and after the War and then declining, largely because newly independent countries began to employ indigenous staff and to recruit expatriate officers themselves or via commercial agencies (Figure 7.1).[5] The majority of their work was for Africa, the destination of 85 per cent of those employed in 1954, and, at first, they engaged all technical staff and some non-technical employees, such as police officers, health inspectors and veterinary and forestry workers (Appendix 4).[6] In 1944, however, the appointment of engineers was transferred to the Colonial Office, which already filled similar professional jobs, and, in 1948 on the establishment of the Colonial Engineering Service, vacancies for architects and surveyors were also dealt with by the CO.[7] The Agents were thus left with the 'NCOs and other

4 CAOG 13/187, memo, 29 Dec. 1964. To ensure that newly appointed senior officers were aware of the Agency's business, from 1959 they were given a brochure that summarised the services offered, and, in some cases, given a tour of the Millbank offices (CAOG 13/152).

5 L 1, M Dept. report, 1965; L 18/9, p. 3; CAOG 13/3, memo, 9 June 1961. Ghana began recruiting its own staff in 1957, Malaya in 1958, Cyprus in 1959 and Nigeria in 1960 (CAOG 13/152).

6 CAOG 13/148, memo, 15 Nov. 1955; *ibid.*, memo, 1 Nov. 1955; *Crown Colonist*, 3 (1933), p. 345; OD 20/410, meeting, 7 April 1965. In 1929, 35 per cent of vacancies handled were for police officers, 20 per cent for railway posts, 18 per cent for positions in Public Works Departments, and 8 per cent for postal, telegraph and marine jobs (CAOG 13/31, memo, 31 Jan. 1930).

7 PP 1947/8, vii, q. 5451; CAOG 13/3, memo, 9 June 1961.

ranks' – engine drivers, plate fitters etc – who lacked a degree or professional qualification.[8] Their role then again changed in the early 1950s, when they began to recruit senior technical staff for the colonial quasi-government bodies and local authorities which were increasingly springing up and for which the CO could not act, and, in the early 1960s, when they started to appoint such people for newly independent territories.[9] During these years, they also had a series of acrimonious arguments with the Department of Technical Co-operation (DTC) over the supply of technical staff to those territories that remained under British control. The DTC increasingly began to recruit subordinate workers, prompting the Agents to accuse them of 'empire building', and, in 1961 and 1962, the CAs demanded to be allowed to take over the appointment of all professional engineers in these countries, arguing that they could perform the work more efficiently and cost effectively than the DTC.[10] Not surprisingly, the DTC, which was also facing a shrinking workload, was unconvinced by these arguments and rejected the Agents' demands, though some Overseas Service Aid Scheme recruitment work was transferred to the Agency in 1971.[11]

During the colonial period, the Agents found the recruitment of good quality officers difficult, though the extent of the problem varied geographically and over time, becoming more formidable at times of full employment. In 1949, when the UK economy was overheating, for example, just over half of all the vacancies reported to the Agency remained unfilled, but in 1945, when unemployment levels were relatively high, candidates were found for all the posts advertised. Likewise, greater difficulties were encountered in finding people to work in West Africa and the West Indies, where 55 per cent and 63 per cent of vacancies were untaken in 1949, than in more 'civilised' areas with pleasant climates, such as East Africa, where only 40 per cent of vacant posts remained unfilled in that year.[12]

The failure to recruit staff was partly the result of Colonial Office restrictions, which prevented the employment of non-British subjects, until 1959 home civil servants, and, after the First World War, former soldiers who had been discharged on medical grounds or had suffered shell shock.[13] Blame also lay with colonial administrations, which sometimes required candidates to possess unnecessarily exacting qualifications, and provided relatively poor employment and living conditions.[14] Vacancies were often for short-term non-pensionable posts, and, because of the poor state of government finances, the salaries offered were usually insufficient to 'attract competent professional people away from Western fleshpots', and, in some cases, were lower than the rates of remuneration

8 OD 20/410, meeting, 7 April 1965.

9 *Ibid.*; CAOG 13/187, memo, 23 Dec. 1964.

10 CAOG 13/187, memo, 30 Dec. 1964; L 12, meeting, 20 March 1963, memo; CAOG 13/187, memo, 22 Nov. 1961.

11 L 35, 1971, no. 18.

12 CAOG 13/148, memo, 16 Dec. 1949.

13 CAOG 13/135, memo, approx. 1955; CAOG 13/136, memo, 26 March 1949; *ibid.*, CAs to CO, 15 May 1959; WN 2, M/SA 1056/8.

14 WN 3, M Gen. 127/11.

attached to similar UK based positions.[15] Many colonies, meanwhile, did not possess adequate housing for Westerners and those recruited therefore had to live in cramped and squalid conditions, and, in the Far East in the 1920s, married men were not allowed to bring out their wives and families and single men had to sign an undertaking not to get married during their period of service.[16]

Colonial governments further reduced their chances of finding employees by their adoption of a virulently racist recruitment policy. There was 'an unwritten law' that the Agents should appoint only 'white' candidates for the jobs advertised, as past experience had clearly demonstrated that subordinate expatriate white officers would not take orders from 'coloured' superiors, whose lives would be made so unpleasant that they would eventually be forced to resign.[17] The Agents thus rejected all applications from black candidates, finding 'some excuse to turn them down on the score of competition'.[18] Thankfully, as local politicians gained more power, this bias gradually disappeared, and, by the late 1950s, colonies such as Nigeria were directing the Agents to encourage more ethic minorities to apply for posts.[19]

Recruitment became even more difficult after independence.[20] The Agents' clients often turned to them 'as a last resort' after their own attempts to fill vacancies had failed, and, as their economies developed, they increasingly required highly skilled workers, who were more difficult to locate.[21] At the same time, candidates were less willing to apply for positions. There was a fear that sudden changes in the political leadership of employing countries would cause expatriate officers to lose their posts or pensions and put their personal safety at risk, and financial problems reduced the salaries on offer, and, along with the political costs of employing 'white' expatriates on long term contracts, prompted employers to provide only short-term temporary contracts.[22] Many potential recruits were also unwilling to work for superiors who were often political appointees with little or no professional knowledge, whose actions would prevent them successfully performing their work and thus damage their reputations and ability to gain future employment.[23]

The recruitment problem was solved in a number of ways. Much to the chagrin of their clients, the Agents employed relatively poor quality candidates,

15 WN 2, M/SA 933/1; CAOG 12/148, memo, 15 Nov. 1955; CAOG 22/31, Hayes. 26 March 1973; WN 3, M Gen. 113/15; Norman Miners, *Hong Kong Under Imperial Rule, 1912–41*, Oxford 1987, p. 181. Colonial administrations feared that paying newcomers the current market rate would damage the morale of serving officers on lower incomes and prompt some to find employment elsewhere (WN 3, M gen. 113/15). Rates increased after 1962 and the introduction of the OSAS, under which the UK government contributed to the cost of maintaining expatriate staff in participating overseas territories (CAOG 13/152).

16 See, for example, WN 3, M Gen. 115/10; *ibid.*, M Gen. 127/11; WN 2, M/SA 930/8.

17 CAOG 13/311, memo, 25 March 1927; *ibid.*, memo, 31 Jan. 1922; *ibid.*, memo, 28 Feb. 1930.

18 *Ibid.*, meeting, 23 Jan. 1930.

19 CAOG 13/134, Nigeria to CO, 25 March 1955.

20 L 1, M Dept. report, 1965.

21 *Ibid.*; WN 5, M Gen. 511/9, vol. 1.

22 L 1, M Dept. report, 1964; *ibid.*, 1965; WN 3, M Gen. 133/2, vol. 3; T 317/1498, *The Economist*, 19 Sept. 1970.

23 WN 18, R Nig. railway 6.

failed to brief applicants fully about those local conditions that could discourage them from taking up posts, which increased turnover, and encouraged colonies to offer higher salaries and various perks.[24] They also sought to arrange secondments from industry and the Civil Service, began to employ foreigners, and tried to recruit people from the colonial private sector and the Voluntary Service Overseas (VSO) programme. The CAs' first secondment scheme involved the Great Western railway and operated from 1920 to the early 1930s, when it was terminated because the GWR needed to reduce its workforce and there was unpleasantness in the colonies between seconded officers and permanent staff members who had been made redundant.[25] After the war, similar agreements were negotiated with British Rail, the British Electrical and London Port Authorities, the National Coal Board and the Inland Waterways Executive.[26] Civil servants began to be seconded from the late 1940s. The secondments lasted up to a year, during which time the colonial employer made contributions to the officer's pension, and, in some cases, became permanent.[27] Among other government departments, the Inland Revenue, the Post Office, and HM Customs all provided staff.[28]

Foreigners began to be appointed after the war. From 1954 to 1956, a number of Italians were recruited for East African colonies.[29] All were English speakers, worked in technical positions and were employed on short-term contracts.[30] Attempts were also made to attract people from companies operating in the colonies and from VSO, a scheme founded in 1958 that allowed young people to work for short periods in developing countries. These initiatives, however, were largely unsuccessful. Colonial companies fought to retain their expatriate staff, the Bank of British West Africa appealing to the Governor of Sierra Leone to force the Agents to sign an agreement not to poach their employees, and, despite much effort, only one VSO volunteer became a permanent colonial employee.

In addition to recruiting colonial staff, the Agents arranged their journeys to and from the colony, paid their salaries and pensions, and adopted a training role. Their transportation duties largely involved them booking passages for colonial officers taking up jobs in the colonies or going to and from Britain on leave. In addition, they organized the repatriation of destitute seamen from Ceylon, Mauritius and the Seychelles, and chartered ships on behalf of British Guiana for the transportation of East Indian coolies to India.[31] In 1922, 4,610 passages were booked on behalf of colonial officers, and, by 1958, this figure had risen to 30,274 (Figure 7.1).[32] Where available, the Agents always used British

24 For example, L 198, Bing to Hart, 21 March 1975; OD 20/119, British Antarctic Survey to CO, 7 Dec. 1962; WN 3, M Gen. 140/9. Officers serving in the Falkland Islands received free peat! (WN 3, M Gen. 109/2).

25 PP 1947/8, vii, q. 5440.

26 WN 5, M Gen. 528/1; *ibid.*, M Gen. 526; *ibid.*, M Gen. 530; CAOG 13/75; CAOG 13/77.

27 CAOG 13/136, memo, 28 Sept. 1949.

28 PP 1947/8, vii, q. 5439.

29 CAOG 13/135, CAs to Home Office, 16 Jan. 1954; WN 2, M/SA 925/5.

30 CAOG 13/135, memo, approx. 1955.

31 CO 323/1099/15, memo, Jan. 1930; CO 323/1177/4, memo, 19 Jan. 1932; WN 2, M/SA 944/17.

32 CAOG 13/338; L 1, M Dept., 1963.

shipping companies and airlines, from which they obtained generous rebates, as their custom was large and regular and carriers believed that the discounts generated much colonial goodwill.[33] To circumvent an International Air Transport Association regulation that restricted concessions to travel agents, air tickets were booked through the British and Commonwealth Shipping Co., which then passed half of the commission obtained onto the Agents; a 'dubious' arrangement that the Passages Department believed would not 'sustain its legality in the face of a determined challenge by another member'.[34]

As with recruitment, the demand for passages fell after independence. Newly independent territories employed fewer expatriate staff and preferred to arrange journeys themselves or via travel agents. In 1965, the CAs booked only 11,582 passages and were losing £20,000 pa on the business.[35] They were nevertheless reluctant to abandon the work or to raise charges believing that this 'would be an abdication of [their] duty to their principals' and that the service created much goodwill among colonial officers and helped 'to steer desirable business in [their] direction'.[36] Passages thus continued to be booked and additional funds were obtained via two dubious ploys. The CAs raised their recruitment charge, but transferred the additional money earned to the Passages Department, and credited to their Office Fund the £8000 pa they obtained in half rebates from the British & Commonwealth Shipping Co, which should really have been passed onto those clients whose tickets were booked through the company.[37]

The Agents' remittance work involved the payment of the salaries of officers on leave in Britain, allowances to colonial residents studying in the UK, and the pensions of retired officials who had served in the colonies, and, from 1971, those who had worked in Burma, India and Pakistan.[38] They also collected the bonds paid by some officers as guarantors of their fidelity and dealt with the estates of serving officials and pensioners who had died in the colonies.[39] By 1966, they were making 322,779 pension and salary remittances per year (Figure 7.1) and, from 1923 to 1967, they helped wind up 13,925 estates.[40] The number of payments then fell, largely because fewer expatriate staff were employed and a number of clients completed the work themselves.[41]

As with recruitment and the booking of passages, the work was thought to generate goodwill and the Agents therefore performed it at a loss, charging no fee until 1958, and, thereafter, a 1 per cent commission, and did all they could to ensure that recipients received 'courteous and detailed attention' and thus

33 CAOG 17/21, Parl. question, 25 Nov. 1931; OD 20/410, meeting, 29 April 1965; CAOG 11/141, CO to CAs, 29 March 1950.

34 OD 20/410, meeting, 29 April 1965; L 35, 1965, no. 24.

35 L 1, M Dept. report, 1963 and 1965; OD 20/410, meeting, 29 April 1965.

36 L 35, 1965, no. 24.

37 *Ibid.*; L 36, meeting, 5 Jan. 1965.

38 CO 323/1099/15, memo, Jan. 1930; L 35, 1969, no. 6; Crown Agents, *Handbook for Colonial Municipalities, Native Administrations and Other Public Authorities*, London 1946, p. 6; L 35, 1971, no. 18.

39 *Crown Colonist*, 3 (1933), p. 350; Crown Agents, *Handbook*, p. 6; CAOG 15/41.

40 *West Africa*, 19 Sept. 1953, p. 865.

41 L 18/9, p. 3; WN 19, O Singapore 1b.

obtained 'a good impression' of the Agency.[42] Particular care was taken to avoid fraud through the careful checking of all payments, which greatly increased costs. Nonetheless, there were a number of cases of fraudulent claims - relatives occasionally kept the death of a pensioner secret, and, in the mid-1970s, it was alleged that the CAs' made remittances to a number of fictitious claimants.[43]

The Agents first began to train colonial staff in the mid-1960s, when they allowed purchasing officers to spend between a few days and several months in their procurement departments.[44] Training was then formalized with the 1969 establishment of a training division that began to run residential nine-week courses on supplies and materials management at a new study centre in Worthing.[45] It was believed that the introduction of such courses would improve the efficiency of clients' procurement activities and thus save them money, but would also contribute to the survival of the Agency.[46] Training would improve the standard of indents sent to the CAs, reducing their indent processing costs, and course graduates would be more likely to buy goods through the Agency, though there is evidence that some clients and students used the knowledge acquired to set up their own procurement agencies.[47] The courses were thus, at first, financed from the Office Fund, and, though fees were later introduced, they continued to be provided at a loss.[48]

Engineering duties

During the colonial period, the Agents' engineering role involved a number of tasks. They firstly examined and approved designs for mechanical and electrical engineering equipment drawn up by client Public Works Departments (PWDs) or Consulting Engineers (CEs) and prepared detailed order specifications, which were sent to manufacturers.[49] In addition, they acted as consultants to clients on the operation of completed railways, commenting on annual reports and general proposals, and, if required, providing civil engineering designs, and helped principals to build new infrastructure, largely railways and harbours, but also sewerage and water schemes, public buildings etc.[50]

The work undertaken as regards infrastructure projects depended on the manner of construction – whether a new scheme was built departmentally, that is by the local Public Works Department, or by a private contractor. The departmental system was adopted when a PWD was engaged on a long-term building

42 L 18/11, pp. 3–4; L 18/8, doc. b.

43 CA (m) 104, Accidents of business, Aug. 1974; SA, File on Coopers & Lybrand report, meeting, 10 June 1975.

44 L 35, 1967, no. 12.

45 L 38, 1975, no. 86; *Trade and Industry*, 11 May 1972, p. 227.

46 L 35, 1966, no. 18.

47 *Ibid.*; L 3, G Dept. report, July 1967; L 18/22, vol. 1, p. 4.

48 L 35, 1970, no. 3; L 38, 1975, no. 86.

49 CO 323/1099/15, memo. Jan. 1930.

50 See, for example, CAOG 10/42, CAs to CO, 17 Sept. 1928; CAOG 10/20, CAs to CO, 29 Jan. 1935; CAOG 10/40, Barbados to CAs, 28 Jan. 1933.

programme and possessed the expertise, the personnel and the equipment necessary for the completion of the work.[51] Its main advantage was that that the final cost of the project excluded a contractor's profit margin, which had to take account of unknown risks and was often relatively large in undeveloped countries, contractor claims for extra payments and any related litigation expenses, and the cost of creating a contract specification. Sections of railways could also be brought into use and earn revenue as soon as they had been completed, the employment of indigenous construction workers by the colony's political staff had a less disturbing impact on the local labour market than contractor recruitment, and the system was relatively flexible. Designs and routes could be altered during construction without extra payment claims and the building of a railway line could begin as soon as the survey of the first section had been completed.[52]

The Agents' role in department construction varied according to the expertise of the local Public Works Department. Where the PWD lacked surveying and design skills, they would use a member of their own engineering staff or employ an engineer to undertake the initial survey of a railway route, complete the design of small civil engineering structures, such as bridges and buildings, themselves, and for large works or projects that required considerable expertise, such as water and drainage schemes, recruit a Consulting Engineer or Consulting Architect, who would embark on the survey and design the whole project.[53] As with suppliers, only a small number of prestigious Consulting Engineers/Architects were used and the Agents choice was almost always accepted by the constructing colony.[54] Generally, the work of the firms employed was well received, though, on occasion, there were criticisms of the fee paid, which was usually calculated on a time basis, and of the quality of survey reports and designs.[55] It was also claimed that some CEs possessed inadequate knowledge of the local environment, assigned junior and inexperienced partners to colonial schemes, and created excessively large projects in order to enhance their remuneration, especially where they were to be employed as construction consultants.[56]

During the building phase of a project, the CAs recruited a Resident Engineer, the individual in charge of construction, if a suitable person was not available in the colony; employed contractors to complete specialist works, such as aqueducts and swing bridges; and, where the PWD's engineering knowledge was weak, again employed a Consulting Engineer, generally the same firm that designed

51 *Crown Agents' Review*, 1 (July 1947), p. 27; PP 1924, 56, p. 8.

52 CAOG 10/97, CAs to Ceylon, 10 May 1940, enclosure; *Crown Agents' Review*, 1 (July 1947), p. 30; PP 1924, 56, p. 9.

53 CAOG 10/19, CAs to Nigeria, 25 Aug. 1949; CO 323/1099/15, memo, Jan. 1930; *Crown Agents' Review*, 1 (July 1947), p. 27; CAOG 10/19, CAs to Nigerian Railway, 25 Aug. 1949.

54 CAOG 17/20, CO to Lambert, 28 Feb. 1927. An exception was the Gold Coast. For the construction of the Takordi harbour, the Canadian born governor Sir Gordon Guggisberg insisted on the employment of a Canadian firm, whose partners had served with him in the First World War (CO 96/598/26601, Ellis, 9 Feb. 1924; CO 96/651/25605, Lambert, 2 June 1924. See also R. E. Wraith, *Guggisberg*, Oxford 1967, pp. 63–70).

55 CAOG 17/20, CO to Lambert, 28 Feb. 1927; CAOG 17/21, Parl. question, 9 May 1929; CO 96/629/59470.

56 L 163, memo, 6 Nov. 1935; CAOG 10/102, KL to CAs, 12 Dec. 1951.

the project, to monitor progress and to offer help and advice.[57] Usually, the CEs performed their work adequately, though, occasionally, their ability to supervise operations was made difficult by the failure of the Resident Engineer to provide them with sufficient and accurate information.[58] Once construction had started, the CAs kept an eye on the progress of the works through the reports of the CE or Resident Engineer, and, if a CE was not employed, would themselves provide the PWD with any advice or information required.[59]

Private contractors were employed where the local Public Works Department lacked the necessary expertise to build a project itself or the scheme was highly complex or required specialized plant.[60] The advantages of using contractors were that the colony knew the extent of its financial liability at the start of construction (though some builders included penalty and price variation clauses in their contracts) and the project was more likely to be completed on time and at a reasonable cost. Contractors had greater building experience and expertise than PWDs, and were not weighed down by colonial regulations, which often increased the cost of indigenous labour. The use of contractors also signalled that a colonial administration possessed a positive attitude towards private enterprise, which encouraged other private sector companies to apply to work concessions or establish subsidiaries in the colony.[61]

Where infrastructure was constructed by contractors, the CAs either completed the design of the scheme and monitored progress themselves, or, in the case of large projects, employed a Consulting Engineer or Consulting Architect to perform these tasks, generally for a fixed sum.[62] As with the department system, some colonies queried the CAs' choice of CEs, Nigeria in 1949 successfully demanding that the Colonial Development Corporation be appointed; criticised the fees paid to the CEs engaged; and complained that they performed their work poorly.[63] The Agents also employed a Resident Engineer and recruited the contractor - drafting the tender documents, inviting and receiving the bids, choosing the winning firm, drawing up the contract, and, after the completion of the project, dealing with any claims for extra payments.[64] In the case of large schemes, only a few large well-known UK firms were invited to bid, though for smaller jobs under £500,000, in which the major contractors had little interest, a greater number of small-scale UK companies were allowed to compete.[65] Inevitably, the Agents' choice of contractor was occasionally challenged by colonial

57 CAOG 10/97, CAs to Ceylon, 10 May 1940, enclosure; PP 1924, 56, p. 8.

58 CAOG 10/97, CAs to Ceylon, 10 May 1940, enclosure.

59 *Ibid.*

60 *Crown Agents' Review*, 1 (July 1947), pp. 27, 30. Building companies therefore were used for the construction of docks and harbours, some varieties of marine work, large bridges with difficult foundations, and for tunnelling (*ibid.*, p. 30).

61 PP 1924, 56, pp. 9, 11, 12; *Crown Agents' Review*, 1 (July 1947), p. 29.

62 *Crown Agents' Review*, 1 (July 1947), p. 27.

63 See, for example, CAOG 10/19, CAs to Nigeria, 24 Nov. 1949; CAOG 10/90, Nyasaland to CO, 16 Sept. 1948; David George Meredith, 'The British government and colonial economic development with particular reference to British West Africa, 1919–39', Essex Univ., PhD, 1976, p. 169.

64 OD 20/410, meeting, 31 March 1965.

65 *Crown Agents' Review*, 1 (July 1947), p. 29.

administrations, which often preferred the employment of local firms, whose owners were known to them and who were believed to have greater knowledge and experience of local conditions.[66] In return for their efforts, the contractors either obtained one payment for the whole project, or, preferably, set amounts for each piece of work completed e.g. a sum for each embankment built, another for each bridge etc, which tended to reduce the premium added for contingencies.[67] Where infrastructure was required urgently, bonuses were sometimes paid, though these sometimes encouraged builders to cut corners, and, in the long run, could prove expensive. The payment of bonuses to McAlpine to speed up the construction of the Gold Coast Takordi harbour in 1928, for instance, encouraged the firm to use rubble rather than cement to secure the harbour's wharves, which subsequently cracked.[68]

As with purchasing, the CAs' engineering work was the subject of some internal criticism. In 1944, the Agency's branch of the Institution of Professional Civil Servants expressed 'serious concern' at the efficiency of the engineering division, and the 1956 Hicks enquiry believed that neither the CAs' engineering 'supply work nor the consultative function [were] discharged to the best effect'.[69] Reasons for the relatively poor service provided include the low Civil Service salaries paid, which made it difficult to recruit good quality engineers – in 1969 only 28 per cent of the senior officers working in the engineering departments and 16 per cent of other staff possessed engineering degrees – and the organisation of the engineering division.[70] From 1937 to 1947, the division was managed by the CA Sir John Calder, who possessed no engineering experience, and, in 1956, the engineers employed both advised on the purchase of equipment and performed consultative duties.[71] An officer was thus 'continually breaking off from his [consultative] investigations to deal with no less important routine [purchasing] matters' and consequently had difficulty performing either role adequately.[72] The department's staff also lacked an adequate knowledge of conditions in client countries, a defect that was gradually rectified after the Second World War through the employment of ex-PWD engineers and more senior staff visits to clients.[73]

After independence, the Agents' engineering role changed. They began to undertake different tasks, and moved into the private sector, setting up Associated Railway Consultants Ltd and Millbank Technical Services Ltd. The nature of their worked altered as a result of the tendency for newly independent countries to replace expatriate staff in their Public Works Departments with indigenous employees, who lacked engineering experience and expertise.[74] There was thus an increase in the demand from clients for engineering advice and help in

66 See, for example, CAOG 10/26, Central Africa Railways Co. Ltd to CAs, 23 July 1930.
67 PP 1924, 56, p. 30.
68 CO 96/681/6216.
69 L 163, IPCS to CO, 2 June 1944; L 18/8, doc. d.
70 SA, File 1, Senior engineers on 1 Jan. 1969.
71 L 163, IPCS to CO, 2 June 1944.
72 L 18/8, doc. d.
73 Abbott, *A Short*, p. 73.
74 L 35, 1966, no. 1.

the construction of infrastructure, which was provided by the CAs, who in 1965 opened a new advisory department and began to undertake feasibility studies and site surveys, and, in the case of small projects such as roads, managed the construction of works themselves.[75]

Unfortunately, the Agents' changed role was the subject of some criticism. The Association of Consulting Engineers argued that they were taking work from the private sector.[76] The accusation was strongly denied by the CAs, who pointed out that their engineering turnover was minute when compared to that of Association members; that they often captured work that would otherwise have gone to foreign Consulting Engineers; and that they actually generated business for engineering consultancies, always recommending a British CE to a client when advice was required that they could not supply.[77] It was also claimed that they obtained help from the UK government in gaining assignments, encouraged clients to buy unnecessary engineering equipment in order to increase their purchasing workload, charged excessive fees, and accepted bribes from contractors in return for providing them with work.[78]

None of these allegations are correct, though some have questioned the Agents' motives in advising the Maltese government to employ the architect and developer John Poulson to design and build a local hospital in 1966. The CAs had originally refused to put Poulson's name forward, as neither the Royal Institute of British Architects nor the Association of Consulting Engineers were willing to support his appointment.[79] Despite pressure from Poulson himself, high level officials at Vickers Ltd, a CA supplier, Albert Roberts MP, and William Wilson, a high ranking Ministry of Health official, they stood by their decision until October 1966, when a senior officer in the engineering division, A. L. McClure, suddenly performed a volte face and informed the Second Secretary at the Malta High Commission that 'Poulsons do not appear to have carried out work for overseas governments, but this is the only possible drawback that we can see to their engagement'.[80] This endorsement was relayed to Carmelo Caruana, the Maltese Minister of Public Works, to whom Poulson had promised a 'commission' if he won the contract, who used it to force a reluctant Director of Public Works to employ Poulson's company Constructions Promotions Ltd.[81]

The reasons for the Agents' change of heart are not recorded. There is no evidence of bribery and there is a possibility that McClure simply failed to realise that his comments represented an endorsement. Alternatively, the recommendation may have been yet another favour to John Cordle MP, who was employed by Poulson as his representative in Parliament, had earlier introduced Poulson to the Crown Agent Sir James Farquarson and to the Assistant CA Edward Morris, and, as discussed in chapter five, received preferential treatment from

75 OD 20/410, meeting, 31 March 1965; CAOG 22/23, Five year review, 1968/73.
76 CAOG 22/28, Hayes, 20 Aug. 1970.
77 *Ibid.*; CAOG 22/30, Hayes to Peel, 14 April 1972.
78 CAOG 22/28, Hayes, 20 Aug. 1970; CAOG 16/92, Hayes, 9 Feb. 1972; L 35, 1974, no. 4.
79 L 167, RIBA to CAs, 9 Sept. 1966; *ibid.*, ACE to CAs, 9 Sept. 1966.
80 *Ibid.*, McClure, 23 Sept, 1966; Gillard and Tomkinson, *Nothing*, pp. 251, 312.
81 Gillard and Tomkinson, *Nothing*, p. 251.

the Agents.[82] The CAs may also have believed that helping Poulson would gain them the support of Reginald Maudling, an influential Conservative MP and later Home Secretary. Maudling was close to Poulson and was Chairman of International Technical & Construction Services Ltd (ITCC), which was to build the hospital.[83]

Of the two private sector companies set up by the Agents, the least successful was Associated Railway Consultants Ltd, which was established in 1969 with the engineering consultancy Livesey & Henderson and provided advice to overseas railway companies.[84] The Association of Consulting Engineers queried the CAs' right to enter into a partnership with the private firm and the company had difficulty attracting business, and, in 1972, entered voluntary liquidation.[85] Set up in 1967, Millbank Technical Services Ltd was more successful. The company supplied engineering and defence goods with or without credit, provided support personnel for the maintenance of equipment and the training of operatives, and supervised multi-input construction or installation projects.[86] By 1974, it had contracts worth £615m, 96 per cent of which were for the supply of goods, 2 per cent for the provision of services, and 2 per cent for package deals.[87] To facilitate the completion of its tasks, it too established a number of subsidiaries. In 1969, it formed MTS Management Holdings Ltd, which provided language tuition, management training and conference facilities and was sold in 1974. A year later, it acquired 1/5 of the equity of the International Agricultural Development Corp., a marketing agency, and, in 1973, it set up two companies to aid its work in Iran.[88] MTS Iran Ltd dealt with general Iranian contracts and MTS Ordnance Ltd, a joint concern established with the building companies Wimpey and Laing, was concerned with the design and construction of a £550m Iranian ammunition factory complex.[89]

There were a number of reasons for the establishment of the company. It firstly allowed the Agents to provide engineering clients with credit, as it could obtain credit insurance from the Export Credits Guarantee Department, which only provided cover to corporate bodies.[90] The company also facilitated the sale of arms, with in 1974 97 per cent of its turnover deriving from the procurement and servicing of military equipment, which was largely provided by the Defence

82 *Ibid.*, p. 147.

83 *The Times*, 8 Aug. 1972, p. 1; *ibid.*, 4 July 1972, p. 4; *ibid*, 2 Aug. 1972, p. 2. Maudling's family also held 25 per cent of the shareholding of ITCC (the majority of the shares were held by Poulson's wife) and his son was office manager, earning £2,000 pa (Doig, *Corruption*, pp. 135, 152). CA files record that in a 1968 meeting, Maudling asked the Crown Agent Sir Stephen Luke to use his influence to persuade the Bahrain government to employ ITCC to build a prestigious technical institute (L 167, memo, 13 Feb. 1968; *ibid.*, note (in pencil), 10 Feb. 1968).

84 L 35, meeting, 25 Feb. 1969.

85 *Ibid.*, meeting, 25 Jan. 1972; *ibid.*, meeting, 24 May 1972.

86 CAOG 14/73, Cotton, 25 March 1975.

87 L 145, CAs and overseas trade memo, 20 Jan. 1976.

88 CAOG 18/676, Coopers & Lybrand (C & L) interim report on MTS, March 1975, pp. 34, 38, 39.

89 CAOG 18/681, Coopers & Lybrand (C & L) report MTSI, March 1975, p. 12.

90 L 35, 1969, no. 8; L 227, Barley, 23 Feb. 1978.

Sales Organisation (DSO), the commercial arm of the Ministry of Defence.[91] Not obviously associated with the Agency, it allowed the Agents to sell armaments to countries with which the UK government did not wish to be officially associated and to work for the Ministry of Defence without damaging their reputation for independence from the British government.[92] Free from government control, it also enabled the CAs to hire and fire staff as work demanded, to pay relatively high salaries and thus attract good quality employees, to recruit onto its Board directors whose links to the business world could generate extra custom, and to charge commercial rates.[93]

Although successful in attracting business, the company had a number of problems. The most important was that it was overly dependent on just one client; in 1975 96.7 per cent of its turnover and 65 per cent of its contracts derived from Iran.[94] The firm was also unprofitable. The commissions it obtained for its work, between 2 per cent and 6 per cent of contract values, failed to cover its costs, and its relatively small profits, £3m in 1975, largely came from the interest earned on the sums of money it received from clients to pay for supplies, which were often held for long periods before payment occurred.[95] Costs were high partly because of unexpected delays in the completion of contracts, but largely because the company was grossly inefficient. A study of its operations by the accountants Coopers & Lybrand in 1975 found, among other things, that it possessed an inadequate organisation and management structure, which led to poor communications between and within departments; that a number of activities, such as estimating, project planning and the monitoring and control of contracts, were inadequately performed; and that there was a lack of financial control and insufficient management information.[96]

The company's low profits, in turn, resulted in small reserves, £4.1m in 1976, which failed to cover contingent liabilities, though risk was partly minimised by the reproduction of the terms of customer contracts in supplier and subcontractor agreements.[97] The firm also had unsatisfactory relationships with the media, the CAs and the ODM. The liberal press constantly criticized its dependence on the arms trade, and, in the late 1970s, gave much publicity to a court case involving two senior executives of Racal (British Communications Corporation) Ltd, who, between 1971 and 1972, had bribed an employee of the DSO to use his influence to ensure that Iran bought their company's radio equipment.[98] Its relations with the CAs should have been good. It channelled much of its

91 TS 1310, MTS information paper, Jan. 1976, p. 3; Doig, *Corruption*, p. 264.

92 L 121, 1976, vol. 4, no. 52/76; HO 268/509197, Burr, Sept. 1967.

93 L 35, 1967, no. 7; L 35, 1967, no. 8; SA, MTS organization and procedure manual, para. 2.4.

94 TS 1310, MTS information paper, Jan. 1976, p. 3. Other clients included Algeria, Argentina, Bahamas, Bahrain, Barbados, Chile, Guyana, Jamaica, Kenya, Malawi, Morocco, Nigeria, the Philippines, Saudi Arabia, Sierra Leone, Swaziland, and Uganda (CAOG 14/73, Cotton, 25 March 1975; CAOG 18/676, p. 4).

95 CAOG 18/676, C & L report, p. 7, 10; CAOG 18/681, C & L report, p. 8; BT 343/202, Overseas Project Group, Oct. 1976. The MoD allowed the company to defer the payment of its invoices until three months after shipment (CAOG 18/676, C & L report, p. 10).

96 CAOG 18/676, C & L report, pp. 6, 14, 21.

97 BT 343/202, Overseas Project Group, Oct. 1976; CAOG 18/676, C & L report, p. 5.

98 Doig, *Corruption*, pp. 264–5.

purchasing business through the Agents and its profits helped to finance their secondary banking activities. However, it was in direct competition with the Engineering Division and undoubtedly reduced its turnover; it obtained many of its staff from the Division and other CA departments, generally 'taking the cream', the most able employees; and the Managing Director of the company, Raymond Roe was not universally popular.[99] Equally poor relations existed with the ODM. Ministry officials lacked the expertise to successfully monitor the company's activities and were unhappy about the risky nature of some of its contracts. In 1976, a working party was therefore established to consider its connections with the UK government, which recommended that supervision should pass to the Ministry of Defence.[100] In the event, in 1979, the MoD took over ownership of the firm, guaranteeing its losses and giving it a new name, International Military Services Ltd.[101]

Miscellaneous duties

The Agents' most important miscellaneous duties were the sale of client goods in the UK, the granting of concessions, property management, the employment of solicitors, the provision of advice to the Colonial Office, and a number of very minor activities. The Agents sold on behalf of their clients a vast array of goods, including government publications, African ivory, Malawi cotton, Malayan opium, Nigerian coal, and stores purchased by the CAs that indenters no longer required.[102] The most important products sold were stamps. By 1960, the CAs Stamp Bureau acted for 63 countries and was the largest philately wholesaler in the World.[103] Until 1940, the Agents arranged sales between the colonies and UK stamp dealers, but, thereafter, retained a stockpile of stamps that were sold direct to dealers. No attempt was made to promote sales, which were relatively small-scale and only made to UK and US wholesalers on their lists of approved dealers, access to which was closely guarded.[104]

This situation changed in the late 1950s when the New York based Lehmann Trading Corporation Ltd became the philatelic agent of Ghana and began to approach other newly independent countries and to 'sow poison against the' Bureau.[105] The Agents viewed the activities of the company with concern. Its capture of the stamp trade of the undeveloped world would reduce their income and could encourage clients to transfer the printing of stamps from the UK to the USA.[106] There was also a fear that the company would damage the economies of

99 L 35, 1974, no. 4. Roe was 'always forthright in his opinions, kow-towed to no one and did not suffer fools gladly' and was involved in a long-running dispute with Allan Challis, the Head of the Finance (Pen Portraits, Roe, Morris to Knights, May 1991).

100 BT 343/202, meeting, 12 Aug. 1976.

101 Doig, *Corruption*, p. 264.

102 L 18/11, p. 20; WN 11, O Misc. 305; L 36, meeting, 23 May 1967.

103 BT 258/1072, Wright meeting, 20 April 1960.

104 L 35, 1972, no. 8.

105 *Ibid.*; CAOG 14/73, Ferne, 25 May 1970.

106 BT 258/1072, CO to B of T, 24 March 1960; *ibid.*, Wright meeting, 20 April 1960.

stamp producers, some of which earned a large proportion of their annual revenues from philatelic sales.[107] The Corporation charged a commission of 25 per cent, as compared to the Agents ¼ per cent, and it was suspected that it would encourage its clients to increase the number and size of issues, which, in the short run, would boost incomes, but, in the long term, lead to a fall in prices.[108]

The Agents decided to halt Lehmann's progress by increasing the competitiveness of its stamp business. In 1960, the commission charged on sales was raised to 10 per cent, and, in 1971, to 15 per cent, and the extra money earned was used to finance changes in the operations of the Stamp Bureau, which was detached from the General Purchasing Department and headed by an officer with a commercial outlook.[109] Stamps began to be marketed through advertisements and exhibitions, the wholesaler dealer lists were abandoned, and retailers were offered credit and special deals.[110] The Bureau also became involved in 'what might be regarded as questionable practices', and offered clients that agreed to use its services for a given period advances of up to £50,000, which were repaid from the income earned from the sale of the stamps produced.[111]

To further increase its competitiveness, in 1969 the Agency bought a 40 per cent share in Stanley Gibbons Ltd, one of the World's largest private sector stamp retailers. The acquisition generated cost economies and allowed the CAs to 'manipulate the market', giving prominence to their clients' stamps in the Stanley Gibbons London store and using the company's monthly magazine to give 'a favourable puff' to its own wares and to 'play down' those sold through other agencies. It was also a good investment with 'the prospect of considerable capital appreciation'.[112]

Unfortunately, from the early 1970s the Bureau began to lose money. Like other philately agencies, in order to attract and keep clients it had increased the number and size of stamp issues. In 1971, for example, it released 218 new issues and 66 reprinted definitives, as compared to 12 new issues and 30 reprints in 1950.[113] At first, there was a large market for the extra stamps, but over time demand waned and prices began to fall. 'The torrent of issues appearing all over the World' generated a 'general disillusionment amongst collectors', who could no longer afford to purchase complete sets and obtained little pecuniary return from their collections, as the large print runs meant that their contents failed to appreciate in value.[114] Stamp collecting had also become less popular among children, owing to the appearance of 'rival attractions', the early 1970s recession

107 In 1961, half of the annual revenue of Tristan da Cunha and 43 per cent of that of Pitcairn Island came from the sale of stamps (BT 258/1072, *Guardian*, 26 Aug. 1961).

108 BT 258/1072, CO to B of T, 24 March 1960; *ibid.*, Wright meeting, 20 April 1960. Attempts by Manfred Lehman in 1970 to work with MTS in the Bahamas and the Caribbean were blocked by the Agents (CAOG 14/73, Dove, 20 May 1970; *ibid.*, Roe to Watty, 21 May 1970; *ibid.*, meeting, 5 June 1970).

109 L 35, 1972, no. 8; *ibid.*, 1966, no. 21.

110 *Ibid.*, 1972, no. 8; *ibid.*, meeting, 30 March 1971; BT 258/1072, CO to B of T, 24 March 1960; L 36, meeting, 23 Jan. 1968.

111 L 36, meeting, 18 Jan. 1966; L 35, 1967, no. 44.

112 L 35. meeting, 26 Aug. 1969; *ibid.*, 1969, no. 33.

113 *Ibid.*, 1972, no. 8.

114 *Ibid.*; *ibid.*, 1966, no. 3.

reduced collectors' disposable income, and, in 1972, stamps became liable to Value Added Tax.[115] The Bureau's revenues thus fell. At the same time, however, its costs rose. The increase in issues had greatly increased its workload and it was grossly inefficient, its slipshod procedures being embarrassingly revealed during the 1971 prosecution of James MacKay, a British Museum keeper accused of stealing CA proofs.[116] Crisis point was reached in 1972, when losses reached £80,000 pa and there were calls for the closure of the Bureau. In the event, it survived, though in a much slimmed down form, largely because it generated much positive publicity and introduced new clients to the Agency, and it was believed that shutting it down would damage customer goodwill and reduce demand for the CAs' other services.[117]

The Agents other miscellaneous duties included the granting of concessions, largely land and mineral rights, to private sector companies, the purchase or rental of London properties, the employment of solicitors, the provision of advice to the Colonial Office and a number of very minor activities. Their concessions work continued until the late 1930s, when it was taken over by colonial administrations. It involved drafting forms of tender and ensuring that concessionaires were British, had sufficient financial resources to work the concession, many applicants being 'men of straw with vague or non-existent … resources', and that they were not monopolists.[118] In the 1920s, applications from the building firm Balfour Beatty, for instance, were rejected because the company appeared to be attempting to secure monopoly control of Crown colony electricity supplies.[119] The Agents also checked the share prospectuses of applicants that had to raise funds to work a concession, in some cases collected license fees, and negotiated the details of the agreement between the colony and the concessionaire, seeking to ensure that the benefits of exploitation were fairly shared.[120] Generally, preliminary negotiations were carried out by the Colonial Office, which then passed the outline agreement to the Agents, who thrashed out the details of the eventual contract with the applicant. The Colonial Office lacked the time and inclination to become involved in the often tedious detailed discussions, and it was believed that the CAs' business experience and independence from the UK government allowed them to obtain relatively good deals.[121]

The Agents' estate role involved the purchase or rental on behalf of clients of London property, which was used to accommodate embassies, offices, Ambas-

115 *Ibid.*, 1972, no. 8.

116 *Ibid.* During the case, it emerged that that the Agents kept no record of the proofs sent to the Museum, failed to request receipts, had no procedure for the return of lent articles, and dumped large quantities of misprinted stamps on Hackney Marches. These were later retrieved by vagrants and sold onto dealers (SA, Folder 122, Simpson, 26 July 1971; *ibid.*, Simpson, 7 Sept. 1972). The Agents denied that such dumping occurred (*ibid.*, memo, 7 Sept. 1971). There is some evidence that the police wrongly believed J. A. Hayball, the Head of the Bureau, was implicated in the thefts (*ibid.*, MacKay to Hayball, 31 Oct. 1972).

117 L 35, 1972, no. 8; *ibid.*, 1972, no. 10.

118 L 178, memo, the concessions phase.

119 WN 18, O Nigeria 117.

120 L 178, memo, the concessions phase; WN 15, O British Guiana 79; *Crown Colonist*, 3 (1933), p. 350.

121 L 178, memo, the concessions phase; CO 323/1023/12, meeting, 6 Jan. 1929.

sador residencies and students.[122] If the property was leased, the CAs also paid the rent and dealt with all the correspondence with the landlord, managing 49 buildings in this way in 1971.[123] The work was completed for no fee, as it 'nourished good relations' with clients, but was far from easy.[124] Landlords were often reluctant to deal with the Agents' clients, fearing non-payment of rents or objections from racist neighbours, and, occasionally, sought to defraud the Agency.[125] Clients, meanwhile, were sometimes reluctant to come a decision as to whether a property should be bought or rented, and occasionally broke verbal agreements to take accommodation, prompting owners to take legal action, and, in two cases, the CAs to meet the outstanding rent from their Office Fund.[126]

The Agents obtained legal advice for principals from a number of firms, in the 1930s paying the fees from the Office Fund and only recovering them from the client concerned if they were especially large.[127] Until 1913, much of the CAs' legal work was dealt with by Sutton, Ommanney & Oliver, which had been used since the 1850s, presumably because its partners included the brother, nephew, son and uncle of Sir Montague Ommanney, a Crown Agent from 1877 to 1900, and, until 1907, an Under Secretary of State at the Colonial Office.[128] Thereafter, the Agents' involvement with the firm dwindled, as it no longer possessed 'its great protector', and, in 1913/14, it was discovered that one of its partners had been defrauding clients.[129] The company was used only for the recovery of money from colonial officers, and, in 1923, the poor quality of its work meant that it no longer received even these cases.[130] Its main successor was Burchills, which was used until the mid-1940s when it too was dropped, largely because its effectiveness declined after the deaths of Charles and Alfred Burchill and there were suspicions that it charged excessive fees.[131] After its demise, another firm, Turners, took its place, though for specialist work the CAs often turned to acknowledged experts.[132]

The Agents provided advice to the Colonial Office on a range of financial and engineering topics, and such was the usefulness of the information given that the Colonial Under Secretary of State Leo Amery in 1919 considered making them the 'general staff for ... development', and, in 1932, it was unsuccessfully proposed that they should become involved in the determination of all colonial policy.[133] Although they regarded their advisory role as important, believing

122 *FBI Review*, June 1957, no. 8, p. 43.
123 L 35, 1971, no. 14.
124 WN 18, R Nigeria 212, a and b.
125 WN 11, O Misc. 315; WN 20, R Trinidad 81 and 81a. Property owners feared that existing residents would find accommodation elsewhere and the space would be difficult to rent.
126 L 193, 18th batch, weeding note, no. 13; *ibid.*, no. 27; *ibid.*, no. 29.
127 CAOG 17/64, CAs to CO, 26 June 1935.
128 Sunderland, *Managing*, p. 91.
129 *Ibid.*; CO 323/902/19475, Fiddean, 6 April 1923.
130 CAOG 17/64, CAs to CO, 29 March 1923; CO 323/902/19475, note, 5 April 1923.
131 L 233, note, 27 Nov. 1979. In 1924, the company reduced a bill by 15 per cent, and, in 1936, cut all its charges by 25 per cent (CAOG 17/64, memo, 15 April 1924; *ibid.*, CO to CAs, 19 March 1936).
132 L 233, note, 27 Nov. 1979.
133 CO 323/1023/12, meeting, 6 Jan. 1929; Leo Amery, *The Leo Amery Diaries, Vol. 1*, London

that it strengthened their bonds with the Colonial Office, the CAs were fearful that it would damage their independent status and their relationship with their clients.[134] They thus insisted that any correspondence containing advice should be conducted semi-officially, and that their views should never be quoted in CO correspondence with colonial governments.[135]

Minor activities undertaken by the Agents included the provision of general information on those clients that did not possess a London information office, the publication from 1928 to 1932 of the *Crown Agents' Bulletin*, and, from 1947 onwards, the *Crown Agents' Review*, which contained articles on a range of subjects that were of interest to clients, and, during the Second World War, the management of a colonial small arms ammunition reserve, a quinine reserve for malarial zones, and civilian foodstuff stores for Ceylon, Mauritius and West Africa.[136] They also provided the three Currency Boards with secretarial and accounting staff; arranged the valuation of Gold Coast diamonds, though the influence of the Diamond Corporation was such that it was difficult to find independent valuers; and, until 1942, supervised students whose UK studies were funded by colonial government scholarships, work that in later years increased the demand for their services as some of the students attained powerful administrative and political positions.[137]

Conclusion

The Agents undertook many of their miscellaneous duties at a loss, largely because their completion drew the attention of colonial administrations and their staff to the Agency and created much goodwill and thus increased demand for their more profitable services. As in other areas, their role was essentially to prevent service providers and colonial administrators acting dishonestly or inadequately and colonial administrations favouring the local business community. So, for example, they ensured that only reputable Consulting Engineers, contractors and stamp dealers were appointed, that vacancies were filled by candidates who possessed the skills required, that salaries and pensions were paid only to genuine recipients, and that economically viable and cost effective infrastructure was constructed.

Eager to impress, they sought to provide a high quality service, and, in doing so, often acted unethically. For example, to increase the competitiveness of their Stamp Bureau they used their purchase of Stanley Gibbons Ltd to manipulate

1980, 12 Feb. 1919, p. 256; *ibid.*, 15 Oct. 1919, pp. 264–5; Summaries of O/sec. files, O CA 243. Amery believed the CAs were superior to the CO, and, in 1919, wrote in his diary that 'I am not sure that the real solution of the problem of organising the Colonial Office doesn't lie in transferring it to the Crown Agents' (Amery, *The Leo*, p. 264).

134 Summaries of O/sec. files, O CA 243.

135 CO 323/1023/12, meeting, 6 Jan. 1929; Summaries of O/sec. files, O CA 243.

136 Crown Agents, *Handbook*, p. 7; Abbott, *A Short*, pp. 51, 81.

137 WN 11, O Misc. 315; Lee, *Colonial*, pp. 261–2. From 1930 to 1971, the Palestine and the East and West African Currency Boards appointed 68 members of the CAs' staff (CAOG 16/47, memo, no date).

the stamp market, and, from 1965, circumvented the International Air Transport Association's regulation that restricted concessions to travel agents by booking tickets through the British & Commonwealth Shipping Co. As elsewhere, however, attempts to perform their work adequately were hindered by unreasonable colonial demands; changes in the external environment; in the case of Poulson affair, the possible dishonesty of a member of staff; and by their need to keep their fees as low as possible. To minimise charges, costs were reduced to a minimum, which led to the provision of a sub-standard service, and, in the 1960s, when the future of the Agency was in doubt, clients were occasionally defrauded. From 1965, for example, the £8,000 pa obtained in half rebates from the British & Commonwealth Shipping Co. which should have gone to the colonies, was paid into the Office Fund, and money raised from the increase in recruitment charges was actually used to subsidise the cost of arranging passages.

8

The Move into Secondary Banking

In March 1967, the Agency embarked on a new venture as a secondary bank, taking deposits from principals and financial institutions, which it re-lent or invested in equities, gilts, property and the private sector. Unlike its traditional financial service, the new pursuits were conducted on its own account and thus became known as 'own account activities'. The Office acted, not as an agent, which had been the case over the previous 134 years, but as a principal, reaping all the profits from the new business, but also being liable for any losses. Begun by the Senior Crown Agent, Sir Stephen Luke, and carried on by his successor, Sir Claude Hayes, the new business was very much the brainchild of Allan Challis, the Head of the Finance Directorate. Although he had worked in the Agency's finance department since leaving school, Challis had great entrepreneurial flair, and, by March 1973, the CAs' new undertaking had a capitalization of £254m (Figure 8.1).

The new venture was dogged by controversy from the start. The City was soon awash with rumours of corruption and incompetence, the press printed highly critical stories, and a series of damaging questions were asked in Parliament by Labour Party MPs and Peers.[1] Concerned about the Office's new pursuits and wishing to finally resolve the problem of its status, the Ministry in 1972 set up an enquiry chaired by Sir Matthew Stevenson.[2] Its report, only published in 1977, was critical of some of the Agents' lapses and errors of judgment and their lack of accountability, but concluded that they were 'competent and conscientious' bankers and that their new operations were 'reasonably prudent' and should continue.[3] Unconvinced by these findings, the Commons Select Committee on Overseas Development initiated a further investigation, which was abandoned after the appointment of Judith Hart MP, a committee member, as Minister of Overseas Development in early 1974 and her declared intention to reorganize the Agency.[4]

Despite the criticism, the new business was highly successful, helped by an extremely favourable economic environment. In 1971, the Bank of England, wishing to increase investment in UK industry, freed the clearing banks from

1 *The Sunday Times*, 19 April 1970, p. 10; *Guardian*, 5 Aug. 1971, p. 13; *Private Eye*, 10 Sept. 1971, p. 4; *ibid.*, 22 Oct. 1971, p. 8.

2 The government department concerned with the CAs had different names over the period 1961–74 and is therefore referred to as 'the Ministry'.

3 PP 1977–8, 8, p. 91.

4 *Hansard*, 1977–78, 940, 1068.

Figure 8.1. Finvest account, 1970–74

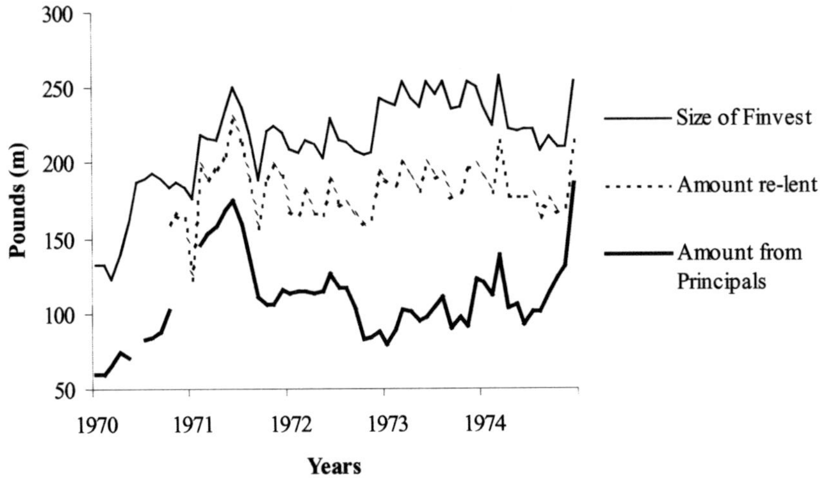

Source. L 1 to L 11, Banking Dept. and F Dept.; HO 268/422, Finvest monthly reports.

their previous credit restrictions. In the event, industry was in the doldrums and failed to take up the new capital, which was lent to secondary banks, and, through them, to the rapidly growing property sector. The following year, Lord Barber, the Chancellor of the Exchequer, again seeking to halt the 'stop-go' progress of the British economy, introduced a policy of cheap and plentiful credit. As before, the new money bypassed industry and instead flowed into the secondary banking and property sectors, which began to expand at previously unseen rates. The Agents reaped the benefits of the boom. Over the period 1969 to 1973, they made net profits of £24.2m and were involved in a number of spectacular business deals.[5] In 1971, for example, they obtained a profit of £12m from the sale of development sites owned by a company in which they had a fifty percent stake, and, over the following eighteen months, obtained a further £1m from the disposal of office and shop developments.[6]

Unfortunately, Barber's 'dash for growth' soon stumbled. Inflation, stoked by the high levels of credit and the tripling of oil prices, forced the government to introduce policies that slowed economic growth and led to a secondary banking crash and devastated the property market. From December 1973 to November 1974, numerous secondary banks and property companies failed in what became the worst financial crisis since the 1930s.[7] The Agency was not immune to the devastation. A number of the companies in which it had invested failed, and, in December 1974, it was declared insolvent and the then Senior Crown Agent, Sir

5 PP 1977–8, 8, appendix xvii.

6 L 8, Banking Dept., April 1972; *ibid.*, Sept. 1972; L 1 to L 11, Banking Dept. reports.; L 9, Banking Dept, Aug. 1973; *ibid.*, Oct. 1973; PP 1977–8, 8, pp. 29, 55, 95.

7 PP 1977/78, 40, p. 4.

John Cuckney, asked the government for financial assistance, receiving a grant of £85m and standby credit facilities of £50m from the Bank of England.

Such was the outcry at the Agents' losses that the government instigated a further enquiry chaired by Lord Fay. After 85 meetings and taking evidence from 46 witnesses, Fay's committee blamed the Agency's collapse on the Agents themselves, and, to a lesser extent, on the government, which had failed 'to inform itself of the developments, to appreciate the risks, and to grasp the need for quick action'. It concluded that the CAs had embarked on their own account activities with insufficient experience and inadequate internal controls, had taken unjustified risks, become involved in unethical and illegal activities, and were personally corrupt.[8] The report resulted in a further barrage of press and Parliamentary criticism. It was claimed that the 'not very bright' 'Clown Agents' were 'a bunch of well meaning amateurs' 'guilty of Walter Mitty like megalomania disastrously combined with bumbling incompetence', and that their corrupt practices 'made the Great Train Robbers look like petty thieves'.[9] At the same time, there developed a belief in Parliament and the media that the enquiry had been 'a cover up'.[10] Harold Wilson MP, then leader of the Opposition, declared in the Commons that in the late 1960s and early 1970s there had been a conspiracy by Civil Servants and the Conservative party to keep the Agents' activities secret, and that attempts by Judith Hart to 'blow the whole thing open' had been blocked by 'the most formidable system of fortifications ... that it is possible to conceive'.[11]

Under pressure from Parliament, the government in 1978 therefore set up a statutory tribunal, chaired by Sir David Croom-Johnson to determine 'who was to blame' for the crash.[12] The tribunal 'laboured long', hearing testimony from 106 witnesses over 260 days at a cost of £2.5m, but, it was generally agreed, brought 'forth a mouse'.[13] The 604-page 1982 report again censured the Agents, in particular Hayes and Challis, and criticized the behaviour of the Ministry, the Treasury and the Bank of England. Rather than a conspiracy of silence, however, it concluded that there was 'a great deal of activity [among government departments and the Bank regarding the Agents] with many papers passing to and fro' and 'many meetings both departmental and interdepartmental'. Unfortunately, these 'concealed the fact that nothing was being achieved', and that, lacking 'common sense' and 'initiative', neither the departments nor the Bank had been willing to take 'the lead' and 'grapple with the problem'.[14]

The actions of government departments and the Bank of England and the impact of the 1973/4 secondary banking crisis on the Agency are discussed in chapter nine. The rest of this chapter investigates the three primary criticisms of the Agents' own account activities put forward by the Fay and Croom-Johnson enquiries - that they involved excessive risk, many were unethical and illegal, and

8 *Ibid.*, 8, p. 173.

9 *Daily Telegraph*, 2 Dec. 1977, p. 18; *Daily Mail*, 7 Dec. 1977, p. 2; *Sunday Telegraph*, 4 Dec. 1977, p. 20; *Hansard*, 1977–78, 940, 736.

10 *The Sunday Times*, 4 Dec. 1977, p. 17.

11 *Hansard*, 1977–78, 940, 1055.

12 PP 1981–2, 364, p. 3.

13 *The Times*, 27 May 1982, p. 13; *Daily Telegraph*, 27 May 1982, pp. 19–20.

14 PP 1981–2, 364, p. 521.

that CA staff benefited personally from their duties. The discussion concentrates on the period 1967 to December 1973, when the trading environment was relatively stable, and makes use of Crown Agent, Ministry and Treasury papers, and, to a lesser extent, Bank of England documents.[15] To put the investigation into context, these sections are preceded by an examination of the Agents' new role and the reasons why it was adopted.

Description of own account activities and the reasons for their adoption

Own Account activities

The Agents' secondary banking venture was undertaken by the Finance Directorate and Four Millbank Investments Ltd (FMI), a Crown Agent subsidiary company, and bankrolled by the Finance Department Investment Account, known as Finvest, though FMI also obtained loans from UK and American banks on its own behalf (Appendix 5).[16] On average, around half of the money in the Finvest account came from the Agents' overseas clients in the form of short-term deposits, the proportion varying according to the strength of sterling and the availability of other funds (Figure 8.1).[17] Most of the remainder was borrowed on a short term basis from UK financial institutions, that is the clearing banks, London branches of continental, American and international banks, insurance companies and pension funds, at an interest rate above bank rate.[18] Extremely small sums were also obtained from Millbank Technical Services, which in 1973 had £14m of short-term deposits with Finvest; the Marine Insurance Fund, approximately £100,00 of which was placed in the account; and, from January to June 1974, the Joint Funds.[19] Although it had been laid down that call deposits placed in the Joint Funds should not be invested in Finvest, such was the demand for money at the height of the secondary banking crash that the rule was circumvented by the Agents, who advanced sums from these Funds to the Burston & Texas Commerce Bank, which, in turn, re-lent them back to the Agency.[20]

The money raised by Finvest was invested by the Finance Directorate or advanced to Four Millbank Investments Ltd. The principal Finance Directorate investment activity was the relending of funds (Figure 8.1). The Agents had an average monthly turnover of loans of £490.9m and generally borrowed long and lent short, that is borrowed money for a time period longer than that for which it was lent, which increased returns.[21] The rates of interest charged were

15 The Bank of England refused the author access to its post-1964 papers, though some of these were presented as evidence to the enquiries and have been seen. A small number of Ministry, Treasury and CA papers lodged at the National Archives are still closed.

16 E.g. L 35, 30 Aug. 1972 meeting; L 48, 11 Mar. 1974; *ibid.*, 7 Aug. 1974; L 50, minutes, 3 Sept. 1973.

17 L 118/5, p. 37.

18 L 35, 1968, no. 38; HO 268/327, memo, 19 Nov. 1970.

19 L 35, 30 Oct. 1973 meeting; L 246, memo, A. L. Batchelor, 17 Oct. 1974.

20 L 118/6, p. 77.

21 L 35, 1968, no. 38; L 1 to L 11, Banking Dept. and Finance Dept.; L 5, Finance Dept., Sept. 1969. Short-term loans carried a relatively high interest rate.

Figure 8.2. Finvest lending, 1971–74

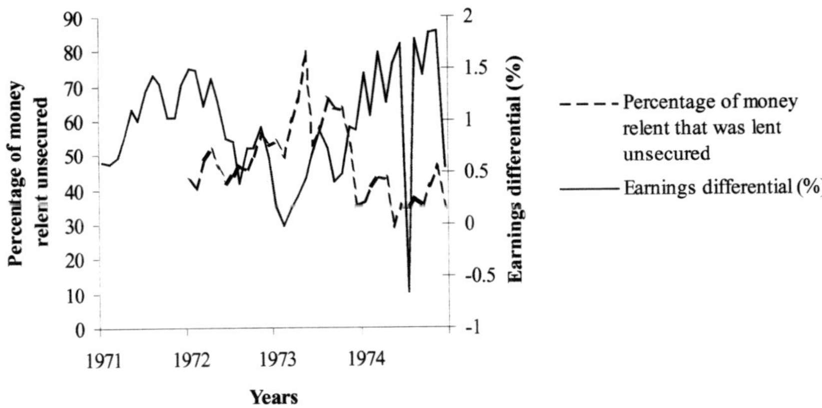

Source. L 1 to L 11, Banking Dept. and F Dept.; HO 268/422, Finvest monthly reports.

slightly higher than those at which the sums had been borrowed to give a 'turn', an average earnings differential, of 0.9 per cent (Figure 8.2).[22] Borrowers were banks, which in May 1971 obtained 46 per cent of the funds lent, finance houses (9 per cent), commerce and industry (15.7 per cent), local authorities (1.1 per cent), property companies (7.9 per cent), overseas clients (2.2 per cent), and those companies in which FMI had shareholdings (18 per cent).[23]

Other Finance Directorate activities included investment in gilts and equities, the trading of currencies and commodities, underwriting, and the purchase of property in Britain, Cyprus and Gibraltar. In December 1971, 0.39 per cent of Finvest funds was invested in gilts, 1.14 per cent in UK equities, and 2.74 per cent in foreign equities, the Agents having portfolios in Australia, Hong Kong, Jamaica, Malaysia, Singapore, South Africa and the US.[24] Currency and commodities trading and the purchase of properties generally accounted for around 3 per cent of the Finvest investments, and, as time passed, became less important. The buying and selling of commodities, such as silver, sugar and cocoa, halted in 1969 when £300,000 was lost on silver trades, and, from March 1971, the Agency disposed of its property portfolio.[25] The majority of the 22 property developments were transferred to English & Continental Property Co. Ltd, a company in which FMI had a large shareholding, and the remaining properties were sold off to a number of developers over an 18 month period.[26]

Four Millbank Investments Ltd took large and long-term equity holdings in individual companies. Its capital rose from £1.074m at the end of 1968 to £10.458m in December 1971 and £18.32m in December 1973, and was

22 The earnings differential is the difference between the rate of borrowing and the rate of lending.

23 L 188, file 1, memo, no date, approx. May 1971.

24 L 227, memo, 'Objectives for..', 1 Feb. 1972; L 7, Investment Dept., April 1971.

25 L 35, 1970, no. 5; PP 1981–2, 364, p. 46.

26 L 188, file 1, meeting, 4 Aug. 1971; L 7, Banking Dept., March 1971.

invested in the UK banking industry, overseas merchant banks, two property development concerns in Australia and Singapore, and a variety of UK quoted and unquoted firms (Appendix 5 and 6). All of these companies then received further loans from the Finvest account, and, as already discussed, in some cases the JCF/JMF and colonial investment Funds bought their shares and, in the case of the banks, made deposits.[27] In the UK banking sector, FMI had a 40 per cent shareholding in the small merchant bank E. D. Sassoons Banking Co. Ltd, which later merged with Wallace Bros, and owned 33 per cent and 10 per cent respectively of the secondary banks Sterling Industrial Securities Ltd (SIS) and First National Finance Corporation Ltd (FNFC).[28] Its involvement in overseas merchant banks was concentrated in Australia, Canada, SE Asia, and the West Indies. In the West Indies, it purchased 40 per cent of the Caribbean Bank and later took a stake in Crown Continental Merchant Bank Jamaica Ltd, which, in 1971, obtained control of the Jamaica Building Society in partnership with the Commonwealth Development Corporation.[29] In SE Asia, 24 per cent holdings in Malaysian International Merchant Bankers Berhad and Singapore International Merchant Bankers Ltd were acquired, in Canada a minority stake was taken in CGA Capital Corporation, and, in Australia, it bought 17 per cent of Westralian International Ltd and 20 per cent of Commercial Continental Ltd.[30]

FMI's Australian and Singapore property ventures were conducted through Abbey Orchard Property Investments Ltd and Orchard Square Development Corporation Ltd respectively. The company owned 33 per cent of the Australian firm, which became one of the largest property developers in the country, and 75 per cent of the Singapore concern. [31] In the UK, it took stakes in a variety of companies, ranging from one of the World's largest postage stamp retailers to an air charter company. Of particular relevance, was its 51 per cent holding of English & Continental Property Co. Ltd, which it formed with others in 1969 with the intention of eventually taking it public.[32] By 1972, the firm owned £100m of properties, including Manchester's Central Railway Station, and, in London, Bush House, the former Westinghouse Works at Kings Cross, and the Port of London's Cutler Street warehouse.[33] After the sale of many of its sites to the Post Office Superannuation Fund in November 1971, a new company, English & Continental Investments Ltd, was formed to take over the non-income producing assets that were not included in the Post Office deal.[34]

Reasons for the new venture

The Agents' motives for embarking on the own account project were personal and organizational self-interest and a desire to help their traditional clients. Both the staff of the Finance Directorate and the Senior Crown Agents personally

27 CAOG 12/127, FMI accounts, 1967 to 1973. See chapters three and four.
28 L 18/24, p. 7; PP 1981–2, 364, pp. 45, 142.
29 L 50, minutes, 21 Aug. 1969; *ibid.*, 24 April 1972.
30 PP 1977–8, 8, p. 30; L 50, minutes, 25 June 1973.
31 L 35, 1971, no. 19; *Guardian*, 5 Aug. 1971, p. 13.
32 PP 1977–8, 8, pp. 28–9; PP 1981–2, 364, p. 87.
33 PP 1977–8, 8, p. 93.
34 PP 1981–2, 364, p. 96.

gained from the Agency's new role. Challis and his colleagues acquired great satisfaction from the performance of their new duties, which were far more interesting and exciting than the Agents' traditional financial activities.[35] Luke and Hayes, meanwhile, obtained an opportunity to amass 'directorships within and outside the City to sustain [them] during [their] retirement', and the leadership of a successful organization increased their professional and social standing.[36]

As regards organizational self-interest, the new project ensured the Agency's survival by enabling it to build up its contingency reserves, which were low owing to the Colonial Office requirement in 1946 that it distribute any annual net profits to its overseas clients. Reserves needed to be raised because the Agents' accountant in a 1966 Board paper predicted that, if losses continued, they would be exhausted by 1970, and the Office was vulnerable to a sudden fall in its receipts.[37] As most of its traditional clients were primary producers, a sudden downturn in the World economy could rapidly reduce demand for its services, and there was the ever-present danger that it could lose a major client for political reasons.[38] A client country could cut its links with the Agency as a protest against some UK government policy or as a result of a regime change, as occurred in Iraq and Ghana. When the Agents' customers were colonies, such a fall in income would have been unimportant, as the UK government accepted financial responsibility for the Agency. But by 1966, the majority of their principals were independent countries, and it was assumed that the CAs had lost UK government support and were 'on their own'.[39] They thus believed that they had no option but to raise their reserves to guard against such losses. Secondary banking being chosen as the vehicle for the generation of the income needed, partly because they possessed financial expertise in the sector, which was known to be lucrative, and partly because their experience over the past five years had amply demonstrated that any increase in their traditional business would be difficult to achieve and that demand for these services was highly price inelastic, with any increase in their charges leading to a disproportionately large fall in demand.

At the two enquiries, the Ministry, seeking to avoid any blame for the debacle, questioned this motivation, arguing that the CAs had no need to raise their reserves because the UK government had always accepted a financial obligation for the Agency. It was claimed that there was no record of a Ministry official ever informing the Agents that the 'government had washed its hands of them', and, in April 1970, Hayes had been told by the Minister that the Treasury had concluded that HMG did have a residual responsibility.[40] Although the two enquiries believed the Ministry's version of events, the CAs' insistence that the

35 PP 1977–8, 8, p. 38.

36 Pen Portraits, E. A. Morris, 10 July 1996; *ibid.*, E. A. Morris's pen portrait of Hayes.

37 PP 1981–2, 364, p. 29.

38 OD 20/410, Luke's memo on the CAs, Nov. 1964. There was also an increased likelihood that the CAs would be sued by clients or suppliers. Independent administrations were more inclined than colonies to take legal action if mistakes were made in the provision of services and were more likely to default on the payment of bills (L 35, 1965, no. 50).

39 Statement, Hayes, Aug. 1993, p. 17.

40 PP 1977–8, 8, p. 4.

government had abandoned them seems the more credible. From 1954 onwards, the Colonial Office had repeatedly disclaimed any responsibility for transactions undertaken by the Agents on behalf of independent countries, and, when the Office came close to bankruptcy in 1961/2, the government failed to come to its rescue. Before his appointment as Senior Crown Agent, Hayes had been a Principal Finance Officer at the Ministry and had understood that the government would not financially back the Agency, and numerous witnesses confirmed to the enquiries that Luke had been told 'in 1963 or thereabouts' that 'the CAs were now on their own feet and that HMG would not be responsible for its obligations'.[41] Although there appears to be no record of this statement being made, there is a memo that suggests that this was the view of the Ministry and that it was conveyed to Luke. A minute dated 3rd April 1963 records that, at a meeting between Luke and Dennis Vosper, the Secretary of State, Vosper made no comment when Luke mused that he 'did not think' that there was 'much of a chance' of public support if a crisis arose, and that Vosper privately believed that government assistance would be 'entirely wrong' and that the Ministry should 'visualise the demise of the CAs within ten years'.[42]

The Ministry's assurance to Hayes in April 1970 that the government had a legal responsibility for the Agency was limited to large losses that would result in bankruptcy, and was, in any case, not believed by the Agents. [43] Hayes suspected that it was part of an attempt by Ministry officials to increase their control of the Agency and asked to see the relevant legal papers.[44] All of his requests were refused, largely because, as he discovered from his contacts, neither the Ministry nor the Treasury had obtained authorative legal advice on the matter.[45] The extent of the government's responsibility, as later admitted by Sir Geoffrey Wilson, the permanent secretary, was that it had only a 'moral obligation' to meet the Agents' debts, and then only as a 'last resort'.[46]

The second purpose of the own account project, hardly mentioned by the enquiries, was to help the third world. The Agency's traditional clients gained from its new role in a number of miscellaneous ways. For example, by placing deposits in the Finvest account they earned higher returns than if the money had been lodged in the Joint Funds or commercial banks, many received Finvest loans directly or through MTS, and the CAs' purchase of equities in Singapore, Malaysia, Hong Kong and Jamaica promoted the development of equity markets in these territories.[47]

More importantly, the new venture permitted cross-subsidisation and invest-

41 SA, Report on Croom-Johnson Tribunal, Hayes, para. 14; PP 1977–8, 8, p. 4; L 160, Hayes memo, 19 Aug. 1970.

42 OD 20/119, memo, 3 April 1963.

43 L 118/5, p. 22. The Ministry 'agreed that it is prudent for the CAs to build up a reserve' (PP 1977–8, 8, p. 190). See also Croom-Johnson Tribunal evidence, Wilson d.162. 45f and King d.167. 29.

44 The Ministry's wish to take control of the Agency is discussed in chapter eight.

45 Report on Croom-Johnson Tribunal, Hayes, para. 14. Hayes' contacts at the Ministry were such that in 1972 an official asked 'do the CAs run a private investigation service as part of their own account activities' (OD 20/514, memo, 18 Dec. 1972).

46 L 160, Hayes memo, 19 Aug. 1970.

47 L 118/5, p. 37; L 188, file 1, memo, no date, approx. May 1971.

ment in companies that could prove useful to developing countries. Cross-subsidisation involved Finvest profits being used to subsidise the Agents' loss-making traditional activities, preventing the increases in charges and the cost cutting and associated falls in efficiency that would otherwise have been necessary. At the same time, the extra funds enabled the CAs to improve and expand the services offered and to extend their business to other developing countries.[48] As regards company investment, FMI tried to become involved in firms that would improve or add to the services provided by the Agency, give it access to new clients, or assist the economic and social development of customers.[49] In the case of the Australian property company, it also hoped to get clients to directly invest in the concern and thus benefit from that country's property boom.[50] In the event, only Singapore became involved, investing $15m, for which it obtained a return of 7.5 per cent per annum, a 15 per cent stake in the company, plus a slice of the profits.[51]

FMI company investments sought to improve both the Agency's financial and non-financial services. The performance of its financial role was enhanced by the stakes in Sassoons and overseas merchant banks. The part-ownership of Sassoons and the connection with Wallace Bros. enabled the Office to supply more sophisticated banking services, for example in the fields of investment advice and foreign exchange, in London, the Bahamas (where Sassoons had a branch office), and, through Wallace Bros., in the Far East.[52] Central bank clients, whose authorizing legislation or articles only allowed them to deal with banks, were also finally able to gain the benefits of banking with the Agents, and the Office obtained access to Export Credit guarantees, only available to banks or exporters, and could thus offer clients package deals that provided engineering or technical services, along with the necessary finance.[53] The move into international merchant banking, similarly, improved and extended the financial advice and services that could be offered to clients. In addition, the banks gave customers access to finance, improved the Agents' management of their principals' and their own local investments, and contributed to the growth of private capital markets and thus promoted development.[54]

FMI's non-financial investments variously gave the CAs' clients access to a charter airline, a railway engineering consultancy, a management company, and a firm whose data capture technology could be used in medical research. Investment was particularly concentrated in the area of communications, thought to be an important aspect of development, by the Agency taking stakeholdings in Crown Communications Ltd, Television Recordings Ltd and Crown Cassette

48 Johns to Sunderland, 6 Dec. 2004, enclosure, p. 3; L 50, minutes, 17 May 1971; PP 1981–2, 364, p. 29.

49 L 50, minutes, 17 May 1971; CAOG 21/194, Towse to Davidson, 5 June 1973. A side effect of development was greater demand for the CAs' services and higher profits.

50 Author's interview with Johns, 20 Jan. 2004.

51 CAOG 24/16, Hewins to Singapore, 13 Nov. 1969.

52 PP 1977–8, 8, p. 12; HO 268/327, memo, 3 June 1970.

53 L 36, 25 July 1967; CAOG 16/93, Hewins, 5 Feb. 1973; L 36, 26 Sept. 1967; T 317/1498, report, approx. Sept. 1969. See also HO 268/378, memo, 13 Dec. 1971.

54 CAOG 21/188; L 50, minutes, 7 May 1971; HO 268/330, memo, no date.

Ltd. Crown Communications Ltd, a partnership with the British Post Office, allowed the CAs to give advice on the establishment of satellite earth stations.[55] From Television Recordings Ltd, a production company, they gained up-to-date knowledge of modern studio techniques and colour transmission, and hoped 'in due course' to be able to 'provide advice on and material for [educational] programmes'.[56] And Crown Cassettes Ltd gave them access to video cassette technology, which would allow these programmes to be seen in those countries with primitive television services.[57]

Development was directly promoted via investment in development and mining companies and a number of other commercial firms. Development companies with which FMI became associated included the Malaysian Industrial Development Finance Corporation, the Development Bank of Singapore, the British Bangladeshi Trust, and, more significantly, ILCO Holdings Ltd and SIFIDA. The Agents owned 25 per cent of ILCO, which was formed to provide a channel for investment in Singapore and S.E. Asia, and 12 per cent of SIFDA, a company that sought to promote private investment in Africa.[58] They were joined in SIFDA by financial and industrial corporations from thirteen other countries, and, by 1973, the company had invested in ten schemes including a fibreboard plant in Kenya and a cement factory in Zaire.[59] To aid the exploitation of natural resources, stakes were taken in Amscot Oceanic Ltd, Hartog Oil Ltd, Eastern Copper Mines Ltd, and Chenderiang Tin Dredging Ltd. The latter company was a mining investment house, which by 1974 was involved in the development of tin mines in Malaysia and Indonesia and oil fields in Nigeria and Abu Dhabi, and was considering a partnership with a Hong Kong company that would have allowed it to extend its activities into the SE Asian oil industry.[60] Holdings were also taken in firms that would promote smaller local industries, often at the request of clients. For example, in 1969, after consultation with the Malta Development Corporation, the CAs bought 13 per cent of Britannia Studios International Ltd, which provided sound and other facilities for film making on the island, and, in 1970, acquired 4 per cent of and gave a £100,000 loan to International Hotels Kenya Ltd 'as a gesture to the Kenya government' and its attempt to promote tourism.[61]

55 L 76, overseas trade memo no. 28/69, 15 Oct. 1969.

56 HO 268/509, Luke to Cohen, 14 March 1968; *ibid.,* Hayes to Wilson, 18 Aug. 1969. It was hoped that the company would allow the Agents 'to offer the sort of comprehensive service that the Thompson organization provides in developing countries – only better!' (HO 268/509, Luke to Cohen, 14 March 1968).

57 CAOG 9/295, Clark to Lord Hill, BBC, 4 Feb. 1971.

58 CAOG 21/188.

59 *Ibid.*; L 50, papers, 29 Jan. 1973.

60 L 50, papers, 23 July 1973; *ibid.*, minutes, 19 Nov. 1973; *ibid.*, 29 July 1974; HO 268/328, B of E memo, 21 March 1974.

61 CAOG 21/188; T 317/1498, report, approx. Sept. 1970.

Risk

Both Fay and Croom-Johnson strongly believed that the Agency's own account business incorporated excessive risk and that loans to and investment in poor quality companies made its downfall during the 1974 secondary banking and property crash inevitable. Risk was supposedly maximised by a number of factors, each of which will be discussed in turn. It was claimed that the Finance Directorate entered its new activities with inadequate reserves, little experience and a reluctance to take advice from others. Lending was inadequately controlled, directed at high risk institutions and excessively concentrated in the property sector, and the Agents took stakes in failing firms operated by morally dubious individuals, whose performance went unmonitored.

Lack of reserves and experience

In criticizing the Agency's lack of reserves, the two enquiries compared its reserve ratios ie. the size of its reserves in relation to its liabilities to those laid down in the Bank of England's banking regulations. In 1967 and 1969, the Agents had ratios of 64 to 1 and 106 to 1 respectively, as opposed the Bank's required 10 to 1.[62] As the Bank itself admitted, however, the problem of a lack of reserves did not arise if, as the Ministry insisted, the government had ultimate financial responsibility for the Agency, or if its non-own account investments were taken into account.[63] The Agents, meanwhile, questioned the Bank's refusal to accept 'property in own occupation' as part of reserves and rejected the argument that they should have followed its ratios. It was pointed out that during the property boom their offices, approximately 1,000 yards from the Houses of Parliament, could have easily been sold off for a large sum and then leased back, and that they were not an authorized bank and thus not subject to the Bank's recommendations, and, in any case, required lower reserves than most banks.[64] They advanced a large proportion of their funds to financial institutions, less likely to default than the private customers to whom the clearing banks largely lent.[65] They also spread their lending among a large number of borrowers, kept the size of their liabilities under constant review, and, by 1973, their reserves, inclusive of the value of their offices, were such that the Bank's 10 to 1 ratio would have been comfortably met.[66]

Those members of the Directorate's staff seeking to escape blame for their supposed transgressions enthusiastically acknowledged the enquiries' conclusion that the Finance Directorate lacked financial experience. Denis Clark, the Head of Finance and later Banking, told the Fay investigation that he was 'completely inadequate for the job'; Peter Sly, the Property Investment Manager, informed them that his 'experience of property investment was nil', and Eric Osgodby,

62 PP 1981–2, 364, p. 52.

63 T 316/186, Hodges, 13 Dec. 1971; *ibid.*, Page, 13 Dec. 1971.

64 L 118/5, pp. 26–27; L 121, 1979, no. 42/79.

65 L 118/5, p. 30.

66 L 118/18, p. 42; L 118/5, p. 32; CAOG 16/93, Barley, 13 Dec. 1973. Reserves in December 1967 were £36.5m (L 118/5, p. 27).

Deputy and later Acting Head of Banking, claimed that that he was neither 'professionally or temperamentally qualified for the post'.[67] Lack of experience was compounded by a shortage of staff. The relatively low Civil Service salary scales and the Agency's penury prevented the payment of high wages, causing the most talented people, once trained, to move to comparable jobs in the City 'for substantially better terms'.[68] The Agency was thus forced to turn away a 'considerable amount of profitable business', and the remaining staff and particularly the senior officers were overworked and performed their roles less efficiently.[69]

The lack of expertise was the direct result of the Office's promotion policy, which was to fill a vacancy with the next senior person in the organization irrespective of technical background. Thus Clark had previously managed the Shipping Department and Osgodby had run the Private Office and the General Stores Department.[70] A further factor was the Agency's inability to recruit externally. The low wages paid made it almost impossible to obtain individuals with banking experience and such appointments would have created internal friction.[71] Hayes, who wished to appoint a CA board member with financial knowledge also faced resistance from the Ministry, which wished to slow the growth of the Agency's own account activities and thus ruled that no such appointment could be made until the Stevenson committee had reported, and, after the report had appeared, until the Agency's constitutional position had been resolved.[72]

The CA's inadequate experience, however, must not be exaggerated. Alan Challis, Norman Hewins, the Investment Manager and later Deputy and Head of Banking, and David Johns, the International Fund Investment Manager and later Challis's assistant, had spent most of their careers in finance, as had many of the Directorate's junior staff.[73] As shown in the previous chapters, the Agents had successfully managed their principals' investments for over a century, and for many years had dealt with their London property requirements.[74] All members of staff also received intensive training. Employees were sent on outside training courses, seconded to investment brokers and merchant banks, studied for the Stock Exchange exams, and attended investment seminars and conferences.[75] Senior staff were given seats (unpaid) on the boards of associated companies, which enabled them to gain 'valuable' commercial 'insight', and one of the reasons for the acquisition of a property portfolio was to allow the Banking

67 PP 1977–8, 8, p. 16, 21, 93, 161; PP 1981–2, 364, p. 53.

68 L 9, Investment Dept., Feb. 1973.

69 SA, Croom-Johnson Tribunal, Doc. Evidence, b/ca/6/2 p. 57, Wheatley, 20 May 1969; Statement, Hayes, Aug. 1993, p. 19. Such was the 'considerable strain' that by 1970 the Heads of the Directorate were 'increasingly inclined to dream dreams of retirement' (Knights' Papers, Shuter to Knights, 25 April 1970).

70 L 118/5, p. 56; PP 1977–8, 8, pp. 16, 93.

71 L 118/7, p. 12.

72 Report on Croom-Johnson Tribunal, Hayes, para. 7; SA, Hayes Papers, Hayes to Hobson, 8 March 1975.

73 PP 1981–2, 364, p. 53.

74 Challis believed the Agents to be 'as good as anybody in the sterling money market' (L 118/5, p. 46).

75 L 118/5, p. 54; L 50, minutes, 17 May 1971. For example, L 7, Banking Dept., June 1971; HO 268/509, Hayes to Ministry, 11 July 1969; L 9, Investment Dept., Sept. 1973.

Department to gain basic property development experience, which would allow it to monitor effectively the progress of those property companies in which FMI took a stake.[76]

Certainly, others did not share the enquiries' lack of faith in the CAs' expertise. The very fact that the City was willing to entrust the Agency with its funds suggests that it had confidence in its abilities and this belief was expressed both verbally and through offers of employment.[77] Not only was there a constant movement of junior staff to the City, but senior officers were also offered posts. Hills Samuel, for example, tried to 'head hunt' David Johns; both the American bank Continental Illinois and FNFC attempted to recruit John Shuter; and D. Barnes, an investment manager, Peter Sly and Alan Challis all eventually took posts elsewhere.[78] Plaudits also came from the Bank of England, which in 1969 had sufficient confidence in the CAs' abilities to suggest that they set up their own banking subsidiary.[79] Officials thought Challis to be a 'remarkable individual', 'a well regarded City figure' and 'shrewd and very able', though lacking in experience 'in some of the financial fields in which he is now leading the CAs'.[80] Wheatley 'was obviously shrewd, a quick mind', and the Bank's Governor spoke 'favourably of Mr Hewins to the point of suggesting that the appointment of an outside banker to the CA board may not be necessary'.[81]

The Agency sought to counter its lack of expertise in those areas in which it had no previous experience by seeking external advice, though the enquiries identified a distinct disinclination to seek out such help.[82]. As regards their investment in UK equities, the CAs were in daily contact with their brokers. To ensure that they obtained the best independent help available, they employed five of the most prestigious London broking houses, plus two firms based in the provinces.[83] They also made use of the Equity Advisory Panel and the Equity Research Unit, discussed in chapter three. Their investments in foreign equities, meanwhile, were managed by leading foreign stockbrokers and their trades in commodities

76 HO 268/509, Hayes to Ministry, 11 July 1969; L 35, 1971, no. 14. The sale and transference of the properties to English & Continental Property Co. Ltd occurred partly because it was judged that sufficient expertise had been acquired (L 118/5, p. 191).

77 Wheatley, for instance, was 'highly respected in the City' (L 118/7, p. 63). See also Sly, Personnel file, memo, approx. 1970; L 36, 23 May 1967.

78 Author's interview with Johns, 20 Jan. 2004; Author's interview with Shuter, 20 Oct. 2004.

79 HO 268/330, memo, 28 July 1967; *ibid.*, memo, 4 Aug. 1967.

80 Croom-Johnson Tribunal, Doc. Evidence, b/be/5/1 p. 14, Keogh, 19 Nov. 1971; T 326/1368, Hillis, 8 Sept. 1969; HO 268/327, memo, 7 May 1970.

81 L 118/5, p. 55; Hayes Papers, notes on meeting between Hayes and Coopers & Lybrans, 28 Feb. 1975.

82 PP 1977–8, 8, p. 164; PP 1981–2, 364, p. 23. A supposed example of this disinclination was that the Agents failed to obtain an independent valuation of the UK properties they transferred at cost value to English & Continental Property Co. Ltd in May 1971. In fact, no valuations were obtained because they had been informally told by surveyors that they would not suffer a loss on the transfer, as the properties had recently been acquired and were of poor quality. A professional valuation would therefore have been an unnecessary expense (L 118/5, p. 191; L 118/7, p. 51).

83 James Capel, W. Greenwell & Co, Phillips & Drew, J. & A. Scrimgeour, Simon & Coates, Haliday Simpson of Manchester, and Parsons & Co of Glasgow (L 188, file 1, staff circular, Feb. 1972).

were carried out with the assistance of Messrs Czarnikow, widely regarded as one of the best commodity brokers in the World.[84]

In other areas, their use of specialists was restricted by the high fees charged by merchant banks and accountants, and a suspicion that any advice provided by banks or the Bank of England, with whom they were in direct competition, could be biased.[85] Nevertheless, on selling English & Continental Property Co. Ltd guidance was obtained from the merchant bank S. G. Warburg, before becoming involved with Capital & Counties Property Ltd, Sassoons and Television Recordings Ltd reports on these companies were commissioned from the accountants Price Waterhouse, and the Bank of England was consulted regarding the acquisition of Sassoons and its later merger with Wallace Bros.[86]

Far more help came from the Agents' solicitors Davies Arnold & Cooper, Sassoons, Sterling Investment Securities, FNFC and Westralian Ltd, and, in the case of property, partnerships with experts.[87] In Australia, the CAs collaborated with Felix Fenston, a leading property developer, and his company Pennine Co Ltd. In England, they formed the company English & Continental Property Co. Ltd with Jack Walker of Davies Arnold & Cooper and Ramon and Lionel Greene, developers and house builders. In each case, the Agents provided all the capital required, and their partners supplied the necessary expertise for a return of 50 per cent and 49 percent of the profits respectively.[88]

These latter sources of help were heavily criticized by the enquiries. Davies Arnold & Cooper supposedly provided poor quality and biased advice and the CA property deals were said to be overly generous. Davies Arnold & Cooper were a relatively inexperienced firm of solicitors, and had a conflict of interests in that they introduced their own clients to the CAs as potential borrowers (in one case taking a fee for the introduction and in another having an interest in a borrowing company), and, at the same time, acted for the Agency in assessing and processing the loan security provided by borrowers.[89] In defence, the Agents stated that they had been perfectly satisfied with the information provided by the firm, pointing out that the prestigious City solicitors Freshfields appointed in 1974 to manage their dealings with the Stern Group had given them negligent advice.[90] It was also pointed out that it was not against Law Society rules for a

84 L 35, 1970, no. 5. US equities were managed by Continental Illinois and Kuhn Loeb, Australian equities by IOS, and the Singapore/Malaysia portfolio by Singapore International Merchant Bankers Ltd (L 227, Statement, Barley, 23 Feb. 1978; L 188, 7 April 1971; L 7, Investment Dept., April 1971).

85 Statement, Hayes, Aug. 1993, p. 19; Report on Croom-Johnson Tribunal, Hayes, para. 10.

86 PP 1981–2, 364, p. 96; L 118/5, p. 46, 306; L 36, 25 July 1967; PP 1977–8, 8, p. 12; HO 268/327, memo, 3 June 1970. Fay's claim that the decision to enter the agreement with Capital & Counties was made before the report was received misrepresents the true state of affairs (PP 1977–8, 8, p. 65). The decision was made after Price Waterhouse had telexed a summary of the report's findings (L 118/5, p. 307).

87 T 317/1498, report, approx. Sept. 1969. For example, CAOG 21/194, Towse to Sheldon, 20 Sept. 1973; L 118/5, p. 280.

88 PP 1977–8, 8, p. 25; PP 1981–2, 364, p. 90.

89 L 147, memo, 28 Sept. 1976; PP 1977–8, 8, pp. 55–6, 165.

90 Council's opinion was that the firm was guilty of gross negligence (L 224, memo, 10 June 1975).

solicitor both to recommend clients for investments and to check the security, and that the borrowers introduced were safe risks. The firm had accurate knowledge of their financial state, and, since the company earned far more from the Agents than from its clients, it always put 'the CAs' interests first'; it being 'far more beneficial' for it to 'preserve ... [its] relationship with the Agents than with any ... single ... client'.[91]

The generosity of the property deals were criticised by the Stevenson and Croom-Johnson committees. Fay, on the other hand, accepted that partnerships between capital and expertise were prevalent in the property world, and that it was 'not uncommon for a partnership to be on a 50–50 basis'.[92] Indeed, the Church Commissioners, who were also heavily invested in property, often obtained only 40 per cent of profits.[93] Fay, however, did severely criticize the Australian deal on another point. Soon after the Agents came to the arrangement with Pennine, the owner Felix Fenston died. But instead of renegotiating or abandoning the agreement, which included a non-competition clause, the CAs ratified it, even though its only advantage, Fenston's expertise, had disappeared.[94] In reality, Fenston, before his death, had completed his selection of sites and work had already begun on a number of plots. The Agents were thus committed in law to the deal and demands for renegotiation would have resulted in costly legal action, which would have halted development, damaged their business reputation, and, if they had lost the case, led to the payment of damages and even the loss of the sites.[95]

Secured and unsecured lending controls

The main criticisms of the Agents' new lending role were that it was subject to inadequate internal controls, loans were made to high risk institutions, and excessive amounts were directed to the property sector. In fact, the Agency did possess strong controls over both secured and unsecured lending. Between January 1972 and December 1974 an average of 52 per cent of loans were secured, that is advanced in return for security, generally marketable financial instruments or property valued by an independent surveyor (Figure 8.2). The guidelines for such lending were that advances were to be no more than 10 per cent of the recipient's net assets less intangibles, not more than 5 per cent of total lending was to be to one institution, and the security given had to be worth at least 33 per cent more than the proposed loan.[96] Given the provision of security, there was no requirement to investigate the viability of clients. Officials, nevertheless, were expected to make enquiries about new borrowers and those that had previously obtained money from low status secondary banks.[97]

Critics of the guidelines argued that, when property was given as collateral, valuations were sometimes unduly optimistic and provided by a surveyor

91 PP 1977–8, 8, p. 56.
92 *Ibid.*, p. 166.
93 CA (m) 61, Personal and Confidential (P & C), annex d, p. 10.
94 PP 1977–8, 8, p. 25.
95 L 118/5, p. 302.
96 *Ibid.*, p. 101.
97 L 18/24, p. 11; L 118/5, pp. 96, 102, 111.

employed by the borrower and the form of security accepted was occasionally invalid. The mortgage given to secure a £5m loan to develop Ethelburga House in London in 1969, for instance, was neither stamped nor registered at the Land Registry.[98] The 33 per cent security rule was also on occasion ignored, and the Agents, in at least three instances, gave individuals loans that were used to make payments to the Agency.[99]

Most of these complaints, however, can be easily rebutted. Liberal valuations were common in the early 1970s and the use of estimates made by surveyors employed by the borrower was an accepted practice.[100] In certain circumstances, the CAs' guidelines permitted the breach of the 33 per cent rule. Loans in excess of two thirds of the security value could be given where short dated marketable securities were provided, and when the return was likely to be high.[101] Many other banks gave their investment managers such discretion and some secondary banks routinely made loans in excess of 75 or 80 per cent of the security given. Property prices and thus collateral values were rising rapidly, and, given the boom conditions, few loans were not repaid.[102] Likewise, the acceptance of temporarily invalid security was acceptable where 'to wait for security with the i's dotted and the t's crossed might well mean waiting too long to achieve the financial success that was desired'.[103] The few loans given to finance payments to the Agency were also made for valid commercial reasons. For example, in 1973 the Agents gave William Stern short-term loans totalling £8.5m to allow him to purchase from them a property development in Epsom because the price he offered for the site was attractive, the Agents were certain that Stern, one of the largest property developers in the UK, would have no difficulty in making the repayments, and it was believed that the deal, which had taken months to negotiate, would collapse if the advance was not provided.[104]

As regards loans advanced without security, prior to 1971 the Agency compiled a list of institutions that could borrow on an unsecured basis and Wheatley had discretion to make loans to these concerns provided that the advance did not exceed 10 per cent of the borrower's net assets and not more than 5pc of such loans went to one institution.[105] The list was reviewed weekly and comprised specific categories of borrowers, that is banks, discount and finance houses, insurance companies and local authorities, and later named companies, whose eligibility for inclusion was dependent on status and credit worthiness as appraised by the Banking Department. Factors taken into account by the appraisers included

98 PP 1977–8, 8, p. 26.

99 L 18/24, p. 1.

100 Peter Scott, 'The new alchemy: Veblen's theory of crisis and the 1974 British property and banking crisis', *Journal of Economic Issues*, 30, 1 (1996), p. 5; L 118/7, p. 18. The tribunal's expert witness confirmed that this was the case.

101 L 118/5, p. 101.

102 *Financial Times*, 23 Jan. 1979; Margaret Reid, *The Secondary Banking Crisis, 1973–75. Its Causes and Course*, London 1982, p. 65. All the CA loans due before December 1973 were repaid.

103 L 118/18, p. 9.

104 L 118/6, pp. 48, 52–3. The Agents were also anxious to sell the site as the development had aroused local hostility (L 118/6, p. 42). In the event, the property crash prevented the repayment of the loans (PP 1977–8, 8, p. 111).

105 L 118/5, p. 98

the ability of the borrower to obtain unsecured loans from other lenders, the healthiness of its balance sheet, in particularly its cash flow and asset value, press comment and City rumour, and the general outlook of the business in which the company was engaged.[106]

In 1971, the loss of £500,000 when the Vehicle & General Insurance Co Ltd went bankrupt, led to a tightening up of the lending procedure.[107] A credit committee was established, comprising senior members of the Directorate, who reviewed the existing list, considered new applications for loans, and laid down a credit limit for each list company based on its size and general performance. The committee sat until mid-summer 1973, when it was disbanded, largely because it had completed its review of list companies and there were no new borrowers seeking funds. Despite its disappearance, its limits remained in force.[108]

As with their secured counterparts, the guidelines for unsecured loans were occasionally breached. The Agents continued to provide Barclays Hotels Group with loans, even though the company refused a full examination of its books, largely because the firm's healthy state was vouchsaved by the CAs' main broker and their solicitors, who part-owned a subsidiary of the group.[109] They also ignored the credit ceilings and by-passed the credit committee in loans to the Stern Group. Hewins, who made the loans, however, had requested and examined the firm's accounts, which had revealed huge net assets, and had closely questioned the owner, William Stern, about his operations. Like others who lent to this and other property companies, he had also obtained a personal guarantee from Stern.[110]

The companies to which the Agency lent were not of the highest quality, not because of poor judgment, as suggested by its critics, but because it had difficulty obtaining deposits and was therefore forced to pay relatively high interest rates to attract them. To gain a decent margin of profit it was thus obliged to go 'down market' and re-lend the funds to the secondary banking sector and property companies, which, carrying greater risk, could be required to pay even higher rates of interest.[111] Its difficulty in procuring deposits was related partly to increasing competition for funds from the rapidly expanding secondary banking sector, and partly to its lack of authorized banking status. It thus possessed little banking credibility, deposits did not count as reserve assets, lenders would find it difficult to sue the Agency to recover debts, and central banks and other potential depositors were prevented from depositing funds by their authorizing legislation and articles of association.[112] Potential depositors were further deterred by the rumours of corruption and ineffectiveness circulating the City and the govern-

106 L 118/5, p. 96; L 188, File 1, memo, unsecured lending, approx. May 1971.

107 The CAs had renewed the loan, even though market reports indicated that it should be called in (Statement, Hayes, Aug. 1993, p. 30).

108 L 18/24, p. 11; L 118/5, p. 113.

109 PP 1977–8, 8, p. 57.

110 L 118/6, p. 35; L 118/5, pp. 253–4; *Daily Telegraph*, 7 Dec. 2004, p. 21. Hewins also claimed that Challis had told him to treat Stern as a special case. Challis denied this (L 118/6, p. 35; L 118/5, p. 251).

111 Hayes Papers, meeting between Hayes and Coopers & Lybrans, 28 Feb. 1975.

112 CAOG 16/93, Hewins, 5 Feb. 1973.

ment's refusal publicly to accept financial responsibility for the Office.[113] It should also be noted that the Agency was not the only high status institution to lend funds to the secondary banking and property sectors. Other prestigious concerns also lent vast amounts.[114] The Israeli-British Bank, for example, received loans from Barclays and the International Westminster Bank, and Cedar Holdings obtained advances from Unilever, Phoenix Insurance and the National Coal Board pension fund.[115]

The CAs not only lent large sums to the property sector, but also supposedly 'placed too many eggs in too few baskets', namely English & Continental Investments Ltd, the Stern Group and Abbey Orchard Property Investments.[116] English & Continental Investments Ltd was the company formed by the Agents, Jack Walker and the Greene brothers to hold the developments not bought by the Post Office Pension Fund. It was decided that the sites, known as the 'rump', would be developed and then sold off, and, in order to finance development, the Agents made a series of loans to the company, which by September 1973 totalled £4m.[117] As already discussed, the Stern Group was regarded as a safe investment by the CAs, who like many others were charmed by its charismatic owner. Loans to the Group increased from £2m in January 1973 to £21m by December of that year.[118] Advances to Abbey Orchard, the CAs' Australian property company, meanwhile, rose from £4.2m in 1970 to £36m by December 1973. [119]

Large sums were lent to the property sector and invested in the Agents' own portfolio because property was regarded by analysts and commentators alike as a safe investment.[120] Although 'the number of people who foresaw the ... disaster and did not reveal the fact until afterwards would fill the Albert Hall', until 1973 there were few warnings that the sector carried a high risk.[121] Property was also seen as a hedge against devaluation and the spiraling inflation of the late 1960s/early 1970s that would otherwise have eroded the Agency's reserves. Given that 'they were no longer manufacturing land', property values were expected to rise at rates equal to or greater than retail prices.[122] More importantly, property could deliver large profits. Interest rates on loans to property companies were high and the value of prime developments could multiply several times in one year. Like other institutions, the Agents reaped large returns from their investments.[123] In

113 L 18/24, p. 7.

114 L 100, *Daily Telegraph*, 27 March 1982.

115 SA, Press clippings, *Guardian*, 16 Sept. 1975; David Kynaston, *The City of London. Vol. iv. A Club No More, 1945–2000*, London 2001, p. 487.

116 PP 1977–8, 8, p. 163.

117 PP 1981–2, 364, p. 96; L 118/6, p. 18.

118 L 118/6, p. 35; PP 1977–8, 8, p. 140.

119 PP 1977–8, 8, appendix xvii, table 3; L 118/5, p. 276.

120 Challis believed property to be as 'safe as houses' (L 121, 1979, 81/79).

121 Statement, Hayes, Aug. 1993, p. 18.

122 L 6, F Dept., Jan. 1970. Inflation rose at an average of 3.6 per cent pa from 1965 to 1967; 5.58 per cent pa from 1968 to 1970; and 8.62 per cent pa from 1970 to 1973. From 1968 to 1970, property returns averaged 10.65 per cent pa in excess of inflation, and, from 1971–3, 14.2 per cent pa in excess of inflation (Scott, 'The new alchemy', pp. 3, 4).

123 Keyser Ullman holdings, for example, took over Central and District Properties in April 1972 for £69m and sold it 17 months later for £97m (Reid, *The Secondary*, p. 63).

1972/3, they obtained profits of £931,000 on the sale of office and shop developments in Altrincham, Bristol, London, Middlesborough and Walsall, and in 1971 the sale of most of the development sites owned by English & Continental Property Co. Ltd to the Post Office Pension Fund brought in a profit of £34m, £12m (after tax) of which went to the CAs.[124]

The extent to which the Agents 'over-invested' in property, can also easily be exaggerated. Compared to many institutions, they had a diverse investment portfolio. Funds were placed in equities, gilts, UK secondary banks, overseas merchant banks and a range of commercial companies. Nor were their advances to English and Continental Investments Ltd and Stern overly excessive, at least in December 1973. Large loans were only poured into these two companies in 1974, and, as will be seen, these advances were part of the Agency's desperate attempt to survive the crash of that year. Furthermore, in heavily investing in property, the Agents were merely following the general trend. Bank advances to the sector rose from £343m in November 1970 to £2,834m in November 1974 and constituted 20 per cent of total commercial bank lending. Participants in the bubble included not only the secondary and American banks, but also high street clearing banks and merchant banks, which invested both directly and indirectly, lending funds to secondary banks, which then passed the funds onto property companies.[125]

Ironically, unlike other institutions, the Agents in 1972–3 sought to reduce their exposure to property, at least in Britain. The Australian and Singapore commitments were regarded as long-term investments and unlikely to be affected by falls in UK prices.[126] On the sale of the English & Continental Property Co. Ltd sites to the Post Office pension fund, Hayes informed the Ministry that the 'CAs were coming out of the property market at what they hoped would prove to be the top of the boom', and that the company's 'rump' of sites would be disposed of during 1972.[127] Unfortunately, profitable sales were not possible until building had been completed, and, before this occurred, the company was engulfed by the 1974 crash. In August 1973, the Agents resolved to avoid further speculation in domestic housing, and, in November of that year, Hayes suggested that all investments in property should be reduced and Hewins later that month asked Stern not to request renewals of short-term loans.[128]

Investment controls

Critics of the FMI's involvement in private sector companies claimed that the risk quota was heightened by an absence of controls. Deals were settled on the telephone on the basis of casual acquaintanceships and wholly inadequate information.[129] The result was that the 'gullible … Millbank innocents' backed schemes that were little more than 'fine sounding rubbish' and became involved

124 L 8, Banking Dept., April 1972; *ibid.*, Sept. 1972; L 1 to L 11, Banking Dept. reports; L 9, Banking Dept., Aug. 1973; *ibid.*, Oct. 1973; PP 1977–8, 8, pp. 29, 55, 95.

125 Reid, *The Secondary*, p. 61; A. R. Goobey, *Bricks and Mortals*, London 1992, p. 21.

126 *Ibid.*, p. 284.

127 PP 1981–2, 364, p. 96.

128 L 35, 29 Aug. 1973; PP 1981–2, 364, p. 342.

129 Christopher Hood, 'The Crown Agents affair', *Public Administration*, 56 (1978), p. 301.

with 'a who's who of people to avoid in the financial world'.[130] Poor investment decisions were then compounded by a failure to monitor the companies, which subsequently performed poorly and engaged in dubious activities.[131]

The Agents certainly depended on a small network of associates for the discovery of business opportunities. As already shown, their traditional activities had always been conducted through such networks. Moreover, when they began their own account activities in 1967, they lacked access to City investment circles, which supplied members with private information not found in company accounts regarding the profitability of potential business partners. Deprived of this information, the CAs were thus forced to take stakeholdings in companies of which they had personal experience or firms recommended by service providers and friends, whose judgments they could trust and who would be unlikely to risk their own lucrative relationship with the Agency through the recommendation of poor quality proposals.

The consequence of this investment strategy was that almost all of the companies in which the Agents took a stakes were linked to them in some way. They had used FNFC for money market dealings, discounted Treasury bills through a company owned by Sidney Finley, with whom they later formed SIS, and had leased property through a firm managed by Ian Abrahams and David Roe in whose Television Recordings Ltd they took a holding.[132] Abrahams and Roe also recommended to the CAs' the solicitors Davies Arnold & Cooper, who introduced the Agents to clients requiring loans and to the Greene brothers, with whom they set up English & Continental Property Co. Ltd, and to Ralph Yablon, one of their partners in Sassoons.[133] The management of Sassoons, in turn, recommended investment in the Canadian merchant bank CGA Capital Corporation and the association with the Australian property development company Pennine Co. Ltd, one of whose directors, Prince Radzewill, introduced them to Col. William Sterling, with whom they entered the UK oil industry.[134]

All decisions to take or sell holdings were made by the board of Four Millbank Investments Ltd after receiving paper and verbal reports on the company concerned from Finance Directorate staff. Very occasionally, when speed was of the essence, decisions were taken by Hayes, who took counsel from those FMI directors who were available.[135] Investigation of proposals was generally thorough. In the case of the Australian property venture, for example, much criticized by Fay, the CAs in 1968 sent their solicitor Jack Walker to Australia to investigate the initial proposal, and, in the following year, Walker, Johns and Hewins. On both occasions, the CA representatives, before completing their reports, consulted leading figures in the construction world, local government, industry, and stock broking, as well as estate agents, accountants, architects and structural and quantity engineers, and investigated all aspects of the invest-

130 *Private Eye*, 10 Sept. 1971, p. 4; *The Times*, 2 Dec. 1977, p. 21.
131 PP 1981–2, 364, p. 54; PP 1977–8, 8, p. 164.
132 PP 1977–8, 8, pp. 12, 27; PP 1981–2, 364, p. 112;
133 PP 1977–8, 8, pp. 11, 12; PP 1981–2, 364, p. 88.
134 L 35, 5 June 1973; L 118/5, p. 273; L 201, Cuckney to Hart, 5 March 1975.
135 171, Board minutes, vol. 2, 17 May 1971.

ment.[136] A similar in-depth examination and discussion was conducted prior to the decision to invest in English & Continental Property Co. Ltd, and, in the case of the Agents' investment in Investico, a report on the company was obtained from their brokers Scrimgeours and information requested from the Board of Trade.[137]

The charge that the CAs only became involved with poor quality firms is simply not true. As Appendix 6 demonstrates, many of the companies were relatively prestigious or had good track records, others had high status directors or managers, and a large number were co-owned by leading merchant banks or financial institutions. A number of their ventures also proved highly lucrative. The Agents recouped their investment in Eastern Copper within a week by selling a mere 15 per cent of their holding.[138] In 1972 they sold off part of their shareholding in FNFC for a profit of £969,000, and as already discussed, the sale of sites owned by English & Continental Property Co. Ltd in 1973 brought in £12m. If the secondary banking crash had not occurred, it seems likely that they would have reaped similarly large profits from their investments in North Sea oil and video cassettes and their association with David and Frederick Barclay. The value of KCA Drilling, in which they had a major stake, increased from £3m in 1974 to £76m in 1981.[139] The production of video cassettes, which the Agents believed in 1970, to the amusement of many, were 'the third wave of the electronic-appliance age following radio and TV', did indeed become a billion dollar industry.[140] The Barclay brothers, meanwhile, who obtained loans totalling £25m from the Agency, today control a vast business empire and have a combined wealth of £1,200m.[141]

It cannot be denied that some of the firms with which the Agents became associated subsequently gained a dubious reputation. However 'what [was] obvious [when the enquiries were held was] not obvious at the time', a view supported by the prestigious nature of the Agents' co-investors and the Bank of England's belief in 1971 that their associates, though not 'first class names', were not 'out and out rogues'.[142] Except in the case of Sidney Finley and Sidney Davidson, discussed below, where there were suspicions regarding a potential partner, the CAs either refrained from investing or disposed of their holdings.[143] They also did not have a monopoly of bad investments. Unlike other City institutions, they had no involvement with Slater Walker, United Dominions Trust, Dawney Day and a host of other companies that were later regarded with distaste.[144]

In order to monitor their investments, the Agents had regular meetings with

136 L 118/5, pp. 273, 285–6, 288–94.
137 L 118/5, p. 187; CAOG 22/20, Scrimgeours to CAs, 3 Jan. 1969; *ibid.*, CAs to B of E, 3 Feb. 1969.
138 L 5, Finance Dept., Nov. 1969.
139 *The Times*, 30 May 1981, p. 20.
140 CAOG 9/295, Clark to Hayes, 4 Sept 1970. Video recorders were first sold to the public in 1978.
141 PP 1977–8, 8, p. 12; *The Sunday Times Rich List, 2005*, p. 16.
142 L 118/5, p. 339; T 317/1632, Wicks, 6 Aug. 1971.
143 For example, L 51, 28 Oct. 1974.
144 Reid, *The Secondary*, p. 45; *The Independent*, 3 Sept. 2004, p. 42.

the managements of associated companies and generally placed one or more CA nominees on their boards, usually senior Finance Directorate officials.[145] Where possible, they also invested in companies that had other institutional shareholders, whose directors would monitor events and 'safeguard [CA] interests'.[146] Within the Agency, the progress of the concerns was followed by the Finance Directorate in their monthly meetings and by the board of Four Millbank Investments Ltd, which comprised Hayes, some members of the CA board and the heads of the main finance departments. Until 1971, the board met quarterly and discussed prepared reports on their investments. Thereafter, it met monthly, and, at each meeting, as well as considering the latest published accounts and recent events, it examined one specific area of investment, which allowed the entire portfolio to be reviewed each quarter.[147]

Unethical and illegal behaviour

One of the reasons the collapse of the Agency reaped such media and Parliamentary attention in the 1970s and the 1980s was that the press, parliament and the two enquiries accused the Agents of unethical and illegal commercial behaviour and personal corruption. Before these accusations can be investigated, it is necessary to consider a campaign of disinformation waged by Ralph Yablon, from which many of the allegations arose. Although, the committees of enquiry were well aware of Yablon's activities, they failed to mention them in their reports, partly because they feared legal action, but largely because they wished to blacken the name of the Agents.

Yablon's campaign against the Agency

Ralph Yablon was a multi-millionaire, owner of the Provident Clothing Co. and several property and commercial firms, and Vice Chairman of the Provident Financial Group.[148] The Agents first met him in 1968 when they became involved in a consortium set up to obtain the Yorkshire television franchise.[149] Yablon was a member of the syndicate and when the application failed, aware that the Agents were seeking involvement in a secondary bank, he suggested that they join him in making a bid for Sassoons. The Agents agreed, but met opposition from the Bank of England, which was concerned about Yablon's 'questionable ... early reputation' and feared that this 'very sharp and impatient man' would 'trade upon' the Agents respectability and seek to take control of the company.[150] After further discussion, the Bank, convinced that the Agents would

145 L 118/5, p. 243; PP 1977–8, 8, p. 27. In 1971 Challis had ten directorship or chairmanships and his staff a further seven (L 48, 31 Dec. 1971).

146 L 50, minutes, 17 Sept. 1970.

147 L 18/24, p. 4, 10; L 50, minutes, 28 Aug. 1969.

148 OD 18/240, Luke to Cohen, 7 Feb. 1968; *The Times*, 23 May 1967, p. 17; *ibid.*, 9 April 1976, p. 7.

149 PP 1977–8, 8, p. 12.

150 HO 268/330, memo, 28 July 1967; *ibid.*, memo, 4 Aug. 1967; HO 268/509, Burr, 4 Aug. 1967.

go ahead with the partnership with or without its consent, dropped its opposition, but succeeded in persuading them to take a 40 per cent rather than the initially proposed 30 per cent stakeholding in the company, leaving Yablon and the American bank Continental Illinois with 25 per cent each and the Sassoons family with 10 per cent.[151]

Yablon had a number of motives for his campaign against the Agency. The most important arose out of his involvement in Sassoons. After the formation of the company, relations between Yablon and the Agents rapidly soured. Yablon's intention, when purchasing his stake, appears to have been to use the bank as his personal investment vehicle, with the CAs as sleeping partners, merely providing the necessary capital. It quickly became apparent that this was not to be. Although the Agents invested in the Provident Clothing Co., they decided not to deposit their principals' liquid money with the bank or to permit it to conduct their own account money market activities, which greatly reduced its funds.[152] Attempts by Yablon to use the company to finance his own activities were blocked by the Agents and Continental Illinois, and his efforts to appoint his own people to the board and higher management were strongly opposed.[153]

In December 1968, he invited J. P. Martin-Bates, Principal of the Administrative Staff College at Henley, to replace Luke as a director of the company without first obtaining the consent of the Board. Hayes objected and the appointment did not go ahead.[154] There were further clashes over the role of his son-in-law, Michael Gillis. During the partnership negotiations, the Agents had opposed Yablon's request that Gillis become Managing Director of the company.[155] The position would give Yablon day-to-day control of the bank and Gillis's honesty and ability were questioned. The Agents believed Hills Samuel, his former employer, had requested his resignation, and he had 'made a less than favourable impression with Continental Illinois'.[156] In July 1968, however, the Managing Director of the bank left, and Yablon persuaded the other shareholders that Gillis, who had become the bank's Euro-Dollar Manager, should take over the role.[157]

Relations between the Agents and Yablon collapsed completely in early 1969 over Sassoon's placing of the shares of Gramco Management Ltd. Shortly after the operation had been completed, it was discovered that Gillis had allocated 26,000 shares to Kommerzialbank, a firm he controlled and which would make a profit of $500,000 when the shares were sold. Moreover, he had authorized a loan from Sassoons to the company to enable it to buy some of the shares.[158] The

151 HO 268/327, memo, 7 May 1970; HO 268/330, memo, 12 Sept. 1967; L 36, 22 Aug. 1967.

152 CA (m) 61, P & C, Annex e1, p. 2. On 31 Dec. 1970, the JCF held £1.5 of Provident shares, the CAs' Office Fund 21,500 shares and five colonial Funds 17,500 shares (CAOG 21/67; CAOG 21/68; CAOG 21/71).

153 CAOG 22/28, Hayes, 4 Dec. 1968.

154 *Ibid.*, Hayes, 3 Dec. 1968.

155 HO 268/330, memo, 4 Aug. 1967.

156 SA, Notes, Hayes, day-to-day Croom-Johnson evidence, CA reliance on B of E section, no. 78; HO 268/330, memo 27/7/67.

157 HO 268/330, memo 8/8/67; HO 268/330, Sassoons to B of E, 19 July 1968.

158 OD 20/514, memo, 9 Feb. 1972; CA (m) 61, P & C, Annex e1, p. 2; L 204, Gillis, no date.

Agents, perhaps seeing this as an opportunity for removing Gillis and Yablon, demanded his immediate resignation, which was duly given.[159] On discovering that this had occurred, Yablon became incandescent with rage. Denying that Gillis had acted unethically and claiming that the charge was an attempt to force him out of the company, he appointed the solicitor Lord Goodman to fight his case, persuaded Gillis to retract his resignation and also obtain legal representation, and sought to persuade the other directors that 'a grave injustice' had been done.[160] After threatening the Agents and Continental Illinois with legal action, he then sought to buy them out of the company, and, when the offer was rejected, sold his own holding and 'left the bank with threats of "revenge"'.[161] Needing a new investment vehicle, he later took a 60 per cent interest in the ill-fated secondary bank Thames Guaranty. This company collapsed in March 1976 and its chief executive, one Michael Gillis, was investigated by the Director of Public Prosecutions for breaches of exchange control regulations.[162]

Another motive for Yablon's vendetta was the Agents' defence sales to the Arab states, discussed in the previous chapter, to which Yablon, a Jew 'deeply involved in Israel', objected.[163] He also had a 'venomous dislike of Hayes', partly related to the patronizing manner with which Hayes conducted his dealings with him and partly because he believed Hayes should never have been made Senior Crown Agent.[164] There is some evidence that Yablon may have regarded himself as a candidate for the position. After the announcement of his retirement, Luke, a personal friend, introduced him to Sir Andrew Cohen, the Ministry's permanent Secretary, as an 'energetic' individual who was 'now in the mood for public service', and, at his first meeting with Cohen, Yablon presented him with a detailed memo on the future of the Agency. In the event, Yablon was merely asked to supply names of possible candidates. Along with Luke, he particularly favoured J. P. Martin-Bates and informed him that his name had been put forward before consulting Cohen. This presumption appears to have outraged the Permanent Secretary, who eventually chose Hayes.[165]

Yablon's 'sustained campaign to denigrate the CAs' was directed at the City, Parliament, the press and the Ministry. Rumours were spread in the City that the Agents were incompetent, acted in an unethical and illegal manner and were corrupt, specifically that they favoured a particular broker, and, in return, received a 'consideration'.[166] It was indeed true that half of the Agency's money business was channelled through the broker Kirkland-Whittaker, but

159 CA (m) 61, P & C, Annex e1, p. 2; CAOG 21/151, Minute of Sassoons board meeting, 8 Aug. 1969. Out of respect for his father, a Judge, the shareholders agreed not to reveal the reasons for Gillis's resignation (CA (m) 61, P & C, Annex e1, p. 4).

160 L 204, Yablon to Fitzgerald, 2 Aug. 1969; CAOG 21/151, Gillis to Fitzgerald, 5 Sept. 1969; *ibid.*, Yablon to Baker, 28 Aug. 1969; *ibid.*, Martin Banks to Fitzgerald, 8 Sept. 1969; *ibid.*, Goodman Derrick & Co. to Fitzgerald, 5 Sept. 1969.

161 CAOG 21/150, Hayes, 5 Jan. 1973; OD 20/514, memo, 9 Feb. 1972.

162 *The Times*, 9 April 1976, p. 7; Press clippings, *Daily Telegraph*, 2 April 1979.

163 Notes, Hayes, day-to-day Croom-Johnson evidence, other factors section, no. 77.

164 Pen Portraits, Morris to Knights, 22 Nov. 1990.

165 OD 18/240, Luke to Cohen, 7 Feb. 1968; *ibid.*, Cohen, 13 Feb. 1968; *ibid.*, Luke to Cohen, 29 Jan. 1968; *ibid.*, Yablon to Cohen, 12 March 1968; *ibid.*, Cohen, 13 March 1968.

166 CAOG 21/150, Hayes, 10 May 1972; CA (m) 61, P & C, Annex e1, p. 4.

such concentration of business was not unusual and occurred because the firm had built up valuable experience of its business.[167] Such allegations received a warm welcome in the City. Not part of financial networks and recruiting their staff internally, the Agents were already distrusted by many institutions. Further suspicions were generated by their supply of arms to the Arab states, with a large number of merchant banks having pro-Israeli allegiances, and their connections to secondary banks, which were mostly operated by individuals whose careers had begun far away from the Square Mile.[168] Competitors, meanwhile, saw the spread of the rumours and their repetition to the press, MPs and the Treasury as a way of ridding the City of an organization that they believed had no right to encroach on commercial territory and possessed 'unfair advantages' in the form of an implicit Crown guarantee and exemption from the payment of tax.[169] It was also assumed by some that the end of the Agents' own account activities would lead to the fire sale of their holdings at bargain prices.[170]

To encourage parliamentary questions hostile to the Agents, Yablon made allegations about the Agency to MPs and Peers, in particular to George Cunningham and Lord Peddie.[171] Cunningham, who having worked under Hayes at the Ministry possessed an intense dislike of the man, asked a series of questions critical of the Agency, many of which contained false allegations.[172] In 1973, for example he claimed the Agents gave 'many millions of pounds' to the slum landlords John Chalk and Timothy Gwinne Jones and the following year suggested that a director of Keyser Ullman was influencing the Agents' equity purchases through his membership of the Equity Advisory Panel.[173] The Labour Peer Lord Peddie questioned the CAs' integrity in the Lords on the same day a critical *Guardian* article was published, later passed Yablon's allegations to the Ministry, and implied that the Agents, via their sale of the English & Continental Property Co. Ltd sites, had contravened the government's pay and prices policy.[174] Five months after he contacted the Ministry, Peddie became a shareholder and director of Emblasan Ltd, a venture capital company set up by Yablon, which subsequently heavily invested in a production control system produced by a company whose board was chaired by Peddie.[175]

As in the City, Yablon's allegations were welcomed by the Labour Party,

167 CAOG 22/28, Clark 18 Oct. 1971.

168 Kynaston, *The City … Vol. iv*, pp. 460, 482.

169 T 317/1498, Kelley, 31 Dec. 1970; T 316/187, Wicks to Downey, 5 April 1972.

170 CA (m) 61, P & C, p. 51.

171 Croom-Johnson Tribunal, Doc. Evidence, ba/ca/6/7, p. 109; OD 20/514, Hayes to Walker, 14 March 1972. Hayes also suspected that Yablon 'was in close touch' with Judith Hart MP (SA, File PQ, Hayes to Pearson, 14 Dec. 1972).

172 *Who's Who, 1988.*

173 It was FNFC that invested in Chalk and Jones's company (FCO 86/138, CA press release, 28 Sept. 1973). The individual had ceased to be a member of the Equity Advisory Panel in 1967 prior to joining Keyser Ullman (Croom-Johnson Tribunal, Doc. Evidence, b/odm/1/15c, p. 624, Hayes to Pearson, 14 Jan. 1974).

174 This was untrue (CA (m) 61, P & C, Annex e1, p. 11).

175 Press clippings, *Financial Times*, 15 May 1972; CA (m) 61, P & C, Annex e1, pp. 5, 9. The Labour Peer Lord Mais believed that Peddie did not realise that he was being 'used' (CAOG 21/150, Mais 31 July 1972).

which had its own reasons for wishing the to see the downfall of the Agency. The Party regarded the City as its 'implacable enemy' for ideological reasons, because it was believed that financiers had deliberately engineered the series of crises that had destroyed the previous Labour government, and because of the strong connections between the Square Mile and the Conservative party.[176] The Agents thus proved a useful stick with which to strike the City and demand reform. Labour MPs were also opposed to the exploitation of poor tenants by slum landlords, had been appalled by the Agents' purchase of arms for the Nigerian Federal government during the Biafran war and 'were influenced by their feelings towards Israel'.[177]

Yablon spread his insinuations to the press via the reporter Charles Raw, whose critical 1971 *Guardian* article contained a series of 'twisted, titillated, misunderstood and misrepresented' facts and painted 'an impressionable picture ... of disintegration'.[178] His criticisms were quickly taken up by others in Fleet Street, who were attracted to the story by the Agents' 'secretive, insular and rather mysterious set-up', and printed further inaccuracies. One of the critics was the *Investors Review*, whose article on the Post Office pension fund's purchase of English & Continental Property Co. Ltd sites was referred to by Peddie in his House of Lord's question on the sale, and was believed to be part-owned by Yablon's son.[179]

One of the results of Yablon's activities was the setting up of the Stephenson enquiry. In December 1971 Peddie wrote to the Ministry proposing that Yablon give evidence to the committee, and, despite CA protests, this was permitted, though the information he provided was later judged to be outside the enquiry's term of reference.[180] During his appearance, Yablon made four detailed allegations against the Agents. These were that they illegally provided Continental Illinois with loans prior to the devaluation of the pound in 1967, that an unnamed CA official had demanded a £1,000 bribe for arranging the takeover of Sassoons, that Jack Walker had taken a 5 per cent stake in the Agents' Singapore property consortium, and that Luke had informed him that they suspected that Wheatley was corrupt. On being informed of the allegations, the Agents appointed the senior partner of the prestigious solicitors firm E. F. Turner & Sons to investigate them. His report, along with the accompanying documentary evidence, was then passed to the Ministry, which undertook a further thorough investiga-

176 *The Banker*, Dec. 1973, p. 1433. For example, the Chairman of Keyser Ullman from 1970 was Edward du Cann MP (Kynaston, *The City... Vol. iv*, p. 462); Peter Walker MP was a founder of Slater Walker Securities; the former MP Sir John Foster QC, chaired Northern Commercial Trust (Reid, *The Secondary*, pp. 35, 45); Peter Brooke MP had connections with Continental Illinois (*Hansard*, 1977–78, 940, 1079); and Ronald Lyon, a Conservative Party donor, was a close friend of William Stern and managed two property development companies supposedly created to generate income for the Party (*Private Eye*, 28 June 1974, p. 22 and 1 Nov. 1974, p. 5).

177 PP 1981–2, 364, p. 351; Croom-Johnson Tribunal, Doc. Evidence, b/odm/1/15d, p. 701, Lord MacPherson to Wood, 22 Nov. 1973.

178 CAOG 21/150, Maynard, 11 May 1972; OD 20/514, memo, 9 Feb. 1972; CA (m) 61, P & C, Annex e2, p. 16.

179 SA, Stevenson enquiry and aftermath, part 2, D. N. Maynard, 21 Feb. 1973.

180 OD 20/514, Peddie to Jay, 29 Dec. 1971; CA (m) 61, P & C, Annex e1, p. 6.

tion, obtaining the advice of the Treasury, Bank of England, the Ministry's own solicitor and the Treasury solicitor. Turner's and the Ministry's findings were that the Continental loans were made after devaluation and thus did not contravene exchange control regulations; a bribe to arrange the takeover of Sassoons was unlikely, as all the parties involved had wished the merger to go ahead; that Walker's participation in the Singapore consortium was neither illegal nor unethical; and that Luke had made no statement regarding Wheatley's honesty to Yablon.[181] Needless to say, Yablon refused to accept the Ministry's findings and sent a number of belligerent letters to Ministry officials.[182]

The damage to the Agents caused by Yablon's campaign and the Stevenson enquiry was immense. In the London money market a number of depositors, including the Midland Bank, National Westminster Bank and National & Grindlays Bank reduced their CA borrowing limits and refrained from renewing loans.[183] By July 1972, deposits were £100m less than in the same month the previous year and the Agents had to pay more for the money they borrowed and thus lend it to more high-risk concerns. Although their overseas clients remained broadly supportive, a number questioned their abilities, the Bank Negara of Malaysia delayed placing funds until after the Stevenson committee reported, and the Central Bank of Cyprus withdrew $14m.[184] Within the Office, staff morale fell, key employees obtained jobs elsewhere, adding to the staffing problems, and much time was wasted rebutting the various allegations and collecting the large volume of information requested by Stevenson.[185]

To counter the accusations and limit the damage caused, the Agents mounted a counter-attack. Public relations were improved. In October 1971, an Information Office was established, which issued press releases and provided information to members of both Houses of Parliament and political party research officers.[186] Hayes began to hold Chairman's lunches, to which government ministers, senior civil servants, major financial figures and opinion formers were invited.[187] Challis arranged a number of meetings with the journalist Charles Raw and the Head of the Information Office lunched with the Managing Editor of the *Guardian*.[188] Hayes, meanwhile, built close relationships with a number of sympathetic MPs, largely through the provision of gifts. Lord Shackleton, leader of the Labour Party in the House of Lords, was given two medallions, eight sets of stamps, and companies with which he was associated were granted favours. A subsidiary of Warburgs was allowed to view the Agent's new computer and Hayes drew the attention of the Agents' subsidiary, MTS, to the benefits of using the serv-

181 OD 20/514, record of discussion between Yablon and Stevenson, 14 Jan. 1972; *ibid.*, memo, 9 Feb. 1972; *ibid.*, Smith to Treasury, 21 March 1972; *ibid.*, B of E to Treasury, 19 April 1972; *ibid.*, report to Minister, no date. As will be discussed below, Wheatley was indeed corrupt.

182 For example, OD 20/514, Yablon to Fifoot, 15 Sept. 1972.

183 L 50, 22 May 1972; CAOG 21/150, Hewins 30 June 1972.

184 CAOG 21/150, Hayes, 17 July 1972; *ibid.*, Hewins, 30 June 1972; *ibid.*, Hayes to Challis, 23 June 1972.

185 L 188, Shuter, 28 Dec. 1973.

186 L 35, 1974, no. 14.

187 L 145.

188 CAOG 21/150, Maynard, 11 May, 1972; *ibid.*, Hayes, 12 May 1972; *ibid.*, memo, 11 May 72.

ices of Rio Tinto Zinc.[189] Hayes, likewise, encouraged associated companies to contribute to a favoured charity of Bernard Braine MP, reversed a decision not to allow the company Capital & Counties Property Ltd to become partners in the Agents' Australian property venture after representations had been made by Sir Richard Thompson MP to the Minister, and partly invested in the British Bangladesh Trust in order to gain the support of its chairman, John Stonehouse MP, and the Conservative party, many of whose financial backers were also involved in the bank.[190] The Agents may also have expected to politically benefit from investments in and loans to other concerns in which MPs had associations.[191]

Criticism was further avoided through costly policy decisions. In October 1971, the Agents reduced the proportion of its money market business that went through Kirkland-Whittaker, allowing other brokers 'a larger slice of the cake'.[192] Two years later, they sold a potentially lucrative site at Epsom, fearful of local hostility, and 'to avoid a political nightmare' refused to allow the South African bank Schlesinger to take a 40 per cent stakehold in SIS.[193] They also, through Lord Mais, warned Lord Peddie 'against sponsoring a vendetta', made it clear to the main City broking firms and their Association that rumours of CA corruption damaged their own as well as the Agents' reputation, and placed great pressure on the Ministry to issue a statement that disparaged Yablon's allegations.[194] The Ministry was reluctant, claiming that such an announcement 'would ... only have the effect of putting [the accusations] into circulation'.[195] After a long series of memos, however, the Minister eventually agreed to defend the CAs' honour and expressed his full confidence in their integrity in answer to a planted supplementary question.[196]

Commercial unethical behaviour

Both the Fay and Croom Johnson reports devote many pages to criticisms of the Agents' supposed unethical, and, in some cases illegal, commercial behaviour. In fact, the activities the enquiries condemn were common in the City, well within the law, and regarded by most financial institutions as acceptable business practice. They could only be seen as unethical if the Agents were public servants. But, as has already been discussed, this was not the case. The Agents had never been Civil Servants, and, throughout the 1960s and early 1970s, believed their

189 CAOG 22/29, Hayes to Shackleton, 21 March 1971; *ibid.*, Shackleton to Hayes, 16 May 1972; CAOG 21/150, Hayes, 10 May 1972; CAOG 22/30, Hayes to Paine, 1 Aug. 1972.

190 CAOG 22/30, Hayes to Braine, 8 Feb. 1972; L 160, notes on a meeting between Challis and Coopers & Lybrand, 6 March 1975; PP 1977–8, 8, p. 113; *Private Eye*, 24 Jan. 1975, p. 18. From 1966to 1967, Stonehouse had been the Parliamentary Under Secretary for the Colonies (*Oxford Dictionary of National Biography*, Oxford 2003).

191 The Agents lent money to Keyser Ullman, whose Chairman was Edward Du Cann MP, and London & County, which had Jeremy Thorpe MP as a director (Kynaston, *The City... Vol. iv*, p. 462).

192 CAOG 22/28, Clark 18 Oct. 1971.

193 PP 1977–8, 8, p. 109; CAOG 22/37, Hayes to Davidson, 22 Oct. 1973.

194 CAOG 16/93, Hayes, 2 May 1973; CAOG 22/35, memo, 26 Oct. 1971; CAOG 21/150, Hayes to Challis, 23 June 1972.

195 CAOG 21/150, Walker to Hayes, 7 July 1972.

196 *Hansard*, 1971/2, 841, 1313–1314.

office to be on the verge of becoming an incorporated company. They and their staff rather saw themselves as 'merchant bankers' 'engaged in entrepreneurial commercial activity', who followed the ethical norms of the City rather than those of Whitehall.[197] A self-image that was accepted by the Bank of England, which believed the 1971 *Guardian* article on the Agents contained no evidence of malpractice, and, in November 1970, was no 'more uneasy about the CAs than about some of the other financial conglomerates, such as Hill Samuel, Slater Walker etc'.[198] The enquiries also judged the Agents according to the moral norms of the late 1970s and early 1980s, which were very different from those of a few years previously, and failed to put their supposed crimes into context.[199] Unlike, other denizens of the City, the CAs did not offer free gifts with loans, lend funds to pyramid selling investors, or engage in such activities as 'flat breaking', the purchase of blocks of flats which were then sold off individually minus their tenants.[200] When offered deals that breached accepted financial moral norms, they declined to become involved. In 1973, for example, a proposal by Sidney Davidson that if the Agents took a stake in Rawson Trust Co. Ltd, a company part-owned by Davidson, SIS would invest in Sassons was emphatically turned down.[201]

The enquires accused the Agents of six unethical activities – the provision of comfort letters, involvement in back-to back-loans, the avoidance of UK taxation, the acceptance of a secret commission, and the rigging of share prices. Comfort letters were sent to institutions that had indicated a willingness to lend to English & Continental Investments Ltd and stated that the Agents would repay the proposed loans and any accrued interest if the company was unable to do so. Letters were issued from April 1971 to April 1973 and 'guaranteed' 182 loans, with an aggregate value of £38m, £27.5m of which was outstanding by the end of November 1973. The enquiries argued that the letters were guarantees, without which the company would have had difficulty raising funds, and that their existence was a major reason for the Agency's eventual downfall in that it was forced to honour the pledges during the 1974 crash. It was also claimed that the CAs used the letters rather than actual guarantees because, not legal instruments, they did not have to be disclosed in their accounts. The Finance Directorate was therefore able to conceal their existence from the CA Board, the Ministry and the Bank of England, who would have objected to the size of the liabilities to the company, and from the City, which, believing the firm borrowed on its own name, was encouraged to advance more money and would have been more willing to support the intended public flotation.[202]

Of all the accusations made against the Agents, this appears to be the weakest. The claim that the company would have been unable to attract funds without the letters is patently false. The firm's predecessor had made a profit of £34m

197 L 118/18, p. 20; L 118/5, p. 196.
198 T 317/1632, Wicks, 6 Aug. 1971; HO 268/327, memo, 19 Nov. 1970.
199 Jim Slater, *Return to Go: My Autobiography*, London 1977, p. 3.
200 Press clippings, *Guardian*, 4 Feb. 1978, *The Sunday Times*, 4 June 1978.
201 CAOG 21/194, Davidson to Hayes, 15 Nov. 1973.
202 PP 1977–8, 8, pp. 61, 63–4, 92, 97; PP 1981–2, 364, pp. 92–4, 101. The 1974 crash prevented the flotation occurring.

in 1971 on the sale of a number of its sites and the period 1971 to 1973, when the letters were issued, was the height of the property boom, when even the most inefficient property developer could and did gain funds. It therefore seems highly unlikely that without the letters the company would have been deprived of money, particularly as the provision of such pledges was 'common practice' and they were not regarded as guarantees.[203] The Agents obtained the idea of using the letters from Barclays bank, which like its counterparts, made great use of them in relation to loans for subsidiaries and associated companies.[204] The letters acted as 'a considered second opinion on the proposed borrower', indicating the sender's faith in its financial strength.[205] It was understood by all that there was no legal obligation on the signatory to repay the loans themselves, only that he would place pressure on the borrower to repay, if necessary forcing the sale of assets.[206]

Similarly, there was no attempt to conceal the letters. It is unlikely that the CA board, Ministry or Bank of England would have objected to their issue. The Ministry and the Bank used similar letters to support loans from the Midland Bank to the Crown Agents in October 1975, April 1976 and May 1977, and the Bank, in any case, was told of the Agents' practice of making such pledges in 1972.[207] Given their widespread use and communication between financial institutions, it is also extremely unlikely that the City was unaware of their existence. As regards their contribution to the Agency's downfall, the company repaid most of the loans covered by the letters. The Agents financed the firm in 1974 because lenders refused to renew loans, and, as will be discussed in the next chapter, because the failure of the company would have damaged the Agency and worsened the property crash.[208]

Back-to-back loans involved one institution lending a certain sum to another concern, which, at the same time, advanced the same amount to the lender at a slightly higher rate of interest. The Agents generally became involved in such arrangements in order to allow clients to 'window-dress', that is enhance, their balance sheets. In 1971, for example, in order to improve the end-of-year accounts of the finance house N. H. Wooley & Co Ltd, the Agents accepted a loan of £7.25m from the company, which it lent to SIS, which then made its own loan of £7.25m to the firm. Two years later, the CAs agreed to borrow £5.5m from the Nation Life Insurance Co Ltd, in which Stern Family Holdings had a 70 per cent stake, and then to lend this sum to Stern Family Holdings at an interest rate one per cent higher. An arrangement that Fay claimed was a clear contravention of

203 PP 1977–8, 8, p. 62.

204 L 118/6, p. 21; L 118/15, p. 3.

205 Press clippings, *Financial Times*, 7 June 1979.

206 L 121, 1978, no. 76/78; A. and G. Sutherland, 'Does Gate Gourmet make comfort letters binding?', *International Finance Law Review*, 23 (8) (2004), pp. 45–6. The acceptance of the view that they were not legal guarantees explains why the Agents did not seek legal advice as to their status, for which they were criticised by the enquiries (PP 1981–2, 364, p. 93).

207 L 152, briefing note, 29 Nov. 1977; HO 268/337, Decca to B of E, 5 June 1972.

208 L 118/6, p. 23; SA, Price Waterhouse Report on English & Continental Property Co. Ltd, April 1972, para. 109.

the Insurance Companies Amendment Act of 1973, which prohibited an insurance company investing in a connected company.[209]

In three other cases, the loans were made to benefit the Agency itself. In 1970, to encourage others to invest in English & Continental Property Co. Ltd and perhaps to circumvent banking department limits on CA loans to the company, Peter Sly arranged to lend money to the secondary bank Edward Bates & Sons Ltd, which would then re-lend the same sums at a slightly higher rate to English & Continental Property Co. Ltd.[210] Three years later, as already discussed, the Agents came to a similar agreement with the Burston & Texas Commerce Bank, which enabled them to borrow from their Joint Funds Account. And in May 1974, to hide their support of the property company Oldham Estates, which could have political consequences if revealed, the Agents lent money to a merchant bank, which then advanced a similar amount to Oldham Estates.[211]

Such back-to-back loans were not illegal. Fay's contention that the Nation Life agreement breached the Insurance Companies Amendment Act was incorrect. As the Croom-Johnson committee admitted, the legislation came into effect after the advances had been made, and, even if this had not been the case, the arrangement would still not have contravened the Act.[212] The Agents provided such loans to clients because they were financially rewarding and they acted as a gift or favour, which would eventually be reciprocated. Although Challis accepted they were not 'nice', the Agents had to 'live in the world as it is' and such arrangements were very common in the City at the time.[213] Back-to-back advances were provided and received by some of the major merchant banks, and the Bank of England fully accepted the practice; the Agents loan to Oldham Estates being partly arranged by the Bank.[214]

The remaining three allegations made against the Agents – tax avoidance, the acceptance of a secret commission and the rigging of share prices – are as lacking in credibility as the two just discussed and suggest that the Fay committee, in particular, had difficulty finding evidence to support its contention that the Agency behaved unethically in its commercial dealings. The Agents sought to elude the payment of tax on a number of occasions. In 1970, it was decided that, to avoid capital gains tax on sales, investments in companies likely to be disposed of would be purchased not by Four Millbank Investments Ltd, which was liable to the tax, but by the Crown Agents, who possessed Crown exemption.[215] In the following year, English & Continental Investments Ltd specifically transferred a development site to the Crown Agents in order to avoid the payment of the tax

209 PP 1977–8, 8, pp. 59, 107, 109. The enquiries discovered two other instances in which the Agency had window-dressed clients' account (L 118/5, p. 310).

210 L 222, Sly to Walford, Edward Bates & Sons Ltd, 13 July 1970; Author's interview with Johns, 20 Jan. 2004.

211 HO 268/329, B of E, 22 May 1974. Oldham Estates was owned by Harry Hyams, who controversely had left four of his office blocks, including London's Centre Point, unlet (*The Times*, 18 July 1972, p. 15; *ibid.*, 19 July 1974, p. 2).

212 PP 1981–2, 364, p. 156.

213 PP 1977–8, 8, p. 59.

214 L 118/18, p. 47; David Whitby, 'Conspiracy and cover up', *Crime, Law and Social Change*, 5 (2001), p. 37; HO 268/329, B of E, 22 May 1974.

215 L 50, minutes, 12 Feb. 1970.

on its disposal, and, in 1973, FMI considered buying and then leasing an oil rig in order to reduce its income tax bill.[216] The enquiries appear only to have been aware of the 1972 site transfer, which they believed demonstrated the Agents' 'low ethical standards'.[217] In response, Challis quite rightly pointed out that 'there was nothing illegal in the arrangements', that tax avoidance was common in financial circles, and that over the years large numbers of public bodies had also sought, often successfully, to limit their tax liabilities. [218]

The secret commission was accepted in September 1969, when FNFC asked the Agents to underwrite a Hambros bank share issue and to take up a small amount of the stock. To ensure that the CAs accepted the offer, FNFC paid them an additional commission from its own fee, failing to inform either the other underwriters or Hambros that the payment had been made. The Fay committee believed the arrangement to be 'morally reprehensible' and a breach of section 44 of the Companies Act, which stated that all statements in a share prospectus had to be true.[219] In fact, as the Croom Johnson enquiry accepted, the Act had not been broken as the offer document was not a prospectus, and, even if it had been, it was highly unlikely that the failure to mention an extra underwriting commission would have resulted in legal action.[220] The fee was paid simply because FNFC wanted an institutional shareholder and believed that the Agents inclusion as lead underwriter would increase the take-up of the shares. It was kept secret from the other underwriters to avoid them requesting similar additional payments and from Hambros because it was not their concern.[221]

Fay's allegation that the Agents rigged share prices related to their supposed 1971 purchase of FNFC shares when the share price temporarily fell, which was made in response to a request from Patrick Mathews, the Chairman of the company.[222] In reality, as the Croom-Johnson committee admitted, although Matthews asked the Agents to purchase the shares, none were actually bought, as the price rose naturally before the buy instruction had been issued.[223] Even if shares had been acquired, such an operation would have been neither illegal nor improper, and, as has been shown in previous chapters, the Agents had long supported colonial loans with the full knowledge of both the Colonial Office and the Bank of England.[224]

Personal corruption

Criticisms of the personal morality of the CAs' finance staff revolved around their relationship with Sidney Finley, the acceptance of gifts, the purchase of shares, the movement to positions in associated companies, and fraud in the Agency's Australian office. Three members of the Agents' staff had unethical dealings

216 PP 1981–2, 364, p. 102; CAOG 21/194, Towse to Sheldon, SIS, 20 Sept. 1973.
217 PP 1977–8, 8, p. 165.
218 *Ibid.*, p. 101; L 118/5, p. 196.
219 PP 1977–8, 8, p. 28; PP 1981–2, 364, pp. 143–4.
220 PP 1981–2, 364, p. 143; L 118/14, p. 9.
221 L 118/5, p. 228; L 118/14, pp. 6, 22, 24, 26.
222 PP 1977–8, 8, p. 58
223 PP 1981–2, 364, p. 143
224 L 118/14, p. 29.

with Sidney Finley – Bernard Wheatley, Alan Challis and Edward Morris. Finley was the owner of Anchor Investments (Personal Loans Finance) Ltd, a money lending company. The firm employed only two part-time staff, and, apart from collecting past debts and an involvement in the fixed deposit market from 1969 to 1970, made loans only to Sidney Finley and to individuals nominated by him.[225] From March to September 1969, Anchor held at least £300,250 of FMI deposits and appears to have received loans from another of Finley's companies, Big City Finance Ltd, which was also associated with the CAs.[226] Between December 1968 and December 1969, Big City was permitted to purchase £1.5m worth of trade bills from the Agents, and, from September 1969 to February 1974, it obtained a series of loans from their Banking Division – £850,000 by the end of 1969, a further £150,000 in April 1971, and £750,000 in February 1974.[227] Finley was also the part owner of the finance house Sterling Industrial Securities Ltd, which he established in April 1969 with FMI and the solicitor Sidney Davidson, each of the three partners putting up a third of the £100,000 share capital.[228] The Agents lent Finley the money with which he bought his part of the equity, and, after the formation of the company, helped it to obtain business and gave it loans, which totalled £7.15m by the end of 1969, £3m in December 1971, £5.6m in December 1973 and £12.2m at end of 1974.[229]

In September 1968, Finley, via Anchor Investments, gave Edward Morris a loan of £1,000 on the security of a bill of exchange maturing within 180 days, which was repaid in March 1969.[230] Four months later in January 1969, again through Anchor Investments, he gave Challis a loan of £6,000 at normal interest rates, which was repaid in September 1973.[231] The advance was to be used to build a house for Challis's parents-in-law and was secured on this (unbuilt) property. Given the inadequacy of the collateral, it was highly unlikely that the loan could have been obtained from a bank or a building society, and, even if one had been forthcoming, it would almost certainly have carried a premium interest rate.[232] Three months earlier, Finley had also done Challis a professional favour, for which he had been promised 'an unspecified quid pro quo', by agreeing to appear to support the CAs in setting up Interservice Mediterranean Ltd, a company that provided film facilities in Malta. Borrowing the money from the Agents, he invested £100,000 in the firm, even though he was 'unable to see any profit in the endeavour' and 'if the proposition had been put to him by

225 CAOG 21/91, meeting, 9 Sept. 1975.

226 CAOG 21/113, Barclays to Wheatley, 12 March 1969; CAOG 21/91, Finley's defence statement 11 Nov. 1975.

227 HO 268/435; HO 268/447, Fay's supplementary report, 26 Aug. 1977.

228 PP 1981–2, 364, p. 45. Davidson became Managing Director of the company, Finley a director and Wheatley the CAs' representative director (CAOG 21/91, Counsel's written opinion, 24 Sept. 1975).

229 PP 1981–2, 364, pp. 45, 115; CAOG 21/194, Towse to Davidson, 30 May 1973; L 118/5, p. 244.

230 OD 59/33, Eaton to Pearson, 10 Jan. 1975; OD 20/503, Charlton, Treasury Solicitors Dept., to Smith, ODM, 15 Oct. 1971.

231 OD 59/33, Eaton to Pearson, 10 Jan. 1975.

232 HO 268/447, Fay's supplementary report, 26 Aug. 1977.

anyone else … he would have thought they were joking'.[233] Finally, in September 1969 and again via Anchor Investments, Finley gave Wheatley a loan of £1,000, which carried no interest, and was the first of 11 advances he was to receive from this source over the following five years.[234]

It seems highly likely that the loans given to Morris, Challis and Wheatley and the Interservice Mediterranean 'investment' were designed to encourage the CAs to place business with Anchor Investments and Big City, to provide Finley with the wherewithal to purchase his SIS shares, and to become involved in SIS. The latter decision, to say the least, was not without controversy. Finley had a reputation for dishonesty and was distrusted even by Davidson, and his group of companies 'was a ramshackle edifice supported largely on borrowed money, …which would have been evident to anyone at the CAs who had insisted on seeing up-to-date accounts'.[235] Davidson, meanwhile, had to borrow the money to buy his SIS shareholding, and, in 1956, had been suspended from practicing law for, among other things, 'utilising, for the purpose of certain clients and for his own purpose, money belonging to and received by him on behalf of clients'.[236] Challis was well aware of these past misdemeanours, but, nevertheless, allowed the investment to go ahead, later claiming that the CAs' solicitors had assured him that the offence was not serious and was the fault a managing clerk.[237]

In order to encourage the CAs to continue to lend to Big City and SIS, Wheatley over the next four years received a further 10 loans from Anchor Investment totalling at least £217,531.[238] SIS in September 1969 also paid the insurance on one of his two cars; in January 1970, gave him the use of a Jaguar car owned by the company, which he later bought with an Anchor Investment loan; allowed him two bridging overdrafts of £1,000 and £300 on his SIS deposit account; and, in September 1974, reimbursed him £205, which he claimed he had spent on three one guest lunches with clients of the company.[239] The two largest Anchor Investment loans were given in November 1973 and January 1974. The 1973 loan was for £122,368 and was used to buy shares in the finance house Wintrust Securities Ltd.[240] Shortly after making the purchases, Wheatley in his role as CA Money Market Manager began to place large deposits with the company, £900,000 by June 1974, even though it had few assets, 'some doubtful associations and would not have been described as an institution of first class standing'.[241] Such deposits

233 PP 1977–8, 8, pp. 26, 112.

234 CAOG 21/91, Counsel's written opinion, 24 Sept. 1975. The loan was repaid in August 1970 (*ibid.*).

235 PP 1981–2, 364, pp. 117–18, 120.

236 PP 1981–2, 364, p. 115; HO 268/447, Fay's supplementary report, 26 Aug. 1977.

237 PP 1981–2, 364, p. 115.

238 HO 268/447, Fay's supplementary report, 26 Aug. 1977.

239 PP 1981–2, 364, p. 137; HO 268/421, Police statement, Abbott; HO 268/333, memo, 20 Sept. 1974. Wheatley had a current and two deposit accounts with SIS (HO 268/421, Police statement, Abbott).

240 CAOG 21/91, Osgodby, 9 Dec. 1974.

241 CAOG 21/208, Wintrust to CAs, 25 June 1974; *ibid.*, White, 25 July 1980.

were presumably made to increase the value of his shares, and because he 'had in mind to try to join Wintrust' when he left the Agency.[242]

The February 1974 advance was directly financed by a £750,000 CA loan Wheatley made to Big City earlier that month, which Finley had then transferred to Anchor Investments. This company had then lent £168,725 to Wheatley, plus a further £14,000 in April 1974, £30,000 to Finley and £250,000 to Davidson, who appears to have been well aware of the source of the money.[243] The Davidson loan was made on inadequate security, at the market interest rate, rather than the premium rate the poor quality collateral should have demanded, and was repaid in June 1974 with the proceeds of a further £250,000 Anchor loan, the memorandum of which did not comply with the Money Lenders Act, making it impossible for the advance to be recouped using the legislation.[244] The loans to Wheatley, meanwhile, were unsecured, carried no interest, were again invalid under the Money Lenders Act, and no doubt were made as a reward for making the £750,000 loan to Big City and for the CAs' continued support of SIS, which was in financial difficulties by this time.[245]

When, in late 1974, Finley found that he could not repay his Big City debts, Wheatley's loans were also unsuccessfully used to encourage the Agents not institute bankruptcy proceedings against the company. In December 1974, Finley visited the Agents, made a clean breast of his relationship with Wheatley, and claimed that he could not pay the £1.75m Big City owed the Agency because he could not obtain repayment from Wheatley, either for the February and April 1974 advances, which were unsecured, nor for the £126,368 he had lent him in 1973.[246] The latter loan had been secured by the deeds of Wheatley's house and the shares in Wintrust purchased with the advance, but neither the deed nor the shares had been lodged with Anchor Investments – Wheatley having used the shares to secure an overdraft elsewhere. Finley also maintained that he had personally taken over the February and April 1974 loans, as Wheatley had informed him that 'the CAs were carrying out an investigation and that it would look bad if he was shown to have a loan from Anchor', a claim that he failed to substantiate.[247] The motivation for his uncharacteristic honesty was no doubt to prevent the Agents from winding up Big City, as by taking legal action they would reveal that one of their senior officials was corrupt, which would damage their reputation in the City and their ability to attract deposits.[248] In fact, unknown to Finley, the CA's own bankruptcy was about to be announced and they therefore would soon have little reputation to loose. They thus began liquidation proceedings against Big City and passed Finley's confession onto the police, who brought criminal charges against both him and Wheatley.[249]

242 *Ibid.*, Frood, 28 July 1980.
243 PP 1981–2, 364, pp. 127–8; CAOG 21/91, Counsel's written opinion, 24 Sept. 1975.
244 CAOG 21/91, Counsel's written opinion, 24 Sept. 1975; PP 1981–2, 364, pp. 129, 133.
245 PP 1981–2, 364, p. 128.
246 CAOG 21/91, Osgodby, 9 Dec. 1974.
247 *Ibid.*; *ibid.*, meeting, 9 Sept. 1975.
248 *Ibid.*, Osgodby, 12 Dec. 1974.
249 *Ibid.*, Osgodby to Buckley, 2 Jan. 1975. Finley received a sentence of one year's imprisonment. Wheatley died of a heart attack on the morning of his trial (Reid, *The Secondary*, p. 101).

Finley's accusations against Wheatley do not seem to have come as a great surprise to the Agents, and it seems likely that they had known or strongly suspected that he was corrupt for many years. It was common knowledge that he was 'a gambling man' and that he lived beyond his means, there were rumours in the City that he accepted bribes as early as 1967, and, the Agents were told about his excessive SIS expense claims by a former SIS employee in September 1974.[250] The CAs, however, dismissed the rumours as 'nasty rubbish' and neither increased supervision of his activities nor removed him from his post.[251] His work went unmonitored by Challis, Hewins and Clark, all of whom claimed that they lacked the necessary time and did not fully understand the technicalities of his duties.[252] Challis made half hearted appeals to Personnel in 1967, 1970 and 1973 to transfer him to another department, but failed to demand action when his requests were rejected.[253]

The Agents adopted a laissez faire attitude because they believed that the loss of Wheatley would damage the Agency's business. Wheatley was 'an excellent money market manager whom the CAs could not easily replace' either internally or externally.[254] His membership of the gambling club Crockfords and of the Casanova club gave 'him an entrée into the society of men who could prove of value to the CAs' and impressed particularly Arab principals, whose representatives when visiting London often accompanied him to the gaming tables and became close friends.[255] His transfer or dismissal would also have confirmed City rumours of corruption, weakening confidence in the Agents. The cost to the Office of his removal from his post would therefore have been far greater than the loss resulting from his 'loans', which, by comparison, were 'peanuts', and, it was hoped, might eventually be repaid.[256] In addition, it seems likely that the Agents feared the reaction of the Ministry to the admittance that a senior official was corrupt, and that some internal support was motivated by long friendships and feelings of loyalty, and, in the case of K. W. Barley, the Head of Personnel, who was moved away from his post as Head of Finance to make way for Challis, a desire to make his replacement's life as difficult as possible.[257]

Other criticisms of the Agents' ethics related to their acceptance of gifts and positions in associated companies, their acquisition of shares, and the fraudulent activities of two of their Australian employees. In 1972 and 1973, four members of the Agents' staff received Christmas gifts from William Stern. In 1972, A. J. Blundell, the Foreign Money Market Manager, received an attaché case and a book worth in total £34; Wheatley and Hewins £56 desk sets; and Challis a silver tea service valued at £400. The following year, Blundell, Wheatley, and Osgodby were given £36 pen and pencil sets and Hewins a gold pen and

250 L 118/18, pp. 10, 12; L 118/6, p. 85. See also PP 1981–2, 364, p. 137.
251 CAOG 22/28, Clark, 18 Oct. 1971.
252 L 118/5, p. 90; L 118/7 p. 71; L 118/6, p. 15.
253 L 118/5, p. 68; PP 1977–8, 8, p. 160.
254 L 118/7, p. 63. See also L 118/18, p. 15.
255 PREM 16/349, *Investors' Chronicle*, 17 Jan. 1975; L 118/18, pp. 10, 18–19.
256 *Ibid.*, pp. 8, 32.
257 Barley had been reluctant to leave the Finance Directorate (Pen Portraits, Barley).

pencil set worth £99.[258] In addition, some members of the Finance Department attended Christmas parties hosted at the Savoy Hotel London by David Garner of the Manchester stockbrokers Halliday Simpson, where 'the birds and the booze' flowed.[259] The provision of such gifts at Christmas was and still is a common practice in the City, designed to build 'sound friendly business relationships' rather than to corrupt.[260] Stern's presents were slightly more expensive than the norm because, as an orthodox Jew eating only kosher food, he could not offer ordinary hospitality to business acquaintances during the rest of the business year.[261] There was also in the early 1970s a general inflation in the value of business gifts related to 'the booming economic growth'.[262]

The Agents were not the only beneficiaries of Stern's largess. In 1972, Stern gave gifts worth £10,500 to 526 people, 200 of whom were executives of financial institutions, including four of the clearing banks, twelve were local authority officers, and one a Bank of England employee.[263] Nor were the CAs happy to receive the gratuities. Morris and Challis wrote to Stern pointing out that those in public service were not allowed to accept such emoluments and requesting that no more be sent. Both kept their gifts 'in the spirit of friendship', fearful that their return would damage business relations with Stern.[264]

Only two senior officials took positions in associated companies. Allan Challis became Joint Deputy Chairman of FNFC and later Chairman of United Merchant Securities, a firm operated by Ramon Greene and Jack Walker, joint owners with the CAs of English & Continental Property Co. Ltd., and Peter Sly accepted a senior post at Star West Investment Holdings Ltd, which was owned by Remo Dipre, who had received a profit of £2m when a property site he had developed with the Agents in Epsom was sold off in June 1973.[265] In defense of the moves, Hayes claimed that Challis's and Sly's former connections with the Agency were of no use to their new employers, and that having such 'a powerful voice [as Challis's] in the City [would] ... be of great benefit to the CAs and perhaps to the establishment when [they were] attacked by [their] enemies'.[266] In fact, Challis made much use of his knowledge of his former employer's business in his new post, in January 1974 attempting to purchase from the Agency its equity share in E. D. Sassoon & Trust International Ltd.[267] As regards directorships, on leaving the CAs Luke joined the Sassoon's board, Morris became Chairman of

258 PP 1981–2, 364, p. 489.

259 Source wishes to remain anonymous; *Private Eye*, 7 Feb. 1975, p. 2. Halliday Simpson was one of the Agents' brokers. After the parties, 'a few select clients would adjourn to continue the celebrations at the Dorchester' (*Private Eye*, 7 Feb. 1975, p. 2).

260 L 118/18, p. 20.

261 *Daily Telegraph*, 27 May 1982, p. 22

262 L 118/18, p. 8.

263 Press clippings, *The Observer*, 28 Jan. 1979.

264 Pen Portraits, Challis; PP 1981–2, 364, p. 491.

265 PP 1977–8, 8, p. 133; Press clippings, *Daily Telegraph*, 8 Dec. 1977; Sly, Personnel file, memo, 21 Jan. 1974.

266 OD 59/15, Hayes to Walker, 9 Aug. 1973.

267 CAOG 21/390, Wallace Bros. to Hewins, 3 Jan. 1974. When Sly joined Star West, the CAs cut all business dealings with Dipre 'in case an enemy might make something of it' (Sly, Personnel file, memo, 21 Jan. 1974).

Nation Life Insurance Co., part of the Stern Group, and Challis continued to chair the board of English & Continental Investments Ltd. However, Morris's chairmanship lasted only a few weeks and Challis left the English & Continental board within a year of resigning from the CAs.[268] As the Ministry accepted, the taking of directorships and posts in associated companies was also neither against Civil Service rules nor unusual. Of those leaving senior administrative posts in the Civil Service in 1973, 17 per cent took up business appointments, and, from 1979 to 1983, retired permanent secretaries and military chiefs took 113 directorships and consultancies.[269] Sir Douglas Wass, a Treasury official who dealt with the Agents, became a director of Barclays bank, Coopers & Lybrand, Equity Law & Life and De La Rue, and John de Loynes, a Bank of England official, shortly before retirement, sought to gain employment with the Crown Agents.[270]

Criticism of the CAs' shareholdings arose in August 1971 when the *Guardian* revealed that Luke, Hayes and Challis had each taken 250 shares in Gramco Management Ltd during the placing of this company by Sassoons, and that Morris in October of that year had bought 5,000 shares in SIS. Unknown to the press, a number of other senior staff also owned shares in companies associated with the Agency, though their shareholdings were relatively small and none were active traders, and, in September 1974, prior to his retirement, Hayes bought 1,000 FNFC shares for a family trust.[271] Such purchases were said to be against the Civil Service rule that public office should not be a source of profit.[272] In fact the Civil Service ruling was that, where the purchase of a shareholding in a company might raise the possibility of conflict, an officer should seek the decision of a superior officer as to whether the transaction should occur.[273] The CAs had always adopted this rule, and, in November 1971 added a further control. All share transactions had to be made through one of the Agents' seven brokers, who then sent a copy of the contract to Head of the Investment Department.[274]

Neither of the specific allegations made by the *Guardian* stand up to close scrutiny. Hayes and Challis bought the Gramco shares because, along with all the other directors and managers of Sassoons, they were strongly pressured to do so by Ralph Yablon and Michael Gillis, who falsely claimed that director support of placings was routine practice in the City. Hayes, unaware of Gillis's inten-

268 CA (m) 64, Abbot on past CAs, no date; CAOG 21/126, Osgodby, 13 Aug. 1974.

269 A. Doig, 'Public service and private gain', *Public Money*, 4 (3) (1984), p. 54.

270 CAOG 22/28, Hayes, 27 June 1969. De Loynes informed Hayes that he had also 'worked up extra-mural jobs with Spinks and other high class art dealers and with one or two expensive West End hotels and restaurants' (*ibid.*).

271 OD 59/15, King to Hayes, 4 Sept. 1974. Challis, Towse and Shuter had very small holdings in FNFC; Clark owned a small number of Stanley Gibbons Ltd and Crown Communications Ltd shares; Morris had an interest in City of London Assurance Co., part-owned by SIS; and Challis also held some English & Continental Property Co. shares (L 50, minutes, 7 May 1971; *ibid.*, 1 July 1970; Shuter, Personnel file, memo, 4 Feb. 1975). Hayes had been advised by the Ministry to avoid investments in companies associated with FMI (L 50, vol. 2, 23 Sept. 1974).

272 PP 1977–8, 8, pp. 77, 83; *Guardian*, 5 Aug. 1971, p. 13.

273 OD 20/503, Smith, 21 Oct. 1971.

274 L 69, memo, Nov 1971.

tion to benefit personally from the placing, accepted the argument, but following Civil Service rules, obtained permission for the purchases from the Permanent Secretary and lodged his shares with Sassoons, with the instruction that they be sold at a time when the sale would result in neither profit nor loss.[275] Morris received permission from Hayes to buy the holding in SIS, even though this was not strictly necessary since he intended to buy the shares after his retirement, when he believed he would become a director of SIS in his own capacity and would be expected to take an interest in the company.[276] In the event, after he bought the shares he was asked by Hayes to delay his retirement and to stay in post on an unestablished basis to deal with the extra work generated by the Stevenson committee.[277]

The Ministry accepted that Morris's purchase was not in breach of Civil Service rules, and would have let the matter rest if it had not discovered more about Morris's activities. It emerged that in February 1971, again in anticipation of his retirement, he had purchased, according to Hayes without permission, £1,000 of shares in Metropolitan Property Ltd, which had links with SIS and the Stern Group, and had become unpaid chairman of the company.[278] The Ministry had also obtained his tax returns for the period 1968 to 1971 and found further links with SIS and discovered that he had failed to declare to the Inland Revenue his holdings in SIS and Metropolitan Property.[279] Fearful that this information would be made public, the Ministry asked Morris to retire immediately. Morris refused, pointing out that his ejection from the Agency would damage his reputation and chances of obtaining the promised SIS directorship and declaring that he had done nothing wrong. Hayes had given permission for the purchase of the Metropolitan shares and he had not declared his shareholdings as Hayes had advised him there was no necessity to do so.[280] The Ministry, however, remained unconvinced. After a series of threats and counter threats, Morris retired at the end of December 1971, taking revenge on Hayes, who he believed had betrayed him, by supplying information to Ralph Yablon from whom he received an offer of a directorship, and to Judith Hart, who, in a Parliamentary question, later sought to clear the way for his SIS directorship.[281]

Finally, there were two cases of fraud in the CAs' Australian office. In 1968, John Sharman, a locally engaged accounts clerk was discovered to have embezzled

275 OD 20/503, memo, 6 Sept. 1971; *ibid.*, Hayes to Walker, 8 Sept. 1971; *ibid.*, Hayes to King, 13 Aug. 1971; *ibid.*, Smith to Treasury Solicitor, 1 Oct. 1971.

276 PP 1977–8, 8, p. 83; OD 20/503, Hayes to King, 13 Aug. 1971. The shares were bought with his retirement gratuity.

277 PP 1977–8, 8, p. 83.

278 OD 20/503, Charlton to Smith, 15 Oct. 1971; *ibid.*, Smith, 26 Nov. 1971. Metropolitan Property was part-owned by SIS and Freshwater Family Holdings Ltd, the managing director of which was William Stern (*ibid.*, Smith, 21 Oct. 1971).

279 *Ibid.*, Charlton to Smith, 15 Oct. 1971. He had current and deposit accounts with SIS (*ibid.*).

280 L 50, minutes, 7 May 1971; OD 20/503, memo, Smith, 21 Oct. 1971. Morris had agreed not to realise profit from the shares whilst employed by the Agents (*ibid.*).

281 OD 20/503, Pearson to Hayes 12 Dec. 1972, Hayes to Pearson, 14 Dec. 1972; OD 20/514, Hayes to Walker, 15 Dec. 1972. Hayes succeeded in getting SIS to withdraw the invitation to take a directorship by informing Lord Mais, the Bank's Chairman, of Morris's relationship with Yablon and Hart (OD 20/514, Hayes to Walker, 15 Dec. 1972).

$6,000 and was subsequently convicted for the falsification of accounts, and, later that year, W. Walters, the CAs' representative in Australia, admitted that he had stolen $23,000 from Abbey Orchard Property Investments Ltd to finance share and gambling debts.[282] Unlike Sharman, however, his crime was not reported to the police nor to the Civil Service Department, as the CAs feared that the resulting publicity would damage their reputation within the City and in Australia, where there was already political criticism of their involvement in the property sector. Walter's crime thus remained unpunished, though he was eventually asked to resign from the Agency.[283]

Conclusion

Sir Claude Hayes summarized the conclusions of the two enquiries as 'some devil got into the Crown Agents and compelled them to do things against all common sense'.[284] In reality, the Agents' decision to establish a secondary bank and their methods of operation were perfectly rational and did not mark a significant break with the past, and, if they were possessed, it was with nothing more sinister than a desire to do good. It is undeniable that the Agency 'exhibited a remarkable will to live' and that its staff embarked on their new venture out of self-interest.[285] This is not unusual. All organizations and particularly bureaucracies have strong survival instincts and the adoption of a new role is just one of many strategies adopted to ensure continued existence. For the Agents, survival depended on increasing their reserves. The UK government had effectively abandoned their office, and because of previous Colonial Office policy 'there was not enough fat on the beast to preserve it in the lean times'.[286] Given the state of their traditional business and their expertise, the obvious way of achieving this goal was to enter the secondary banking sector.

A more important reason for the new role, however, was to help the Agency's traditional clients through the privatisation of aid. Although the Fay committee dismissed this explanation as 'one of the armoury of propaganda weapons … used by the CAs in their dealings with Whitehall', it appears in numerous internal documents and reflects the Office's almost evangelical belief in 'the rightness and goodness' of its work.[287] From the start, it was intended that the income derived from the own account venture would be used to subsidise the provision of traditional services, enabling them to be improved and extended, and that money would be invested in companies and banks whose businesses could assist the economic development of clients. If the initiative had succeeded, the Agency today would be a very different organization and its overseas principals arguably far more prosperous. Private sector funds and, as in the colonial era, the clients'

282 L 147, Lousley, 29 March 1976; PP 1977–8, 8, p. 114.
283 Statement, Hayes, Aug. 1993, p. 40; PP 1977–8, 8, p. 114.
284 Notes, Hayes, day-to-day Croom-Johnson evidence, Rebuttable presumptions, no 36.
285 PP 1977–8, 8, p. 4
286 L 118/18, p. 44
287 PP 1977–8, 8, p. 163; Author's interview with Shuter, 20 October 2004.

investments would be used to finance Third World economic and social advancement. The Office would provide a far wider range of services, many at below cost. Clients would obtain advances at reasonable interest rates and perhaps without the strings attached to loans from international aid organisations. The Agency's network of merchant banks, which would no doubt have spread across the continents, would continue to promote the growth of private capital markets, and the skills and expertise of hundreds if not thousands of private sector companies, in which the Agents had a financial interest, would be directed at solving economic and social problems. That the underdeveloped world has been deprived of these benefits is nothing less than a tragedy.

The methods used by the Agents in their new venture were adequate, though far from perfect. The failings resulted from the constraints imposed on the Agency by the government, the activities of Ralph Yablon, and its own culture. The CAs' Civil Service salary scales prevented the employment of professionals and led to staff shortages, and its ambiguous constitutional status forced it to pay high rates for deposits and to relend the money to relatively risky secondary banking and property companies. Yablon's campaign of disinformation reduced staff morale and increased staff turnover, forced the Agents to waste time and effort refuting his allegations, and further reduced City confidence in the Agency, making it even more difficult for it to attract funds. Its culture, meanwhile, ensured that some Finance Directorate staff had little or no relevant experience and encouraged the Agents to operate within small networks composed of individuals and firms that they trusted.

The Agency's procedural defects, however, were much exaggerated by the two enquiries, which judged its actions from the standpoint of the public sector. In fact, the Agents were not and did not regard themselves as Civil Servants, but as 'merchant bankers who spoke the language of the money market'. It was 'an era of risks', 'the temper of the times [being] in favour of a dash for growth', and to be successful, speculation was unavoidable, 'caution ... scarcely [being] the requisite of a successful tycoon'.[288] The Agents' procedures were therefore necessarily far less stringent than those adopted by a Civil Service department, but no worse, and, in many cases, far better than those of other secondary banks.

The two enquiries, similarly, used Civil Service moral norms when judging the ethics of the Agency. Again, the CAs followed the ethical norms of the City rather than those of the public sector, though taking care not to act illegally. If they had acted otherwise, they would have been far less successful. Full payment of UK taxation would have reduced profits, without comfort letters English & Continental Investments Ltd would have found it more difficult to attract funds, and favours, such as the provision of back-to-back loans, generated trust and were usually reciprocated. The adoption of such norms was by no means a new development. As has been seen in previous chapters, in their provision of their traditional services the Agents had frequently failed to follow the Civil Service moral code, often with the Colonial Office's blessing. Only in the case of Bernard Wheatley did the Agents exceed both public service and City norms. It seems

288 L 118/18, pp. 7, 8; L 118/5, p. 328.

likely that they were well aware that he was corrupt, but chose to do nothing. This, however, was a rational, and, from a business point of view, arguably the correct decision. It would have been almost impossible to replace Wheatley, who was a highly regarded money market manager, and the discovery of his crimes would have further damaged City confidence and the Agency's ability to gain deposits.

9

The Collapse of the Secondary Banking Venture

Having decided that the Agents' own account activities had been carried out in an unacceptable manner, both enquiries placed part of the blame on the failure of internal and external control mechanisms. It was claimed that within the Agency neither the CA Board nor the Senior Crown Agent effectively monitored the activities of the Finance Directorate, and that outside the Office, the Ministry, the Treasury, the Bank of England and the Exchequer & Audit Office all adopted a policy of laissez faire. The Agency's supposedly high-risk pursuits were therefore neither restricted nor brought to a halt. As a result, when secondary banks and later property companies began to fail from December 1973, the Agents' own collapse was inevitable. The chapter examines the extent to which the CAs' activities went unsupervised, and investigates their 'orgy of lending' during the secondary banking crisis, which both enquiries believed contributed to the Agency's insolvency in December 1974.[1]

Control mechanisms

Agency-wide control

The two enquiries argued that control of the Finance Directorate's activities by the CA Board and Sir Claude Hayes was weak because the Challis failed to inform them of its actions. The Crown Agent Board was established in 1965, in anticipation of the expected incorporation of the Agency, and comprised Hayes and Morris and the heads of all the Office's various departments.[2] It met monthly and was an advisory body only. Decisions taken by department heads could only be approved by the Senior Crown Agent, either personally or in his role as Board Chairman.[3] The Board received a large amount of finance information. Each month it obtained a report from the Directorate, which contained a summary of its money market transactions and details of 'interesting and important developments'. From January 1969, Challis gave a brief oral report of the progress of Finvest at each meeting, and, the following year, it received a quarterly list of all the companies in which the Agents had an equity interest, which included infor-

1 PP 1981–2, 364, p. 179.
2 L 18/24, p. 3.
3 L 141, Luke, 16 Nov. 1967; L 118/5, p. 13.

mation on the capital structure of each firm, the value of the investment and any advances made, and the names of the nominee directors.[4] A number of Board members were also on the FMI Board and attended the Finance Directorate monthly meetings and all of them had access to informal information flows.

Nonetheless, a certain amount of information was kept from the Board. Minor decisions and actions were rarely reported because its members lacked the time to fully consider them. The Board supervised all the work of the Agency, and, in 1967, asked the department heads to limit the length of their monthly reports to 'a couple of pages'.[5] Some larger decisions were also concealed, though it seems likely that Morris, who informed the enquiries that he knew little of the Directorate's activities, exaggerated his and the Board's ignorance. Morris had a tendency to 'indulge in hyperbole' and his claim freed him from blame for the supposed failures of the Division, throwing responsibility instead onto Challis, for whom he possessed a deep dislike.[6] The few major developments kept hidden were concealed because they were extensions of existing activities and so did not require the specific approval of a higher authority, or because Challis preferred to obtain consent from Hayes himself, fearing that the Board lacked the necessary financial expertise to understand them.[7]

Like some Board members, Hayes insisted to the enquiries that he was ignorant of many of the activities of the Finance Directorate and thus could not be held responsible for its failures.[8] He certainly knew little of the minutiae of the Agents' financial work. The Senior Crown Agent had always been responsible for matters of general policy, rather than the day-to-day management of the Agency, and, in any case, he lacked the time to immerse himself in the work of just one department.[9] He headed a business with twenty activities, was often absent on overseas visits, had to devote a great deal of time and effort to the development of a new constitution, and received little help from his second in command, Morris, who avoided 'at any cost ... making firm decisions'.[10] Pleas to the Ministry for administrative support were brushed aside.[11] On joining the Office, he had also been told that he 'need not worry about finance', and he therefore concentrated on those traditional activities, such as procurement, which were making large losses.[12] Furthermore, unlike his predecessor, he had little or no access to informal information flows. The belief that he had been appointed by the Ministry as their 'spy' and 'agent for a take-over ', along with his 'icy rudeness', short temper and brusque manner stopped staff 'telling him anything'. [13] Morris, who should

4 L 3, memo, 9 Jan. 1967; L 35, 21 Jan. 1969; *ibid.*, 29 June 1971.

5 L 3, memo, 9 Jan. 1967.

6 L 118/1, para. 145. Morris resented Challis's power, which had reduced the prominence of his own role (L 118/5, p. 124).

7 PP 1981–2, 364, pp. 23, 38

8 *Daily Telegraph*, 27 May 1982, p. 22.

9 Notes, Hayes, day-to-day Croom-Johnson evidence, Rebuttable presumptions, no. 13.

10 Report on Croom-Johnson Tribunal, Hayes, para. 3; Pen Portraits, Morris. Many believed he devoted excessive time to overseas visits (Pen Portraits, Morris to Knights, 2 May 1990).

11 Report on Croom-Johnson Tribunal, Hayes, para. 19.

12 Statement, Hayes, Aug. 1993, pp. 4–5.

13 *Ibid.*; Notes, Hayes, day-to-day Croom-Johnson evidence, Hayes management section, no. 51; PP 1981–2, 364, p. 21; Pen Portraits, Knights to Morris, 26 Oct. 1990.

have been his 'eyes and ears' and possessed an intricate network of Office 'spies', favourites who had benefited from his patronage, gave him no help whatsoever.[14] His dislike of his superior was such that 'his presence on most occasions repelled' him.[15] Having been promised the post of Senior Crown Agent by Luke, he was intensely jealous of Hayes, who often acted without consulting him, subjected him to constant verbal attack, and had effectively transferred his previous overall control of the Finance Directorate to Challis.[16]

On the other hand, there seems little doubt that Hayes was aware of the major financial developments. He was the Chairman of the CA and FMI Boards, often attended the meetings of the Equity Advisory Panel, and had frequent meetings with Challis, who appears to have discussed most aspects of his work with him.[17] Unfortunately, like the Board, he had no financial expertise with which to make value judgments and 'happily accepted Challis's dominion of the finance department'.[18] Challis possessed the expertise that he lacked, and it was important that he was not offended, lest he take his talents elsewhere or use his banking contacts to scupper Hayes' ambition to obtain 'a top job in the City' on retirement.[19] Moreover, even if Hayes had possessed the knowledge and inclination to take a more hands-on role, it seem unlikely that he would have halted the Agency's more dubious activities, as he regarded the Directorate as a City institution that followed City practices and norms.

External control

Government control was provided through the Ministry, the Bank of England, the Treasury, and the Exchequer & Audit Department. The two enquiries blamed the failure of these departments to supervise the Agency partly on the CAs' reluctance to provide them with the necessary financial and other information, and partly on the Office's fringe status and the absence of inter-departmental communication. Neither the Treasury, Ministry nor Bank were prepared to take primary responsibility for the Agency's actions nor devote a great deal of time and effort to its supervision, preferring instead to eliminate its constitutional ambiguities by devising a new constitution. Independent entities, they also failed to share the limited information they managed to acquire, with the result that a full picture of the extent of the Agents' supposed inadequacies failed to emerge.

Within the Ministry, there were two opposing views as to the amount of control the Minister should exert on the Office. The various Permanent Secretaries believed supervision should be relatively light, and the Agency should only provide information on major new initiatives, significant extensions of existing

14 Pen Portraits, Knights, Jan. 1997; Author's interview with Shuter, 20 October 2004.

15 Pen Portraits, Morris to Knights, 2 May 1990.

16 Statement, Hayes, Aug. 1993, pp. 4–5; File no. 54, Morris to Abbot, 3 May 1968; L 118/5, p. 124; Pen Portraits, Morris to Knights, 2 May 1990.

17 PP 1981–2, 364, p. 21.

18 Pen Portraits, Hayes.

19 PP 1977–8, 8, pp. 73, 75; Pen Portraits, Hayes. Hayes believed challis 'stood head, shoulders and waist above everyone else' (PP 1977–8, 8, p. 75).

ventures, and actions that could have political repercussions.[20] The Agents largely dealt with independent territories, their own account activities made no use of government funds, they were believed to be competent and honest, and the Ministry lacked 'the commercial expertise to supervise their activities in any meaningful sense'.[21] There was also a fear that excessive government interference would weaken the Agency's links with its principals and damage its traditional business, which contributed a great deal to the UK economy, and impair its relations with the City, harming its secondary banking activities.[22] For Sir Geoffrey Wilson, Permanent Secretary 1969–71, a further reason for avoiding confrontation was the personality of Sir Claude Hayes, whose capacity for argument and invective was such that 'opponents gave way out of pure fatigue or for the sake of peace'.[23]

Conversely, Ministry officials, in particular E. C. Burr, M. G. Smith, Sir Richard King and D. L. Pearson, believed that they should receive detailed information from the Agents and closely supervise their work.[24] There are a number of explanations for this supposition. First, they possessed an intense dislike of Hayes, having worked with him before he moved to the Agency, and saw constant intervention in his new role as the perfect opportunity for revenge.[25] Secondly, they were extremely hostile to the Agents' own account activities, which they regarded as 'a nettle which has to be grasped – and killed'.[26] The hostility partly arose from the fact that they were career Civil Servants, with no business experience, and, in the case of Burr and Smith, possessed a strong religious faith.[27] They were therefore suspicious of commerce, disliked change and had high moral standards, which the Agents failed to meet. They also had real doubts about the necessity for the CAs' move into banking and commerce, which they believed involved excessive risk, led to unethical behaviour, had the potential to embarrass the Minister and themselves, and could end with the government having to 'bail [the Agents] out if they got into financial difficulties'.[28]

According to Hayes, a further motive was the Ministry's wish to take over the Agency's role either by increasing their direct control of the Office or by engineering its demise. As with the Agents, decolonisation had reduced the need for a Colonial Office/Ministry, and, from the early 1960s, officials constantly feared that it would be abolished or subsumed into another Ministry. These worries

20 Croom-Johnson Tribunal, Doc. Evidence, b/odm/1/7, p. 312, Wilson to Minister, 21 Dec. 1970; L 160, Hayes, 19 Aug. 1970; Statement, Hayes, Aug. 1993, p. 25.

21 PP 1977–8, 8, pp. 39, 42; Croom-Johnson Tribunal, Doc. Evidence, b/odm/1/7, p. 312, Wilson to Minister, 21 Dec. 1970.

22 PP 1981–2, 364, p. 22; PP 1977–8, 8, p. 39; OD 59/27, memo, 19 Nov. 1973.

23 PP 1981–2, 364, p. 22.

24 L 160, Hayes, 19 Aug. 1970. Burr was an Assistant Secretary, King a Deputy Secretary, and Pearson and Smith Under Secretaries.

25 CA (m) 67, vol. 1, Abbott, 12 Aug. 1980.

26 PP 1977–8, 8, p. 126.

27 Hayes private papers, Knights to Hayes, 28 Feb. 1996. Burr had joined the Colonial Office at the age of 17 and was a member of the Plymouth Brethren (John Gretton, 'Crown Agents and civil servants: A failure of control', *Public Money*, 2 (2), (1982), p. 23; Notes, Hayes, day-to-day Croom-Johnson evidence, Ministry's hostile attitude to CAs, no. 46).

28 PP 1977–8, 8, pp. 37–8, 169.

were heightened in June 1970 when the Ministry, renamed the Overseas Development Administration, was subordinated into the Foreign and Commonwealth Office. The reorganization was a 'red light' that the Ministry could disappear altogether, and strengthened the long-held belief that control of the Agents was their only 'salvation', giving them a 'big executive function other than aid, which the FCO could not themselves takeover'.[29]

Having worked at the Ministry, Hayes was well aware of its wish to gain control of the Agency, which was clearly reflected in its behaviour. As discussed in chapter eight, the Ministry effectively abandoned the Office in the early 1960s, planning to take over some of its work if it disappeared.[30] In the event, it survived, but the Ministry, nevertheless, sought to obtain its recruitment of professional engineers, and subsequently succeeded in carrying off some of its passage duties and engineering consultancies.[31] In 1973, King proposed that the Senior Crown Agent and Deputy Crown Agent posts be occupied by serving Ministry officials, and, early in the following year, suggested that Burr be made a temporary Deputy Crown Agent.[32] Prior to Hayes' retirement, this idea resurfaced and King strongly advocated the appointment of W. A. C. Mathieson, an Undersecretary, and M. G. Smith as Principal and Deputy Crown Agent respectively, but was overruled by the Treasury.[33]

The Ministry's hostility towards the CAs' own account activities and its incessant demand for information, which greatly increased the Finance Directorate's workload, were seen by Hayes as part of its 'slow and long' plan to take over a weakened Agency.[34] Similarly, Burr et al's numerous interferences were regarded as attempts to sabotage the Agents' business. Much anger was particularly generated by the discovery that officials had queried their tax position with the Inland Revenue, attempted to block a Ministry of Technology grant towards the cost of their new computer, and had failed to mention in a press releases their contribution in the 1971 East Pakistan relief operation.[35] In retaliation, the Agents refused to provide the information demanded by officials, in the hope that this would reduce their ability to intervene. The consequent protests further damaged relations, which eventually degenerated into a form of 'trench warfare'.[36]

According to the enquires, the Bank of England failed to oversee the Agents and was thus largely unaware of their supposed defects, and failed to pass onto the Treasury and Stevenson enquiry those few concerns that it did have about

29 Notes, Hayes, day-to-day Croom-Johnson evidence, ODM wish to absorb CAs, no. 5; Hayes private papers, Hayes to Sir Robin Butler, 30 Sept. 1982.

30 OD 20/119, memo, 3 April 1963.

31 WN 4, M gen. 141/2, vol. 1; L 118/1, para. 16.

32 Croom-Johnson Tribunal, Doc. Evidence, B/odm/1/14b, p. 501, Pearson, 2 July 1973; Report on Croom-Johnson Tribunal, Hayes, para. 9; OD 59/27, King, 11 Oct. 1973; *ibid.*, memo, 19 Feb. 1974. The officials would have combined their new CA roles with their Ministerial duties. Hayes refused to countenance the proposals (Notes, Hayes, day-to-day Croom-Johnson evidence, Odm – King, no. 39).

33 Croom-Johnson Tribunal, Doc. Evidence, odm 1/16, p. 125, memo, 7 March 1974; HO 268/337, Treasury to B of E, 27 Feb. 1974.

34 Notes, Hayes, day-to-day Croom-Johnson evidence, What went wrong, no. 6.

35 L 160, Hayes, 19 Aug. 1970; L 35, 31 Aug. 1971.

36 Hood, 'The Crown Agents', p. 300.

their activities. The Agency was supposedly poorly supervised because it was not a bank, and the Discount Office, the Bank's supervisory body, performed its duties poorly.[37] The Discount Office had a staff of only fifteen, no mechanisms for supervision, and was managed by Jim Keogh, a mercurial heavy drinking Irishman, who many at the Bank believed lacked the abilities of his predecessor.[38] In fact, the Bank appears to have closely monitored the Agency and to have had a good understanding of its operations. The Bank received details of its receipts and payments at the end of each day and monthly and quarterly summaries of its assets and liabilities, and, from December 1970, the CAs agreed to supply the Bank with the same information it received from merchant banks.[39] After the April 1970 *Sunday Times* article, Challis spent a whole day explaining the Office's activities to Keogh, and, subsequently, in order to 'improve contact', Challis and Keogh had regular informal meetings at the Bank, and met each other socially, becoming good friends.[40] The Discount Office also tracked the Agents' progress through its covert sources of information – discount houses, merchant banks, clearing banks etc.[41]

The Bank's anxieties regarding the Agents were relatively minor and merely a continuation of a disquiet that dated back to the 1920s. Prior to December 1973, concern was expressed about their intention to acquire a stakeholding in Sassoons, the quality of seven commercial bills purchased in March 1969, their failure to balance their current account in September 1971, and, as discussed in chapter four, their injudicious purchase of Treasury bills and supposed disregard of exchange controls.[42] The Bank also had 'qualms' about Finvest and the CAs' lack of accountability.[43] Strangely, it failed to broach these concerns in its evidence to the Stevenson enquiry and was reluctant to make them known to the Treasury. Officials assured the Stevenson committee that the Bank had 'no particular worries about the nature of the CAs' activities', 'and there had never been any suggestion in the market that their name was other than good'.[44] When questioned about their reticence by Fay and Croom-Johnson, officials gave a variety of self-contradictory explanations. One denied that the Bank had failed to convey its 'generalised unease' to the committee. Others claimed that it had

37 L 118/2, p. 27.

38 Michael Moran, *The Politics of Banking. The Strange Case of Competition and Credit Control*, London 1984, p. 86; Stephen Fay, *Portrait of an Old Lady. Turmoil at the Bank of England*, London 1987, p. 62; Kynaston, *The City … Vol. iv*, pp. 462–3. Keogh became the Bank's scapegoat for the 1973–4 crash, and, in 1975, he took early retirement (Fay, *Portrait*, p. 62; Alan A. Block, 'Introduction', *Crime, Law and Social Change*, 5 (2001), p. 4).

39 SA, Hayes' Fay committee notes; Croom-Johnson Tribunal, Doc. Evidence, b/tr/2/1, p. 26, Treasury paper, 10 Oct. 1969. The daily information was provided to allow the CAs' account at the Bank to be balanced.

40 HO 268/327, memo, 19 Nov. 1970 and Deputy Governor, 20 Jan. 1971; L 118/5, p. 134; CAOG 21/80, Davidson to Wheatley, 20 Nov. 1973. Keogh and Challis had similar personalities and both were physically disabled, Challis as a result of polio and Keogh from a war wound (Kynaston, *The City … Vol. iv*, p. 463).

41 For example, HO 268/337, B of E Drawing Office, 7 Aug. 1969.

42 HO 268/327, memo, 24 March 1969; HO 268/337, B of E, 6 Sept. 1971.

43 Croom-Johnson Tribunal, Doc. Evidence, b/be/5/11, 7, Fforde, 19 May 1970; T 326/1368, Hillis, 8 Sept., 1969.

44 PP 1977–8, 8, p. 91.

been assumed that its members were already aware of the concerns, that the worries were not significant enough to be mentioned, and that the Bank had little faith in the enquiry and did not want to 'contaminate' its involvement in the post-enquiry discussion of the Agents' future.[45]

The Bank was equally reluctant to pass their 'qualms' onto the Treasury. In May 1970, in response to a Treasury query, the Deputy Governor expressed disquiet about 'the risks the CAs were running' and their lack of accountability, and seven months later voiced some concern to Sir Frank Figures, the Treasury's Second Permanent Secretary.[46] The warnings, however, were so oblique that the Treasury did not construe them as such, and the Bank failed to sound any further alarm bells. Indeed, on several occasions it expressed its confidence in the Agency.[47] Asked why it had not taken further action, the Bank insisted that its expression of concern in 1970 was more than sufficient, pointing out that responsibility for the Agency lay with the Government and not itself.[48]

A more realistic explanation for the Bank's coyness is that the Agents' practices were common in the City, and Bank officials were 'no more uneasy about the CAs than about some of the other financial conglomerates'.[49] Informing the Treasury of these concerns would not only have brought Lord Barber's 'dash for growth' to a shuddering halt, but would have damaged the Bank's own reputation as an architect of the policy of cheap money and as a strong City regulator. Told that the Agents had embarked on high risk strategies, the Treasury would have investigated whether other institutions were behaving in the same manner and perhaps introduced a general crack down on the City. At the very least, it would have required the Agents to relinquish their new activities and could even have demanded the abandonment of their traditional financial role. The resultant withdrawal of funds would have destabilized the money and property markets and led to Parliamentary and press queries as to the universitality of the CAs' methods, which would again have resulted in greater regulation.

The Treasury had sources of information other than the Bank, and in 1969 Sir Robert Armstrong, the department's Under Secretary, was so concerned about the Agents' new role that he commissioned an in-house report on the Agency, and, as seen, asked the Deputy Governor if he had any worries about its activities.[50] The Department, however, failed to act on its anxieties, partly because the Ministry kept it as 'far as possible at arms length' in order to protect its responsibility for the Agency, and partly because the establishment of the Stevenson committee appeared to demonstrate that the Ministry had begun to take the matter more seriously.[51] Another reason was the knowledge that the CAs' own account activities were subsidising their traditional services, which benefited the UK economy, and the belief that without this extra income there

45 *Ibid.*, pp. 91–2; *Sunday Times*, 30 May 1982, p. 55; L 118/2, p. 58.
46 L 118/2, p. 51.
47 For example, T 317/1632, Wicks, 6 Aug. 1971.
48 PP 1977–8, 8, p. 45; L 118/2, p. 11.
49 HO 268/327, memo, 19 Nov. 1970.
50 T 326/1368, Armstrong, 2 July 1969.
51 T 316/186, Hodges to Boothroyd, 2 Dec. 1971; PP 1977–8, 8, p. 46.

was a possibility that the Exchequer could be asked to make a contribution.[52] There were also strong personal links between the Treasury and the CAs. Hayes had begun his career in the department and the father of Sir Frank Figgures had spent most of his working life at the Agency as successively a messenger and office keeper.[53]

The Exchequer & Audit Department expressed concern at the CAs' lack of accountability in a letter to the Treasury in 1969, but otherwise completely failed in its monitoring role.[54] The Agents' accounts were rarely published on time. Those for 1971 only appeared in August 1973 and the 1972 accounts were over two years late. Moreover, prior to 1971, they did not reflect the overall financial position of the CAs. Separate accounts were created for the Joint funds and the Office Fund, and the latter only gave a net figure for their own account activities, detailed results being relegated to the notes page.[55] Part of the blame for these inadequacies lay with the Agents. The CA accountant was never '100 per cent' physically fit; had little time to devote to the production of the accounts, which were highly complex; had difficulty obtaining accurate figures, owing to the computerisation of the Office's activities; and claimed, at least at the Fay enquiry, that he had received little support from higher management, who 'regarded the accounts as a bore'.[56] But the main culprit was the Exchequer & Audit Department, which was understaffed, had a reputation for inefficiency and gave the Agents' audit a low priority, as their accounts were not presented to Parliament and there were no statutory or other requirements that they be produced by a set date.[57] Concerned at the department's 'shallowness', the Agents sought on a number of occasions to follow the lead of the Post Office and others and appoint a commercial firm of accountants.[58] These bids for freedom, however, were halted by the high cost of commercial audits and opposition from the Auditor-General, who, unofficially, made it clear that he would fight such a move.[59]

The Crown Agents and the secondary banking and property crises

In late 1973, the Barber boom went bust. High levels of credit had increased demand beyond the capacity of British industry and led to an increase in prices, which was further stoked by the Yom Kippur war of October 1973 and the trebling of oil prices by the Arab states. In order to damp down demand and protect the value of the pound, the government raised interest rates, imposed an incomes policy on industry, introduced rent control on commercial proper-

52 T 316/187, Hodges, 27 April 1972; T 317/1756, evidence to Stevenson Committee, no date.

53 *Guardian*, 5 Aug. 1971, p. 13; L 147, Lousley, 13 Dec. 19/77.

54 PP 1977–8, 8, p. 36.

55 PP 1977–8, 8, p. 119; PP 1981–2, 364, p. 61.

56 Pen Portraits, Hayes; L 118/5, p. 171; PP 1977–8, 8, p. 120. At the tribunal, he retracted this claim.

57 PP 1977–8, 8, p. 121; G. Ganz, 'Parliamentary accountability of the Crown Agents', *Public Law*, 1980, p. 456.

58 L 35, 1967, no. 53

59 *Ibid.*; Notes, Hayes, day-to-day Croom-Johnson evidence, Other factors section, no. 42.

ties, and, in December, announced its intention to impose a development land tax. The Bank of England, meanwhile, asked banks to reduce loans to property developers, and, to further limit lending, required clearing banks to pay it special deposits. The economic impact of these initiatives was disastrous. The high interest rates slowed growth, accelerating the fall in equity prices that had begun earlier in the year, the policies to reduce property lending devastated the property market, and the incomes policy brought the miners out on strike, forcing the government to take emergency powers and institute a three-day working week. The clearing and secondary banks, both of which had overlent to the property sector, began to suffer liquidity problems, and, by the end of the year, three secondary banks had collapsed.[60]

For the Bank of England, the failure of these banks raised the possibility of financial meltdown. The resultant loss of confidence could prompt other financial institutions to call in loans, leading to further collapses and to the withdrawal of foreign funds from London and a fall in the value of the pound. To prevent such a scenario, the Bank established a support group of banks, known as the 'lifeboat'. The consortium gave assistance to concerns suffering a lack of liquidity, though only if they had a reasonable chance of survival and they were engaged in deposit taking, either in or near the banking sector. Over the following year, it provided loans totaling £1,200m to 26 companies, eighteen of which were still trading in 1976.[61]

As the economic outlook was worsening, the Agents were undergoing a crisis of their own. In July 1973, Challis resigned, 'fed up' with the domineering managerial style of Hayes and the lack of progress on the Agency's constitution and no doubt attracted by the £15,000 pa salary offered by his new employers, FNFC.[62] Five months earlier, Peter Sly had left the Office, and, in October 1972, David Johns, the Assistant Director of Finance had been posted to Australia and thence to Singapore.[63] The loss of Challis was a disaster for the Agents. He was 'the planner, architect and builder' of the own account venture, and, without him, the Directorate was directionless.[64] Moreover, neither he nor Sly and Johns were replaced. Hayes later claimed that only the Ministry could appoint a successor to Challis, and that it and the Bank of England had decided to delay making a decision until they had chosen and consulted the person who would succeed Hayes, who was due to retire in early 1974.[65] This explanation is supported by Hayes' numerous memos to the Ministry on the subject. The Ministry and Bank, on the other hand, argued that Hayes could have made the appointment himself, but decided not to do so until the Agency was incorporated and because he wished to use the situation to force them to raise his salary and final pension.[66] Whatever the reason, Challis's and the other positions remained unfilled, and, in the meantime, it was decided that the various departmental heads would run

60 PP 1977–8, 8, p. 138; PP 1981–2, 364, p. 60; Scott, 'The new', p. 7; Reid, *The Secondary*, p. 106.
61 PP 1977/78, 40, pp. 2–3, 4–5, 9.
62 Pen Portraits, Challis; Press clippings, *Daily Telegraph*, 8 Dec. 1977.
63 PP 1977–8, 8, p. 136; Pen Portraits, Shuter to Knights, 5 June 1999.
64 Challis, Personnel file, Hayes, 21 Nov. 1973. See also HO 268/327, memo, 7 May 1970.
65 Report on Croom-Johnson Tribunal, Hayes, para. 5, 16, a6.
66 PP 1977–8, 8, p. 135; L 118/2, p. 164.

the day-to day business of the Directorate, seeking the approval of the Managing Director, Ron Newman, in cases of special importance.[67] To Challis and others, the decision was 'quite ridiculous' and 'it would have been better to have made a bad appointment'.[68] The Directorate was 'rudderless' and the departmental heads overworked and isolated, lack of time causing them to halt the monthly Finance Directorate meetings.[69]

As their equity and gilt holdings were purchased with borrowed money, the Agents' response to the fall in equity and gilt prices was to sell their portfolios. Sales of equities began in July 1973, and the CAs undoubtedly minimized their losses by baling out early.[70] Unfortunately, they were heavily invested in those sectors that experienced the largest falls, secondary banking, investment trusts and North Sea Oil, and, in many cases, the decline in value was so great that it was not rational to liquidate holdings.[71] Consequently, by December 1973, Finvest had lost £1.23m.[72] Sales of gilts and overseas equities occurred in 1974. By August of that year, apart from £1.4m invested in long-term stock, the Office had disposed off most of its gilts and local authority bonds.[73] It had also sold most of its overseas equities, encouraged to do so by the Bank of England, desperate to increase the liquidity of the London market, who Shuter believed through their 'legendary "nod and wink" policy [were] tacitly telling [him] to "go and sin no more"'.[74]

The Agents' reaction to the secondary banking crash was to seek to assist associated companies. This support can be divided into assistance given at the urging of the Bank of England and that undertaken purely to prevent the Stern Group and English & Continental Investments Ltd going under and taking the Agency with them. The Agents' unofficial involvement in the lifeboat is the subject of some controversy. According to the CAs, they were encouraged by the Bank to support three types of institution. Concerns that were being rescued by the lifeboat committee, companies that were part of the lifeboat and were rescuing others, and 'institutions which might become lame ducks if they were to suffer major withdrawals'.[75] Their assistance took two forms – passive and active.[76] Passive support involved the Agents agreeing not to withdraw funds from institutions falling into the three categories, and during 1974 they assisted 18 companies by failing to demand the repayment of £71.55 m of loans.[77] Active support entailed them placing more funds with an institution than 'we might otherwise

67 PP 1977–8, 8, p. 136.
68 *Ibid.*, p. 137.
69 L 188, file 2, Hewins, 30 July 1974; *ibid.*, 28 Dec. 1973. The meetings were resumed in August 1974.
70 *Ibid.*, Shuter, 28 Dec. 1973.
71 CAOG 21/377, Shuter 14/2/74
72 *Ibid.*, Shuter, 20 Feb. 1974.
73 L 188, file 2, 21 Aug. 1974 meeting.
74 L 10, Investment Dept., April 1974; Pen Portraits, Challis.
75 L 152, Hewins to Hayes, 8 April 1974.
76 L 152, Hayes to King, 11 April 1974.
77 G. T. White (£14.8m); London & County Securities (£1.5m); Moorgate Mercantile Holdings (£753,000); British Banglash Trust, Northern Commercial Trust, SIS, Western Trust & Savings, Morris Wigram, Edward Bates, and Dawnay Day etc (£25m); Keyser Ullman (£5m); FNFC

have done'.[78] In 1974, the Agency lent £17m to two subsidiaries of the Burston Group, which was receiving the support of the lifeboat.[79] Despite being told by the Bank of England that the 'group was safe and [that they] would retrieve [their] money in due course', the company subsequently went bankrupt and the Agents lost £9m.[80] The CAs also advanced £5m to Triumph investments, another company receiving help from the lifeboat, and lent £10m to two 'lame ducks' – Wallace Sassoons and Tulone investments.[81]

The Agents were not part of the lifeboat and the Bank of England's requests to support companies were not made officially. Rather a Bank official contacted his CA counterpart and 'by a nod and a wink' made it clear that the Agents' assistance would be appreciated.[82] The Agency was not the only institution asked to provide such support. Bankers were persuaded not to call in loans to property companies and secondary banks, and insurance companies and pension funds were cajoled into purchasing sites from failing property concerns.[83] Their help reduced the financial burden of the support group and maintained confidence in the companies assisted, with the revelation that the lifeboat was propping up a firm causing it to lose much of its creditworthiness.[84]

Wishing to avoid responsibility for the Agents' collapse, the Bank at the two enquiries flatly denied, except in the case of Triumph investments, that it had asked them to deposit new loans with companies, and claimed that any encouragement not to withdraw funds that may have been made did not constitute support.[85] They therefore valued the Agency's unofficial contribution to the lifeboat operations at just £10m. The two enquiries put the figure at £26m and the actual figure was probably £110m.[86] Inevitably, such support contributed to the Agency's eventual collapse. In April 1974, Hayes admitted to the Minister that 'if we had felt free we should have withdrawn a good deal of this money on maturity', and the evidence suggests that this would have occurred.[87] The Agents had begun to withdraw from the equity and gilt markets at the first sign of price falls; in December 1973, prior to the Bank's requests, the CA board had decided 'not to put more money out' and to 'get as liquid as quickly' as possible; and on

(£20.5m plus £2.5m of shares) (PP 1977–8, 8, p. 138; Reid, *The Secondary*, p. 100; L 152, Hewins to Hayes, 8 April 1974; Press clippings, *The Bankers Magazine*, Feb. 1978).

78 L 152, Hayes to King, 11 April 1974.

79 PP 1977–8, 8, pp. 144–8.

80 L 118/16, p. 28; PP 1977–8, 8, p. 148.

81 L 152, Hewins to Hayes, 8 April 1974; *ibid.*, Lonsley, 24 Nov. 1977.

82 PP 1977–8, 8, p. 147; L 118/16, p. 28; L 35, 30 April 1974; HO 268/540, Treasury, 10 May 1974. See also OD 59/32, Newman to King, 8 March 1974; *ibid.*, Hayes to King, 11 April 1974. In February 1974, the Ministry's Bank of England contact, S. D. N. Brearley, privately informed them that the Bank had persuaded the Agents to provide support, and, in May 1974, the Prime Minister was told that 'the CAs participated in the fringe bank rescue operation' (OD 59/32, note, 22 Feb. 1974; PREM 16/349, Hunt to Prime Minister, 22 May 1974).

83 Scott, 'The new', p. 9; Moran, *The Politics*, p. 109.

84 L 118/2, p. 152; Kynaston, *The City … Vol. iv*, p. 492.

85 L 152, Somerset, 25 Nov. 1977; L 118/2, p. 152.

86 PP 1977–8, 8, p. 148; L 152, Lonsley, 24 Nov. 1977.

87 L 152, Hayes to King, 11 April 1974.

7th December 1973 the Agents refused a request from Moorgate Mercantile for a further loan and the following March called in all of their loans to FNFC.[88]

The CAs, of course, could easily have refused the Bank's requests for assistance, and it seems likely that this would have happened if Challis had remained in post. In his absence, the person in control of lending was Norman Hewins, the Head of Banking, who lacked Challis's confidence and close relationship with the Bank of England, and whose judgment was always 'inclined to be muddled', and, no doubt, was further weakened by the strain of 'living in a waking nightmare'.[89] Moreover, he had to make all the decisions himself, with little help from colleagues, Hayes or the Ministry. The other Department Heads were overworked and Ron Newman had no financial expertise, possessed 'a reluctance to take decisions', and 'lacked any serious initiative'.[90] Hayes was financially illiterate, spent March 1974, the height of the crisis, 'joyriding about the pacific' on yet another official tour, and, an establishment figure, strongly believed that 'a senior member of [the secondary market] cannot responsibly walk away from the front line'.[91] Ministry officials, meanwhile, were not officially aware that support was being given until 11 April 1974. Hayes failed to inform them of the Agents' unofficial involvement in the lifeboat, as he believed that it did not constitute a change of policy and he correctly surmised that they would oppose the initiative as the support of domestic institutions was not part of the Agents' role and would damage clients' confidence and lead to political repercussions.

The loans to English & Continental Investments Ltd amounted to £36.73m by the end of 1974, and, on its collapse in May 1974, the Agents had lent the Stern Group £40m, £13m of which was unsecured and £5.5m advanced on William Stern's personal guarantee.[92] The Agents did not support Stern alone. When his Group crashed, it owed £180m to 40 financial institutions, including Nat West bank (£30m), Lloyds bank, the International Credit bank, the Anglo-Portuguese bank (£11.48m), the American International Marine bank (£10m), FNFC (£9.8m) and Keyser Ullman (£20m).[93] Nor was the Agency the only institution that had taken William Stern's personal guarantee; almost £100m of his Group's debt had been secured on his personal assurance that it would be repaid.[94]

A small part of the Agents' loans to Stern were lent in response to a request from the Bank of England and a promise that the help would be reciprocated. At a meeting on 11 April 1974, the Bank's Governor asked the Agents and Barclays bank to 'nurse Stern into viability again … and indicated that the Bank would support [them]'.[95] As a result of the promise, the CAs ploughed a further £3.25m

88 Statement, Hayes, Aug. 1993, p. 45; PP 1977–8, 8, p. 138; L 118/5, p. 222.
89 Norman Hewins, Personnel file, Barley, 23 Feb. 1973; *Daily Telegraph*, 27 May 1982, p. 22; PP 1977–8, 8, p. 141.
90 L 118/6, p. 59; Pen Portraits, Newman.
91 CA (m) 67, vol. 1, Abbott, 12 Aug. 1980; L 152, Hayes to King, 11 April 1974.
92 L 118/5, p. 203; HO 268/540, Bridgeman, 3 May 1974; HO 268/335, B of E, 8 April 1974.
93 Reid, *The Secondary*, p. 106; Kynaston, *The City … Vol. iv*, p. 497; Press clippings, *Sunday Times*, 4 June 1978.
94 Reid, *The Secondary*, p. 106.
95 L 118/6, p. 66.

into the Group.[96] There was also a belief that the Agents had a duty to the City to support Stern and English & Continental Investments Ltd, and that both would survive the crash. In the early months of 1974, it was generally accepted that the lifeboat would bring the crisis to a rapid end. Stern had assured the Agents that his financial difficulties were merely a temporary embarrassment, and, even if this was not the case, Hewins was confident that other institutional shareholders would join the Agents' in ploughing more money into the company.[97]

A further motivation for the support was self-interest. Hewins believed that the Agents 'were walking a tight-rope of confidence' and that a disclosure of bad debts would sound their 'death knell'.[98] Depositors would call in existing loans and refuse further advances, overseas clients would reduce the traditional financial and procurement work they gave the Office, and Yablon and the Agents' critics in Parliament and the press would clamour for the reform or the abolition of the Agency.[99] In the event, none of these events occurred, and such thinking, again, demonstrates Hewin's poor judgment. As with the assistance given at the prompting of the Bank of England, Hewins also lacked the support of Hayes and the Ministry. Hayes was only informed of the loans made to the Stern Group on 8 April, when the collapse of the company seemed imminent. Hewins, who may have coveted the vacant post of Head of Finance, believed that it was his duty to solve the problem himself, and 'was very afraid of crying wolf', of the verbal whip lashing that he would receive when he informed the Senior Crown Agent and of Hayes' subsequent actions, which he believed would only worsen the situation.[100] The Ministry remained in ignorance until 3 May. Hayes failed to inform them of the 11 April meeting with the Bank of England, as the Governor had insisted on complete secrecy for the operation for fear that it would leak out and because it suspected that the new Labour Minister, a severe critic of property developers, would block the advances.[101]

On 6 May, the Agents and Nat West halted their loans to the Stern Group, having read a report by the accountancy firm Peat Marwick that they had earlier commissioned, which concluded that the company was in terminal decline.[102] Neither the lifeboat, which only assisted banks, nor the Treasury were willing to provide further support, and it was thus only a matter of time before the firm went bankrupt, and, it was assumed, depositors would begin to call in their loans to the Agency.[103] Despite its earlier promise to 'support' the Agents if they continued to lend to the Stern Group, the Bank declined to come to their assistance if such a run occurred. It claimed that the word 'support' had been used in

96 PP 1977–8, 8, p. 142.
97 PP 1981–2, 364, p. 343; L 118/16, p. 23; L 118/6, p. 18.
98 PP 1977–8, 8, p. 141.
99 PP 1977–8, 8, pp. 138, 141; HO 268/540, Bridgeman, 3 May 1974; HO 268/335, B of E, 8 April 1974; *ibid.*, B of E, 16 April 1974.
100 PP 1977–8, 8, p. 143; L 118/6, pp. 62, 82.
101 PP 1981–2, 364, p. 351; L 121, 1979, no. 81/79. The Bank's later denial of the charge is undermined by the fact that it only informed the Treasury of the operation on 1 May 1974 (PP 1981–2, 364, p. 372).
102 PP 1977–8, 8, p. 142.
103 *Ibid.*; PP 1981–2, 364, p. 354.

the sense of taking any blame for the loans, that it lacked sufficient resources to mount its own rescue operation, and that the Agency did not fulfill the criteria for assistance from the lifeboat committee - it was not a bank and it was unlikely to survive, even if assistance was given.[104] The Treasury, however, suspected that, by transferring responsibility for the Agents to the government, the Bank was seeking revenge for the Chancellor's earlier refusal to support failing property companies and parts of the secondary banking system.[105]

On 13 May, representatives of the Bank, Crown Agents, Treasury and Ministry met to discuss the situation. What was said at this meeting was to be the subject of intense dispute. The Deputy Governor of the Bank, Sir Jasper Hollom, later insisted that he informed all those present that the Agents were 'bust or were capable of being bust', and strongly denied that anyone present could have believed the problem was one of temporary illiquidity as opposed to imminent insolvency.[106] Everyone else at the meeting, however, had a different recollection of what occurred. The Ministry and Treasury representatives were convinced that Hollom had merely stated that the Agents lacked liquidity and that they would be insolvent only if depositors began to call in loans.[107] To prevent such a run, at a second meeting, it was decided that the Chancellor would issue a statement declaring government backing of the Agents if funds began to be withdrawn.[108]

Stern went bankrupt on 6 June, but the expected run on the Agents failed to occur. The Ministry and Treasury, believing that the crisis was over, returned to the problem of the Agency's constitution and the CAs continued to trade until the end of the year. Strangely, neither the Agents nor the Bank addressed the Office's insolvency. Hayes believed that the government expected them to 'work [their] own salvation and that they should seek to trade their way out of trouble'.[109] It was hoped that, if the Stern Group could be salvaged and the secondary banking sector stabilized, the Agency could survive, though Hewins later accepted that 'he might in part have been shutting his eyes to the possibility of insolvency as being a prospect too horrible to contemplate'.[110] Bank of England officials, although convinced that the Agency was bankrupt, actively encouraged it to keep trading and failed to prompt the Ministry or Treasury to take action.[111] It was claimed that they believed that both government departments were aware of the Office's insolvency and that they had more than fulfilled their duty by informing them of the true situation at the 13 May meeting.[112]

This explanation for their inaction, however, is undermined by the records of

104 L 118/2, p. 122; PP 1981–2, 364, p. 357.

105 Croom-Johnson Tribunal, Doc. Evidence, b/tr/2/3, p. 100, Bullock, Treasury, 13 May 1974; *ibid.*, p. 93, Downey, 10 May 1974.

106 PP 1977–8, 8, p. 145; L 118/2, p. 114.

107 PP 1981–2, 364, p. 357, 360; L118/3, p. 45.

108 PP 1977–8, 8, p. 146.

109 PP 1981–2, 364, p. 359.

110 *Ibid.*, pp. 359–60.

111 Croom-Johnson Tribunal, B of E submissions, p. 144; L 118/2, p. 144; HO 268/329, B of E, 3 July 1974.

112 L 118/2, pp. 115, 140, 171.

a meeting with the Ministry and Treasury held on 3 June to discuss the Agents' future status. During the meeting, S. D. N. Brearley, the Assistant Principal of the Bank's Discount office, stated that the Agents would have no difficulty in finding the necessary capital for a proposed banking subsidiary.[113] The Bank later claimed that Brearley was unaware of the Agents' insolvency because it was regarded as sensitive information, and that he was not told of it before the meeting as there was no reason to believe that the matter would be raised.[114] A more cynical interpretation is that the Bank at the 13 May and later meetings deliberately hid the Agency's insolvency from the Ministry and Treasury, and sought to give them the impression that the Agents were solvent.

The reason for this subterfuge was that it was in the Bank's interest for the Agents to trade as normal. The financial crash was far from over. The failure of Stern prompted rumours that other property companies were in trouble and that 'something nasty [was] about to happen'.[115] In August, there were whispers that a number of insurance companies were about to collapse, and, in November, the financial viability of Nat West was questioned.[116] The Bank believed that an announcement that the Agents had lost hundreds of millions of pounds would devastate City confidence. Depositors would pull-in their loans, forcing the Agents to withdraw their own funds from a myriad of institutions, and the Agency's overseas clients would require their non-own account investments to be sold, causing prices to fall even further, and would transfer the proceeds overseas.[117] The resultant financial collapse would increase the burden of the lifeboat committee, and, from August 1974, any support would have to be met by the Bank itself. Alarmed at the actual and potential cost of their rescue operations, the members of the lifeboat committee capped their support at £1,200m, requiring the Bank to meet the cost of any assistance given above that figure.[118]

Another reason for the Bank's wish that the Agents trade as normal was that they could continue to provide unofficial support to institutions in difficulty, again reducing the likelihood of further collapses and minimizing lifeboat costs. Hollom argued that such support was unavoidable, as, if it came to a sudden halt, questions regarding the CAs' viability would have been asked, which could have led to a run on their deposits.[119] The Bank, nonetheless, failed to inform the Treasury of the assistance. It was assumed that Treasury officials were already aware of its existence, and it was claimed that it was not the Bank's duty to enlighten them even if this was not the case.[120]

From May to December 1974, the Agents provided passive or active assistance to at least five companies, partly financing the operations through the sale of gilts, which, if retained, could have been sold at a later date at recovered

113 PP 1981–2, 364, p. 372.
114 L 118/2, pp. 170, 173.
115 Kynaston, *The City … Vol. iv*, p. 497; *Financial Times*, 25 May 1974, p. 10.
116 Kynaston, *The City … Vol. iv*, pp. 505, 510.
117 L 118/2, p. 148; HO 268/329, B of E, 9 May 1974.
118 Kynaston, *The City … Vol. iv*, p. 504.
119 L 118/2, p. 148.
120 PP 1981–2, 364, p. 365.

prices.[121] At the end of July, they agreed to a Bank request not to withdraw £9m of loans to the Burston Group, which subsequently went bankrupt.[122] In August, in a meeting with the CAs and the directors of SIS, Hollom informed the CAs that 'he would not wish to dissuade [them] from continuing to give whatever support was necessary' to SIS, and the following month they invested £1m, which again disappeared, along with their £10m of deposits, when the bank went into receivership in early 1975.[123] The Agents also lost a $2m loan to the Israeli-British Bank, lent a further £6.2m to English & Continental Property Investments Ltd, which subsequently went into voluntary liquidation, and, as already discussed, was inveigled by the Bank into making a £14.3m back-to-back loan to Oldham Estates.[124] In total therefore the Agents' support operations from May 1974 increased their losses by at least another £18.2m.

The curtain was eventually brought down on the Agency at the end of 1974. On Hayes retirement in October, the Ministry appointed Sir John Cuckney as his replacement. The Treasury's and the Bank of England's preferred candidate, Cuckney was an ex-member of MI5, who had sorted out the problems of the crisis ridden Mersey Docks & Harbour Board and reorganised the Property Service Agency, and, after his stint at the CAs, went on to be chairman of the defence company Westland and of International Military Services.[125] Ironically, both the Property Service Agency and International Military Services were later found to be far more corrupt than the Agents.[126] One of Cuckney's first acts on taking office was to require the Banking Department to turn away 'poor quality money market loans', with the result that by the end of October the Agency faced a liquidity problem.[127] Allowed by the Ministry to pay the going rate, he also recruited specialists from outside the organization, and, doubtful of the information supplied by the Finance Directorate, he asked the accountants Coopers & Lybrand to investigate the Agents' financial position.[128] Their report confirmed

121 Author's interview with Shuter, 20 Oct. 2004.

122 PP 1981–2, 364, pp. 180–1, 234.

123 *Ibid.*, p. 364; CAOG 21/194, Wheatley, 19 Sept. 1974.

124 PP 1977–8, 8, p. 150; PP 1981–2, 364, p. 103; HO 268/329, B of E, 20 May 1974; *ibid.*, B of E, 22 May 1974.

125 Hart had preferred Aubrey Jones or Harry Walston as Hayes' successor, but was overruled (Prem 16/349, France, Treasury to Armstrong, 18 June 1974; *ibid.*, Healey to Hart, 26 July 1974; *ibid.*, Armstrong to Prime Minister, 30 July 1974). Peter Wright, *Spycatcher. The Candid Autobiography of a Senior Intelligence Officer*, London 1987, p. 31; *The Times*, 3 Sept. 1974, p. 11; Magnus Linklater and David Leigh, *'Not with Honour'. The Inside Story of the Westland Scandal*, London 1986, p. 49; P. Fitzgerald, 'Why are we waiting?', *New Statesman and Society*, 8 (381) (12 Jan. 1995), p. 16.

126 A 1978 government report cited 49 incidences in which Property Service Agency employees had taken bribes from contractors, stolen government property, or submitted fraudulent expense claims. A total of 61 employees were sacked for various irregularities between 1976 and 1982, ten of whom were prosecuted and convicted (CA (m) 67, vol. 1; clipping, *Daily Telegraph*, 6 Oct. 1978; *ibid.*, Abbott, 9 Dec. 1980). During Cuckney's period of office, International Military Services was found to have paid large bribes to Nigerian government officials in return for orders (Whitby, 'Conspiracy', p. 30).

127 L 188, 31 Oct. 1974; L 35, 26 Nov. 1974.

128 HO 268/329, Brearley, B of E, 18 Oct. 1974. Morgan Grenfell were appointed initially as managers of the CA money market operations, but with a more general and continuing

the Bank's conclusion seven months earlier that the Agency was insolvent and concluded that it lacked sufficient cash to continue operating.[129]

Unable to obtain capital from the private sector, Cuckney explored the possibility of the Bank of England purchasing the Agents' assets, investing in the proposed banking subsidiary, providing a standby facility of £50m, or approving the segregation of the Agency's dubious assets into a realization agency.[130] Despite the Agency's unofficial support of the Bank's rescue operation, which was one of the main causes of its insolvency, the Bank rejected all the proposals. It claimed that it lacked the resources to purchase the assets or a banking stake, lifeboat criteria prevented the support of an insolvent concern, and the approval of a realization agency was a matter for the government.[131] Hayes and others suspected that the true reason for its reluctance to help was a wish for the Agency to disappear and its financial work to be transferred to the Bank.[132] As discussed in chapters three and four, over the previous forty years the Bank had made numerous attempts to capture the Agents' investment business, in the 1960s had persuaded a number of central banks to abandon them, and, in September 1975, it unsuccessfully proposed that it take over their banking role.[133] After over a century of disputes, the Bank also perhaps sought revenge for the many slights that it had suffered at the hands of the Agency.

Having no other option, Cuckney asked for government assistance. After a number of meetings, it was decided that the Agents should be given a recoverable cash grant of £85m, increased to £175m in 1978, and that the Bank of England should indeed provide standby facilities.[134] Freed of the danger that depositors would withdraw their funds, Cuckney began to dispose of the Agents' own account investments. Sales reduced the likelihood that the Agency would be involved in another scandal, further damaging its and Cuckney's reputation, and minimized government interference, which damaged the confidence of overseas clients in the Agents' independence.[135] By April 1975, £59m of assets had been sold and sales continued into the 1980s. Some of the investments, such as the Australian property portfolio, were disposed off at a small profit.[136] The majority, however, were offered at prices far lower than could have been obtained if the Agents had struck better bargains or had waited for the market to recover and

responsibility for advice on banking matters (L 35, 28 Nov. 1974). In November 1974, Cuckney recruited a former colleague at the Property Services Agency as Deputy Chairman and Managing Director of Millbank Technical Services. (*The Times*, 19 Nov. 1974, p. 21).

129 L 35, 28 Nov. 1974.

130 *Ibid.*, 26 Nov. 1974; *ibid.*, 28 Nov. 1974; *ibid.*, 7 Nov. 1974.

131 HO 268/329, B of E, 2 Dec. 1974; L 35, 7 Dec. 1974.

132 Hayes private papers, Hayes to Sir Robin Butler, 30 Sept. 1982.

133 L 38, no. 69, Kirkness to Cuckney, 26 Sept. 1975.

134 L 35, 17 Dec. 1974.

135 Author's interview with Johns, 20 Jan. 2004; Press clippings, *West Africa*, 3 May 1976. The Bank of England, however, continued to secretly 'influence' the Agents' actions. In February 1975 the Bank 'put it into [the CAs'] minds the possibilities for lending by Brunei and others to the UK public sector', and two months later asked them not to demand repayment of loans given to FNFC (CAOG 21/124, meeting, 27 Feb. 1975; *ibid.*, B of E to Cuckney, 7 April 1975; *ibid.*, Cuckney to B of E, 8 April 1975). Cuckney fulfilled both requests.

136 Press clippings, *Daily Telegraph*, 27 Nov. 1981; Author's interview with Johns, 20 Jan. 2004.

prices to rise.[137] By 1977/8, losses amounted to £212m, reduced to £195.4m in 1982.[138]

For the staff of the Finance Directorate the disaster of the own account experiment did not end in 1974. All had to give evidence to the two enquiries and a number were severely criticized in the press. The Bank of England ensured that Challis was forced to resign his position at FNFC, and the reputation of Hayes was left in tatters.[139] They also received little sympathy from the Crown Agents. In 1977, the Agency attempted to seize the pensions of Challis and Hayes, and, in the following year, sought to take civil action against them for the recovery of funds.[140] Both initiatives were eventually abandoned when the Treasury Solicitor and the Attorney General pronounced that there was no evidence that either was guilty of negligence or breach of duty.[141] Of the Department Heads, Hewins was forced to retire early; G. R. Towse, the Controller of Financial Services, was 'very firmly ... encouraged to find another job' and subsequently left the Agency 'an unhappy and embittered man'; it was made clear to Johns, Shuter and Osgodby that they were 'unlikely to have much future in the office', and R. C. Dorrington, the Assistant Money Market Manager, was moved to another department.[142]

Conclusion

Both the CA Board and Sir Claude Hayes appear to have been given adequate information by the Finance Directorate, but lacked the expertise and knowledge to determine whether its activities were excessively risky or unethical. Although, even if they had possessed the necessary experience, given the tenor of the times and the Agency's view of itself as a business organisation rather than a government department, it seems unlikely that they would have objected to any of Challis's decisions. The Bank of England and the supervisory government departments, similarly, to varying degrees were aware of the Offices' activities. They failed to initiate change because, in some cases, it was not in their interests to do so, and they understood that the Agency was the victim of a disinformation campaign.

The Bank of England knew that there was little difference between the operational methods of the Agents and those of the rest of the secondary banking community, but failed to raise the alarm. It accepted that the Agents followed City norms and suspected that Treasury knowledge of the Agents' activities

137 Press clippings, West Africa 3 May 1976; Author's interview with Johns, 20 Jan. 2004; Croom-Johnson Tribunal. General Correspondence, Walker's evidence to the Fay committee; T 317/2018, Unwin 12 Dec. 1974.

138 PP 1977–8, 8, p. 2; *Financial Times*, 27 May 1982, p. 13.

139 Challis's offer to resign from FNFC had been unanimously rejected by his fellow directors. The B of E then informed Pat Matthews, Managing Director of the bank, that it was 'in the long term interests of FNFC to part with [Challis] ... sooner rather than later' (HO 268/329, memo, 19 Dec. 1974).

140 L 226, 6 Oct 1977 meeting.

141 *Ibid.*, and Hall to Eburne, 14 July 1978; *ibid.*, Hall to Eburne, 21 Aug. 1978.

142 Personnel file, Norman Hewins, Cuckney, 16 Sept. 1977; *ibid.*, Cuckney, 13 Sept. 1977; SA, 1973 CA provisional accounts and 1974 CA profit forecast, Knights, no date.

would lead to the reform of the Agency and the withdrawal of its own account and perhaps investment funds from the market, which would slow the Barber boom. It also perhaps feared criticism of its own regularity role and a general crack down on the City. The supervisory departments followed the Bank's lead. The Treasury, though kept in the dark by Bank officials about certain practices, was still broadly aware of the Agents' new role, which it accepted. The department wanted the Agency to continue to supply its traditional services, which benefited the UK economy, but wished to avoid any Exchequer contribution to their provision. The Ministry's higher officials opposed heavy control of the Agents, not wishing to disturb the Agency's links with its traditional clients. Their subordinates, on the other hand, fearful for the survival of the Ministry, attempted to closely supervise the Office, but were blocked by the Agents who deprived them of information. As for the Exchequer & Audit Department, time spent on the Agency's audit would have caused them to miss the auditing deadlines of those accounts that had to be presented to Parliament on specific dates, which would have resulted in criticism, loss of some clients to the commercial sector, and possible reform.

It seems equally unlikely that the Agency would have failed if there had been no secondary banking collapse, and it is possible that it could even have survived the crisis. It succumbed because it failed to call in loans and continued to lend money to a number of companies that subsequently became insolvent. Some of the blame for the provision of the advances lies with the Agents. Hewins feared that the failure the Stern Group and English & Continental Investments Ltd would lead to the collapse of the Office, and possessed a misplaced optimism that the market would recover and that these companies would survive. The Ministry and the Bank, however, were equally culpable. The Ministry blocked attempts by Hayes to replace Challis with a specialist from outside the Agency, and the Bank exploited the CAs' loyalty to the City by encouraging them to unofficially help the lifeboat committee. The resultant active and passive support, which continued even after the Agency was bankrupt, ultimately cost the Agents over £100m.

Strangely, neither the Fay nor Croom-Johnson committees explicitly state that support of the lifeboat was responsible for the Agency's downfall. The enquiries had other failings. Their evidence was never published and the reports often exclude the Agents' explanations for their actions. The Agency's successes are downplayed and its flaws, however minor, are highlighted, often at great length and in mind-numbing detail. Its staff are criticized both for being financial innocents lacking entrepreneurial drive and for being City sharks obsessed with money-making and conducting labyrinthine financial scams. Favourable documentary evidence is often ignored, and, on a number of occasions, the Fay committee incorrectly accuses the Office of breaking the law.

It seems that the main purpose of the enquiries was to conceal the true reasons for the Agency's insolvency. Knowledge that the Bank of England had deliberately used the funds of the Agents' overseas clients to prop up the British financial system would have had political consequences and prompted many of the Agency's customers to take their business elsewhere, which would have damaged the UK economy and particularly the weak financial sector. Likewise, if the unethical, and, in many cases, illegal activities of the secondary banking sector had been revealed, overseas confidence in the London market would have fallen and funds withdrawn. It also seems likely that neither the Bank of England nor the main political parties wished to remind the British public of their own contributions to the crisis. It was a Conservative government that had introduced the policy of cheap money that led to the Barber boom and a Labour government whose actions had halted the rapid economic growth. The Bank of England, meanwhile, had contributed to the expansion of credit by its removal of clearing banks' credit controls in 1971 and had subsequently failed to regulate the City.

The investigations of the Agents' collapse were used to deflect demands for a wider enquiry into the crisis, and were 'a classic Civil Service muffling strategy, enabling the Treasury and the Bank of England to retreat into silence on the convenient plea' of sub judice, and, in the meantime, ensure that the events would not reoccur.[143] In 1979, a new Banking Act gave the Bank of England stronger regulatory powers, and, within the Bank, the Discount Office was completely reorganized.[144] Given its ambiguous constitutional status, the eventual reports could reasonably depict the Agency as a unique organisation with little in common with other City institutions, and, a newcomer to the secondary banking sector, its failure could be blamed on inexperience and incompetence.

143 *Sunday Times*, 4 Dec. 1977, p. 17.
144 *Sunday Telegraph*, 30 May 1982, pp. 19–20.

Conclusion

The activities of the Crown Agents over the period 1920 to 1974 can perhaps be best understood in the context of principal-agent theory, which suggests that agents possess a number of interests. Their official goal is the completion of the task for which they are retained; in the case of a builder employed to construct a garage, for example, the completion of the building. Agents with more than one principal, however, may have a number of such interests that contradict each other; the builder may be employed by two people, one of whom wants a cheaply built garage and one who would prefer a building constructed to the highest specification. As well as these official goals, agents also have unofficial interests, generally the survival and growth of their businesses, which may be incompatible with their official objectives or the general interests of their principal; the pursuit of such interests being termed moral hazard. Our builder, for instance, may want to rapidly expand his business, and, to achieve this aim, he may use substandard materials or overcharge his customers. At the same time, the staff who work for agents have their own personal interests, the fulfillment of which may be detrimental to their employer and his clients. The labourers engaged by our builder, for example, may fail to complete a full day's work or pilfer building materials.[1]

All of the participants in the development of the colonies had official, unofficial and staff interests. The official goal of colonial administrations, the Colonial Office and the Crown Agents was to protect the interests of the colonies; that of the Bank of England and the Treasury was to safeguard the UK economy; and that of the Agents' suppliers and service providers was to meet their contractual obligations. In reality, some of these agents served two or more principals and possessed two or more, sometimes contradictory objectives. The Bank of England additionally represented the City of London; colonial administrations, the Colonial Office and the Crown Agents were agents of the UK government; and High Commissioners and Governors were expected by local legislatures to act in the interests of the local business community.[2] All of these agents, furthermore, possessed unofficial goals, generally the growth and survival of their particular organisation, and their staff had their own interests, usually the maximization of their income, power and status.

The Agents' contribution to development during the period covered by the book was thus determined by two factors. First, the extent to which they acted in

1 Richard M. Kreps, *A Course in Microeconomic Theory*, London 1990, chs xvi, xvii; Paul Milgrom and John Roberts, *Economics, Organisation and Management*, Princeton 1992, chs v, vi.

2 The Colonial Office was a government department, colonial Governors and High Commissioners were essentially British government employees, and the Colonial Secretary of State recruited the Agents, set their salaries and service charges, had the power to dismiss them, and, if he so wished, to close down the Agency.

the interests of their clients and prevented suppliers, service providers and local administrations fulfilling those official, unofficial and staff goals that were detrimental to their customers. And second, their success in overcoming pressure to act in the UK government's interest, in preventing the Bank of England and the Colonial Office fulfilling unofficial aims that harmed their clients, and in fighting their own desire to meet similarly detrimental unofficial and staff objectives.

CAs acting in the interests of clients

Generally, the Agents followed the interests of their clients, partly because their staff strongly identified with the colonies, but largely because by doing so they fulfilled their wish for the Agency to survive and grow. It was well understood that if they failed to meet their principals' needs, some administrations would use their services less or not at all and that they would have difficulty attracting new customers. Discharging their clients' interests also generated further work. The successful issue of a colonial loan, for example, added to their loan management and Sinking Fund investment business; permitted them to make JCF and JMF advances, some of which would be spent on goods ordered through themselves; encouraged other colonial governments to make flotations; and usually enabled the issuer to embark on a new infrastructure project, which brought in even more work. The CAs had some involvement in the construction of such schemes, bought a large proportion of the building materials required, and, when the project was completed, recruited the technical operating staff and benefited from the extra income generated, which permitted the constructing colony to make even greater use of their services.

The Agents helped their clients in four ways. They prevented suppliers and service providers acting in their own interest, as opposed to that of the colonies, and, on occasion, treated them unfairly, and stopped colonial administrations and administrators acting contrary to the interests of the territories they governed.[3] A number of strategies were adopted to restrict supplier and service provider self-interest. The CAs, firstly, used only a limited number of firms, which they trusted, and, in the case of suppliers, they had thoroughly investigated. The companies were often relatively small, relying on the Agency for a large part of their turnover, and had a good reputation, which they would lose if they acted fraudulently. Generally, they were employed for long periods, fifty years was not unusual, and, once recruited, their actions were closely monitored. The CAs also actively acted against self-interest. To avoid paying the extortionate prices demanded by cartels, for example, they bought goods from firms outside the ring or from foreign companies, and, in the 1930s, they prevented City dealers selling and buying stock for colonial Investment Funds at respectively relatively low

3 The CAs attempts to avert moral hazard by suppliers, service providers and administrations was partly motivated by their own self-interest. Any exploitation of the colonies by the private sector would damage the Agency's relationship with the Colonial Office and reduce its ability to retain and gain clients, and moral hazard by colonial administrations would reduce colonial revenues and demand for its services.

and high prices by completing all deals secretly through Edward Bickerstethe. Mostly, these attempts to restrain self-seeking behaviour were successful, though inevitably there were failures. The CAs were unable, for instance, to avoid the payment of underwriting and overriding fees nor halt the inclusion in procurement contracts of price variation clauses.

Whilst insisting that their suppliers and service providers treat the colonies fairly, the Agents had no compunction occasionally exploiting these people themselves if it was in their clients' interest. For example, to defeat the cement cartel they gave preferential treatment to firms operating outside the ring; they circumvented the International Air Transport Association ruling that restricted the provision of concessions to travel agents; and they frequently acted against the interests of those investors who bought colonial loans.[4] If it benefited their clients, they were also willing to turn 'a blind eye' towards their service providers' exploitation of customers and business associates, and, in some cases, helped them to take advantage of them. So, for instance, nothing was done to prevent Scrimgeours and their underwriters giving the impression to private investors that a loan was much in demand by putting in their own applications, and, during the secondary banking adventure, the Agents helped companies that provided Finvest with funds to take advantage of shareholders and business partners, no doubt hoping that their favours would be reciprocated. On various occasions, they made back-to-back loans to firms, allowed them to 'window-dress' their accounts, and, in the case of FNFC, were willing to buy shares to artificially raise the company's share price.

Such behaviour, along with their tendency to ignore or circumvent UK government instructions discussed below, was regarded by the Colonial Office and the Treasury as unethical. They acted in this way largely because they were not a government department and were therefore, unlike their Colonial Office and Treasury counterparts, under no obligation to follow public sector ethical norms. These demand impeccable conduct, as Civil Servants spend public money, are answerable to Ministers and Parliament, and their behaviour is thought to influence the moral values of society in general.[5] Instead, the Agents followed the moral norms of private sector companies, which are duty bound only to maximize the interests of their owners and thus can act in a less honest manner. The CAs dealt with the private sector on a day-to-day basis and thus absorbed its values, and their adoption of these norms helped them to form stronger relationships with their suppliers and service providers by clearly signalling their independence.

As well as safeguarding colonies from supplier and service provider self-interest, the Agents also protected them from themselves. There was a constant danger that colonial government staff would seek to defraud their colonial employers, and, more importantly, that administrations would act in the interests of domestic business elites rather than the colonies they governed. Local business

4 For example, loan proceeds were occasionally used for purposes not stated in the prospectus and Supplementary Sinking Funds were raided.

5 Richard Chapman, *Ethics in Public Service for a New Millennium*, Aldershot 2000, pp. 219, 227; C. W. Lewis and S. C. Gilman, *The Ethics Challenge in Public Service*, New York 2005, p. 22.

communities were well represented on legislative councils and there was a possibility that British administrators would come under their influence. Governors and High Commissioners socialised and often formed strong attachments with local businessmen, who through their UK connections could provide them with valuable directorships on retirement, and they needed the commercial community's support for the smooth operation of their colonies, on which their reputation at the Colonial Office and their future career prospects rested.

The Agents sought to reduce both types of behaviour. Their existence, along with the requirement that most government goods had to be purchased through them, prevented administrations buying expensive and poor quality materials from local merchants and defaulting on their debts, and stopped local administrators accepting bribes from suppliers in return for orders. Their supervision of development projects, meanwhile, averted the construction of overly expensive infrastructure, their management of the JCF and the JMF reduced the likelihood that administrations would run overdrafts, and their issue of public loans and inter-colonial loans ensured that external finance was only raised for development projects that were economically viable. Unfortunately, the Agents' efforts were not completely successful. There were a number of cases of fraud by colonial administrators; JCF overdrafts were common, particularly after independence; and many colonial governments simply ignored the colonial procurement regulations, or, after demanding that tenders be held simultaneously in the colony and the UK, gave local suppliers preference.

CAs acting against the interests of clients

Although they generally tried to help their clients, there were many occasions when the Agents followed the UK governments' or their own interests. Throughout the period, the Bank of England, the Board of Trade, the Colonial Office and the Treasury constantly intervened in the CAs' activities in order to protect the UK economy, for political reasons, or to prevent actions that they considered to be excessively risky. There are numerous examples of the government's attempts to promote the UK economy. Wishing to finance central government expenditure and to reduce the outflow of monies from the UK and thus protect the Balance of Payments, the Treasury, for example, pressured the Agents to purchase UK government stock, which paid relatively low interest rates. As a result, the colonies were less able to support their own loans, which thus commanded lower prices, and they earned relatively meagre returns from their investments. Likewise, the Bank of England and the Treasury sought to ensure the successful issue of loans by UK institutions by forcing the Agents to set low prices for colonial stock, limiting their access to the market during periods of high demand for securities, in the 1930s, halting conversions and the flotation of loans for the early repayment of old issues, and, during and after the Second World War, restricting the use of inter-colonial loans. During the 1974 secondary banking crisis, meanwhile, the Bank of England put pressure on the Agents to use their own and their clients' funds to support UK financial institutions, some of which subsequently went bankrupt.

The government intervened in the Agents' business for political reasons where their actions were contrary to existing HMG policies or would initiate criticism of Britain within client countries. In the late 1960s, the Foreign Office thus blocked the sale of arms to Cyprus, as this was against government policy, and, a few years earlier, the Treasury refused to make the CAs' purchase of aid financed goods obligatory, fearing protests from Third World politicians, who used procurement contracts to reward their political supporters. There were also political motives behind the Colonial Office's and Treasury's attempts to restrain the Agents' more high-risk ventures. Both departments feared that the failure of these undertakings would harm the reputation of the British Empire and the country's diplomatic relations with its colonies. More important reasons, however, were that, like all Civil Servants, Colonial Office and Treasury officials were risk-averse and they feared that a financial crisis would damage the reputations of their departments and result in the British Exchequer having to bail out the Agents.[6] To minimize risk, the Colonial Office variously insisted that the CAs follow the security price restrictions laid down in the Trustee Acts, and opposed the use of running contracts and equity investment. The Treasury, meanwhile, embarked on a long-running campaign to force them to keep a relatively large proportion of the JCF liquid, a crusade that was intensified from 1931, when a rash move into long-term securities almost resulted in the bankruptcy of the Fund.

The UK government's interventions, however, were not always successful and the Treasury sometimes allowed the Agents to disregard the domestic interest. The CAs, on one or two occasions, fought back. In 1941, they refused a Bank of England request to buy more UK government stock, and, in the 1930s, rejected demands to increase Currency Fund liquidity. At other times, they resorted to stratagems that the Colonial Office and the Treasury regarded as unethical. Government instructions were ignored and circumvented and actions hidden. The Bank of England's requirement that all local Treasury Bill issues be halted in 1931 and the 1932 JCF investment agreement, for example, were both flouted, and, in the 1920s, Colonial Office authority to buy 'self stock' for Sinking Funds at a reasonable price was deliberately misinterpreted. Where the UK's interests clashed with its goal of keeping the country's finances in order, the Treasury was also occasionally prepared to permit the Agents to act in ways that favoured their clients. For instance, Treasury officials, allowed the Agency to breach the 1933 ruling that loans should not be floated for the repayment of old issues because they feared that the payment of excessive interest rates on the old loans would cause some colonies to become more dependent on Exchequer funds. Likewise, in the late 1950s, they permitted a reduction in Currency Fund coverage, which made currencies less secure, as the resultant release of monies would reduce the Fund holders' demands for aid.

As well as acting in ways that favoured the UK, the CA staff additionally sometimes performed their duties in ways that benefited the Agency's or their

6 In recent years, successive governments have tried to reduce Civil Servants' aversion to risk. See Paul Du Gray, 'How responsible is "responsive" government', *Economy and Society*, 31 (3) (2002), pp. 461–82.

own interests. They promoted the interests of the Agency over those of their clients through the maximization of revenues and the minimization of costs, and, when purchasing goods, by giving undue priority to quality. In order for the Agency to survive and grow, it was crucial that its fees were kept as low as possible and that colonies did not complain to the Colonial Office about the quality of the service provided. Charges were kept down in two ways. First, by cutting costs to the bone and thus providing clients with a sub-standard service. When buying colonial imports, for example, the CAs made relatively little use of open competition, used a limited number of suppliers and failed to introduce an effective price-checking procedure, and, as a result, paid relatively high prices for the goods purchased. Inadequate staffing levels, similarly, meant that the Engineering Division and the Stamp Bureau provided a relatively poor quality service, and the Agents' decision in the 1960s only to actively manage the larger colonial Investment Funds reduced investment returns. Fee increases were further avoided by diverting monies that should have been passed to their clients to the Office Fund, a practice that became more pronounced after independence when the Agency was fighting for its survival. From 1925 to 1947, the Agents kept the colonies' underwriting commissions, and, during the 1960s, they variously raided the Marine Insurance Fund, continued to charge a fee for the management of the JCF and JMF, even after the introduction of fixed rates, and kept the interest earned on the suspense account and the shared commission obtained from the British & Commonwealth Shipping Company.

As colonial governments had little understanding of financial matters, criticism of the Agents' work was mostly likely to relate to their procurement role, and, more specifically, to the supply of defective goods, which could prove costly to colonies. To protect their reputation for efficiency with the Colonial Office and to prevent clients turning to local merchants, the Agents therefore gave undue priority to the purchase of quality goods, and, in doing so, greatly increased the cost of the materials supplied and delivery delays. Articles were sourced from a small number of trusted and high status firms, which increased prices, and from manufacturers rather than wholesalers, causing clients to wait for their orders to be manufactured, and went through a costly and slow inspection process.

The tendency of CA employees to act in their own personal interest and against those of clients again increased from the early 1960s. The likelihood that the Agency would close down, leaving them unemployed, lessened the loyalty staff felt towards their employer, the Colonial Office's reluctance to monitor an organisation that served independent countries reduced the chances that fraud would be detected, and the move into secondary banking increased the opportunities for dishonesty and caused the ruling ethical norms to be degraded by those of City institutions. During the 1960s, Edward Morris appears to have given preferential treatment to a firm owned by John Cordle MP, A. L. McClure wrongly recommended the architect John Poulson to the Cypriot authorities, and various members of the Finance Directorate accepted gifts and loans from the businessmen Sidney Finley and William Stern. Some of these unethical actions, however, may have been partly motivated by a desire to help the Agency and its clients. The provision and acceptance of favours facilitates the generation of strong trust relationships, and Morris may have believed that his preferential treatment of E. W. Cordle & Son Ltd encouraged Cordle to defend the CAs in Parliament and to drum up orders for them during his frequent trips to West Africa.

Finally, the Agents' clients' position was weakened by the CAs occasionally favouring one colony over another, and the tendency of the Bank of England and the Colonial Office to follow their own unofficial and staff goals. The Agents acted against the interests of one colony in order to help another territory when they believed that the benefit obtained was greater than the cost. For example, when providing desperately needed inter-colonial loans to relatively poor colonies, they often favoured the borrowers by using the Sinking Funds of governments that had not agreed to participate in the programme and by setting relatively low interest rates. Likewise, during the 1931 financial crisis, in order to save the JCF, they sold the contents of some colonies' Sinking Funds at a loss.

Both the Bank of England and the Colonial Office sought to fulfil their own unofficial goals. Throughout the period, the Bank tried to increase its turnover and to capture all or some of the Agents' financial business, and, in doing so, harmed their clients. The Bank, for example, partly objected to the CAs setting high prices for their loans and issuing large amounts of stock during market upturns because the premium prices reflected badly on its own lower priced loans and the clogging of the market threatened the success of its issues. It opposed the CAs' campaign to abandon underwriting, in part, because it wished to retain the goodwill and business of underwriters; it failed to broach its concerns about the Agency to the Stevenson enquiry as it wanted to protect its policy of cheap money; and it allowed the Agency to continue to trade from May 1974 in order to relieve itself of the burden of supporting ailing secondary banks. The Colonial Office and its successors, meanwhile, sometimes gave greater priority to maintaining good relations with colonial governments than to acting in their best interests, and, from the early 1960s, tried to ensure its own survival. Colonial Office staff, for instance, in the 1930s allowed certain administrations to flout the colonial procurement regulations, and, from the early 1960s, made a number of attempts (some successful) to take over the Agents' work. A number of Bank of England and Colonial Office staff also appear to have fulfilled their own personal goals, again to the disadvantage of the CAs' clients. The Bank's governor Montagu Norman and Sir George Grindle, the Permanent Under Secretary, pursued personal vendettas against the Agent Sir Percy Ezechiel; in the late 1960s, personal dislike of Claude Hayes influenced the actions of a number of ODM officials; and, in the 1930s and the 1960s, two Parliamentary Under Secretaries at the Colonial Office required the Agents to employ firms of solicitors with whom they had personal connections.[7]

7 L 233, note on employment of solicitors, 27/11/79; WN 15, O E. Africa 13a & 13b.

Contribution of the CAs to the UK and client economies

The contribution the Agents made to their clients' and the UK economies during the colonial period is difficult to determine. As regards their financial duties, the issue of the colonies' loan stock and the investment of their Funds in the UK by the CAs allowed administrations to obtain most of the finance they required relatively cheaply and to earn relatively high returns. Most colonies had undeveloped capital markets; there were few advantages in issuing loans or keeping Funds in other currencies; and it is doubtful whether another UK financial institution could have fulfilled colonial financial needs better than the Agency. The use of the CAs for the issue of loans, the investment of Funds and the procurement of supplies also allowed the colonies to operate as a self-financing collective. The employment of colonial Investment Funds for the purchase of colonial loan stock ensured that issuing colonies received the money required and allowed the Funds to earn a relatively high rate of interest; in 1939 4.32 per cent as opposed to the 3.71 per cent earned on UK government stock. More importantly, it helped to maintain colonial credit and thus increased the public's demand for Crown colony stock, enabled the securities to be sold at a relatively high price, and permitted less well known territories, for whom the London market would otherwise have been closed, to make issues.

The fact that the Agents managed loan Sinking Funds and the JCF/JMF, meanwhile, allowed a portion of these Funds to be lent to colonies in the form of (respectively) inter-colonial loans and JCF/JMF advances. These loans and advances ensured that JCF/JMF depositors and Sinking Funds obtained a relatively high rate of return; reduced colonial demands on the London market, enabling Crown Colony credit to remain high; and permitted colonies that had little chance of successfully issuing loans on the market to obtain finance at a reasonable cost. They also allowed the Agents to direct capital to development projects that were economically viable and to colonies in most need of money; if used to pay for the early stages of infrastructure construction, increased the chances that a subsequent public loan to finance the whole project would be successful; and, in the case of JCF/JMF overdrafts, ensured that administrations always met their debts, which reduced the likelihood that suppliers and service providers would add a bad debt premium to their prices and fees.

On the other hand, the Bank of England's control of loan prices reduced the amount of money raised from issues, and the Treasury's and the Bank's insistence that Investment Funds be used to purchase large amounts of UK government stock and the Agents' switching inadequacies minimised investment returns. Although it is impossible to put a figure on the amounts lost, if it is assumed that the Bank's actions reduced loan prices by 0.5 and the Treasury's and the Bank's investment rulings and the Agents' poor management of Funds cut rates by a very conservative ½ per cent per annum, the colonies will have been deprived of £1.64m of loan receipts (1920 to 1965) and £68.4m worth of interest payments (1930 to 1960).

Looking at the Agents' financial activities from the UK's perspective, their use of the London market gave work to City institutions and increased the international status and importance of London as a financial centre. Colonial investments contributed to the support of sterling, and, through the purchase of HMG and Local Authority securities, helped to finance UK public sector expenditure, the issue of loans increased UK investor incomes, and the money raised by the Agents, by financing infrastructure construction and opening up territories for commercial development, ultimately increased the profits of British companies operating in the colonies and reduced the cost of primary imports to the UK.[8] On the distaff side, by making up the country's visible trade deficit, the income earned from colonial loans, along with that from other much larger foreign investments, allowed successive governments to postpone the reorganization of UK industry, which was to the long-term detriment of the economy.

It has also been argued that the £328.3m of colonial loans issued from 1920 to 1965 deprived UK industry of funds. However, there is little basis to this claim. There was relatively little demand for capital from British industry, and the UK money that did flow to the colonies did not constitute a loss.[9] Nine per cent of the stock issued (£21.96m) was converted from older higher interest securities and therefore involved no new expenditure, and the outflow of monies was matched by inflows in the form of interest payments, which amounted to £188m from 1926 to 1962, and the repayment of between £42m and £86m worth of old colonial loans. Moreover, much of the colonial stock issued, 63.7 per cent by the end of the colonial era, was purchased by colonial Investment Funds, and even greater outflows of capital were avoided by the CAs' provision of £24.6m of inter-colonial loans and up to £729.5m of JCF/JMF advances.

Turning to the Agents' procurement duties, although the goods purchased were relatively expensive, it seems unlikely that colonial administrations would have obtained cheaper materials from colonial merchants or direct from UK manufacturers. On the other hand, by depriving local merchants of government orders, the Agents probably slowed local economic development and the long delays in delivering orders undoubtedly carried a cost. For the UK, the purchase of up to £1.19bn of goods from 1920 to 1965 from UK manufacturers benefited the domestic economy. The Agents' existence and bias towards British supplies, however, also had a negative economic impact. Their presence made it more difficult for those colonial merchants who sold British goods to meet foreign competition and gave UK manufacturers little incentive to employ overseas representatives. Their UK bias diverted much needed materials away from the post-war British economy, slowing reconstruction, and, along with their reluctance to use competitive tender, helped to prop up declining and uncompetitive industries and delay industrial reorganization. Furthermore, it seems likely that colonial anger at the high prices charged for goods, along with their low investment returns and the low colonial loan prices, fuelled calls for independence,

8 In 1929, imports from the Crown colonies accounted for 4.5 per cent of all UK imports, in 1929 for 18.8 per cent, and, in 1961, for 12.5 per cent (Overseas Development Institute, *British, vol. 5*, p. 86).

9 G. C. Allen, *The British Disease*, London 1976, p. 33; Michael Ball and David Sunderland, *An Economic History of London, 1800–1914*, London 2001, pp. 350–51.

though whether the resultant loss of the colonies was beneficial or detrimental for the British economy is debatable.

As regards the Agents' other duties, these benefited both the colonies and the UK. It seems doubtful that any other institution could have recruited better quality expatriate staff or booked cheaper passages, and the various engineering services they provided did much to reduce the cost of infrastructure construction and to ensure that only economically viable projects were 'green lighted' and that the completed schemes were operated profitably. The UK economy, meanwhile, benefited from the employment of British contractors, Consulting Engineers and expatriate staff, though some argue that the loss of men to the Empire deprived British industry of managerial talent.[10] From 1920 to 1965, the CAs recruited at least 33,104 expatriate staff, arranged at least 479,584 passages on British lines for colonial officers traveling to and from the colonies, and made at least 5.23m salary and pension payments. The Agents themselves also provided employment to thousands of people and made a contribution to the Balance of Payments, earning at least £38.14m in fees.[11]

Decline and resurgence of the Agency

From the early 1960s, the Agency underwent a period of decline, largely because it was no longer advantageous for its clients to use its services. It was often not politically expedient to be seen doing business with the old Imperial power, and, in some cases, it was not in a former customer's economic interests. The Agents could no longer raise funds on the London market and their attempts to cut costs had damaged the quality of their work. Many colonial administrations also lacked the money or foreign currency to purchase UK goods or wished to have the freedom to operate against the interests of suppliers, by paying for materials late or not at all, and to act in their own interests, by buying goods from political supporters and only giving orders to companies that proffered bribes. The Agency survived by obtaining new clients, building closer trust relationships with their existing customers, improving the quality and the number of services offered, and entering the secondary banking sector.

The CAs' move into secondary banking was partly motivated by self-interest. The earnings from their new activities allowed them to build up a large contingency reserve and protect themselves against a sudden fall in receipts, and those who worked in the Finance Division gained great satisfaction from the performance of their new duties and a few obtained gifts and 'loans' from companies with whom they did business. A further reason for the initiative, however, was to help their clients. The income derived from the own account adventure subsidised the provision of traditional services, enabling them to be improved and

10 Bernard Porter, *The Lion's Share. A Short History of British Imperialism, 1850–1983*, London 1984, p. 355.

11 See Figure 7.1; CA (mc) 32; L 18, no. 11, Savage report, March 1962, p. 3, 4; CO 323/1107/13, memo, April 1930. Appointment date for 1941–4 and 1961–3, passage data for 1920–30, pension and salary data for 1920–2 and 1943–46 and CA revenue data for 1963–5 are missing.

extended; administrations that placed deposits in the Finvest account earned relatively high returns; and the companies in which FMI invested could assist in the development of their clients' economies. Unfortunately, the new venture was launched at an unpropitious time. The early 1970s property boom encouraged the Agents to expand their secondary banking activities far too rapidly and the 1974 secondary banking crash caused many of the companies in which they had invested to fail. By December 1974, the Agency was itself bankrupt, with debts of up to £200m, and there was an intense debate as to whether it should be allowed to continue trading.

It survived because it was believed that its disappearance was not in the interests of the government or of the UK. It provided valuable advice to the ODM, reduced the cost of providing essential services to the country's remaining dependencies, helped to link Britain with these territories and with the wider Commonwealth, ensured that bilateral aid was spent on British goods, and, through MTS, enabled the government to influence the supply of arms and thus avoid political embarrasement.[12] It also benefited UK finances and industry. If it ceased to exist, its clients would transfer the management of their Investment Funds to UK or foreign merchant banks, who would move money out of UK government securities and sterling investments, making it more difficult to finance government borrowing and weakening sterling.[13] At the same time, the Agency's fees made a contribution to the UK's invisible exports, and, if it closed, many former purchasers of British goods would turn to foreign manufacturers, weakening the Balance of Payments and damaging the viability of the old staple industries, the collapse of which could significantly raise unemployment.[14]

Having decided that they should continue trading, the government determined that the Agents should have a new constitution. Their quasi-government status was largely redundant, as the bulk of their business was conducted with independent countries, and, by linking them with the UK government, it discouraged some potential clients from using their services. After much discussion, in 1979, the Agency was incorporated as a statutory company monitored by and reporting to the Minister for Overseas Development, who also appointed its Board. Seventeen years later, it was given even more freedom when the undertakings and assets of the statutory corporation were transferred to a new private company managed by a Foundation, whose part-time members were drawn from academic institutions, charities, international development organizations and major companies.

Generally, this new constitution has worked well. Acutely aware of the failings of its recent past, the Agency today is professionally and efficiently run and well respected by the development community. Although the loss of the £3bn Brunei investment portfolio in 1983 reduced the size of its financial activities, it still provides various banking services, particularly in the areas of foreign exchange and money market dealing, manages investment portfolios, and provides investment advice. It also continues to purchase, inspect and ship goods, supply engi-

12 L 121, 1978 information papers, vol. 2, inf. 17/78; L 38, 1975, no. 66.

13 L 38, 1975, no. 66.

14 L 174, Luke to Wilson, 5 Sept. 1968; T 317/1498, report, approx. Sept. 1969.

neering information and train its clients' employees, and has taken on a number of new roles, including public debt management and Custom's modernization. Its success in all these fields is reflected by its annual turnover, £84.5m in 2004, and by the fact that it undertakes work for 147 countries and thirty international bodies and agencies, including the European Development Fund, the Japanese Ministry of Foreign Affairs, the Organisation for Economic Co-operation and Development, the Red Cross, the United Nations, the World Bank, and the World Health Organisation.[15] If its secondary banking venture had been successful, of course, its role in third world development would have been far greater and more significant. However, given its history, its survival and ability to continue to help its clients is itself a remarkable achievement.

15 *CA Annual Review, 2005.*

Appendices

Appendix 1. The Crown Agents, 1920–74

Name	Service as CAs	Education	Previous career
Cameron, Sir Maurice Alexander (1855–1936)	1895–1920	Wellington College; Royal Military Academy	Colonial service
Mercer, Sir William Hepworth (1855–1932)	1900–21	Wadham College, Oxford; Inner Temple	Colonial Office
Thornton, Sir Hugh Cholmondeley (1881–1962)	1920–43	Kelly College, Tavistock; Christ Church College, Oxford	Colonial Office
Ezechiel, Sir Percy Hubert (1875–1950)	1920–37	Bombay; Trinity College, Cambridge	Colonial Office/Crown Agents
Carmichael, Lieut-Col. Sir James Forrest Halkett (1868–1934)	1921–32	Clifton College; Royal Military Academy	Crown Agents
Lambert, Sir Henry Charles Miller (1868–1935)	1921–32	Eton; New College, Oxford	Colonial Office
Fleming, Colonel John Gibson (1880–1936)	1932–36	Haileybury College; Royal Military Academy	Army
Gowers, Sir William Frederick (1875–1954)	1932–8	Rugby; Cambridge University	Colonial service
Bottomley, Sir William Cecil (1878–1954)	1938–43	Tettenhall College; Owens College, Manchester; Trinity College, Cambridge	Colonial Office
Flood, John Ernest William (1886–1940)	1938–40	Portora Royal School, Enniskillen; Trinity College, Dublin	Civil Service/Colonial Office
Calder, Sir John Alexander (1889–1974)	1942–53	Grove and Harris Academies, Dundee; Edinburgh University	Colonial Office
Downie, Sir Harold Frederick (1889–1966)	1943–53	Christ's Hospital; University College, Oxford	Colonial Office
Seel, Sir George Frederick (1895–1976)	1953–59	King's School, Macclesfield; Corpus Christi College, Oxford	Colonial Office
Stooke, Sir George Beresford (1897–1973)	1953–55	Not known	Colonial service
Savage, Sir Alfred William Lungley (1903–1980)	1955–63	Owens School, London	Civil Service/Colonial service
Luke, Sir Stephen Elliot Vyvyan (1905–1988)	1959–68	St George's School, Harpenden; Wadham College, Oxford.	Civil Service/Colonial Office

Farquarson, Sir James Robbie (1903-)	1963–65	Royal Technical College, Glasgow; Glasgow University	Colonial service/ Crown Agents
Bawden, William George	1963–4	Okehampton Grammar School	Crown Agents
Morris, Edward Allan (1910–1997)	1964–70	Hampton Grammer School; LSE	Crown Agents
Hawtrey, John Havilland Procter (1905–)	1965–69	Eton; City and Guilds Engineering College; London University	Colonial service/ Crown Agents
Hayes, Sir Claude James (1912–1996)	1968–75	Ardingly College; St Edmund Hall, Oxford; Sorbonne; New College Oxford	Civil Service/ Treasury/ Colonial Office
Cuckney, Baron John Graham (1925–)	1974–78	Shrewsbury; University of St Andrews	MI5; private sector

Source. *Who Was Who*, London 2001; CA (m) 64, Past CAs, no date.

Appendix 2. Market finance, 1914–68 (£m)

	Publicly issued loans	Loans sold to market	IC Loans	Conversions	Guaranteed loans	Total	Average price	Local loans	Public revenues, 1950
East Africa									
EA High Commission	42.99	2.95	3.50	10.76		60.20	93.57	0.25	
Kenya	33.69	10.53		2.10		46.31	98.60	3.60	13.72
Somaliland									1.13
Tanganyika (Tanzania)	9.16	3.28		1.75	5.57	19.76	97.16		11.60
Uganda	15.08	0.85	0.34			16.28	96.38		11.04
Zanzibar (Tanzania)									1.66
Total	100.91	17.61	3.84	14.62	5.57	142.55	96.42	3.85	
Central Africa									
N. Rhodesia (Zambia)	13.66	1.25		1.25		16.16	97.18		12.16
Nyasaland (Malawi)	2.06				3.57	5.63	98.50		3.55
Total	15.72	1.25		1.25	3.57	21.79	97.84		
West Africa									
Gambia			0.04			0.04	97.00		0.98
Gold Coast (Ghana)	10.83	0.05		2.56		13.45	99.31		20.57
Nigeria	36.46	0.51	0.05	6.80		43.81	100.14		32.79
Sierra Leone	2.03	2.03	0.80	0.88		5.74	97.14		3.27
Total	49.33	2.59	0.89	10.24		63.04	98.40		
Southern Africa									
Basutoland (Lesotho)			0.51			0.51	99.50		
Bechuanaland (Botswana)			1.08			1.08	100.29		
Total			1.59			1.59	99.90		

Northern Africa									
Sudan					13.64	13.64	n/k		
Atlantic									
Falkland islands									0.22
St Helena									0.09
Total									
Mediterranean									
Cyprus	3.16	5.31	0.21			8.67	91.79	3.00	6.17
Gibraltar								1.40	0.82
Malta								1.20	5.72
Total	3.16	5.31	0.21			8.67	91.79	5.60	
Middle East									
Aden		1.33				1.33	98.00		1.32
Palestine					4.48	4.48	n/k		
Total		1.33			4.48	5.81	98.00		
Indian Ocean									
Ceylon (Sri Lanka)	13.26	0.45		3.06		16.76	96.48	9.55	
Mauritius	6.80	0.58	0.21	0.06	0.60	8.24	98.22	2.65	4.62
Seychelles			0.03			0.03	99.50		0.38
Total	20.06	1.03	0.23	3.12	0.60	25.04	98.07	12.20	
Far East									
Hong Kong								1.92	18.23
S.E. Asia									
Federation of Malaya	12.72	7.09	7.00	1.71	1	28.51	94.40	25.60	51.73

N. Borneo (Sabah)			2.44			2.44	n/k		2.52
Sarawak			2.40			2.40	n/k		3.66
Singapore								13.40	12.90
Straits Settlements	9.36					9.36	96.00		
Total	22.07	7.09	11.84	1.71	0.00	42.71	95.20	39.00	
Western Pacific									
British Solomon Islands									0.40
Fiji	0.77	0.33	0.33			1.42	99.56	1.00	2.80
Gilbert and Ellice Islands									0.26
New Hebrides		0.45				0.45	100.00		0.21
Tonga									0.28
Total	0.77	0.78	0.33	0.00	0.00	1.87	99.78	1.00	
West Indies									
Bahamas								1.00	1.58
Barbados	5.36	0.16				5.52	97.59	0.60	2.54
British Guiana (Guyana)	7.72	2.95	0.33	1.35		12.34	98.17	2.77	4.74
British Honduras (Belize)			0.84			0.84	98.11	0.10	1.34
Cayman Islands			0.13			0.13	96.50		0.07
Jamaica	30.22	2.00	0.95	0.34		33.51	97.35	8.00	11.24
Trinidad	10.67	2.80				13.47	95.58	2.70	10.55
Turks and Caicos									0.08
Total	53.97	7.90	2.24	1.69	0.00	65.81	97.22	15.17	

Leeward and Windward Islands									
Antigua		0.47	0.00			0.47	100.00	0.01	0.65
Dominica	0.44					0.44	95.00	0.01	0.33
Grenada		0.78	0.11			0.88	97.71		0.79
Montserrat			0.04			0.04	102.00		0.09
St Kitts and Nevis	0.41		0.00			0.41	99.50		0.47
St Lucia	0.42	1.06	0.12			1.59	97.36		0.67
St Vincent	0.32		0.03			0.35	96.96		0.37
British Virgin Islands									0.03
Total	1.57	2.30	0.29	0.00	0.00	4.17	98.36	0.01	

Source. See Figures 1.1 and 2.1. Guaranteed Loans: CAOG 9/32, list, 31 Dec. 1953; Constantine, *The Making*, p. 296. Local Loans: OV 44/72, No. 39d, table 1; S 1, A156; *ibid.*, A166; *ibid.*, A169; *ibid.*, A239; *ibid.*, A240; S 3, A853; S 4, A1138; S 5, A1230; CAOG 9/330, memo, 1 Aug. 1944; WN 13, summaries of loan files still current and held by B6; *ibid.*, A414802; *ibid.*, A1770. Public revenue, 1950: PP 1951/2, 24.

Appendix 3. Non-market finance, 1920–65 (£m)

	D & W grants & loans	Grants & loans-in-aid	Exchequer loans	ECGD loans	Total	CDC investment	Local resources
Africa							
General	0.58	1.11			1.70		
East Africa							
Non-country specific	17.03	3.59	8.50	2.05	31.17		
EA High Commission							
Kenya	22.25	59.98	22.06		104.29	7.89	27.12
Somaliland	3.10	9.82			12.92		
Tanganyika (Tanzania)	15.70	9.99	3.50	1.25	30.44	6.98	13.87
Uganda	6.01	5.74	11.25	2.40	25.40	1.63	51.60
Zanzibar (Tanzania)	1.82	2.86			4.68		1.67
Total	65.91	91.98	45.31		203.20	16.50	94.27
Central Africa							
Non-country specific	3.53				3.53		
Fed. of Rhodesia and Nyasaland				5.00	5.00		
N. Rhodesia (Zambia)	5.57	2.36	3.00		10.93	1.40	14.75
Nyasaland (Malawi)	9.71	16.01	3.00		28.72	3.99	1.40
Total	18.80	18.37	6.00		43.17	5.39	16.15
West Africa							
Non-country specific	4.44				4.44		
Gambia	4.72	1.90			6.62		0.55
Gold Coast (Ghana)	4.06			7.17	11.23	0.12	143.40
Nigeria	39.75	4.08	3.00	23.50	70.33	5.53	195.33

Republic of Cameroon						1.00	
Sierra Leone	8.20	3.20	3.00	3.50	17.90	0.83	6.84
Total	61.17	9.18	6.00		76.35	7.49	346.11
Southern Africa							
Non-country specific	0.46				0.46		
Basutoland (Lesotho)	4.38	6.18	0.41		10.97		
Bechuanaland (Botswana)	6.44	8.78	1.09		16.31	0.77	
Southern Rhodesia		6.25	3.86		10.10	1.00	
Swaziland	6.39	3.35	2.16		11.90	16.44	
Total	17.66	24.56	7.51		49.73	18.20	
Northern Africa							
Sudan		0.50			0.50		
Atlantic							
Falkland Islands	0.36	4.31			4.67		0.33
St Helena	0.75	1.56			2.30		0.02
Tristan da Cunha	0.12				0.12		
Total	1.23	5.87			7.10		0.35
Mediterranean							
Cyprus	2.50	37.38	1.10	2.00	42.98		5.19
Gibraltar	1.60				1.60		1.22
Malta	21.98	43.41	2.20		67.60		4.05
Total	26.09	80.79	3.30		110.18		10.46
Middle East							
Aden	8.58	12.22	1.00		21.80		10.12
Fed. of Arab Emirates		0.29			0.29		
Iraq		1.73			1.73		

Kamaran		0.02			0.02		
Palestine	0.02	12.42			12.44		
S. Arabia Protectorate		8.24			8.24		
Trans-Jordan		10.59			10.59		
Total	8.60	45.52	1.00		55.12		10.12
Indian Ocean							
Ceylon (Sri Lanka)				2.50	2.50		
Mauritius	4.23	4.65	1.51		10.39		16.01
Seychelles	2.12	0.51			2.63		0.19
Total	6.35	5.17	1.51		13.02		16.19
Far East							
Hong Kong	1.82	5.21			7.02	0.24	
Far Eastern Territories War Damage Compensation Scheme		36.52			36.52		
Wei-Hei-Wei		0.04			0.04		
Total	1.82	41.76			43.57	0.24	
SE Asia							
Non-country specific	0.37				0.37		
Christmas Island		0.02			0.02		
Federation of Malaya	5.22	39.16		2.25	46.64	10.95	11.38
N. Borneo (Sabah)	7.51	3.97			11.48		13.72
Sarawak	5.71	0.01			5.73	4.03	32.67
Singapore	2.59				2.59	0.06	129.02
Straits Settlements (Malaysia)							
Total	21.41	43.16			64.57	15.05	186.78

Western Pacific							
Non-country specific	0.07				0.07		
British Solomon Islands	3.49	4.15			7.64		0.83
Fiji	6.99	0.02	2.00		9.01	0.27	6.77
Gilbert and Ellice Islands	0.96	0.38			1.34		0.26
New Hebrides	0.92	0.01			0.93		0.00
Pitcairn	0.03				0.03		
Tonga	0.01	0.07	0.00		0.08		
Total	12.46	4.63	2.00		19.08	0.27	7.86
West Indies							
Non-country specific	13.03	6.64			19.67		
Bahamas	0.01				0.01		
Barbados	2.30	0.06			2.36		10.16
British Guiana (Guyana)	12.40	6.50	1.25		20.15	1.98	6.89
British Honduras (Belize)	7.22	5.65	1.22		14.08	0.28	0.12
Cayman Islands	0.22				0.22	0.03	
Jamaica	9.43	6.82	1.25		17.50	6.08	8.46
Trinidad	1.62	0.89			2.51	1.80	2.83
Turks and Caicos	0.41	0.51			0.92		
Total	46.63	27.06	3.72		77.41	10.17	28.45
Leeward and Windward Islands							
Non-country specific	1.01	0.03			1.04		
Antigua	2.39	1.86			4.25		0.15
Dominica	3.24	2.37			5.61	0.42	
Grenada	1.90	4.27			6.17	0.29	0.63

Montserrat	0.67	1.44			2.11		0.00
St Kitts and Nevis	1.75	0.69			2.44		1.05
St Lucia	3.85	2.60			6.45		
St Vincent	2.27	1.65			3.92	0.45	0.40
British Virgin Islands	0.47	1.46			1.93		
Total	17.55	16.36			33.91	1.15	2.22
Non-country specific	18.29				18.29	0.02	

Source. PP 1966/7, 52; Civil Appropriation Accounts, 1920–65 (see bibliography); PP 1970–71, 8, p. 50, table 4; Overseas Development Institute, *British Aid. Volume 2*, p. 75; PP 1964/5, 22; PP 1954/5, 4; PP 1956/7, 10; PP 1961/2, 11.

Notes. D & W grants and loans, 1946–65; Grants and loans-in-aid, 1920–65; Exchequer loans, 1959–65; ECGD loans to 31/3/64; CDC Investment, 1948-Dec. 1963. Local resources = Amount allocated to local resources in development plans 1946–64 (includes local loans in Appendix 1).

Appendix 4. 1954 Investment Funds (£m), Wartime gifts and loans (£m), 1936 procurement (£m) and 1954 colonial appointments

	Investment Funds, 1954	Gifts to HMG, 1939–45	Loans to HMG, 1939–45	Procurement, 1936	Appointments, 1954
East Africa					
Non-country specific			0.014		131
East African High Commission					36
Kenya	53.2	0.386	2.958	2.025	405
Somaliland		0.008		0.560	2
Tanganyika (Tanzania)	37	0.421	0.374	2.127	49
Uganda	85.5	0.302	0.702	1.491	45
Zanzibar (Tanzania)		0.041	0.003	0.564	5
Total	175.7	1.158	4.051	6.767	673
Central Africa					
N. Rhodesia (Zambia)		0.41	2.127	0.805	87
Nyasaland (Malawi)		0.164	0.534	0.593	87
Total		0.574	2.661	1.398	174
West Africa					
Gambia	7	0.011	0.028	0.688	8
Gold Coast (Ghana)	111.5	0.362	1.022	4.051	25
Nigeria	179.2	0.409	0.493	3.626	195
Sierra Leone	12	0.149	0.102	0.998	18
Total	309.7	0.931	1.645	9.363	246
Southern Africa					
Basutoland (Lesotho)			0.13	0.224	
Bechuanaland (Botswana)			0.071	0.262	

Cape Coast				0.012	
Swaziland				0.155	
Total			0.201	0.653	
Atlantic					
Falkland Islands		0.072	0.002	0.204	12
St Helena		0.006	0.004	0.125	
Total		0.078	0.006	0.329	12
Mediterranean					
Cyprus	16.7	0.013	1.496	0.624	5
Gibraltar	3.5	0.058	1.17	0.314	
Malta	36.9	0.035		0.608	3
Total	57.1	0.106	2.666	1.546	8
Middle East					
Aden	4.5	0.077	0.405	0.006	13
Iraq				0.701	
Palestine		0.039	0.707	2.002	
Trans-Jordan				0.330	
Total	4.5	0.116	1.112	3.039	13
Indian Ocean					
Ceylon (Sri Lanka)		1.096	5.875	2.403	
Mauritius	14.6	0.302	0.344	0.771	
Seychelles		0.016	0.015	0.221	
Total	14.6	1.414	6.234	3.395	
SE Asia					
Brunei	26.7			0.036	
Federated Malay States	123.5	7.115	2.028	3.795	28
Hong Kong	79.3	0.4		0.700	48

N Borneo (Sabah)	5.8	0.038		0.144	2
Sarawak	14.5	0.316	0.233		6
Singapore	76.8			0.065	3
Straits		9.479	0.059	1.819	
Total	326.6	17.348	2.32	6.659	87
Western Pacific					
British Solomon Islands				0.081	1
Fiji	9.9	0.169	0.512	0.615	1
Gilbert and Ellice Islands				0.064	4
New Hebrides				0.013	
Tonga				0.069	
Total				0.842	6
West Indies					
Bahamas	2.8	0.125	0.45	0.188	1
Barbados	6.2	0.202	0.033	0.210	
Bermuda	4.6	0.344	1.15	0.146	10
British Guiana (Guyana)	12.5	0.129	0.417	0.987	3
British Honduras (Belize)	0.9	0.027		0.222	
Cayman Islands					
Jamaica	17.3	0.223	0.285	1.135	
Trinidad	24.1	0.929	1.681	1.285	4
Turks and Caicos				0.027	
Total	68.4	1.979	4.016	4.200	18

Leeward and Windward Islands	0.8	0.095		1.778	1
Newfoundland				0.112	
Others				1.591	42

Source. Investment funds: T 236/3562. Gifts: PP 1947, 162. Loans: CAOG 9/318, loans to HMG recorded in CAs' books as at 31 March 1945. Procurement: CAOG 12/40, memo, approx. 1936. Appointments: CAOG 13/148, memo, 1 Nov. 1955; *ibid.*, memo, 11 Nov. 55

Notes. Investment Funds include Currency Funds managed by Currency Boards. Gifts: Federated Malay States denotes Federated and Unfederated Malay States.

Appendix 5. CA's own account activities

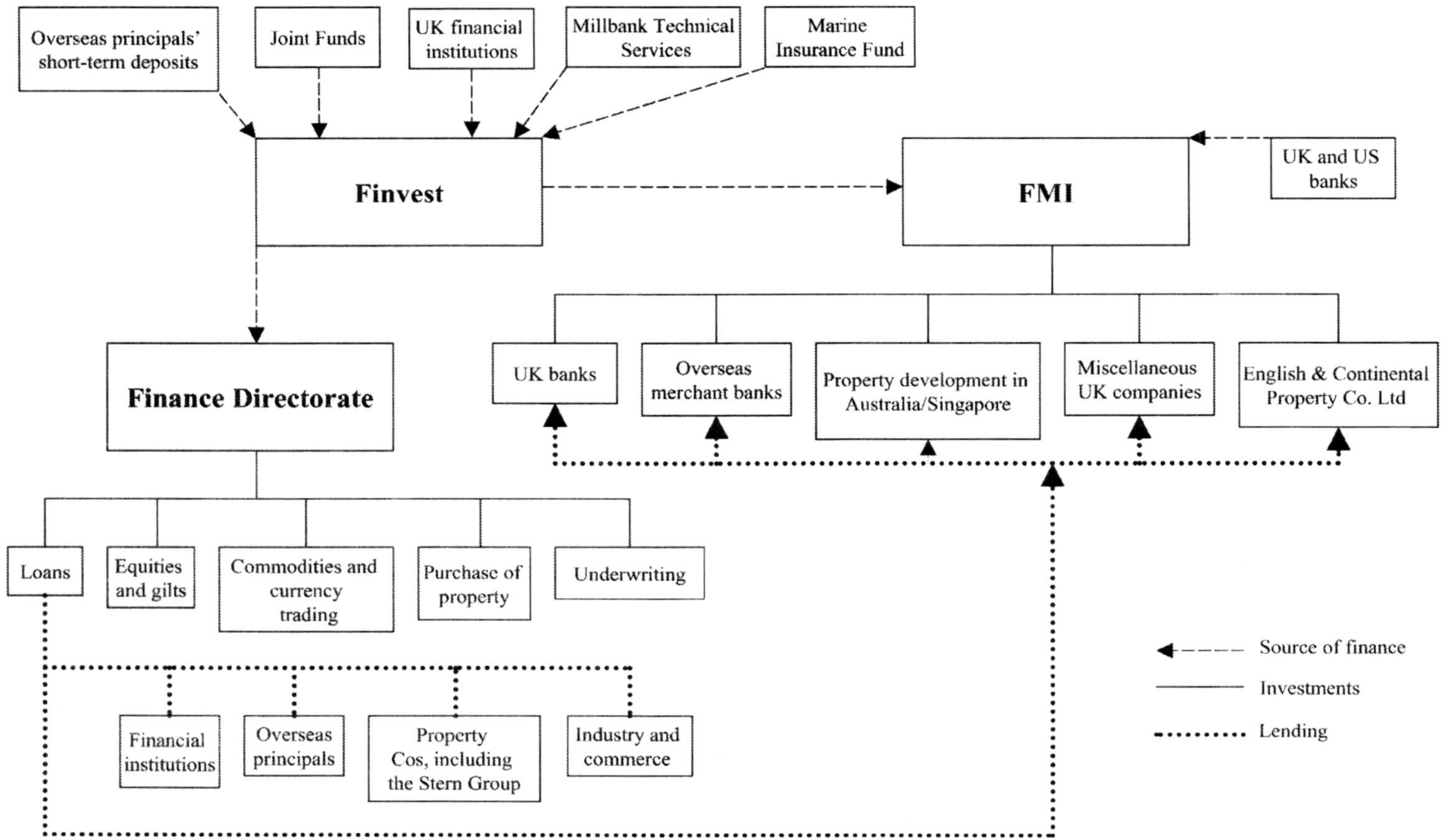

Appendix 6. FMI investment in associated companies, 1969–74

Company	CAs' initial investment	Activity	Benefit to principals	Notes
Abbey Orchard Property Investments	33 pc	Australian property company	1 Increased CA reserves 2 Allowed direct client investment in the Australian property boom	One of the largest property developers in Australia.
Amscot Oceanic Ltd	£500,000	Oil company	Development of oil resources	Co-investors: KCA Drilling Group Ltd, Atwood Oceanic Inc., UK government. Engaged in offshore oil rig contracting, chiefly in the North Sea, in pipe laying and in rig and barge construction.
Associated Railway Consultants Ltd	50 pc	Railway consultancy	Improved advice on railway matters	Co-investor: engineering consultant Livesey & Henderson Ltd. In 1969 the World Bank expressed an interest in using the company.
Britannia Studios International Ltd	13 pc	Provision of visual, sound and other facilities for film making in Malta	Promotion of the local economy	—
British Bangladeshi Trust (renamed London Capital Group)	£100,000 plus £350,000 loan	Provision of banking services to the Bangladesh community and British companies wishing to trade with Bangladesh	1 Promotion of development in Bangladesh. 2 Increased demand for CAs' procurement and engineering services	Co-investors: De La Rue, Plessy, Guest Keen & Nettlefolds, Balli International .
Caribbean Bank Ltd	40 pc	W. Indies merchant bank	1 Increased CA reserves 2 Promotion of private capital market	Co-investor: Continental Illinois, the USA's seventh largest bank and highly regarded by the Bank of England. Profits (1972) $169,759.

Caribbean Bank (Cayman) Ltd		Cayman Islands merchant bank	1 Increased CA reserves 2 Promotion of private capital market	—
CGA Capital Corp.	N/K	Canadian merchant bank	Increased CA reserves	Co-investors included Jack Gilbert QC, E. D. Sassoon Banking Co. Ltd.
Chenderiang Tin Dredging Ltd (later CTD Resources Group Ltd)	32 pc	Mining investment house	Co-ordination of the exploitation of natural resources	Co-investors: K. McMahon Group, Ivory & Sime, Pexamin Inc. (US oil company). Profits (1971) £85,000. In 1974 took a shareholding in Petroleum Exploration & Development Co. Ltd, which owned offshore concessions in East and West Africa.
Commercial Continental Ltd	20 pc	Australian merchant bank	Increased CA reserves	Co-investors: Continental Illinois, Credit Commercial de France, Commercial Banking Co. of Sydney, Mutual Life & Citizens Assurance Co., Sanwa Bank of Japan.
Crown Cassettes Ltd	30 pc	Production of video cassettes	Promotion of education	Co-investors: Longmans Penguin, Industrial Commercial & Finance Corp., and TDC Ltd. Surridge Dawson & Co., the UK's third largest newspaper distributor; Cable & Wireless; Macmillans; Associated Newspapers; Collins; the Thompson Organization; W. H. Smith & Son Ltd and IPC Business Press all expressed an interest in taking a stake in the company when Longmans Penguin pulled out.
Crown Communications Ltd	N/K	Design and operation of satellite earth stations	Provision of advice on satellite communications	Co-investor: British Post Office.
Crown Continental Merchant Bank Jamaica Ltd	N/K	Jamaican merchant bank	1 Increased CA reserves 2 Promotion of private capital market	Profits (1972) $142,613. In 1972 the company acquired control of the Jamaica Building Society in partnership with the Commonwealth Development Corporation.

Development Bank of Singapore	N/K	Provision of development finance	1 Promotion of development in Singapore 2 Increased demand for CAs' procurement and engineering services	—
Diebold Group Ltd	10 pc (later 27.8 pc)	Provision of management consultancy services	1 Improvement of public administration 2 Services could be used by MTS in major projects	Co-investors: Australia & NZ Bank, Hanover Trust Co., Industrial Bank of Japan. Declared insolvent in Jan. 1973.
Eastern Copper Mines Ltd	£950,000	Australian mining company	Development of natural resources	—
English & Continental Investments Ltd	11 pc	UK property company	Increased CA reserves	Co-investors: Continental Illinois, Ramone Green, ICI pension fund, various individuals. Directors included two senior partners in Caplan Hay & Co., a leading firm of surveyors; the senior partner of Silver Altman & Co., the City solicitors; and Brien Levy, another well-known City solicitor.
English & Continental Property Co. Ltd	51 pc plus loans	UK property company with two Cypriot subsidiaries	1. Increased CA reserves 2. Cypriot property development	Co-investors: Ramon and Lionel greene, 'two personalities … with considerable experience in the field of commercial property', and J. J. Walker, CA solicitor. Loans obtained from leading merchant banks (including Singer & Friedlander Ltd, Barclays, London International Ltd, Bank of Adelaide, Standard Bank, Bank of Scotland, Rothschild Intercontinental Bank, Bank of Tokyo) and commercial companies (including Massey Ferguson, Imperial Metal Industries, ICI, Whitbread, Allied brewers).

Fenston syndicate	N/A	Australian property development	Increased CA reserves	F. Fenston was 'a well known property developer in the UK'. Other syndicate members were Prince Stanislaus Radziwell, one time husband of Lee Bouvier, sister of Jacqueline Kennedy Onassis, and L. M. F. Rawlence, a Chartered Surveyor and estate agent.
First National Finance Corporation Ltd	4.9 pc (later 10 pc)	UK secondary bank	Increased CA reserves	Co-investors: the electricity supply industry's pension fund, Hambros, Phoenix Insurance Co. Chairman: Viscount De L'Isle, a former Governor General of Australia. Directors included Jocelyn Hambro, Chairman of Hambros. FNFC was well regarded by the Bank of England, operating the banking rump of London & County with the Bank in 1974.
Greenshields Cowie & Co Ltd	100 pc	Liverpool based shipping agency	Improved CA services	—
Hartog Oil Ltd	N/K	Oil company	Development of oil resources	—
ILCO Holdings Ltd	25 pc	Development bank	1 Promotion of development in Singapore and SE Asia 2 Increased demand for the CAs' procurement and engineering services 3 The connection with Charles Letts and Barclays Unicorn Trust benefited Singapore International Merchant Banking Co. and the CAs' portfolio investments in the region.	Co-investors: Investico Overseas Holdings Ltd, John Swires & Sons, Commonwealth Development Finance Co. Ltd plus two Singapore groups. Holding sold Jan. 1973.

Inter City Investment & Holding Co. Ltd	11.4 pc	Finance	Increased CA reserves	Co-investor: E. D. Sassoons Banking Co.
International Hotels Kenya Ltd	4 pc	Operation of hotels	Promotion of economic growth	Co-investors: El Al Airways, Kenya Tourist Development Corp., Nairobi Hilton Co.
Inter Service Mediterranean Ltd	32 pc	N/K	Increased CA reserves	Co-investors: Sydney Finlay; Douglas Hurn, Morris Stanton.
Kayloch Overseas Ltd	85 pc	Finance	Increased CA reserves	A subsidiary of E. D. Sassoons Banking Co.
KCA Drilling Group Ltd	10 pc	Oil mining company	Development of natural resources	Holding sold July 1974.
Keyser Ullman	410,000 shares	UK merchant bank	Increased CA reserves	Co-investor: Prudential Insurance Co. Chairman: Edward du Cann MP.
Malaysian Industrial Development Finance Corp.	N/K	Investment company	Promotion of development in Malaysia	Co-investors: Malayan Banking Corp, Continental Illinois, Yong Pung How, Malaysian Industrial Development Corp.
Malaysian International Merchant Bankers Berhad	24 pc plus £500,000 credit line	Malaysian merchant bank	1 Increased CA reserves 2 Promotion of private capital market	Co-investor: Continental Illinois. Held large holding in the S.E. Asia Development Corporation. Profits (1972) $516,765.
Metro Industries Ltd (W. Australian company)	27.7 pc	Industrial holding company	Increased CA reserves	Interests ranged over hotels, steel, hardware, neon signs, instruments, retailing, truck sales and plastics. Profits (1972) $657,882.
Moorgate Mercantile	£253,000	Secondary bank	Increased CA reserves	—
Nairobi Hilton Hotel	N/K	Hotel	Promotion of economic growth	—
Northern Commercial Trust Ltd	2.5 pc	Secondary bank	Increased CA reserves	Co-investors included Authority Investments (joint owner Lord Lever, former Labour Cabinet Minister). Chairman: Sir John Foster QC, a former Conservative MP.

Orchard Square Development Corp. Ltd	75 pc	Singapore property company	1 Increased CA reserves 2 Promotion of development	Co-investors: Town & Commercial Properties, J. J. Walker.
Questel Ltd	26 pc (later 33 pc)	Development of new computer technology for the capture of information	Use in medical research	Co-investors: Wm Brandt (merchant bank), UKPI. Sold in Oct. 1972.
Rowan International Fund	£500,000	European unit trust	Increased CA reserves	Established by Rowe and Pitman. Co-investor: Scottish Provident.
Rowe & Pitman Management Ltd	N/K	Stock brokers	Aided investment of principals' and own account funds	'London's premier stockbrokers'. Clientele included the Royal family.
E. D. Sassoon Banking Co. Ltd	40 pc	UK merchant bank	1 Increased CA reserves 2 Improved provision of traditional financial services	Co-investors: Ralph Yablon, Sassoon family, Continental Illinois. In 1968 Barclays bank expressed an interest in taking a stake in the company. Management team included two former directors of Hill Samuels and a former Bank of England official.
SIFIDA	1.2 pc	Investment company	1 Promotion of private investment in Africa 2 Increased demand for CAs' procurement and engineering services	Co-investors: Barclays bank, Booker McConnell Ltd, British American Tobacco, Dunlop Group, Midland bank, Morgan Grenfell, Standard bank, Mitchell Cotts Group.
Singapore International Merchant Bank Ltd	24 pc	Singapore merchant bank	1 Increased CA reserves 2 Promotion of private capital market	Co-Investors: Overseas Chinese Banking Corp., Continental Illinois, Yong Pung How. In Feb. 1974 acquired 24 pc participation of Singapore-Japan merchant bank. Profits (1972) $495,346.
Southern Pacific Properties	£105,000	Property company	Promotion of development	Co-investors: P and O, Jardine Mathieson, Slater Walker.

Stanley Gibbons Ltd	40 pc	Retail sale of stamps	Expertise increased sale of principals' stamps and their incomes	Profits (1972) £141,600.
Sterling Industrial Securities Ltd	33 pc	UK finance house	Increased CA reserves	Co-investors: S. Davidson and S. Finley, financiers, and later Eagle Star Insurance, N.M. Rothschilds & Sons, Franklin National Bank of New York. Chairman: Lord Mais, former Lord Mayor of London and a director of the Royal Bank of Scotland. Profits (1972) £490,000.
Television Recordings Ltd	44 pc	Production of television programmes	Improvement and development of CAs' advisory services	Co-investors: Marine Enterprises, Scaffolding (GB) Ltd. Profit (1968) £38,000. In 1971 a merger with London Weekend Television was discussed.
Toronto & London Investment Co.	10 pc	Finance house	Increased CA reserves	Co-investors: S. G. Warburg ,Jonlab, Samuel Montagu, the Lowson Group of companies..
Tradewinds Airways Ltd	45 pc	Air charter company	Provision of low rate charter services for West Africa	In Aug. 1973 entered co-operation scheme with British Airways. Profits (1973) £19,000.
Westralian International Ltd	17 pc	Australian merchant bank	1 Increased CA reserves 2 Improved local equity investment	Co-investors: Continental Illinois, State Savings Bank of Victoria, Credit Lyonnais, Sassoons, Alexander Discount, Rural & Industries Bank of W. Australia, Mutual Life & Citizens Assurance Co., Western Industries. Profits (1972) $375,000.

Sources. HO 268/378, memo, 29 Sept. 1970; *ibid.*, memo, 17 Dec. 1970. Abbey Orchard; L 35, 1971, no. 19; *Guardian*, 5 May 1971, p. 13; Amscot: HO 268/378, memo, 22 Aug. 1973; L 50, minutes, 23 July 1973; Associated Railway: L 41, 1969 FMI accounts; L 35, 25 May 1969; Britannia Studios: CAOG 21/188; British Bangladesh: L 8, FMI, Nov 1972; Croom-Johnson Tribunal. Documentary Evidence, b/odm/1/14a, p. 242, Pearson, 28 Nov. 1972; Press clippings, Daily Telegraph, 20 Nov. 1972); PP 1977–8, 8, p. 113; Caribbean Bank: PP 1977–8, 8, p. 30; L 50, minutes, 21 Aug. 1969; *ibid.,* minutes, 26 March 1973; L 227, Statement of K. W. Barley, 23 Feb. 1978; HO 268/509, Luke to Hayes, 1 Sept. 1967; Caribbean Bank (Cayman): CAOG 21/186, memo 25 March 1971; CGA: L 35, 5 June 1973 meeting; Chenderiang: HO 268/378, Oct. 1971; *ibid.*, memo, 19 March 1974; CAOG 21/188; L50, minutes, 1 Sept. 1971; Commercial: PP 1977–8, 8, p. 30; Crown Cassettes: CAOG 9/295, Clark to Lord Hill, BBC, 4 Feb. 1971; *ibid.*, Hayes to Faint, 7 Jan. 1971; *ibid.*, Wightman to Challis/Clark, no date; L 41, 1970 FMI accounts; Crown Communications: L 76, overseas trade memo no. 28/69, 15 Oct. 1969; Crown Continental: L 50, minutes, 29 Nov. 1971; *ibid.*, minutes, 24 April 1972; *ibid.*, minutes, 17 Dec. 1973; Development Bank: CAOG 24/16, Ministry of Finance to CAs, 19 March 1969; Diebold: CAOG 21/188; L 41, 1970 FMI accounts; L 50, minutes, 3 Jan. 1973; Eastern Copper: L 50, minutes, 12 Feb. 1970; L 5, F Dept., Nov. 1969; English & Continental investments: L 118/5, p. 200; L 50, minutes, 3 Sept. 1973; *ibid.*, papers, 30 April 1973; English & Continental Property: CAOG 21/126, Osgodby, 29 Aug. 1974; PP 1977–8, 8 pp. 28–9; PP 1981–2, 364, p. 88; CAOG 21/186, memo, approx. Jan. 1972; *Guardian*, 5 Aug. 1971, p. 7; Fenston: PP 1981–2, 364 p. 63; Press clippings, *Investors Review*, 9–20 Dec. 1977; FNFC: PP 1981–2, 364, p. 142; Reid, *The Secondary*, p. 36, 45; Croom-Johnson Tribunal. Documentary Evidence, b/ca/6/2, p. 57, Wheately, 20 May 1969; Kynaston, *The City … Vol. iv*, p. 460; Charles Gordon, *The Cedar Story. The Night the City was Saved*, London 1993, p. 292; Greenshields: HO 268/378, memo, 20 Nov. 1974; ILCO: HO 268/378, memo, 22 Jan. 1973; L 50, minutes, 29 March 1971; CAOG 21/188; Inter City: L 41, 1970 FMI accounts; International Hotels: T 317/1498, report, approx. Sept. 1970; Interservice: L 41, 1969 FMI accounts; Hartog: L 50, minutes, 12 Feb. 1970; KCA: HO 268/378, memo, 22 Aug. 1973; *ibid.*, memo, 22 July 1974; Keyser: L 50, minutes, 1 July 1974; *ibid.*, 1 July 1974; Kynaston, *The City … Vol. iv*, p. 462; Malaysian Industrial: L 50, minutes, 24 Sept. 1973; *ibid.*, 25 June 1973; Malaysian International: HO 268/378, April 1972; PP 1977–8, 8, p. 30; L 50, minutes, 28 June 1971; *ibid.*, 26 March 1973; Metro: HO 268/378, memo, 20 Feb. 1973; L 50, minutes, 30 April 1973; *ibid.*, 30 April 1973; Moorgate: PP 1977–8, 8, p. 138; Nairobi: L 36, 20 Aug. 1968; Northern: L 51, 28 Oct. 1974; Reid, *The Secondary*, p. 38; Reid, *The Secondary*, p. 45; Orchard Square: L 35, 1971, no. 19; Questel: HO 268/378, memo, 25 Oct. 1972; CAOG 21/188; L 41, 1970 FMI accounts; Rowan: HO 268/378, memo, 25 Oct. 1972; L 50, minutes, 28 Oct. 1974; L 51, 28 Oct. 1974; Rowe: L 50, minutes, 26 March 1973; The Times, 10 Jan. 1984, p. 13; *ibid.*, 13 Jan. 1984, p. 16; Sassoons: L 18, no. 24, Coopers & Lybrand report, 13 March 1975, p. 7; HO 268/330, memo, 12 Sept. 1967; HO 268/509, Luke to Hayes, 1 Sept. 1967; SIFIDA: L 50, minutes, 25 Oct. 1971; CAOG 21/188; L 51, 29 Jan 1973; Singapore International: HO 268/378, memo, 19 Feb. 1974; PP 1977–8, 8, p. 30; L50, minutes, 26 March 1973; SIS: PP 1977–8, 8, p. 26; PP 1981–2, 364, p. 45; *Guardian*, 5 Aug. 1971, p. 13; Reid, *The Secondary* p. 45; L 50, minutes, 26 March 1973; Southern: L 180, memo, 23 Dec. 1975; Stanley Gibbons: L 35, 1969, no. 331; PP 1977–8, 8, p. 43; L 50, minutes, 30 April 1973; Television: HO 268/509, Luke to Ministry, 14 March 1968; L 50, minutes, 28 June 1971; *ibid.*, 21 Aug 1969; PP 1977–8, 8, p. 12; Toronto: HO 268/378, memo, 24 July 1973; L 50, minutes, 24 Sept. 1973; *ibid.*, 24 Sept. 1973; Tradewinds: HO 268/378, memo, 22 Aug. 1973; L 35, 27 Jan. 1970; L 50, minutes, 24 April 1974; Westralian: PP 1977–8, 8, p. 30; L 50, minutes, 29 Nov. 1971; *ibid.*, 17 Dec. 1973; *ibid.*, 26 March 1973.

Notes. N/K – Not Known. N/A – Not Applicable.

Bibliography

Periodicals

The Banker; *Crown Agents' Review*; *Crown Colonist*; *Daily Mail*; *Daily Telegraph*; *The Economist*; *FBI Review*; *Guardian*; *Financial Times*; *The Independent*; *Journal of West Africa*; *Ministry of Labour Gazette*; *The Nation*; *New Commonwealth*; *Private Eye*; *Sunday Telegraph*; *The Sunday Times*; *The Times*; *Trade and Industry*; *West Africa*; *Westminster Bank Review*; *Whitaker's Almanac*; *Who's Who*

Parliamentary Papers

Civil Appropriation Accounts PP 1924, 25; PP 1925, 27; PP 1926, 24; PP 1927, 20; PP 1928, 22; PP 1929, 24; PP 1930, 20; PP 1931, 20; PP 1932, 17; PP 1933, 22; PP 1934, 23; PP 1935, 19; PP1936, 20; PP 1937, 248; PP 1938, 476; PP 1939, 711; PP 1940, 949; PP 1941, 5; PP 1942, 72; PP 1943, 131; PP 1944, 194; PP1945, 259; PP 1946, 14; PP 1947, 134; PP 1948, 281; PP 1949, 364; PP 1950, 678; PP 1950–1, 25; PP 1951–2, 23; PP 1952–3, 22; PP 1953/4, 24; PP 1954/5, 12; PP 1955/6, 34; PP 1956/7, 25; PP 1957/8, 23; PP 1958/9, 24; PP 1959/60, 26; PP 1960/61, 26; PP 1961/62, 29; PP 1962/3, 29; PP 1963/64, 24; PP 1964/5, 27

Colonial Development and Welfare Acts. Report on the Administration and Use of Funds Provided Under the Acts. PP 1954/5, 4; PP 1966/7, 52

Colonial Development and Welfare Acts, 1929–70. A Brief Review PP 1970–71, 8

Colonial Development and Welfare Acts. Final Return of Schemes Made and of Loans Approved PP 1970–1, 8, p. 22

Colonial Development Corporation. Annual Report and Statement of Accounts PP 1959/60, 10; PP 1960/1, 10; PP 1961/2, 11; PP 1962/3, 10; PP 1963/4, 10; PP 1964/5, 12; PP 1966/7, 25; PP 1967/8 18; PP 1968/69, 28; PP 1950, 8; PP 1950/1, 10; PP 1951/2, 9; PP 1952/3, 8; PP 1953/4, 10; PP 1954/5, 4; PP 1955/6, 12; PP 1956/7, 9; PP 1957/8, 9; PP 1958/9, 10; PP 1964/5, 22

The Colonial Empire 1939–47, PP 1947, 162

The Colonial Territories PP 1951/2, 24; PP 1956/7, 10; PP 1961/2, 11

Report of the Committee of Inquiry Appointed by the Ministry of Overseas Development into the Circumstances that led to the Crown Agents Requesting Financial Assistance from the Government in 1974, PP 1977/8, 8

Report of the Tribunal Appointed to Enquire into Certain Issues Arising Out of the Operations of the Crown Agents as Financiers on Own Account in the Years 1967–74, PP 1981/2, 364

Report on the Use of Funds Provided Under the Colonial Development and Welfare Acts PP 1958/9, 10

Ronaldshay committee. Private enterprise in British Tropical Africa, PP 1924, 56

Select Committee on the Nationalised Indistries. Sub-committee C. Minutes of Evidence, PP 1977/78, 40

Select Committee on Estimates, Fifth Report, Colonial Development, PP 1947/8, 7
Statement by HMG on the Report of the Fay Committee of Inquiry on the Crown Agents, PP 1977/8, 8

Bank of England Archive

ADM 14 L. P. Thompson-McCausland's papers
C 47 Discount Office (market supervision) files
G 1 Governor's files
OV 44 Sterling and sterling area policy

Crown Agents' Liverpool Archive

L 1 Departmental Annual Reports to CA Board, 1963, 1964 and 1965
L 2 Departmental Monthly Reports to CA Board, 1966
L 3 Departmental Monthly Reports to CA Board, 1967
L 4 Departmental Monthly Reports to CA Board, 1968
L 5 Departmental Monthly Reports to CA Board, 1969
L 6 Departmental Monthly Reports to CA Board, 1970
L 7 Departmental Monthly Reports to CA Board, 1971
L 8 Departmental Monthly Reports to CA Board, 1972
L 9 Departmental Monthly Reports to CA Board, 1973
L 10 Departmental Monthly Reports to CA Board, 1974
L 11 Departmental Monthly Reports to CA Board, 1975
L 12 Budget Committee Papers, 1963, 1964, 1965
L 13 Public Relations Committee. Minutes and Papers, 1964–68
L 18 Investigations into Purchasing Practices - No. 1 Nattriss's report, May 1943; No. 2 Parkin's report, 5 May 1945; No. 3 Curtis's report on G procedure and method, 13 Oct. 1950; No. 5 Guide to the organisation and method of working of the Stores Dept., May 1953; No. 8 Hicks' interim report, 18 March 1957; No. 9 Report of the sub-committee on CA costs, 23 March 1960; No. 11 Savage report, March 1962; No. 14 Dent report, 1970; No. 16 Paper submitted by G Dept. Executive Officers, approx. 1973; No. 22 Review of G. Dept. procurement, Aug. 1973; No. 24, Coopers & Lybrand report, 13 March 1975; No. 25 Coopers and Lybrand report, 16 May 1975
L 35 CA Board Papers, 1965–75
L 36 CA Board Minutes, 1965–74
L 38 CA Executive Board Minutes, 1975
L 48 Four Millbank Holdings Ltd, Board Minutes, 31 Dec. 1971 to 25 Mar. 1987
L 50 Four Millbank Investments Ltd, Board Minutes and Papers, 1969 to 1974
L 51 Four Millbank Securities Ltd, Board Minutes, 1974–77
L 69 Internal Audit. Personal Investment Regulations, 1971–83
L 76 Correspondence with the Department of Trade and Industry, 1971–82
L 100 Press Cuttings, 1982
L 118 Closing submissions to the Croom-Johnson Tribunal - No. 1 Sir Claude Hayes; No. 2 Bank of England; No. 3 Treasury; No. 5 Allan Challis; No. 6 Norman Hewins; No. 7 Dennis Clark; No. 14 Patrick Matthews; No. 15 Peter Sly; No. 16 Eric Osgodby; No. 18 Bernard Wheately
L 121 CA Board Papers, 1976–82
L 141 CA Board, Constitution and Members
L 145 Chairman's Lunches, 1974–82

L 146 Chairman's Visits to the World Bank, 1978; Middle East, 1979; China, 1979; USA, 1980; E. Africa and Seychelles, 1980; S. E. Asia, 1980; Brunei, 1980; Australia, 1981
L 147 Fay Committee of Inquiry, General Papers
L 152 Fay Committee of Inquiry, ODM Briefing Notes
L 160 Coopers & Lybrand Report on the Circumstances Necessitating Government Support, March 1975
L 163 Appointment of Crown Agents, 1935–71
L 166 Monitoring of Sensitive Services to Principals Committee, 1969–82
L 167 John Poulson, Crown Agent Dealings with
L 168 John Cordle MP, Crown Agent Dealings with
L 170 Status and Constitution – Future Projections
L 174 Authority to Act for Independent Principals
L 178 Competitors to the Crown Agents
L 180 Publicity, General Papers, 1974–79
L 181 New Year and Retirement Messages, 1948–74
L 185 JCF Foreign Securities, 1970–74
L 188 Finance Directorate Meetings, 1971–75
L 193 Archives Panel, Reports
L 198 Relations with ODA. Legal and Constitutional Problems, 1974–90
L 201 Croom-Johnson Tribunal, Correspondence, 1976–77
L 204 E. D. Sassoons, Miscellaneous correspondence, 1968–70
L 215 Hong Kong Investment Policy, 1966–81
L 222 English & Continental Property Co. Ltd, 1969–71
L 224 Clifford Turner, Claims against Freshfields, 1975- 78
L 226 Fay Committee of Inquiry, Possible Action Against Individuals
L 227 Fay Committee of Inquiry, Exchange Control Investigation
L 228 History of Banking Operations
L 233 Archives, General, 1977–82
L 245 Marine Insurance Fund. Reserve Fund Enquiry, 1967
L 246 Marine Insurance Fund. General Policy Matters, 1967–74
L 265 Marine Insurance Fund. General Policy Matters, 1927–28
L 266 Notes on investments and rulings
WN 2 Archive List of M Appointments Files and Collective Summaries, File 2
WN 3 Archive List of M Appointments Files and Collective Summaries, File 3
WN 4 Archive list of M appointments files and collective summaries
WN 5 Archive List of M Appointments Files and Collective Summaries, File 5
WN 9 Summaries of O/Sec, CA, O Files
WN 10 Summaries of O/Sec, CA, O Files
WN 11 Summaries of O/Misc, O/Gen, O/Sch and O/O Files
WN 13 Summaries of Loan Files Still Current and Held by B6
WN 15 Summaries of O and R Colony Files, Abu Dhabi to Fort Hall
WN 17 Summaries of O and R Colony Files, Kenya to New Hebrides
WN 18 Summaries of O and R Colony Files, Nigeria
WN 19 Summaries of O and R Colony Files, North Borneo to Swaziland
WN 20 Summaries of O and R Colony Files, Tanganyika to Turks Islands
WN 34 Archive Summaries of Engineering Purchasing Department Files
WN 38 Archive Summaries of O Files and Miscellaneous Files
Allan Challis, Personnel file
Norman Hewins, Personnel file
John Shuter, Personnel file
Peter Sly, Personnel file

Crown Agents' Sutton Archive

CA (m) 25 CA publications
CA (m) 29 Salmon Report, 1949 and internal comment
CA (m) 60 'The Crown Agents as an Issuing House, 1860–1968'
CA (m) 61 Personal and Confidential
CA (m) 64 Biographies of Past Crown Agents
CA (m) 67 Office History from 1974, Vol. 1
CA (m) 102 Salmon Report, 1949 and the introduction of O and M
CA (m) 104 Risk to Office Funds
CA (m) 106 Provision of Credit Facilities
CA (m) 117 External Relations with Principals
CA (m) 118 Iraq
CAOG 14/38
CA provisional accounts 1973 and 1974 CA profit forecast
Croom-Johnson Tribunal. Bank of England submissions
Croom-Johnson Tribunal. Documentary Evidence
Croom-Johnson Tribunal. Evidence
Croom-Johnson Tribunal. General Correspondence
Croom-Johnson Tribunal. Papers from Jan. 1979
CS Bahamas 4 Local and Direct Purchases, 1930–63
CS Kenya 4 Local and Direct Purchases
CS 6852 Commissions to Agents
Engineering Inspection Department. Annual Reports
File 1 Senior Engineers as on 1 Jan. 1969
File 54. Exchanges with E. A. Morris
File on Coopers & Lybrand report
File PQ 18 Dec. 1972, Commons' questions
Folder no. 117 Relationship with UK government Departments
Folder no. 119/120, London Standard Investment Trust
Folder no. 122 Prosecution of James Alexander MacKay
Hayes' Fay Committee notes
JCF and JMF Annual Reports
MTS Organization and Procedures Manual
Notes by Hayes on day-to-day evidence tendered to the Croom-Johnson Tribunal
'Notes for Office History, 1958–65'
'Notes for Office History, 1966'
'Notes for Office History, 1968'
'Notes on the issue of loans by the Crown Agents', 1926
Pen Portraits
Philip Knights' Papers, July 1967 to July 1970
Press clippings
Price Waterhouse Report on English & Continental Property Co. Ltd, April 1972,
RANS report, July 1973
RC 2063 Arab Boycott
RC 2326
Report on the Croom-Johnson Tribunal by Sir Claude Hayes
S 1 Summaries of Finance Department (A) files, 1–300
S 2 Summaries of Finance Department (A) files, 301–600
S 3 Summaries of Finance Department (A) files, 601–900
S 4 Summaries of Finance Department (A) files, 901–1200

S 5 Summaries of Finance Department (A) files, 1201–1500
S 6 Summaries of Finance Department (A) files, 1501–1800
S 7 Summaries of Finance Department (A) files, 1801–2100
Sir Claude Hayes' Papers
Statement by Sir Claude Hayes, Aug. 1993
Stevenson enquiry and aftermath, part 2
Summaries of o/sec files
TS 1310 Classified Documents
'Winding up'

The National Archives, Kew, London

BT 258 Board of Trade, Industries and Manufacturers Department; BT 343 Board of Trade, Overseas Project Group.
CAOG 9, CA Finance Files; CAOG 10, Engineering Files; CAOG 11, Shipping Files; CAOG 12, CA Purchasing Files; CAOG 13, Appointments and Passages files; CAOG 14, External Relations; CAOG 16, CA Staff Files; CAOG 17 Miscellaneous Registered Files; CAOG 18, Investigations by Messrs Coopers & Lybrand; CAOG 21, CA records made available to the Fay Committee and the Croom-Johnson Tribunal; CAOG 22, CA Private Office Files; CAOG 23 Finance Department Registered Files; CAOG 24, CA Investment Dept. Files
CO 83 Colonial Office, Fiji; CO 96 Colonial Office, Gold Coast; CO 323 Colonial Office. Colonies. General. Original Correspondence; CO 537 Supplementary correspondence; CO 852 Colonial Office. Economic General Department
FCO 46 Foreign and Commonwealth Office. Defence Department; FCO 86, Foreign & Commonwealth Office General Dept. Files
HO 268, Home Office, Croom-Johnson Tribunal, Evidence and Papers
IR 79
OD 18, Department of Technical Co-operation, Establishments, Registered Files; OD 20, Department of Technical Co-operation, Finance Dept., Registered Files; OD 39 Ministry of Overseas Development. Malaysia and Singapore Department; OD 59, Ministry of Overseas Development, Organisation Department.
Prem 16, Prime Minister's Office, Correspondence and Papers.
T 161 Treasury. Supply Department; T 213 Treasury. Defense Personnel Division; T 233 Treasury. Home Finance Division. Registered Files; T 236 Treasury. Overseas Finance Division; T 316, Treasury. Management Accounting Unit, Registered Files; T 317, Treasury, Overseas Development Divisions, Registered Files; T 326, Treasury, Finance, Home & General Division, Registered Files

Secondary Sources

Abbott, A. W., *A Short History of the Crown Agents and their Office*, London 1959 (privately published)
Allen, G. C., *The British Disease*, London 1976
Amery, Leo, *The Leo Amery Diaries, Vol. 1*, London 1980
Andromidas, Dean, 'Crown Agents. The Queen's Managers', *The Executive Intelligence Review*, August 22, 1997
Anon, *The Crown Agents for the Colonies. Centeniary*, London 1933
Anon, '*The Crown Agents, London. Their Organization and Functions*, London 1955

Avery, R. W., 'The Crown Agents keep the link', *New Commonwealth*, 31 (1956), pp. 329–32

Ball, Michael and Sunderland, David, *An Economic History of London, 1800–1914*, London 2001

Bangura, Yusuf, *Britain and Commonwealth Africa. The Politics of Economic Relations, 1951–75*, Manchester 1983

Bank of England, *UK Overesas Investments*, London 1950, 1951, 1952, 1953, 1954, 1955, 1956, 1957

Bareau, Paul, *The Sterling Area*, London 1948

Bell, Philip W., *The Sterling Area in the Post War World*, Oxford 1956

Beloff, Max, *Imperial Sunset: Britain's Liberal Empire, 1897–1921*, London 1989

Block, Alan A., 'Introduction', *Crime, Law and Social Change*, 5 (2001), pp. 1–5

Braine, Bernard, 'UK income tax and colonial industrial development', *New Commonwealth*, 17 March 1952, pp. 256–7

Butler, L. J., *Britain and Empire. Adjusting to a Post-Imperial World*, London 2002

Cain, P. J. and Hopkins, A. G., *British Imperialism: Crisis and Deconstruction, 1914–1990*, London 1993

Cairncross, Alec, *The British Economy Since 1945: Economic Policy and Performance, 1945–1990*, Oxford 1992

Calder, Sir John, *Buying and Selling Agents*, London 1947

Chapman, Richard, *Ethics in Public Service for a New Millennium*, Aldershot 2000

Constantine, Stephen, *The Making of British Colonial Development Policy, 1914–40*, London 1984

Crown Agents, *Handbook for Colonial Municipalities, Native Administrations and Other Public Authorities*, London 1946

Darwin, John, 'British decolonization since 1945: A pattern or a puzzle?', *Journal of Imperial and Commonwealth History*, 12 (2) (1984), pp. 187–209

Doig, Alan, 'Public service and private gain', *Public Money*, 4 (3) (1984)

Doig, Alan, *Corruption and Misconduct in Contemporary British Politics*, London 1984

Du Gray, Paul, 'How responsible is 'responsive' government', *Economy and Society*, 31 (3) (2002), pp. 461–82

Fay, Stephen, *Portrait of an Old Lady. Turmoil at the Bank of England*, London 1987

Fieldhouse, D. K., *Black Africa, 1945–1980. Economic Decolonisation and Arrested Development*, London 1986

Fieldhouse, D. K., *The West and the Third World. Trade, Colonialism, Dependence and Development*, Oxford 1999

Fitzgerald, P., 'Why are we waiting?', *New Statesman and Society*, 8 (381) (12 Jan. 1995)

Ganz, G., 'Parliamentary accountability of the Crown Agents', *Public Law*, 1980, pp. 454–80

Gillard, Michael and Tomkinson, Martin, *Nothing to Declare. The Political Corruptions of John Poulson*, London 1980

Goobey, A. R., *Bricks and Mortals: The Dreams of the 80's and the Nighmares of the 90s. The Inside Story of the Property World*, London 1992

Gordon, Charles, *The Cedar Story. The Night the City was Saved*, London 1993

Gretton, John, 'Crown Agents and civil servants: A failure of control', *Public Money*, 2 (2), (1982), pp. 19–26

Hargrave, J. F., 'Competition and collusion in the British railway track fittings industry. The case of the Anderston foundry, 1800–1960', University of Durham, PhD thesis, 1991

Havinden, Michael and Meredith, David, *Colonialism and Development. Britain and its Tropical Colonies*, 1850–1960, London 1993

Hawkins, E. K., 'Marketing Boards and econonomic development in Nigeria and Ghana', *Review of Economic Studies*, 26 (1958), pp. 51–62

Hood, Christopher, 'The Crown Agents affair', *Public Administration*, 56 (1978), pp. 297–303

Houseman, Lorne, *The House that Thomas Built. The Story of De La Rue*, London 1968

Howson, Susan, *Sterling's Managed Float. The Operations of the Exchange Equalisation Account, 1932–39*, Princeton 1980

Hyam, Ronald, *Britain's Imperial Century, 1815–1914: A Study of Empire and Expansion*, New York 1976

Kreps, Richard M., *A Course in Microeconomic Theory*, London 1990

Krozewski, Gerold, 'Sterling, the minor territories and the end of formal Empire', *Economic History Review*, 46 (2) (1993), pp. 239–65

Krozewski, Gerold, 'Finance and Empire. The dilemma facing Great Britain in the 1950s', *International History Review*, 18 (1) (1996), pp. 48–68

Krozewski, Gerold, *Money and the End of Empire. British International Economic Policy and the Colonies 1947–58*, London 2001

Kynaston, David, *The City of London. Vol. iv A Club No More, 1945–2000*, London 2001

Lee, J. M., *Colonial Development and Good Government*, Oxford 1967

Lewis, C. W. and Gilman, S. C., *The Ethics Challenge in Public Service*, New York 2005

Linklater, Magnus and Leigh, David, *'Not with Honour'. The inside story of the Westland Scandal*, London 1986

May, R. S. and Dobson, N. C., 'The impact of the UK's bilateral aid programme on British industry', *ODI Review*, 2 (1979), pp. 1–22

May, R. S., Schumacher, Dieter, and Malek, Mohammed H., *Overseas Aid. The impact on Britain and Germany*, London 1989

Meredith, David George, 'The British government and colonial economic development with particular reference to British West Africa, 1919–39', Essex Univ., PhD, 1976

Milgrom, Paul and Roberts, John, *Economics, Organisation and Management*, Princeton 1992

Miller, J. D. B., *Survey of Commonwealth Affairs. Problems of Expansion and Attrition, 1953–69*, Oxford 1974

Miners, Norman, *Hong Kong Under Imperial Rule, 1912–41*, Oxford 1987

Moran, Michael, *The Politics of Banking. The Strange Case of Competition and Credit Control*, London 1984

Morgan, D. J., *A Reassessment of British Aid Policy, 1951–65*, London 1980

Morgan, D. J., *Developing British Colonial Resources, 1945–51*, London 1980

Overseas Development Institute, *British Aid. Volume 2: Government Finance*, London 1964

Overseas Development Institute, *British Aid. Volume 5: Colonial Development*, London 1964

Oxford Dictionary of National Biography, Oxford 2003

Polk, J., *Sterling: its Meaning in World Finance*, New York 1956

Porter, Bernard, *The Lion's Share. A Short History of British Imperialism, 1850–1983*, London 1984

Reid, Margaret, *The Secondary Banking Crisis, 1973–75. Its Causes and Course*, London 1982

Schenk, Catherine R., *Britain and the Sterling Area. From Devaluation to Convertability in the 1950s*, London 1994

Schenk, Catherine R., 'Finance and Empire: confusions and complexities: a note', *The International History Review*, 18 (4), (1996), pp. 869–72

Scott, Peter, 'The new alchemy: Veblen's theory of crisis and the 1974 British property and banking crisis', *Journal of Economic Issues*, 30, 1 (1996), pp. 1–11

Shonfield, Andrew, *British Economic Policy Since the War*, Harmondsworth 1958

Slater, Jim, *Return to Go: My Autobiography*, London 1977

Spero, Joan Edelman, *The Politics of International Economic Relations*, London 1990

Stock Exchange, *Stock Exchange Official Intelligence*, London, 1921–32, 1939, 1953, 1962

Sunderland, David, *Managing, the British Empire. The Crown Agents 1833–1914*, London 2004

Sutherland, A. and G., 'Does Gate Gourmet make comfort letters binding ?', *International Finance Law Review*, 23 (8) (2004), pp. 45–6

Tomlinson, Jim, 'The Commonwealth, the balance of payments and the politics of international poverty, 1958–71', *Contemporary European History*, 12 (4) (2003), pp. 413–29

Wasserstein, Bernard, *Britain and the Jews of Europe, 1939–45*, London 1979

Whitby, David, 'Conspiracy and cover up', *Crime, Law and Social Change*, 5 (2001), pp. 21–41

Wicker, E. R., 'Colonial development and welfare, 1929–57. The evolution of a policy', *Social and Economic Studies*, 7 (4) (1958), pp. 170–92

Wraith, R. E., *Guggisberg*, Oxford 1967

Wright, Peter, *Spycatcher. The Candid Autobiography of a Senior Intelligence Officer*, New York 1987

Index

Abbey Orchard Property Investments Ltd 91, 184, 196, 218
Abrahams, Ian 198
Abu Dhabi 48, 91, 109, 110, 147, 188
Aden 44 n.11, 92, 148
Addis Ababa 147
Admiralty 125, 134
advances/overdrafts 11, 12, 14, 32, 50–3, 64–5, 66, 67, 97, 98, 100, 103, 104, 105, 107, 108, 242, 248, 249
Africa 9, 36, 47, 115, 161, 173, 188
  see also East Africa, West Africa, South Africa, named countries
African Development Bank 150, 151
Afro-American Purchasing Centre 150–1
Agency for International Development 150–1
aid 1, 9, 33, 39, 51, 52, 55, 57, 58, 59–63, 65, 66, 67, 68, 97,155, 159; procurement financed by 128, 130, 141, 146, 148–51, 153, 245, 251
Amery, Leo 176
Amscot Oceanic Ltd 188
Anchor Investments (Personal Loans Finance) Ltd 211–13
Arab League 146
Arab Legion 146
arms sales 6, 147, 171–2, 202, 203, 251
  intervention of HMG in 148–9, 245
Armstrong, Sir Robert 227
Association of Consulting Engineers 170, 171
Associated Railway Consultants Ltd 169, 171
Australia 88, 94, 99, 129, 130, 135, 184, 229
  colonial investment Funds 73, 82
  corruption of CA staff 217–18
  equity portfolios in 94, 183, 192 n.84
  property investments in 91, 184, 187, 192, 196, 197, 198, 206, 237

back-to-back loans 208–9, 243
Bahamas 89, 172 n.94, 174 n.108, 187
Bahrain 171 n.83, 172 n.94
Balfour Beatty 175
Bank of British West Africa 164
Bank of England
  as competitors to CAs 17, 40, 83, 90, 192, 237, 247
  CA current account 97, 111
  CA move into secondary banking 179, 181, 182, 189, 191, 192, 200, 205, 207–8, 209, 210, 215, 216
  colonial investment Funds 73, 74, 77–80, 83, 87, 89, 90, 91, 92, 93, 94, 95, 96, 248
  control of CAs' secondary banking activities 225–7
  interests of 5, 241, 242, 244, 245, 247
  JCF/JMF/Joint Funds 6, 100, 102–11
  miscellaneous sources of finance 46–7, 50, 51, 54, 55, 66, 67
  public issues 11, 16–18, 21, 22, 25, 28, 29, 32, 33, 35, 36, 40, 248
  secondary banking crisis 7, 229, 230, 231–2, 233, 234–6, 237, 238, 239, 240
  Treasury bills (colonial) 44–5, 102–3
bank deposits 71, 75, 97, 98, 104–6, 109
bank loans to colonies 44, 58, 68
Banque de Paris 94
Barbados 36, 44 n.10, 172 n.94
Barber, Anthony Lord 180, 227
Barclays Bank 35, 43 n.8, 44 n.10, 102, 196, 208, 216, 232
Barclays Hotels Group 195, 199
Barley, K. W. 3 n.10, 214
Barnes, D. 191
Basutoland 49 n.46, 145
Bechuanaland 14, 49 n.46, 145
Belgium 93, 113, 130 n.105
Beresford-Stooke, Sir George 3
Beynon Ltd 131–2
Biafran war 124, 148, 204
Bickerstethe, Edward 27–8, 83–5, 102, 243
Big City Finance Ltd 211–13
Blundell, A. J. 214
Board of Trade 62, 119, 130 n.108, 133, 144, 146, 147, 156 n.102, 159, 199, 244
Botswana
  see Bechuanaland
Braine MP, Bernard 206
Brearley, S. D. N. 235
Britannia Studios International Ltd 188
British and Commonwealth Shipping Co. 165, 178, 246
British Bangladeshi Trust 188, 206, 230 n.77

British Guiana 30 n.127, 35, 45 n.24, 52, 53, 139, 164
British Stockbrokers Trust Ltd (BST) 26–7
Brunei 48, 90 n.133, 91, 237 n.135, 251
Burchills 176
Burma 165
Burr, E. C. 224, 225
Burston & Texas Commerce Bank 182, 209, 231

Calder, Sir John 169
Canada 73, 89, 93, 129, 135, 139, 167 n.54, 184
Capital & Counties Property Ltd 192, 206
Capital Issues Committee 22
cartels 131–3, 136, 242, 243
Caruana, Carmelo 170
Casebourne & Co 132
Cedar Holdings 196
cement 131–2, 133, 135, 243
Cement Marketing Co. Ltd 131–2, 133
Central Electricity Board 103
Ceylon 47 n.38, 89 n.127, 137, 164, 177
  procurement for 118, 139, 145, 154
  public loans of 9, 21, 28, 33–4, 35
CGA Capital Corporation 184, 198
Chalk, John 203
Challis, Allan 91, 111, 173 n.99, 195 n.110, 205, 209, 210, 214, 222, 226
  CA 1970 accounts 111–12
  corruption allegations against 211, 212, 214, 215
  criticism of 181
  directorships/shareholdings of 200 n.145, 216
  expertise of 190–1
  and move into secondary banking 179, 185
  post-CA career of 191, 215, 229, 232, 238
  provision of information to board/Hayes 221, 223
Charles Hendall & Partners 147
Chenderiang Tin Dredging Ltd 188
China 22
Civil service 3, 5, 113, 153, 154, 164, 169, 190, 206, 216, 217, 240, 243
Clark, Denis 189–90, 214, 216 n.271
client unethical behaviour 116, 118, 137, 139, 141, 143, 152, 176, 241, 242, 243–4
Cohen, Sir Andrew 202
Colonial Development Act (1929) 14, 59
Colonial (later Commonwealth) Development Corporation 59, 61–2, 110, 168, 184
Colonial Development Fund 31, 59
colonial investment Funds 5, 29, 32, 33, 35, 37, 39, 49, 52, 63, 113
  colonial sterling balances 85–9
  FMI 184
  investment of 15, 17, 19, 25, 26, 28, 30, 40, 42, 43, 55, 56, 70–6, 100, 111, 248, 249
  investment of after independence 89–94, 251
  Scrimgeours and 83–5
  trading of securities 80–3, 242, 246, 248
  see also Currency Funds, Opium Funds, Pension Funds, Provident Funds, Reserve Funds, Saving Bank Funds, Sinking Funds, Surplus Funds
Colonial Loans Consortium 38, 39
Colonial Office (and successor departments) 2, 137–8, 144, 146, 152, 153, 162, 175, 182, 227, 229
  CA advise to 173, 176–7, 243, 244, 251
  CA move into secondary banking 181, 185–6, 189, 190, 195–6, 205, 207–8, 210, 217
  control of CAs' secondary banking activities 223–5
  desire to control/takeover CA business 161–2, 186, 224–5, 247
  colonial investment Funds 72, 75, 76–7, 78, 79, 81, 82, 83, 88, 89, 92, 94, 95
  interests of 5, 241, 242, 244, 245, 246, 247
  JCF 6, 98, 100, 102, 104
  Millbank Technical Services 172–3
  miscellaneous sources of finance 46, 49, 52, 53, 55, 57, 58, 61, 66
  procurement 119, 121, 133, 138–9, 142, 144, 148–50, 151
  public issues 13, 14, 15, 17, 18, 21, 22, 26, 28–9, 36, 37
  recruitment 161–2
colonial procurement regulations 6, 138–9, 244, 247
colonial sterling balances
  attempts to reduce size of 87–9
  growth of 85–7
Colonial Stocks Acts 14, 38, 46, 49
colony-to-colony loans 48
comfort letters 207–8, 232, 233, 234–5
Commercial Continental Ltd 184
commissions 47, 80, 107, 116, 118, 133–4, 140, 154, 160, 246
commodities trading 183, 191–2
Commons Select Committee on Overseas Development 179
Commonwealth Assistance Loans 31, 62

Commonwealth Relations Office 148
concessions 133, 173, 175
Congo 148
Conservative party 105, 171, 181, 204, 206, 240
Constructions Promotions Ltd 123 n.54, 170
Consulting Engineers/Architects 6, 145 n.14, 166, 167, 168, 170, 250
Continental Illinois 94, 191, 201–2, 204–5
contractor construction of infrastructure 6, 143, 166, 168–9, 250
conversion of loans 9–10, 12, 15, 31, 32, 33–6, 40, 63, 244, 249
Coopers & Lybrand 121, 172, 236
E. W. Cordle & Son Ltd 123–4, 247
Cordle MP, John 123–4, 170, 246–7
Costains 123
credit 45, 67, 151, 153
credit committee 195
Credit Lyonnais 94
creditworthiness of colonies 15, 24, 29, 43, 46, 49, 52, 53, 55, 56, 66, 75, 76, 248
Croom-Johnson report 112, 151, 181, 189, 193, 206, 209, 210, 225, 226, 239
Crown Agents 2, 254–5
Crown Agents board 207, 208, 221–2
Crown Agents Office
  arms sales of 6, 147–9 171–2, 202, 203, 245, 251
  contribution to UK/clients' economies 248–50
  description of 1–2, 241–2
  engineering duties of 166–73
  extent and direction of finance 63–6
  guaranteed and public body loans 45–7
  interests of 241, 242–8
  inter-colonial finance 48–53
  JCF/JMF 97–114
  loans issued in London 9–41, 43
  local bank loans and use of Surplus Funds 58–9
  local issue of colonial treasury bills and loans 53–58
  London bank loans, colonial treasury bills and CA credit 44–5
  miscellaneous duties of 173–7
  personnel duties of 160–6
  post-1974 history of 251–2
  procurement 222, 115–60
  reserves of 185–6, 189
  unethical behaviour of 31, 40, 45, 66, 76, 84, 95, 107, 110, 111–12, 131, 165, 174
  unethical behaviour towards clients 49–50, 91, 93, 100, 103, 108, 137–8, 151, 152–3, 154, 159
Crown Agents staff 3, 152, 119, 145, 154, 155, 190, 246, 250
  corruption/possible corruption 122–4, 170–1, 176, 204, 210–8, 246–7
  culture/norms of 4–5, 207, 219
  inefficiency of 3–4, 121–2, 133–4, 156, 157
  training of 190–1
Crown Cassette Ltd 187–8
Crown Communications Ltd 187–8, 216 n.271
Crown Continental Merchant Bank Jamaica Ltd 184
Cuckney, Sir John 181, 236, 237
Cunningham MP, George 203
currencies 93, 108–10, 183
Currency Boards 24 n.84, 28 n.111, 57 n.112, 58 n.120, 69 n.2, 91, 177
Currency Commissioners 57, 69, 78–9
Currency Funds 5, 37, 57, 69, 70, 71, 72, 74, 77–80, 83, 86, 89, 91, 95, 97, 245
Curtis, Walter 3 n.10, 133, 157
Cyprus 22, 39, 58, 89 n.127, 79, 148, 161 n.5, 183, 205, 245, 246
Cyrenaica 145
Czarnikow, Messrs 192

Daiwa Securities 94
Davidson, Sidney 199, 207, 211, 212, 213
Davies Arnold & Cooper 192, 198
Dawney Day 199, 230 n.77
De La Rue 131, 216
Defence Sales Organisation 171–2
delivery delays 6, 120, 135, 136
  caused by CAs 157–8
  caused by colonial administrations 156–7
  caused by suppliers 15–16, 158
Department of Technical Co-operation *see* Colonial Office
Development and Welfare Act (1940) 60
Development Bank of Singapore 188
departmental system of infrastructure construction 166–8
Deutsch Bank 94
Diamond Corporation 53, 177
Dipre, Remo 215
discount market/houses 97, 111
Discount Office (Bank of England) 226, 235, 240
dividends 12, 21, 31–2, 37, 63, 97, 249
Dobson, N. C. 128
dominion securities/loans 9 n.1, 15, 20, 72, 73, 99
Dorrington, R. C. 238
Downie, Sir Harold 2
drug procurement 120, 129, 135

East Africa 91, 127, 150, 162, 164, 177 n.137
finance of 9, 13, 14, 23, 30, 32 n.140, 43, 46, 47, 48, 53, 57 n.112, 63, 69 n.2
Eastern Copper Mines Ltd 94, 188, 199
Edward Bates & Sons Ltd 209
Egypt 135
Elder Dempster 132, 136
Elders & Fyffes 132
embassies 147
Engineering Purchasing Department 115, 120, 134
engineering role
criticism of performance 169, 170, 246
post-war duties 6, 169–70, 250
pre-war duties 6, 166–9, 250
see also Associated Railway Consultants Ltd, Millbank Technical Services
English & Continental Investments Ltd 184, 209, 216
CA 1974 support of 230, 232–3, 236
comfort letters 207–8
over-investment in 196–7
English & Continental Property Co. Ltd 183, 184, 191 n.76, 192, 197, 198, 199, 203, 204, 209, 215
Epsom development 194, 206, 215
equities 38
colonial investment funds 91–4, 245
JCF/JMF 110–13
own account investment in 179, 183
sale of in 1973/4 230, 231
Equity Advisory Panel 93, 95, 191, 203, 223
Equity Research Unit 191
Eritrea 145
Eurodollar market 38
Evan Cook Ltd 136
exchange control regulations 110, 114, 151, 202, 205, 226
Exchange Equalisation Account 85
Exchequer & Audit Department 112, 228
expatriate staff 143, 153, 160–5
Export Credits Guarantee Department 45, 53 n.75, 62, 66, 149, 171, 187
Ezechiel, Sir Percy 3 n.10, 58, 247

Falkland Islands 164 n.24
Farquarson, Sir James 170
Fay report 112, 181, 189, 193, 206, 208, 209, 210, 218, 225, 226, 228, 239
Federated Malay States 9, 13, 14, 30 n.127, 48, 102
see also Malaya
Fenston, Felix 192, 193
Figures, Sir Frank 227, 228
Fiji 103
Finance Department Investment Account (Finvest) 45, 93, 109, 111, 137, 151, 182–3, 184, 186, 187, 226, 230, 243, 251
Finley, Sidney 198, 199, 210–13, 246
'firm' buying 15, 17, 26, 42, 43, 55, 58
First National Finance Corporation Ltd (FNFC) 184, 191, 192, 198, 199, 203 n.173, 210, 215, 216, 229, 232, 237 n.135, 238, 243
First World War 15, 16, 167 n.54
floating balances 97–8
foreign loans 15, 17
Foreign Office (later Foreign and Commonwealth Office) 91, 145, 146, 148, 159, 225, 245
Four Millbank Investments Ltd (FMI) 93, 110, 182, 183–4, 187–8, 191, 198, 209, 251
France 39, 93, 113, 129
Freshfields 192

A. Gallenkamp & Co 125
Garner, David 215
General Purchasing Department 115, 116, 120, 122, 123, 125, 134, 154
Germany 44, 67, 93, 113, 129, 130 n.105
Ghana 124, 161 n.5, 173
cutting links with CAs 74, 75, 106, 185
see also Gold Coast
Gibraltar 183
Gillis, Michael 201–2, 216–17
Gold Coast 107, 167 n.54, 169, 177
finance of 20, 35, 57, 59
procurement for 138, 152–3.
see also Ghana
Gramco Management Ltd 201, 216
Greene, Lionel 192, 196, 198
Greene, Ramon 192, 196, 198, 215
Grenada 28, 103
Griffin & George Ltd 154
Grindle, Sir George 58, 247
guaranteed loans 13, 22, 23, 39, 46–7, 67, 72
Guardian 148, 203, 204, 205, 207, 216
Guyana 172 n.94.
see also British Guiana
Gwinne-Jones, Timothy 203

Halliday Simpson 191 n.83. 215
Hambros bank 210
Hart MP, Judith 179, 181, 203 n.171, 217
Hartog Oil Ltd 188
Hayes, Sir Claude 122, 181, 190, 197, 218, 228, 229, 236, 238
HMG responsibility for CAs 185–6
and move into secondary banking 179, 185
personal responsibility of 198, 200, 222–3
personality of 2, 202, 203, 223, 224, 229

relationship with Morris 217, 222–3
relationship with the ODA 224–5, 247
secondary banking crisis 231, 232, 234, 237
shareholdings of 216–17
Hewins, Norman 214–15, 238, 190, 191, 195, 197, 198
secondary banking crisis 232, 233, 234
Hicks' enquiry 122, 134
Hills Samuel 191, 200, 207
Holland 39, 93, 113, 129
Hollom, Sir Jasper 234, 235, 236
Hong Kong 58, 188, 82, 89
equity portfolios in 94, 183, 186

ILCO Holdings Ltd 188
indents 115, 125, 153
India 73, 88, 99, 129, 135, 164, 165
India Office 125
Indonesia 188
Inland Revenue 48, 107, 109, 114, 164, 225
insider trading 24, 25, 93
inspection 6, 115, 116, 134–5, 140, 154, 157, 251
inter-colonial loans 13, 32, 35, 46, 48–50, 58, 64, 65, 66, 67, 244, 247, 248, 249
International Agricultural Development Corp. 171
International Air Transport Association 137, 165, 243
International Bank of Reconstruction and Development
see World Bank
International Hotels Kenya Ltd 110 n.95, 188
International Military Services 173, 236
International Technical & Construction Services Ltd 171
Interservice Mediterranean Ltd 211, 212
Investico 199
Investors Review 204
invoice payment 154
Iran 147, 171–2
Iraq 44 n.10, 53, 139, 145, 146, 147, 185
Israel 146, 147, 202, 203, 204
Israeli-British Bank 113 n.114, 196, 236
Italy 93, 129, 130 n.105, 164

Jamaica 131 n.117, 132, 139, 172 n.94, 183, 186
finance of 9, 13, 18, 39, 48, 54, 57
Jamaica Building Society 184
Japan 130
Johns, David 190, 191, 198, 229, 238
Joint Colonial Fund 31, 98, 120, 133, 151, 245, 246
advances 9, 11, 12, 14, 32, 44, 50–2, 58, 64–5, 66, 67, 69, 78, 242, 248, 249
dividend 98, 100, 106
establishment of 98
investment of 5, 72, 93, 94, 98–9
liquidity of 100, 104–6; 1931/2
1930/1 crisis 6, 17, 21, 44, 76, 84, 100–3, 245, 247
overdrafts 52–3, 244, 248
reserve fund 100, 101, 106
situation prior to establishment 97–98
see also Joint Funds
Joint Consolidated Fund
see Joint Colonial Fund; Joint Funds
Joint Funds 108, 209, 228
Finvest 182, 186
fixed term deposits 108–9
FMI 184
foreign currencies 108–10
1971/1974 crises 111–13
other investments 110–12
see also Joint Colonial Fund, Joint Miscellaneous Fund
Joint Miscellaneous Fund 5, 72, 93, 94, 133, 151, 246
advances 9, 69, 44, 50–2, 64–5, 66, 67, 242, 248, 249
establishment of 106–7
overdrafts 52–3, 244, 248
see also Joint Funds
Jordan 52, 139, 145, 147

KCA Drilling 199
Kenya 49, 74, 89 n.127, 90 n.135, 172 n.94, 188
finance of 9, 13, 14, 17, 19, 21, 28, 31 n.132, 32 n.140, 54, 55, 57
procurement for 138, 139, 144
Keogh, Jim 226
Keyser Ullman 196 n.123, 203, 204 n.176, 206 n.191, 230 n.77, 232
King, Sir Richard 224, 225
Kirkland-Whittaker 202–3, 206
Kommerzialbank 201
Korea 21
Kuhn Loeb & Co. 94
Kuwait 147

Labour Party 179, 203–4, 240
Laing 171
Lambert, Sir Henry 2–3
Lehmann Trading Corporation Ltd 173–4
Lesotho
see Basutoland
Libya 52, 123 n.54, 145, 146

lifeboat committee 229, 230–1, 233, 234, 235, 237
Livesey & Henderson 171
loans issued in London 50, 51, 52, 58, 63, 65, 75, 92, 97, 99, 102, 210, 248, 249
  CA purchase of 72, 73, 74, 75
  CA support of 15, 21, 25, 30–3, 192, 248, 249
  interest rates and prices of 15–8, 42–3
  management of 21, 31–6, 74, 242
  prior charges 22–3
  purchase by colonies 18–19
  purpose, size and length of 11–12
  subscription 10, 16, 36–40
  timing of issue 21–2
  transfer and repayment instruments 19–20
  type of asset created 13–14
  underwriting of 23–30
  see also guaranteed loans, public body loans
local authority securities/loans 9 n.1, 18, 20, 27, 72, 73, 82, 98, 99, 105, 106, 249
local loans 39, 53–58, 67
local merchant supply of goods 6, 115, 116, 139–40, 249
London Assurance Co. 137
London Chamber of Commerce 147
London County Council 35–6
London Standard Investment Trust 83
de Loynes, John 216
Luke, Sir Stephen 146, 150, 171 n.83, 179, 185, 186, 204, 215, 216, 223

MacKay, James 175
Mais, Lord 203 n.175, 206, 217 n.281
Malawi 172 n.94, 173
  see also Nyasaland
Malaysia 47, 118, 137, 161 n.5, 173, 184, 188, 205
  colonial investment Funds 74, 75, 79, 83, 89 n.127, 91 n.140
  equity portfolios in 183, 186, 192 n.84
  see also Federated Malay States, Straits Settlements
Malaysian Industrial Development Finance Corporation 188
Malaysian International Merchant Bankers Berhad 184
Malta 52, 53, 79, 188, 211, 170
mandated territories 14, 23, 46, 49
Marine Insurance Fund 6, 115, 116, 137–8, 140, 159, 182, 246
Martin-Bates, J. P. 201, 202
Martins bank 84, 102
Mathews, Patrick 210, 238 n.139
Mathieson, W. A. C. 225
Maudling MP, Reginald 171
Mauritius 32 n.138, 34 n.1, 46 n.32, 49, 63, 103, 164, 177
May, R. S. 128, 141
McAlpine 169
McClure, A. L. 170, 246
Mersey Docks & Harbour Board 236
Metropolitan Property Ltd 217
Midland Bank 205
Millbank Technical Services 4, 66, 151, 169, 171, 205–6, 237 n.128, 251
  establishment of 45, 171–2
  Finvest 182, 186
  problems of 172–3
Ministry of Defence 172, 173
Ministry of Overseas Development *see* Colonial Office
Ministry of Supply 123, 135 n.144, 156
Ministry of Technology 225
Moorgate Mercantile 232
Morris, Edward 133 n.134, 215
  directorships/shareholdings of 215–17
  relationship with Cordle 123–4, 170, 246–7
  relationship with Finley 211, 214
  relationship with Hayes 222–3
MTS Iran Ltd 171
MTS Management Holdings Ltd 171
MTS Ordnance Ltd 171

Nairobi 46
Nation Life Insurance Co Ltd 208, 209, 216
National & Grindlays Bank 205
National Debt Commissioners 38–9, 80
National General Export Merchant Group 147
National Westminster Bank 97, 102, 196, 205, 232, 233, 235
nationalised industries 38, 44, 67
New Hebrides 39
Newman, Ron 230, 232
New Zealand 73, 82, 99, 135
Nigeria 101, 107, 137, 161 n.5, 163, 168, 172 n.94, 173, 188
  colonial investment Funds 74, 76
  finance of 9, 12, 13, 15, 16, 18 n.40, 20, 24 n.84, 26, 28 n.111, 35, 52, 53, 57, 63
  procurement for 124, 150
Norman, Montague 17, 21, 102, 103, 247
North Borneo 48
Northern Rhodesia 100, 102, 103, 117
  finance of 14, 21, 43 n.8, 54, 59
Nowers, P. W. 112, 228
Nyasaland 14, 23, 46, 102, 103
  see also Malawi

Office Fund 45, 53, 100, 107, 108, 111–12, 113 121, 137, 151, 166, 176, 228, 246
Ofori-Arra, Mr 153
oil industry investments 188, 198, 199, 210, 230
Oldham Estates 209, 236
Oman 147, 148
Ommanney, Sir Montague 176
Opium Funds 72
Orchard Square Development Corporation Ltd 184
orders 115, 125
  direct 117, 119–21
  price discounts 125–6, 139
  price variation clauses 125, 126–7, 129, 243
  running contracts 117, 120–1
  suppliers 127–33
  tendering 117–19, 246, 249
Organisation and Methods Division 133 n.134, 155
Osgodby, Eric 189–90, 214, 238
over-riding commission 15, 23, 24, 25, 27, 40, 84, 243
Overseas Development Administration
  see Colonial Office
Overseas Food Corporation 61
overseas merchant banks 184, 187
Overseas Service Aid Scheme 62, 162, 163 n.15
own account venture
  see secondary banking
Overseas Superannuation Fund 92

packing 6, 115, 116, 135–6, 140, 154
Pakistan 165, 225
Palestine 2, 28 n.111, 44 n.11, 46 n.30, 69 n.2, 177 n.137
'par' price 10, 16, 23
Parliament 23, 25, 36, 59–60,84, 100, 115, 124, 128, 132, 147, 170, 179, 181, 189, 200, 203, 205, 227, 228, 233, 243, 246
Pearson, D. L. 224
Peat Marwick 233
Peddie, Lord 203, 204, 206
Pember Boyle 27
Pennine Co Ltd 192, 193, 198
Pension Funds 5, 15, 75, 80, 92
personnel duties
  arrangement of passages 6, 165–6, 250
  payment of salaries/pensions 6, 165, 97, 250
  recruitment 6, 160–5, 242
  training of expatriate officers 152, 166, 250, 252
placings 43
Post Office 38, 144, 164, 188, 228
Post Office Superannuation Fund 184, 196, 197, 204
Poulson, John 123 n.54, 124, 170–1, 178, 246
press 36, 92, 147–8, 153, 172, 179, 181, 195, 200, 227, 233, 238
price variation clauses 125, 126–7, 129, 243
prices of loans 10, 15–18, 40, 42–3, 49, 244, 247, 248, 249
prices of supplies 116, 153, 249
  commission, inspection, packing, insurance and shipping costs 133–8, 140
  corruption 122–4
  determination of 121–2
  direct ordering 119–21
  local merchant supply 6, 139–40, 249
  price discounts 125–6, 139
  price variation clauses 125, 126–7, 243
  running contracts 120–1
  suppliers 127–33
  tendering 117–19, 246, 249
Price Waterhouse 192
principal-agent theory 241
  as explanation of CAs' activities 241–7
prior charges 22–3, 40, 44, 56
private sector
  CA investments in 179, 183–4
  competition from 143–4
  investment in colonies 9, 39, 47–8, 65
procurement 6, 11, 97, 222, 242, 251
  attempts to increase demand from early 1960s 144–53
  attempts to reduce costs from early 1960s 153–55
  colonial regulations 6, 138–9, 244, 247
  commission, inspection, packing, insurance and shipping costs 133–8, 140
  corruption 122–4
  delivery delays 155–8
  determination of prices 121–2
  fall in demand from early 1960s 143–55
  local merchant supply 139–40, 249
  methods of purchase 117–21
  purchasing agreements 125–7
  suppliers 127–3
promissory notes 45, 151
property
  CA investments in 91, 179, 183, 190–1
  management of investments in 173, 175–6
  over-investment in 196–7
Property Service Agency 236
protectorates 13, 46, 49
Provident Clothing Co. 93, 110 n.95, 200, 201
Provident Financial Group 200

Provident Funds 92
public body loans 45–6
public corporations 143, 151
Public Works Departments 6, 143, 161 n.6, 166, 167, 169

Racal (British Communications Corporation) Ltd 172
racism 163, 176
Radzewill, Prince 198
Raw, Charles 204, 205
recruitment of expatriate officers 160–5, 242, 250
repayment of loans 9, 12, 20, 21, 31–6, 37, 46, 49, 63, 245, 249
Reserve Funds 35, 55, 69, 72, 89
Resident Engineers 167, 168
Risk Assessment Panel 154
Roberts MP, Albert 170
Roe, David 198
Roe, Raymond 173
rumour 195, 202, 214
running contracts 117, 120–1, 245
Russia 135

Salmon enquiry 122
Sarawak 48, 150
E. D. Sassoons & Trust International Ltd 215
E. D. Sassoons Banking Co. Ltd 45, 93, 110 n.95, 151, 184, 187, 192, 198, 200, 207, 215, 216, 217
Saudi Arabia 147, 148, 172 n.94
Saving Bank Funds 37, 56, 57, 69, 71, 72, 75, 85, 89
Scandinavia 129
J. & A. Scrimgeours 9, 15, 23–30, 40, 43, 44 n.15, 55, 83–5, 99, 191 n.83, 199, 243
S. E. Asia 9, 54, 163, 184, 188
Second World War 5, 15, 16, 22, 47, 52, 70, 73, 78, 82–3, 85, 95, 155, 177, 244
secondary banking 7, 90, 179–84
  commercial unethical/illegal behaviour 206–10
  corruption 204–18
  crash 228–40, 247
  external controls 223–8
  internal controls 221–3
  investment controls 197–200
  lending controls 193–5
  over-investment in property 196–7
  quality of borrowers/investments 195–6, 199–200
  reasons for movement into 184–88, 250–1
  reserves 189, 196
  risk 189–200
  staff inexperience 189–93
  Yablon 200–6
secondary banking crash
  active support 230–1, 235–6
  causes of 228–9
  disposal of investments 237–8
  impact on CAs 7, 229–38, 251
  passive support 230–1, 235–6, 247
Seel, Sir George 3
Select Committee on Estimates 115
service provider unethical behaviour 84–5, 93, 95, 169, 176, 242–3
Seychelles 58, 164
Shackleton, Lord 205–6
Sharman, John 217–18
shipment of freight 6, 116, 136–7, 138, 140, 251
shipping conferences 136
shipping department 136–7 157–8
Shuter, John 90 n.133, 112–13, 191, 216 n.271, 230, 238
Sierra Leone 21, 32 n.140, 35, 52–3, 54, 57, 164, 172 n.94
SIFIDA 188
Singapore 46, 89 n.127, 94, 184, 188, 229
  equity portfolios in 94, 183, 186, 192 n.84
  procurement for 145, 150
  property investment 91, 184, 187, 197, 204, 205
Singapore International Merchant Bankers Ltd 184, 192 n.84
Sinking Funds 20, 32, 33, 34, 35, 40, 47, 55, 65, 97, 98, 103, 114
  inter-colonial loans 48–50, 247, 248
  investments 30, 69, 70, 71, 75, 76–7, 78, 80, 81, 82, 94, 242, 245
Slater Walker 199, 207
Sly, Peter 188, 191, 209, 215, 229
Smith, M. G. 224, 225
solicitors employed 173, 176, 247
Somalia 145
South Africa 73, 88, 99, 129, 135, 183, 206
South America 22
Spanish Civil War 145
stagging 10, 36
stamp duty 19–20, 40, 49
stamp sales 6, 173–5, 246
Stanley Gibbons Ltd 93 n.158, 174, 177, 216 n.271
Star West Investment Holdings Ltd 215
Sterling, Col. William 198
Sterling Industrial Securities Ltd 113 n.114, 184, 192, 198, 206, 207, 208, 211–14, 216, 217, 236
Stern Group 113 n.114, 192, 195, 217
  collapse of 234, 235
  over investment in 196–7

support of 230, 232–3
Stern, William 194, 204 n.176, 208–9, 214–15, 217 n.278, 232, 246
Stevenson report 179, 190, 204, 205, 217, 225, 226, 227, 247
stock
sales to the market 9, 35, 42–3
types of 13
Stock Exchange 12, 16, 27, 28, 29,42, 43, 54, 84
Stonehouse MP, John 206
Strachan, Mr 123
Straits Settlements 13, 27, 35, 101
see also Malaya
sub-underwriting 24
subscription of loans
attempts to raise demand 38–40
fall in demand 36–8
purchasers 10, 16, 36–7
Sunday Times 226
Supplementary Sinking Funds 12, 20, 32, 33, 34, 35, 243 n.4
suppliers of goods 121, 122, 127–8, 135, 141
cartels 131–3, 242
delivery delays 156, 158
interests 242–3
lists 117, 119, 123, 126, 157, 158, 246
UK bias 128–30, 249
use of manufacturers 130–1, 139, 249
Surplus Funds 12, 35, 51, 58–9, 69, 72, 75, 86, 89, 102
suspense account 151, 159, 246
Sutton, Ommanney & Oliver 176
Swaziland 14, 49 n.46, 145, 150, 172 n.94
Switching
see trading of securities
Switzerland 39, 93

Tanganyika 100, 102, 103
finance of 39, 44, 46, 49, 54, 61
Tanzania 89 n.127
see also Tanganyika, Zanzibar
taxation 31–2, 48, 55, 58, 59, 92
avoidance of 15, 106–7, 209–10
CA non-payment of 73, 203, 225
Taylor enquiry 134
Taylor, Sir Robert 123
Television Recordings Ltd 187–8, 192, 198
tenders 153, 157
check 117, 118–19
competitive 117–18, 139, 249
simultaneous 117, 118
Thames Guaranty 202
Thompson MP, Sir Richard 206
Thornton, Sir Hugh 3
Towse, G. R. 112, 216 n.271, 238
track fittings cartel 131
Trade bills 110
trading of securities
between funds 80–1
on the market 80, 81–3, 242, 246, 248
Treasury 145, 181, 182, 185, 205, 216, 225, 226, 243
colonial investment Funds 74, 77, 78, 79, 80, 86, 87, 94, 95, 248
control of CAs' secondary banking activities 227–8
interests of 5, 241, 242, 244, 245
JCF/JMF/Joint Funds 6, 100–3, 104–6, 107
miscellaneous sources of finance 46–7, 49–50, 51, 52, 55, 59, 60, 61, 67
procurement 129, 144–5, 150, 154
public issues 13, 14, 15, 17, 20, 21, 22, 23, 28, 31, 33, 35, 36, 40
secondary banking crisis 233, 234–5, 236, 240
Treasury bills (colonial) 44–5, 51, 53, 67, 69, 102, 103, 104, 106, 245
Treasury bills (UK) 44, 67, 71, 97, 98, 104, 105, 106, 110, 111, 198
Treasury bonds 103
Treasury Solicitor 205, 238
Trinidad 9, 28, 35, 36 n.161, 44 n.10, 79
Tripolitania 145
Triton Labouchere & Caro 83–4
Triumph investments 231
Trustee Acts 38, 71, 72, 75–6, 82, 94, 95, 245
Trustee Savings Bank 38
trustee status and trustees 13, 14, 16, 37–8
Tulone investments 231
E. F. Turner & Sons 176, 204

Uganda 89 n.127, 100, 102, 103, 172 n.94
finance of 14, 15, 21, 23, 32 n.140, 44, 53, 54, 55, 57
UK government securities/loans 15, 20, 31, 35, 38, 39, 72–3, 74, 75, 78, 79, 83, 95, 99, 106, 113, 244, 245, 248, 249, 251
UK supply bias 128–30, 249
Underwriting
Finvest 183
JCF 98, 99, 114
local loans 54, 55
London colonial loans 11, 13, 15, 16, 17, 19, 21, 23–30, 34, 36, 38, 40, 41, 73, 84, 243, 246, 247
underwriter applications for stock 24, 243
Unemployment Insurance Fund 31
unit trust 92
United Dominions Trust 199
United Merchant Securities 215

United Nations 1, 63, 65, 150, 151, 252
United States 39, 86, 88, 93, 94, 112, 113, 129, 130, 183, 192 n.84

Vehicle & General Insurance Co Ltd 195
video cassettes investment 187–8, 199
Voluntary Service Overseas 164
Vosper, Dennis 186

Walker, Jack 192, 196, 198, 204, 205, 215
Wallace Bros. 184, 187, 192
Wallace Sassoons 231
Walters, W. 218
war loans 73
S. G. Warburg 192, 205
Wass, Sir Douglas 216
Ways and Means Advances 73
West Africa 24 n.84, 47 n.37, 55, 69 n.2, 91, 123–4, 136, 162, 177, 246
West Indies 47, 115, 162, 184
  finance of 9, 51, 54
Westminster Bank
  see National Westminster Bank
Westralian International Ltd 184, 192
Wheatley, Bernard 111, 191, 194, 214
  corruption 204, 211–14
Wilson MP, Harold 181
Wilson, Sir Geoffrey 186, 224
Wilson, William 170
Wimpey 171
Window dressing 208, 243
Wintrust Securities Ltd 212–13
N. H. Wooley & Co Ltd 208
World Bank 1, 31, 39, 62–3, 65, 109, 130, 135, 150, 252

Yablon, Ralph 93, 198, 200–6, 216, 217, 219, 233
Yemen 147, 148

Zaire 188
Zambia 89 n.127.
  see also Northern Rhodesia
Zanzibar 14, 46 n.32, 90 n.133